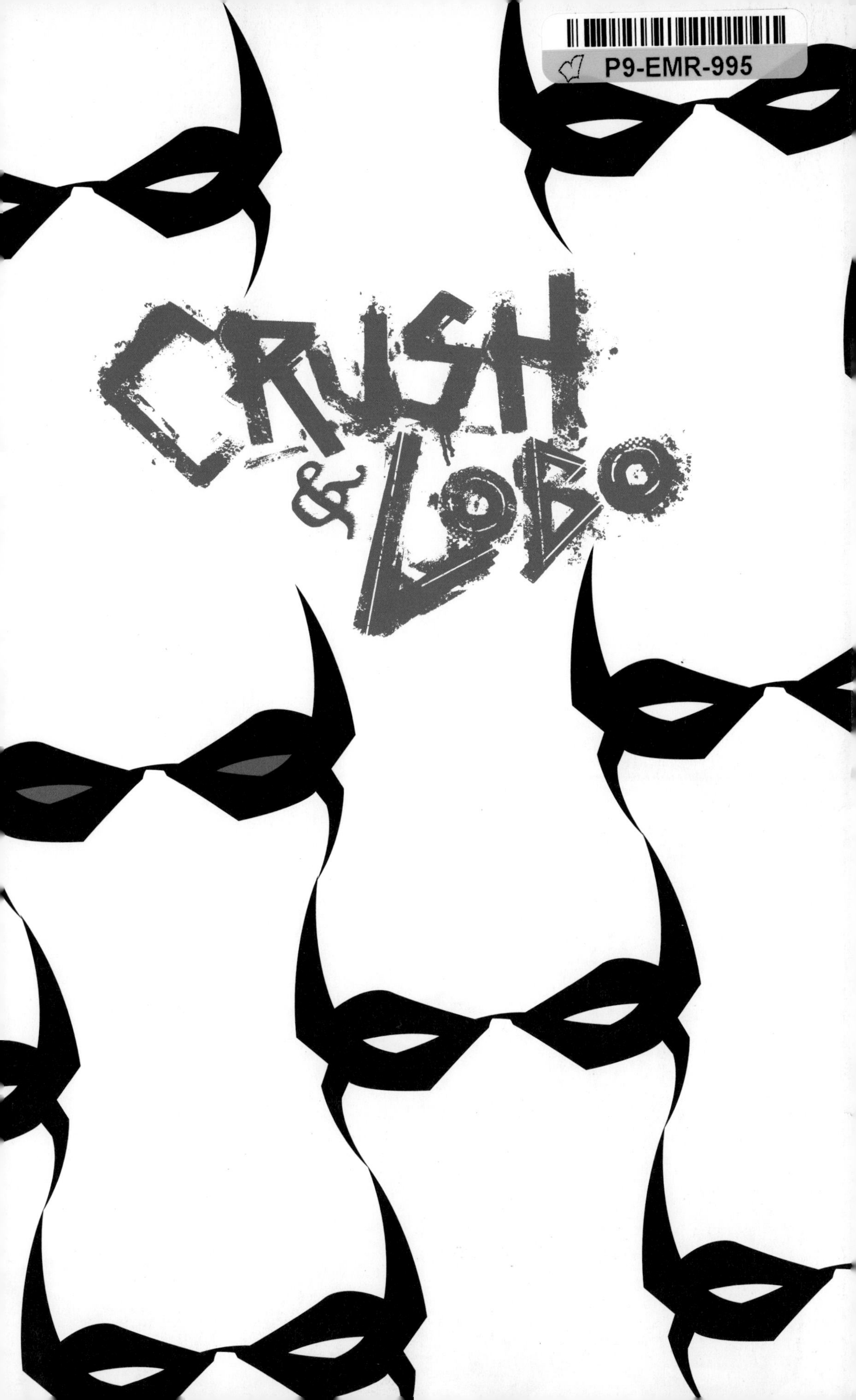
CRUSH
& LOBO

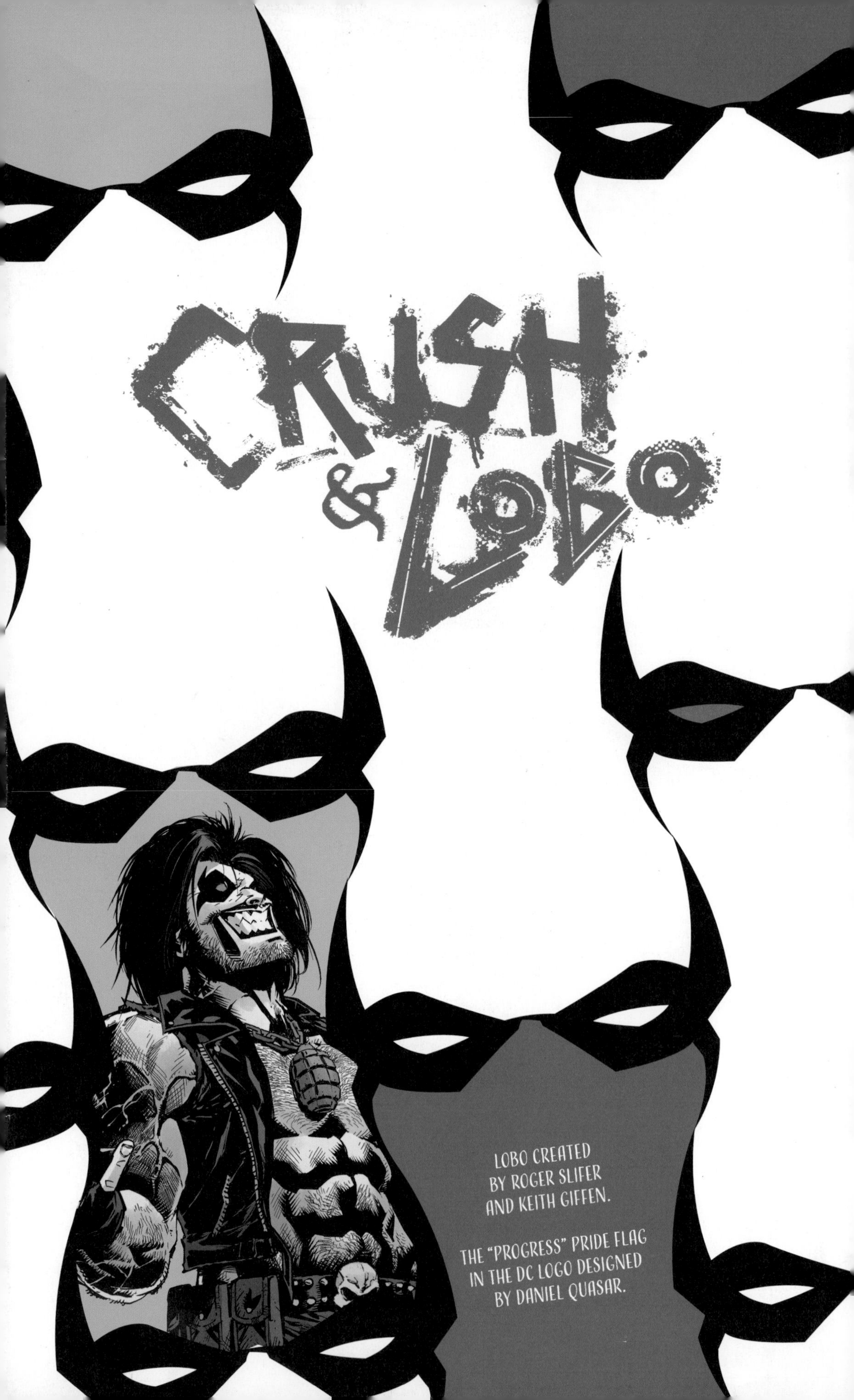
CRUSH
& LOBO

LOBO CREATED
BY ROGER SLIFER
AND KEITH GIFFEN.

THE "PROGRESS" PRIDE FLAG
IN THE DC LOGO DESIGNED
BY DANIEL QUASAR.

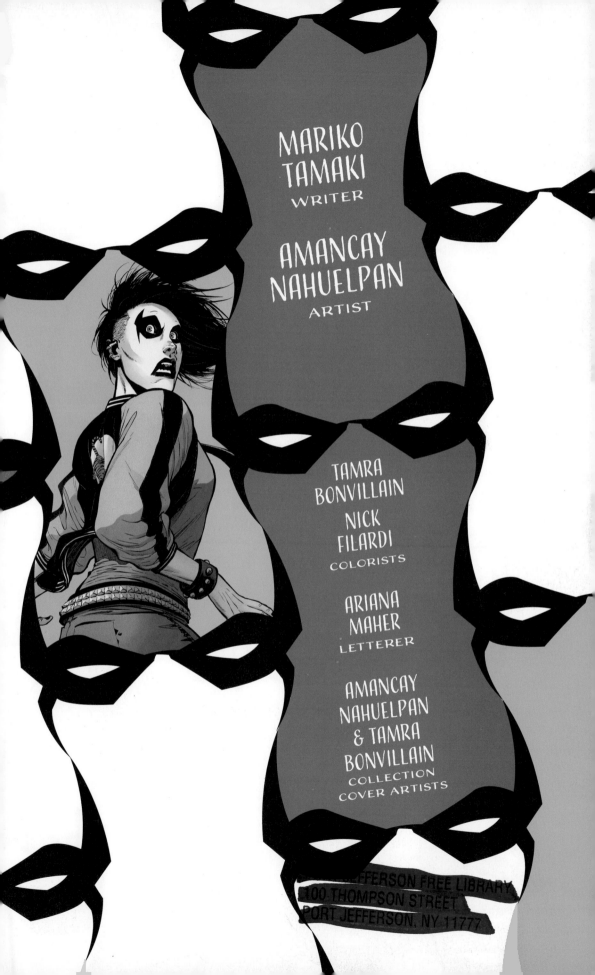

MARIKO TAMAKI
WRITER

AMANCAY NAHUELPAN
ARTIST

TAMRA BONVILLAIN
NICK FILARDI
COLORISTS

ARIANA MAHER
LETTERER

AMANCAY NAHUELPAN & TAMRA BONVILLAIN
COLLECTION COVER ARTISTS

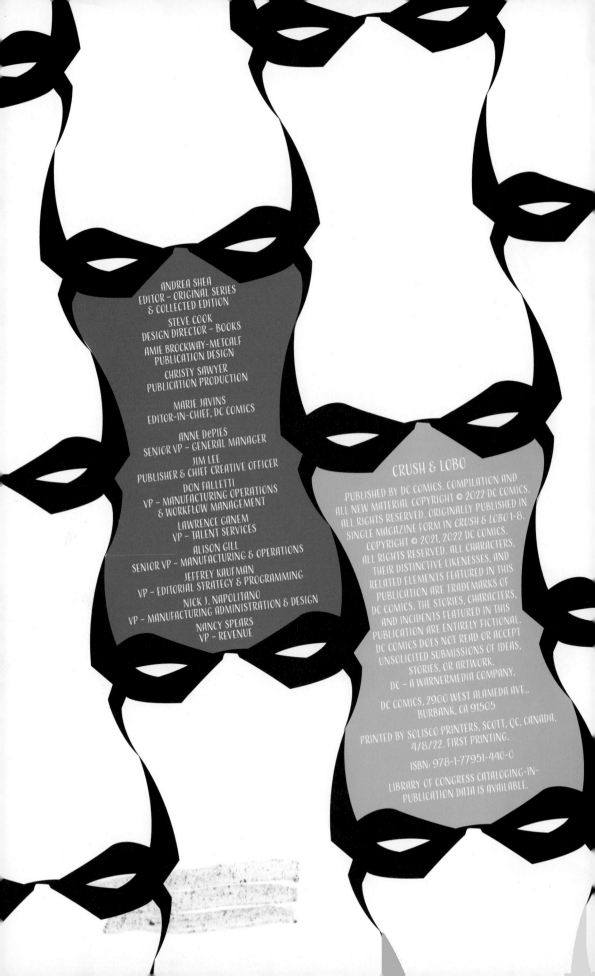

ANDREA SHEA
EDITOR – ORIGINAL SERIES
& COLLECTED EDITION

STEVE COOK
DESIGN DIRECTOR – BOOKS

AMIE BROCKWAY-METCALF
PUBLICATION DESIGN

CHRISTY SAWYER
PUBLICATION PRODUCTION

MARIE JAVINS
EDITOR-IN-CHIEF, DC COMICS

ANNE DePIES
SENIOR VP – GENERAL MANAGER

JIM LEE
PUBLISHER & CHIEF CREATIVE OFFICER

DON FALLETTI
VP – MANUFACTURING OPERATIONS
& WORKFLOW MANAGEMENT

LAWRENCE GANEM
VP – TALENT SERVICES

ALISON GILL
SENIOR VP – MANUFACTURING & OPERATIONS

JEFFREY KAUFMAN
VP – EDITORIAL STRATEGY & PROGRAMMING

NICK J. NAPOLITANO
VP – MANUFACTURING ADMINISTRATION & DESIGN

NANCY SPEARS
VP – REVENUE

CRUSH & LOBO

PUBLISHED BY DC COMICS.
DC – A WARNERMEDIA COMPANY.

DC COMICS, 2900 WEST ALAMEDA AVE., BURBANK, CA 91505

PRINTED BY SOLISCO PRINTERS, SCOTT, QC, CANADA. 4/8/22. FIRST PRINTING.

ISBN: 978-1-77951-440-0

LIBRARY OF CONGRESS CATALOGING-IN-PUBLICATION DATA IS AVAILABLE.

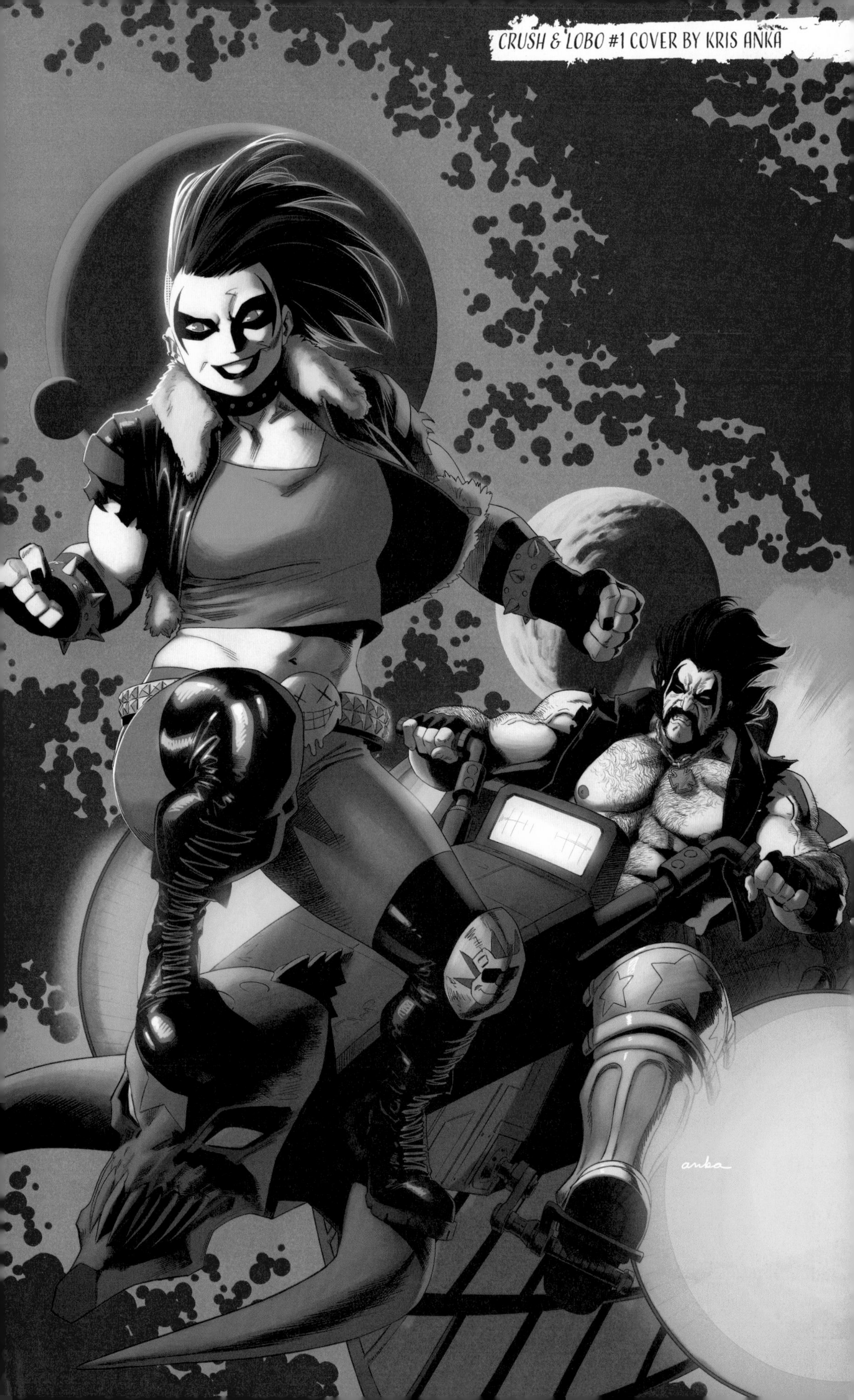
anka
CRUSH & LOBO #1 COVER BY KRIS ANKA

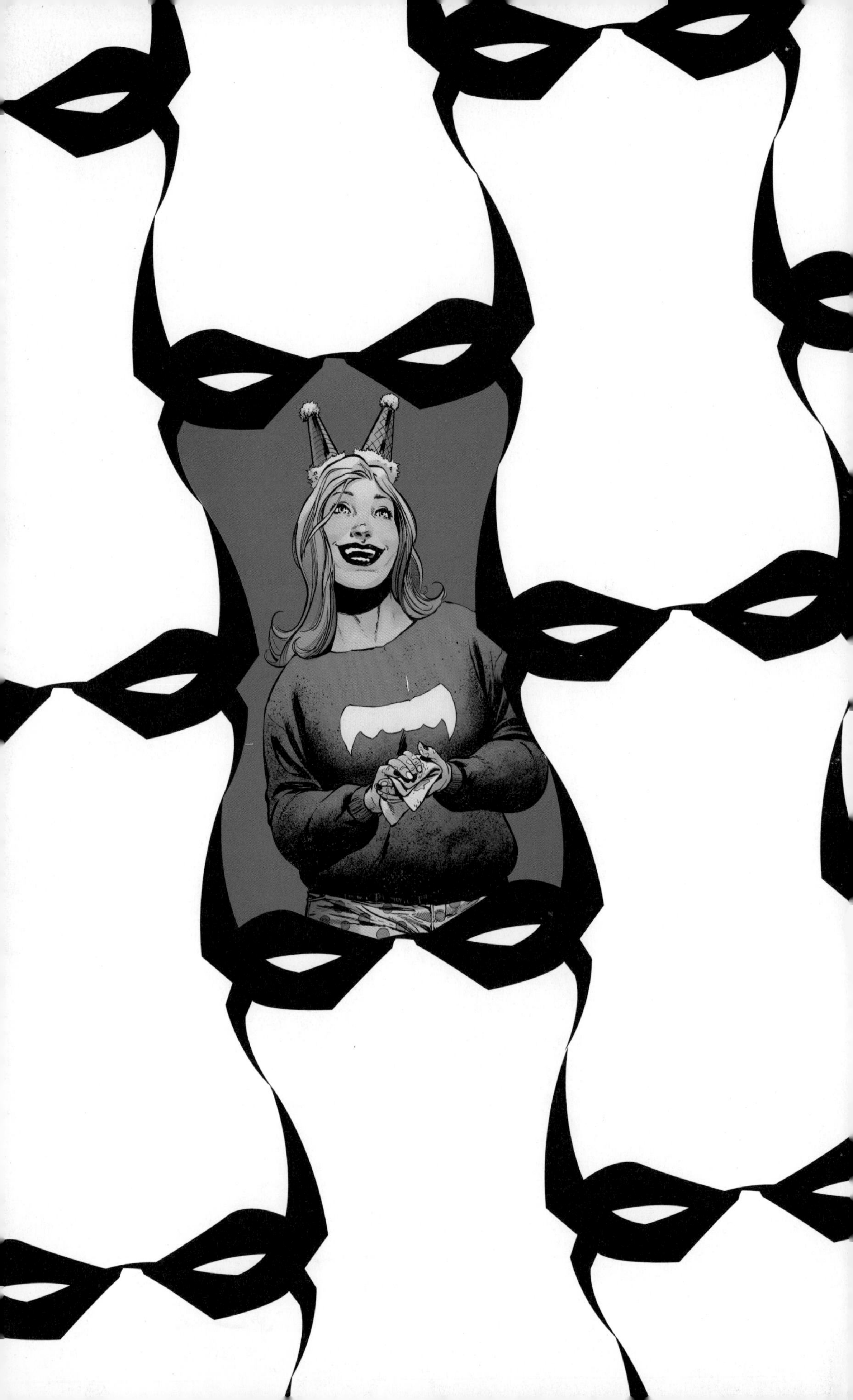

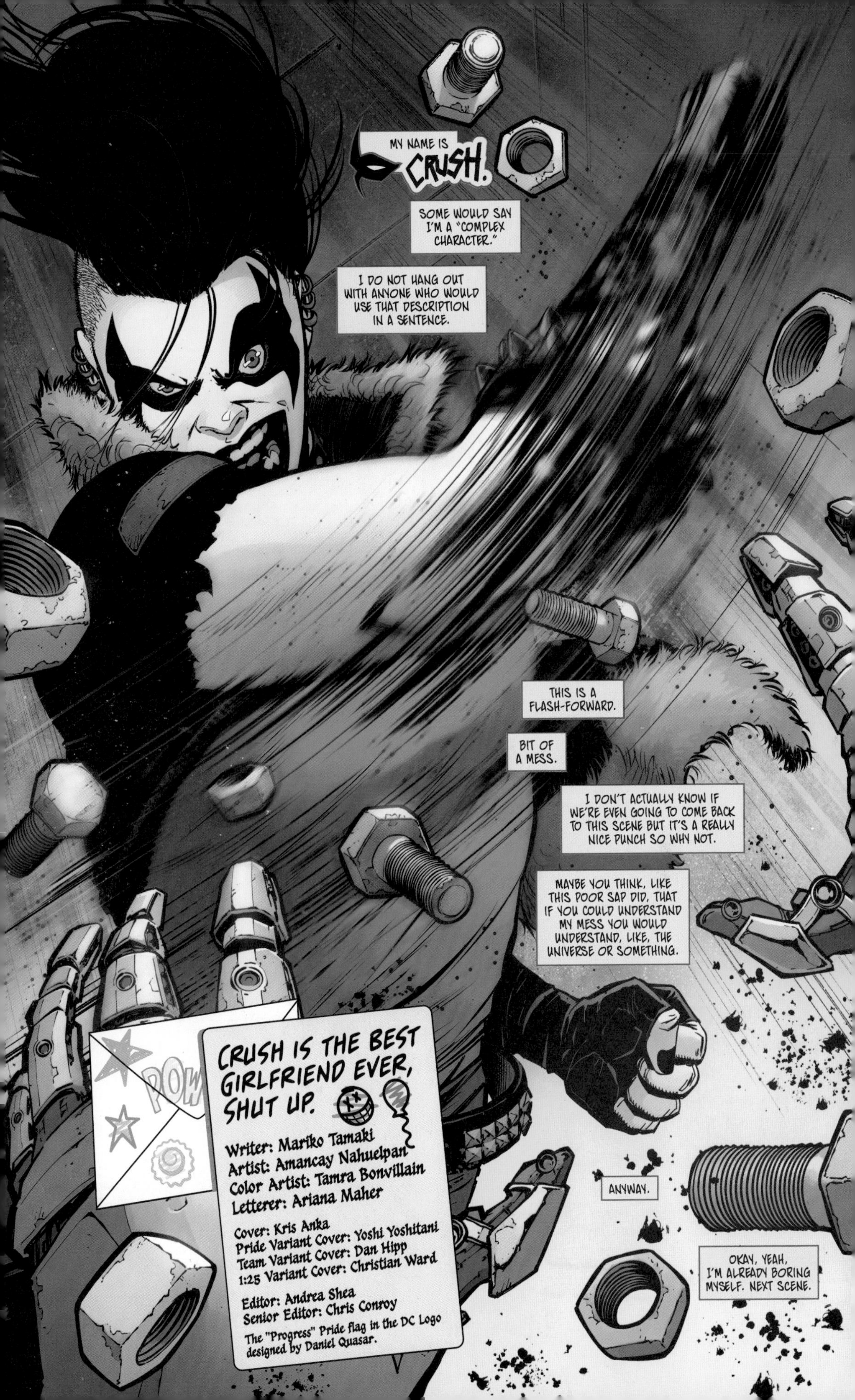
MY NAME IS CRUSH.
SOME WOULD SAY I'M A "COMPLEX CHARACTER."
I DO NOT HANG OUT WITH ANYONE WHO WOULD USE THAT DESCRIPTION IN A SENTENCE.
THIS IS A FLASH-FORWARD.
BIT OF A MESS.
I DON'T ACTUALLY KNOW IF WE'RE EVEN GOING TO COME BACK TO THIS SCENE BUT IT'S A REALLY NICE PUNCH SO WHY NOT.
MAYBE YOU THINK, LIKE THIS POOR SAP DID, THAT IF YOU COULD UNDERSTAND MY MESS YOU WOULD UNDERSTAND, LIKE, THE UNIVERSE OR SOMETHING.
POW
CRUSH IS THE BEST GIRLFRIEND EVER, SHUT UP.
Writer: Mariko Tamaki
Artist: Amancay Nahuelpan
Color Artist: Tamra Bonvillain
Letterer: Ariana Maher
Cover: Kris Anka
Pride Variant Cover: Yoshi Yoshitani
Team Variant Cover: Dan Hipp
1:25 Variant Cover: Christian Ward
Editor: Andrea Shea
Senior Editor: Chris Conroy
The "Progress" Pride flag in the DC Logo designed by Daniel Quasar.
ANYWAY.
OKAY, YEAH, I'M ALREADY BORING MYSELF. NEXT SCENE.

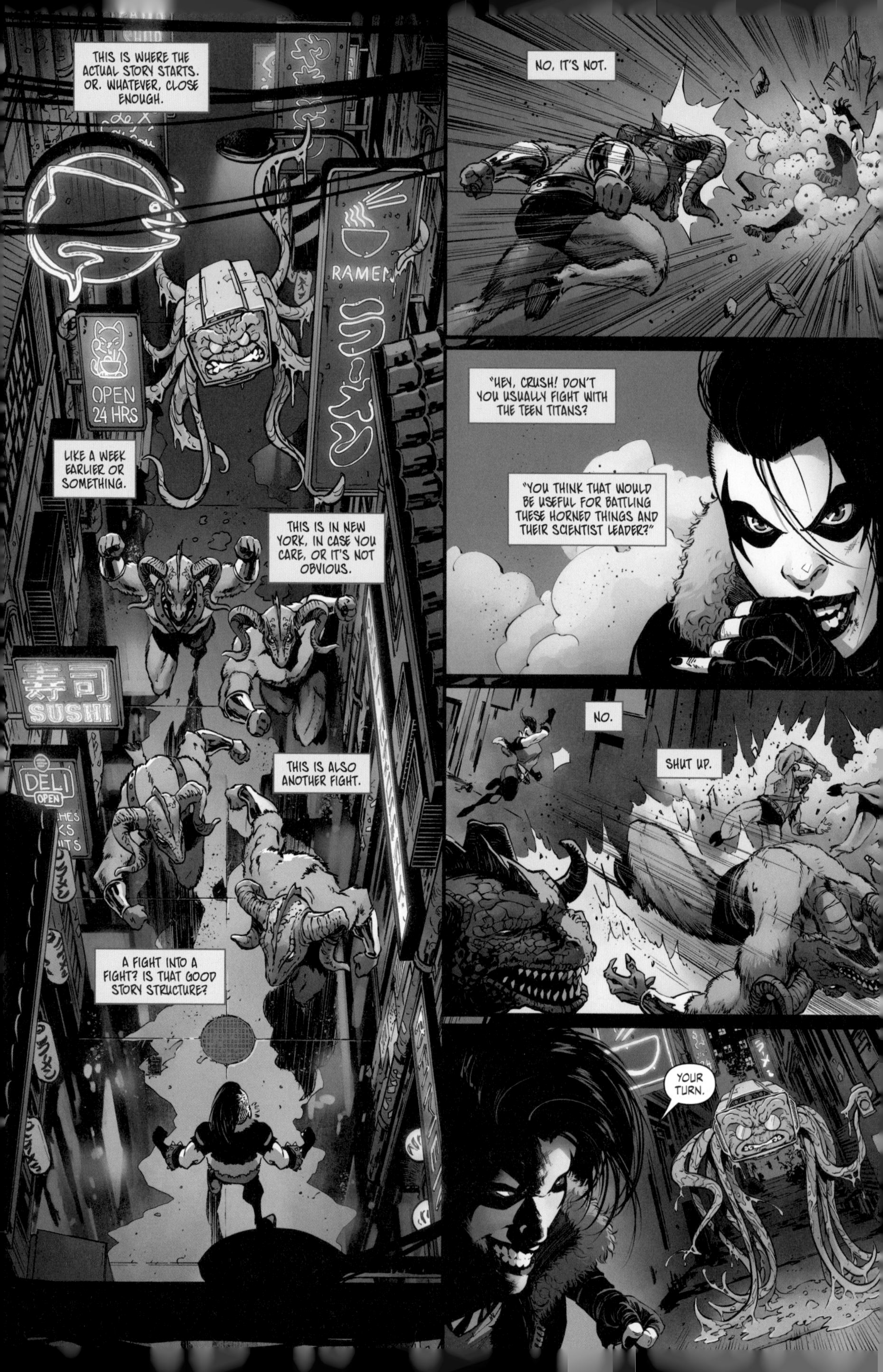
THIS IS WHERE THE ACTUAL STORY STARTS. OR. WHATEVER, CLOSE ENOUGH.
RAMEN
OPEN 24 HRS
LIKE A WEEK EARLIER OR SOMETHING.
THIS IS IN NEW YORK, IN CASE YOU CARE, OR IT'S NOT OBVIOUS.
寿司 SUSHI
DELI OPEN
THIS IS ALSO ANOTHER FIGHT.
A FIGHT INTO A FIGHT? IS THAT GOOD STORY STRUCTURE?
NO, IT'S NOT.
"HEY, CRUSH! DON'T YOU USUALLY FIGHT WITH THE TEEN TITANS?
"YOU THINK THAT WOULD BE USEFUL FOR BATTLING THESE HORNED THINGS AND THEIR SCIENTIST LEADER?"
NO.
SHUT UP.
YOUR TURN.

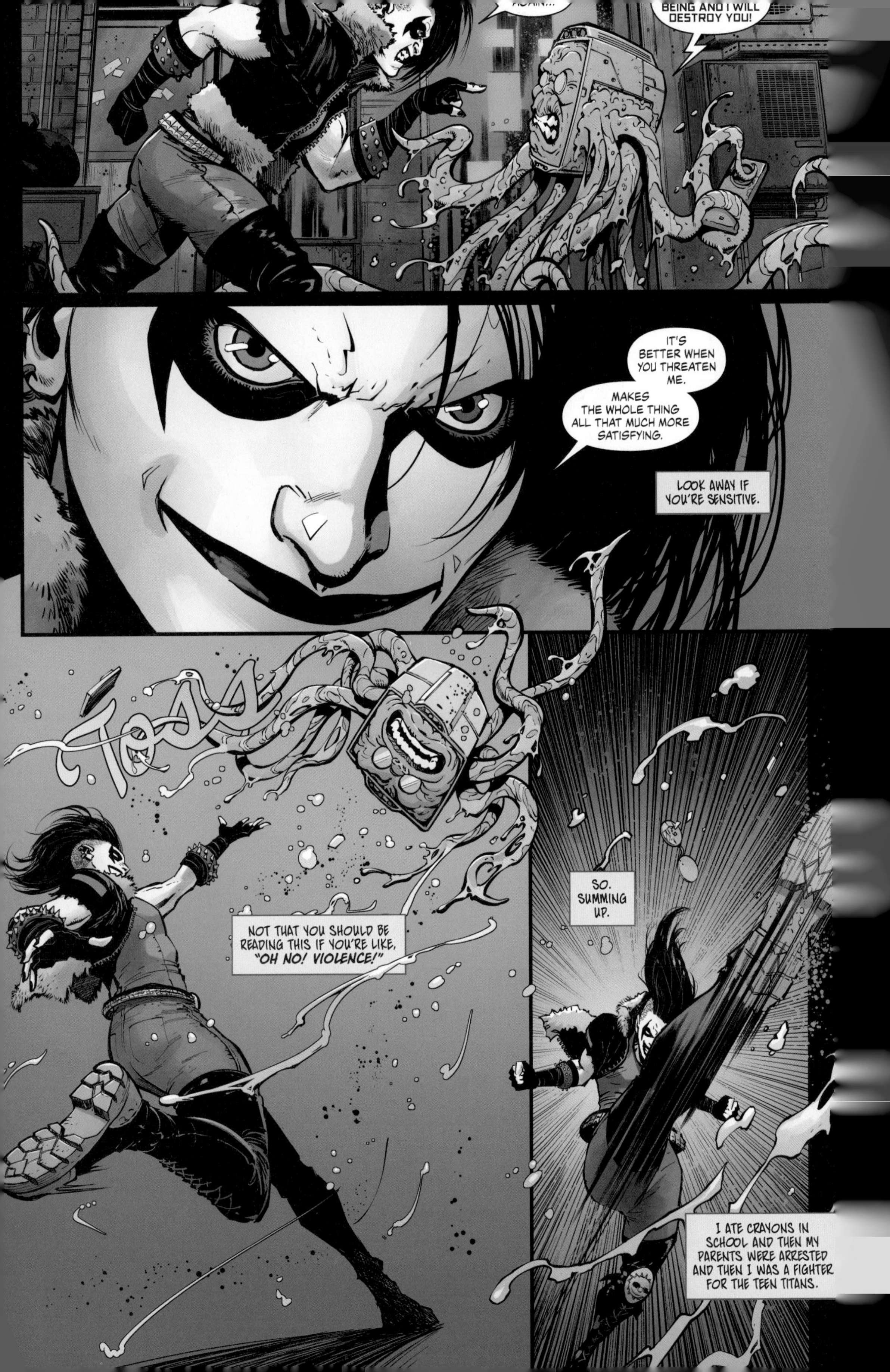
BEING AND I WILL DESTROY YOU!
IT'S BETTER WHEN YOU THREATEN ME.
MAKES THE WHOLE THING ALL THAT MUCH MORE SATISFYING.
LOOK AWAY IF YOU'RE SENSITIVE.
TOSS
NOT THAT YOU SHOULD BE READING THIS IF YOU'RE LIKE, "OH NO! VIOLENCE!"
SO. SUMMING UP.
I ATE CRAYONS IN SCHOOL AND THEN MY PARENTS WERE ARRESTED AND THEN I WAS A FIGHTER FOR THE TEEN TITANS.

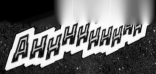

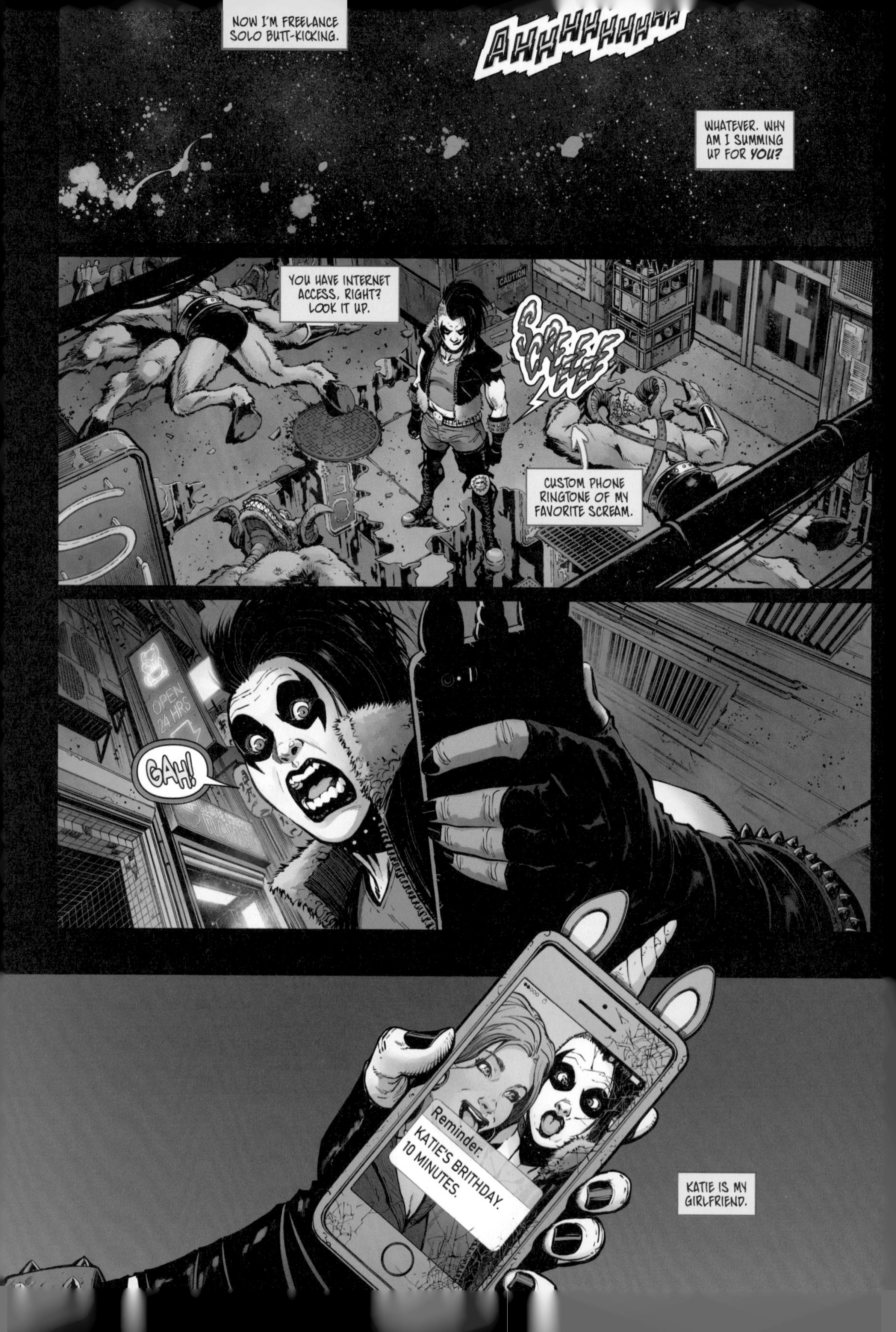
NOW I'M FREELANCE SOLO BUTT-KICKING.
AHHHHHHHHH
WHATEVER. WHY AM I SUMMING UP FOR *YOU?*
YOU HAVE INTERNET ACCESS, RIGHT? LOOK IT UP.
CAUTION
SCREEEEEE
CUSTOM PHONE RINGTONE OF MY FAVORITE SCREAM.
OPEN 24 HRS
GAH!
Reminder.
KATIE'S BRITHDAY.
10 MINUTES.
KATIE IS MY GIRLFRIEND.

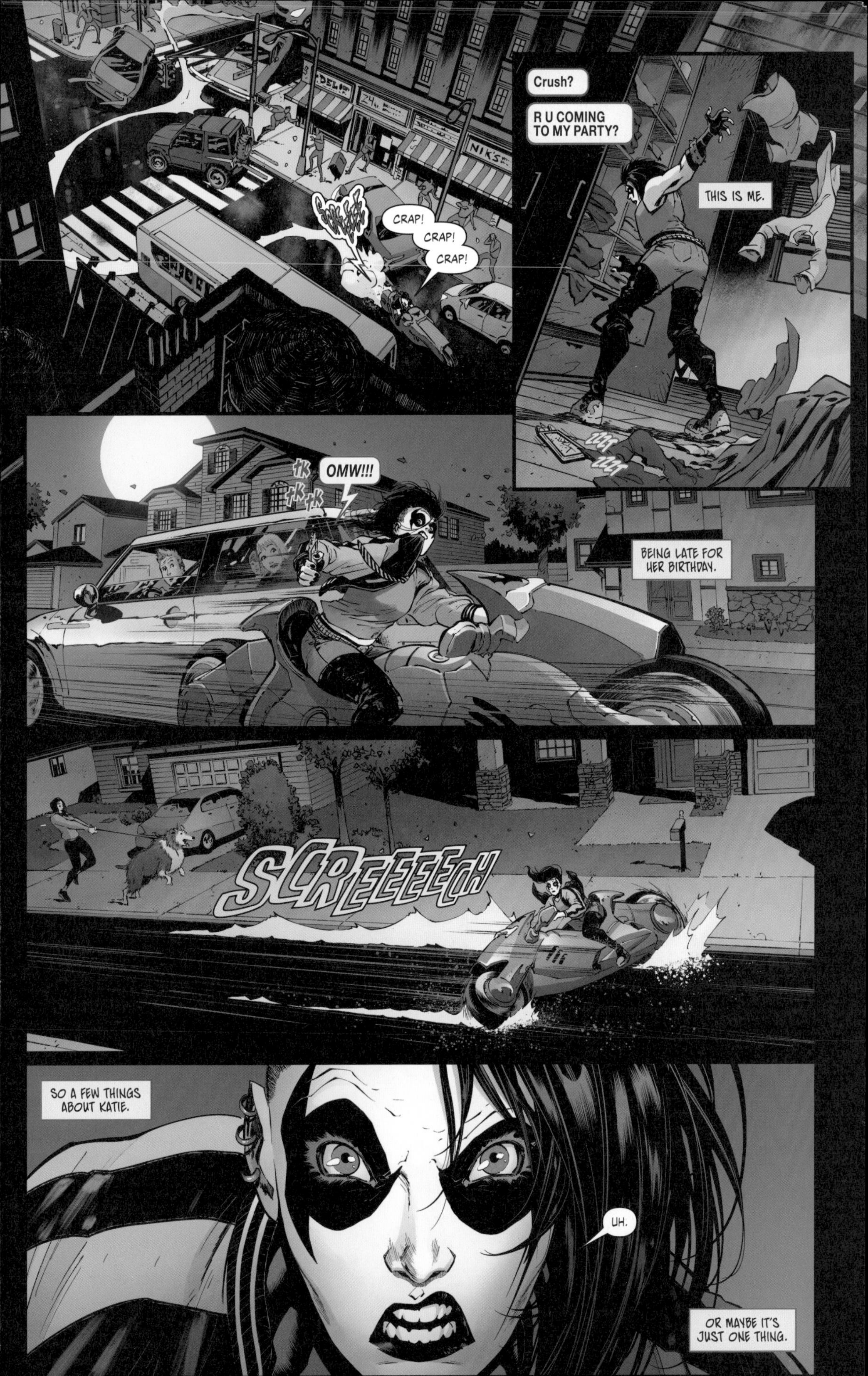

CRAP!
CRAP!
CRAP!
Crush?
R U COMING TO MY PARTY?
THIS IS ME.
OMW!!!
BEING LATE FOR HER BIRTHDAY.
SCREEEEECH
SO A FEW THINGS ABOUT KATIE.
UH.
OR MAYBE IT'S JUST ONE THING.

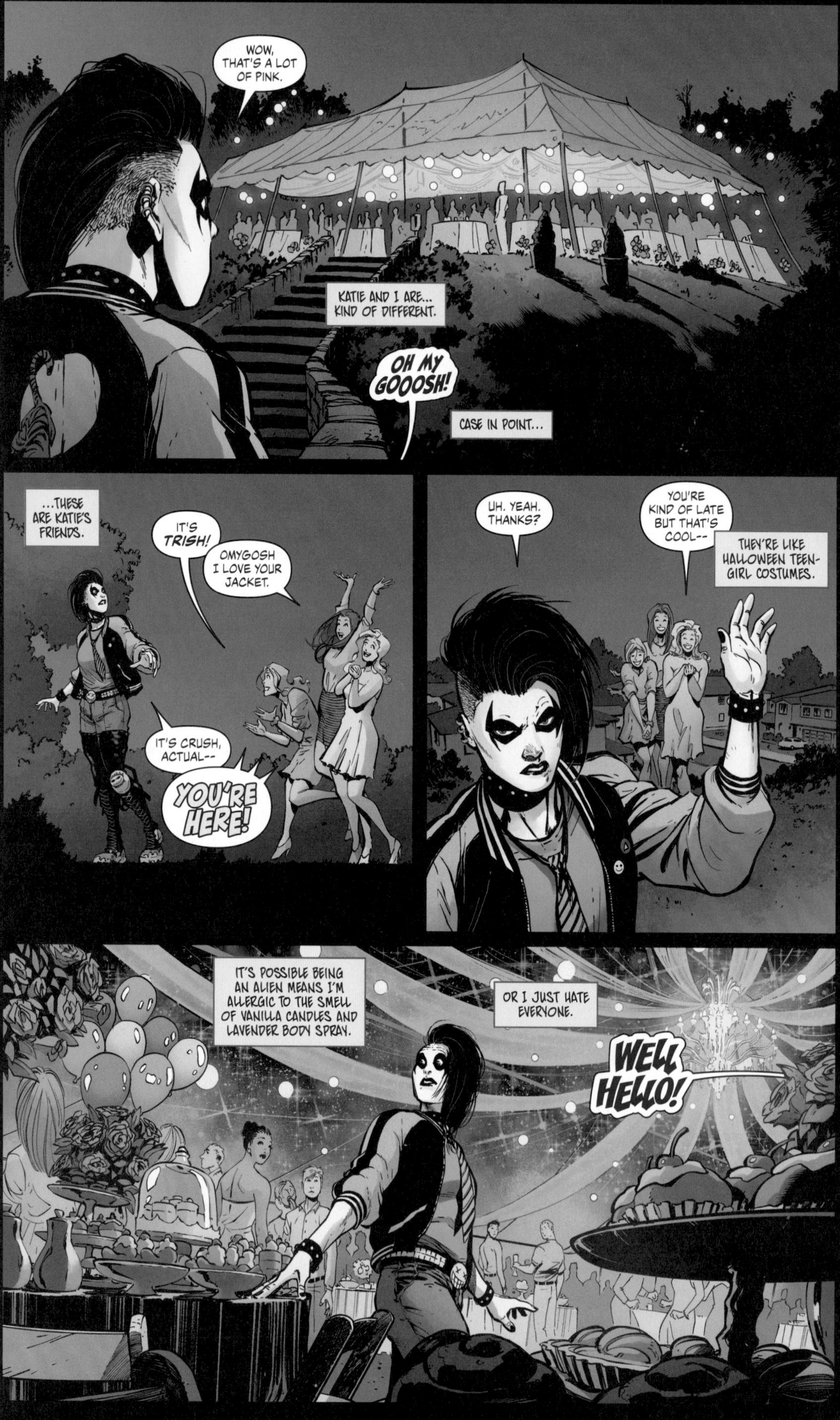
WOW, THAT'S A LOT OF PINK.
KATIE AND I ARE... KIND OF DIFFERENT.
OH MY GOOOSH!
CASE IN POINT...
...THESE ARE KATIE'S FRIENDS.
IT'S TRISH!
OMYGOSH I LOVE YOUR JACKET.
IT'S CRUSH, ACTUAL--
YOU'RE HERE!
UH. YEAH. THANKS?
YOU'RE KIND OF LATE BUT THAT'S COOL--
THEY'RE LIKE HALLOWEEN TEEN-GIRL COSTUMES.
IT'S POSSIBLE BEING AN ALIEN MEANS I'M ALLERGIC TO THE SMELL OF VANILLA CANDLES AND LAVENDER BODY SPRAY.
OR I JUST HATE EVERYONE.
WELL HELLO!

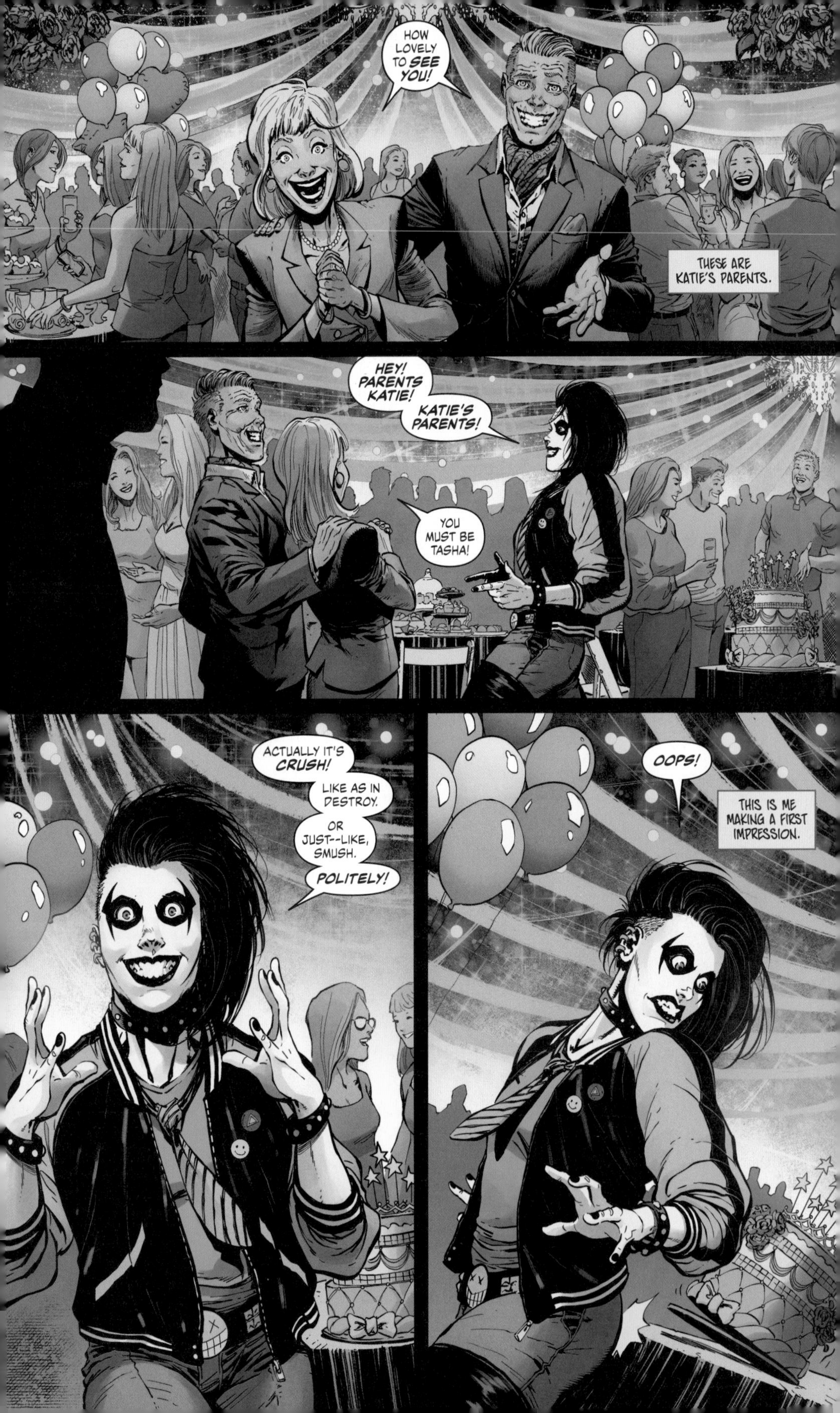
HOW LOVELY TO SEE YOU!
THESE ARE KATIE'S PARENTS.
HEY! PARENTS KATIE!
KATIE'S PARENTS!
YOU MUST BE TASHA!
ACTUALLY IT'S CRUSH!
LIKE AS IN DESTROY.
OR JUST--LIKE, SMUSH.
POLITELY!
OOPS!
THIS IS ME MAKING A FIRST IMPRESSION.

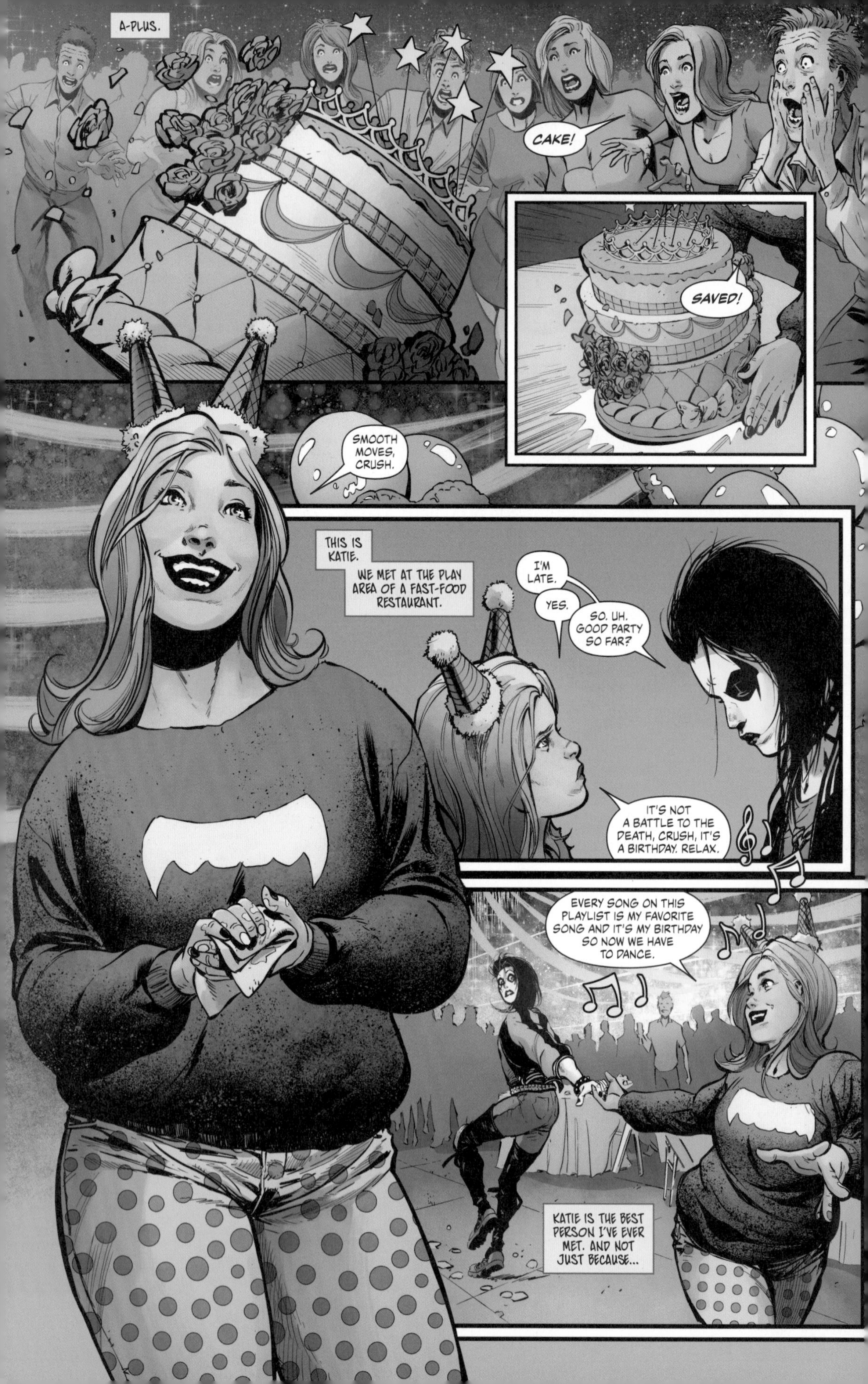
A-PLUS.
CAKE!
SAVED!
SMOOTH MOVES, CRUSH.
THIS IS KATIE.
WE MET AT THE PLAY AREA OF A FAST-FOOD RESTAURANT.
I'M LATE.
YES.
SO. UH. GOOD PARTY SO FAR?
IT'S NOT A BATTLE TO THE DEATH, CRUSH, IT'S A BIRTHDAY. RELAX.
EVERY SONG ON THIS PLAYLIST IS MY FAVORITE SONG AND IT'S MY BIRTHDAY SO NOW WE HAVE TO DANCE.
KATIE IS THE BEST PERSON I'VE EVER MET. AND NOT JUST BECAUSE...

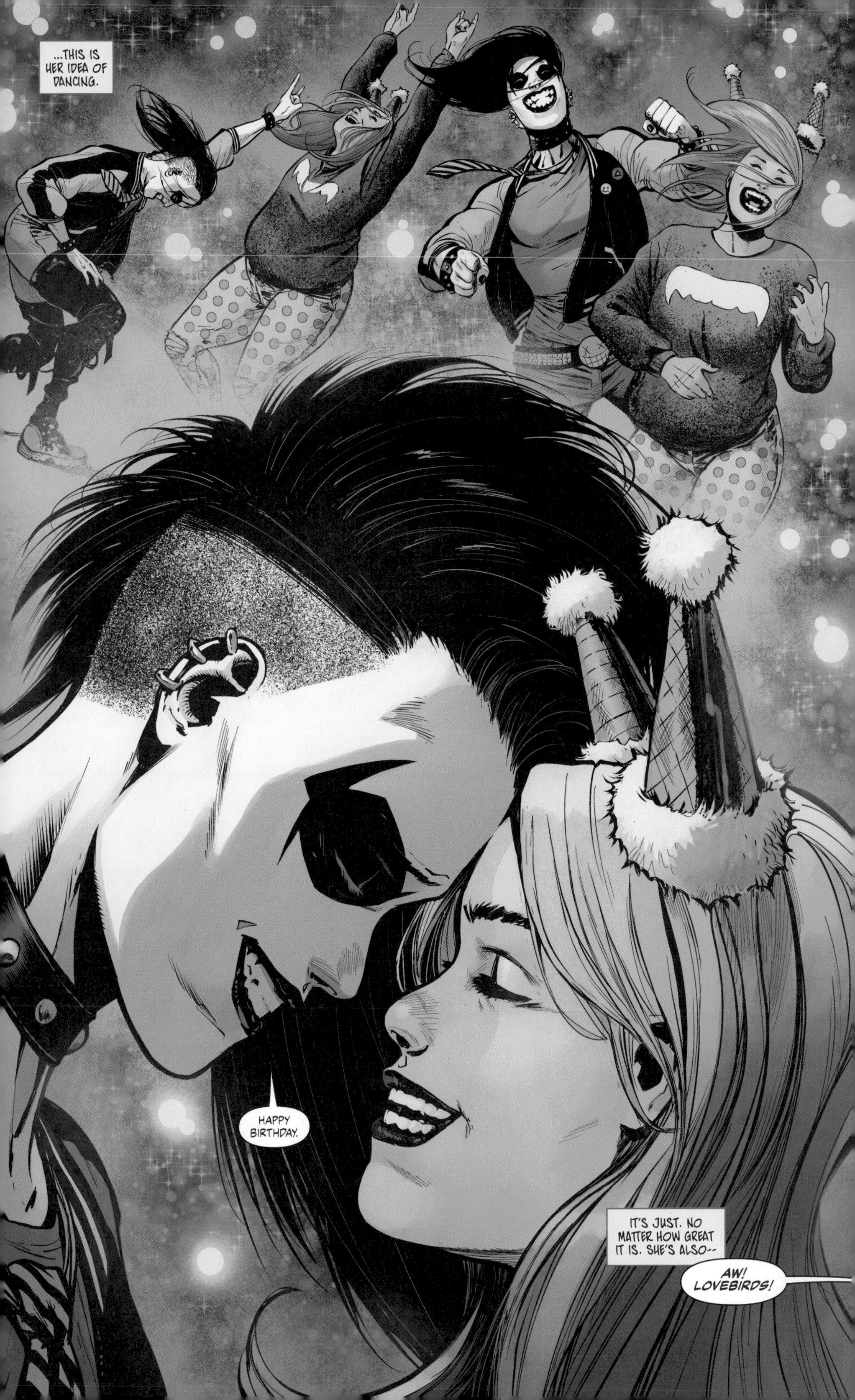
...THIS IS HER IDEA OF DANCING.
HAPPY BIRTHDAY.
IT'S JUST. NO MATTER HOW GREAT IT IS. SHE'S ALSO--
AW! LOVEBIRDS!

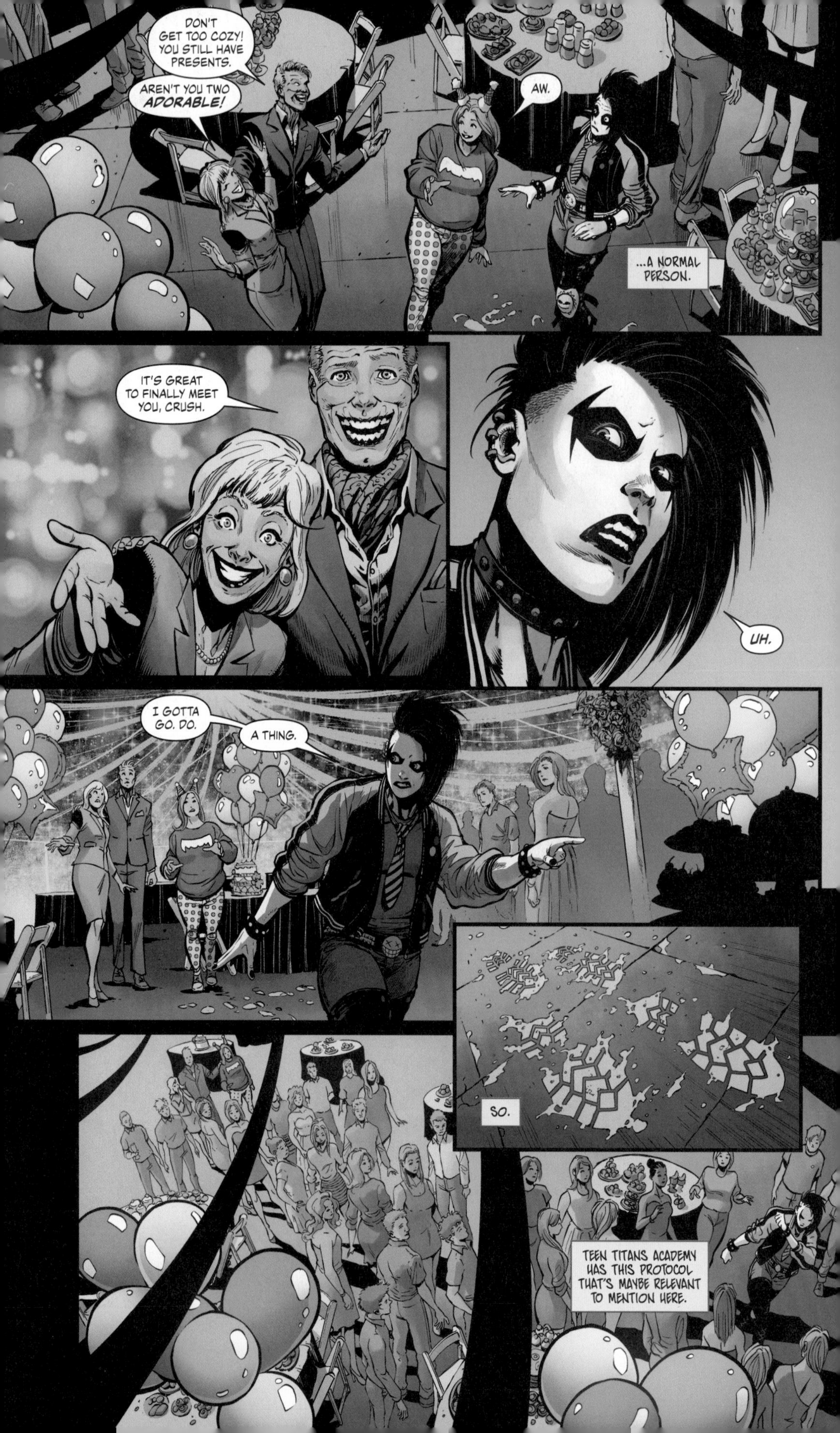
DON'T GET TOO COZY! YOU STILL HAVE PRESENTS.
AREN'T YOU TWO ADORABLE!
AW.
...A NORMAL PERSON.
IT'S GREAT TO FINALLY MEET YOU, CRUSH.
UH.
I GOTTA GO. DO.
A THING.
SO.
TEEN TITANS ACADEMY HAS THIS PROTOCOL THAT'S MAYBE RELEVANT TO MENTION HERE.

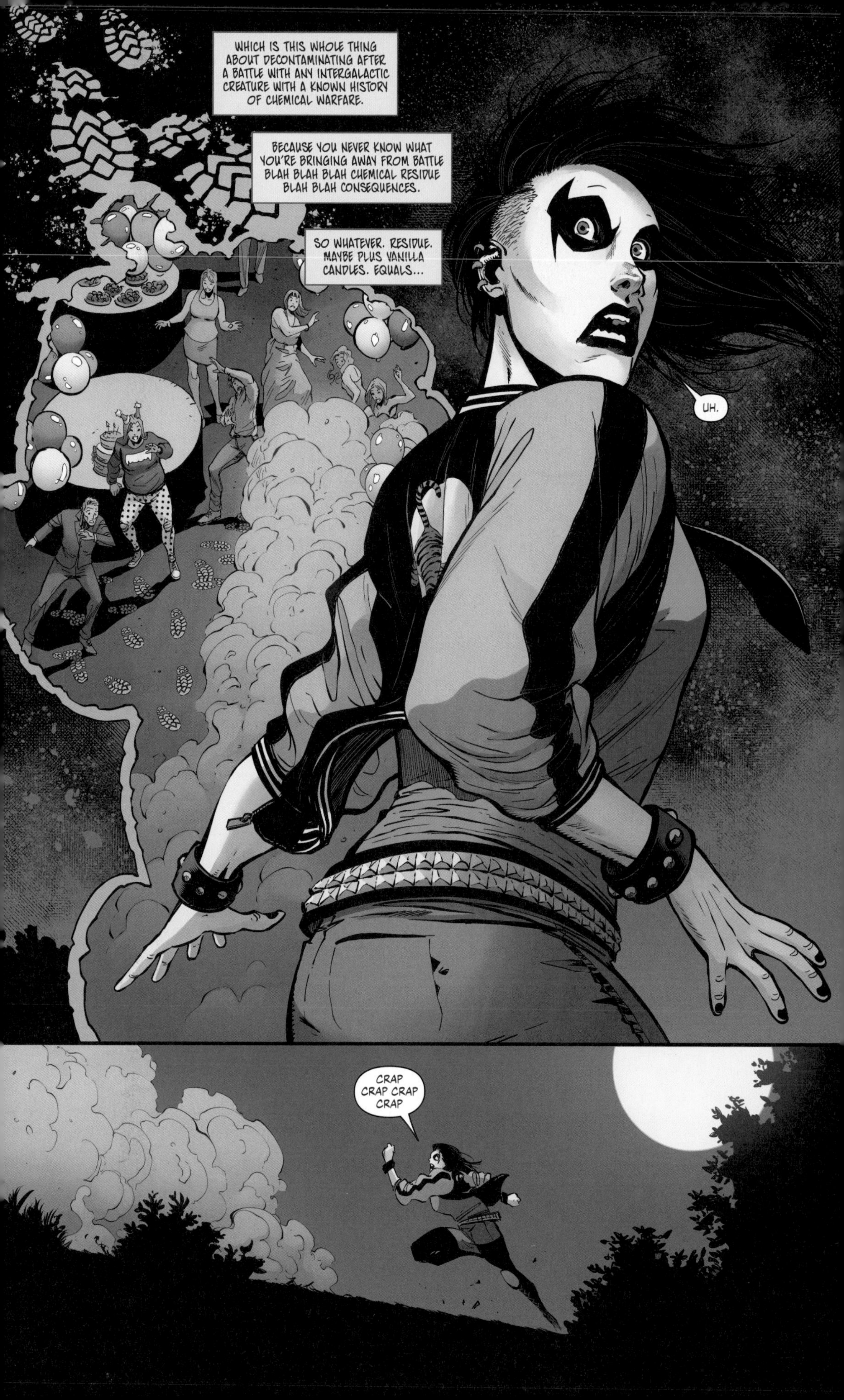
WHICH IS THIS WHOLE THING ABOUT DECONTAMINATING AFTER A BATTLE WITH ANY INTERGALACTIC CREATURE WITH A KNOWN HISTORY OF CHEMICAL WARFARE.
BECAUSE YOU NEVER KNOW WHAT YOU'RE BRINGING AWAY FROM BATTLE BLAH BLAH BLAH CHEMICAL RESIDUE BLAH BLAH CONSEQUENCES.
SO WHATEVER. RESIDUE. MAYBE PLUS VANILLA CANDLES. EQUALS...
UH.
CRAP CRAP CRAP CRAP

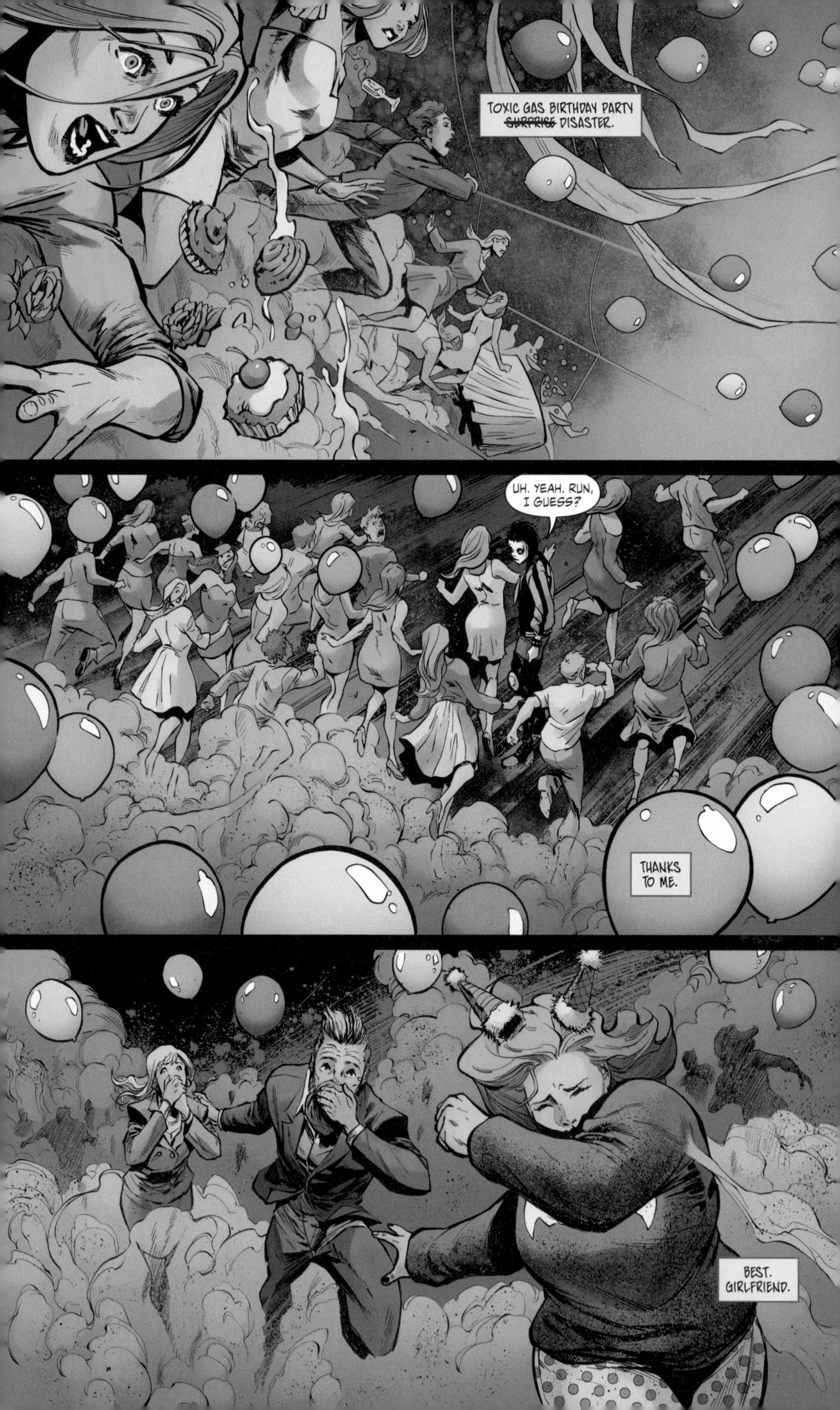
TOXIC GAS BIRTHDAY PARTY SURPRISE DISASTER.
UH. YEAH. RUN, I GUESS?
THANKS TO ME.
BEST. GIRLFRIEND.

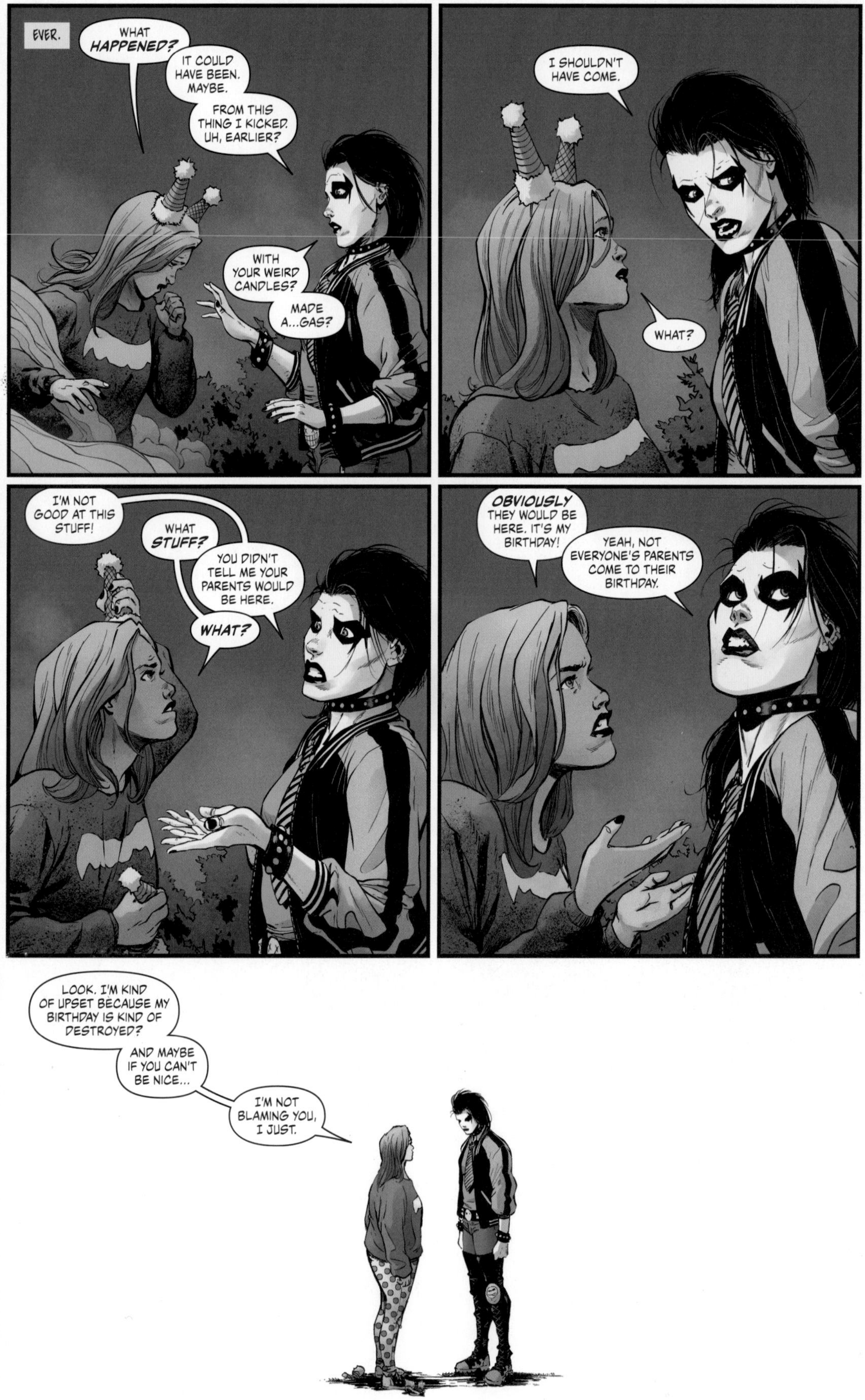
EVER.
WHAT HAPPENED?
IT COULD HAVE BEEN. MAYBE.
FROM THIS THING I KICKED. UH, EARLIER?
WITH YOUR WEIRD CANDLES?
MADE A...GAS?
I SHOULDN'T HAVE COME.
WHAT?
I'M NOT GOOD AT THIS STUFF!
WHAT STUFF?
YOU DIDN'T TELL ME YOUR PARENTS WOULD BE HERE.
WHAT?
OBVIOUSLY THEY WOULD BE HERE. IT'S MY BIRTHDAY!
YEAH, NOT EVERYONE'S PARENTS COME TO THEIR BIRTHDAY.
LOOK. I'M KIND OF UPSET BECAUSE MY BIRTHDAY IS KIND OF DESTROYED?
AND MAYBE IF YOU CAN'T BE NICE...
I'M NOT BLAMING YOU, I JUST.

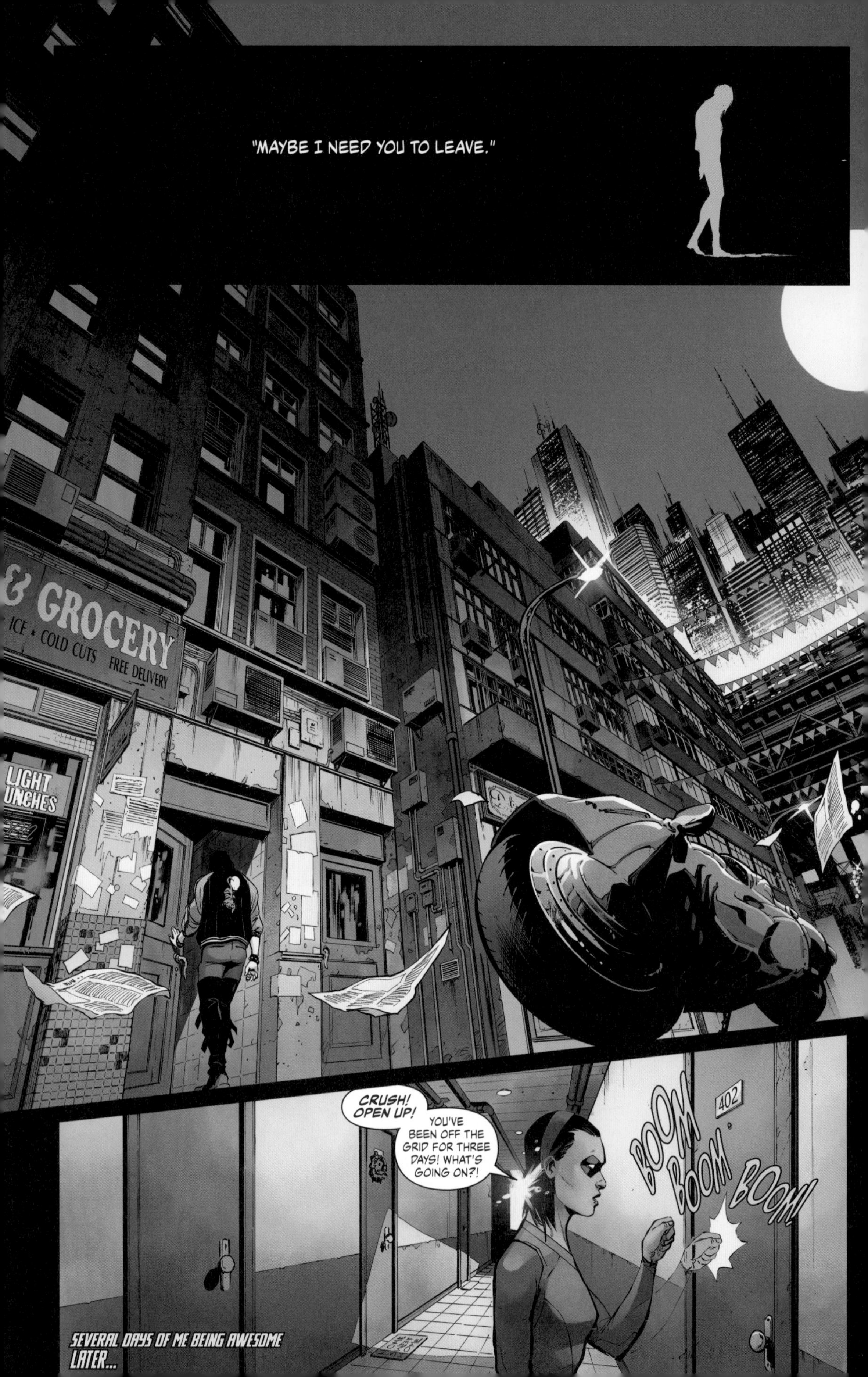
"MAYBE I NEED YOU TO LEAVE."
& GROCERY
ICE ★ COLD CUTS FREE DELIVERY
LIGHT
UNCHES
402
CRUSH! OPEN UP!
YOU'VE BEEN OFF THE GRID FOR THREE DAYS! WHAT'S GOING ON?!
BOOM BOOM BOOM!
SEVERAL DAYS OF ME BEING AWESOME LATER...

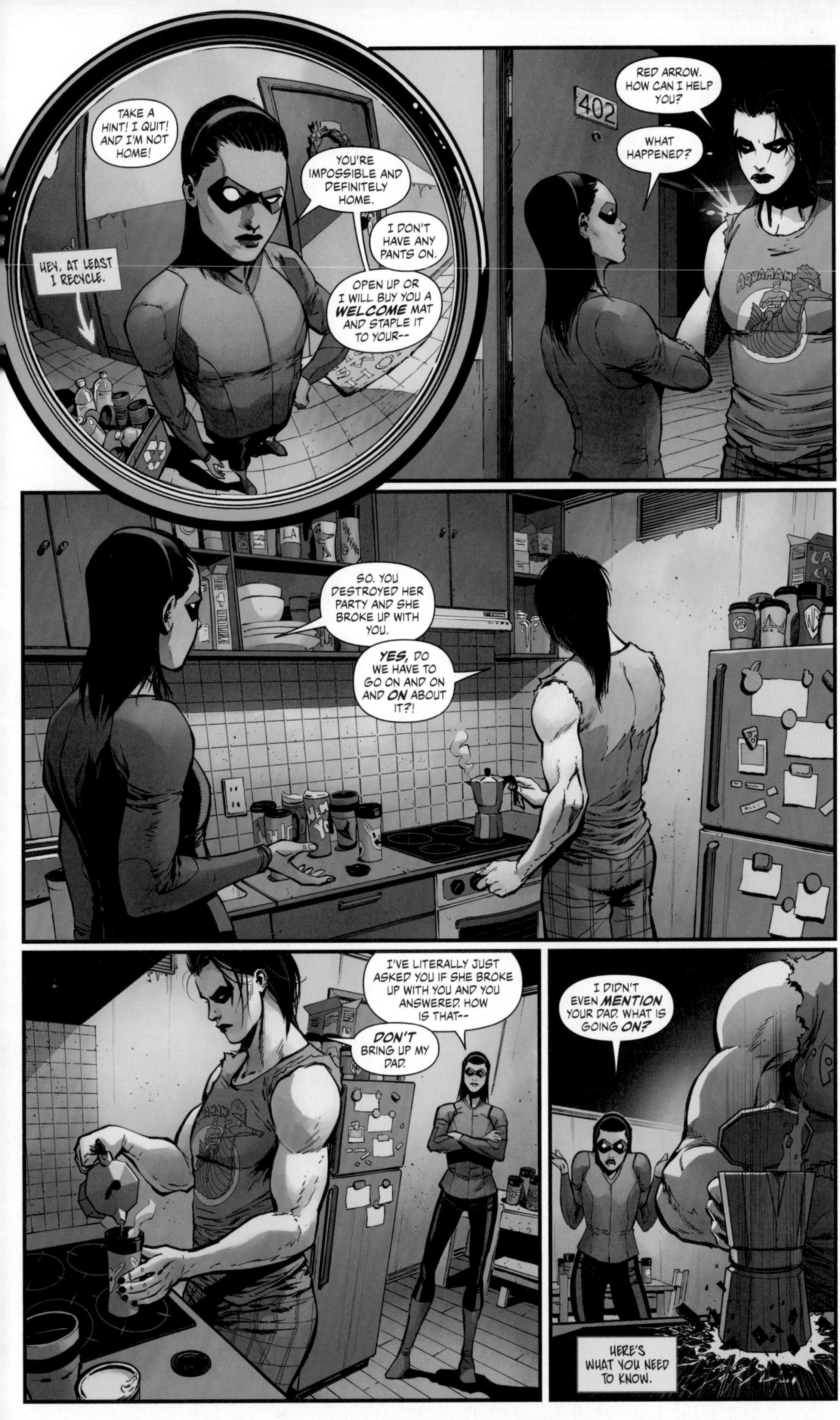

TAKE A HINT! I QUIT! AND I'M NOT HOME!
YOU'RE IMPOSSIBLE AND DEFINITELY HOME.
I DON'T HAVE ANY PANTS ON.
OPEN UP OR I WILL BUY YOU A WELCOME MAT AND STAPLE IT TO YOUR--
HEY, AT LEAST I RECYCLE.
402
RED ARROW. HOW CAN I HELP YOU?
WHAT HAPPENED?
AQUAMAN
SO. YOU DESTROYED HER PARTY AND SHE BROKE UP WITH YOU.
YES, DO WE HAVE TO GO ON AND ON AND ON ABOUT IT?!
I'VE LITERALLY JUST ASKED YOU IF SHE BROKE UP WITH YOU AND YOU ANSWERED. HOW IS THAT--
DON'T BRING UP MY DAD.
I DIDN'T EVEN MENTION YOUR DAD. WHAT IS GOING ON?
HERE'S WHAT YOU NEED TO KNOW.

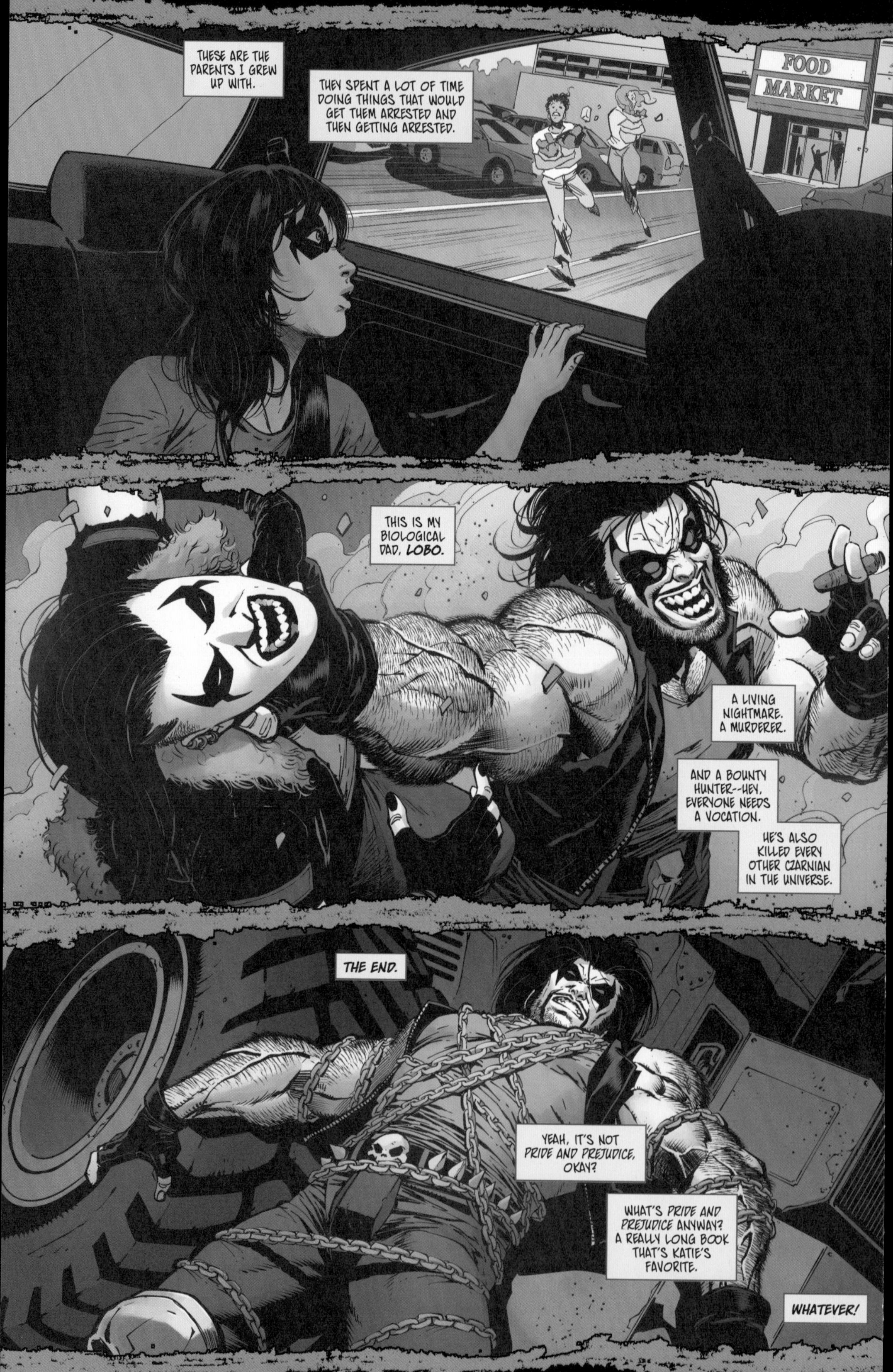
THESE ARE THE PARENTS I GREW UP WITH.
THEY SPENT A LOT OF TIME DOING THINGS THAT WOULD GET THEM ARRESTED AND THEN GETTING ARRESTED.
FOOD MARKET
THIS IS MY BIOLOGICAL DAD, LOBO.
A LIVING NIGHTMARE. A MURDERER.
AND A BOUNTY HUNTER--HEY, EVERYONE NEEDS A VOCATION.
HE'S ALSO KILLED EVERY OTHER CZARNIAN IN THE UNIVERSE.
THE END.
YEAH, IT'S NOT PRIDE AND PREJUDICE, OKAY?
WHAT'S PRIDE AND PREJUDICE ANYWAY? A REALLY LONG BOOK THAT'S KATIE'S FAVORITE.
WHATEVER!

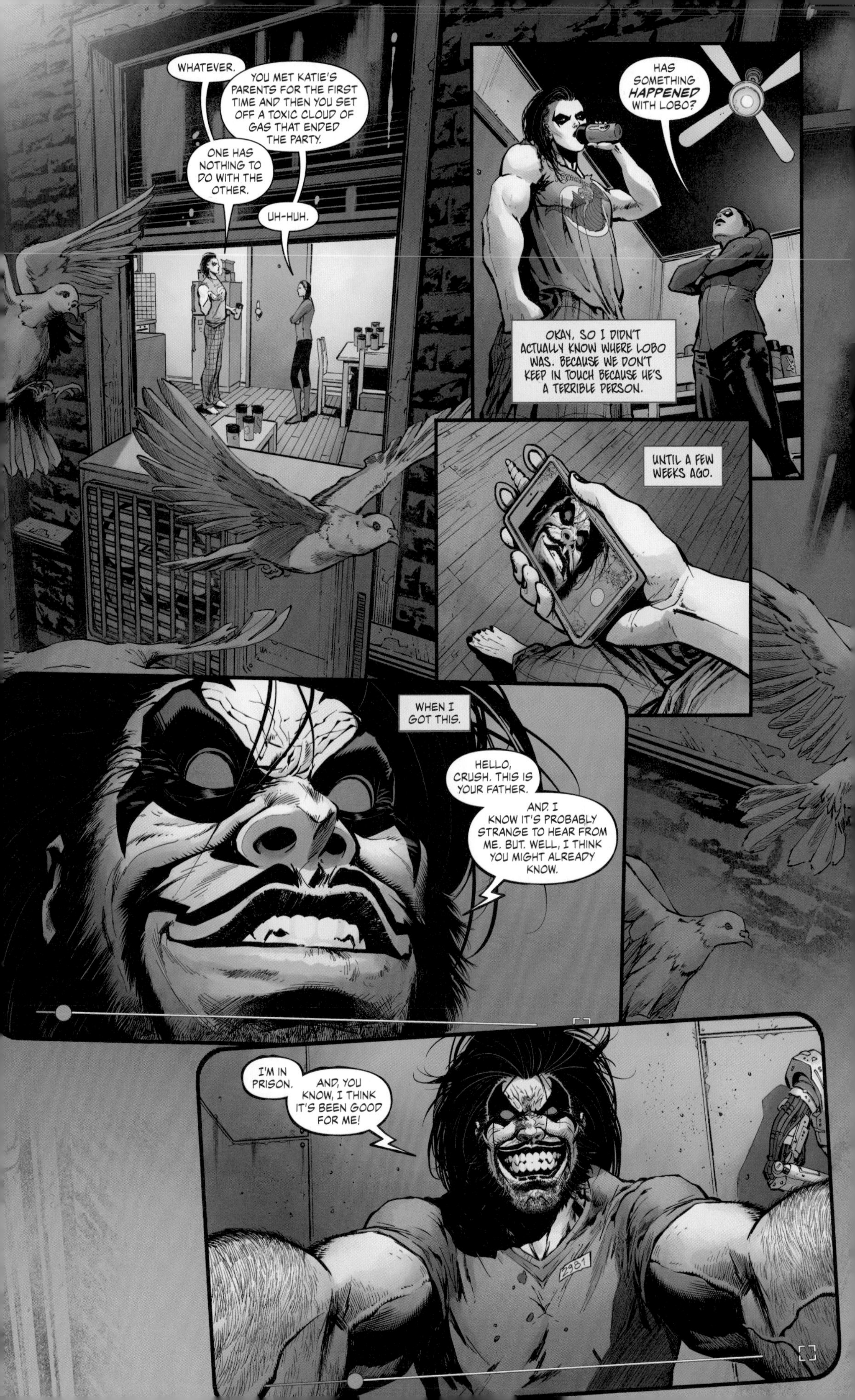
WHATEVER.
YOU MET KATIE'S PARENTS FOR THE FIRST TIME AND THEN YOU SET OFF A TOXIC CLOUD OF GAS THAT ENDED THE PARTY.
ONE HAS NOTHING TO DO WITH THE OTHER.
UH-HUH.
HAS SOMETHING HAPPENED WITH LOBO?
OKAY, SO I DIDN'T ACTUALLY KNOW WHERE LOBO WAS. BECAUSE WE DON'T KEEP IN TOUCH BECAUSE HE'S A TERRIBLE PERSON.
UNTIL A FEW WEEKS AGO.
WHEN I GOT THIS.
HELLO, CRUSH. THIS IS YOUR FATHER.
AND. I KNOW IT'S PROBABLY STRANGE TO HEAR FROM ME. BUT. WELL, I THINK YOU MIGHT ALREADY KNOW.
I'M IN PRISON.
AND, YOU KNOW, I THINK IT'S BEEN GOOD FOR ME!
2981

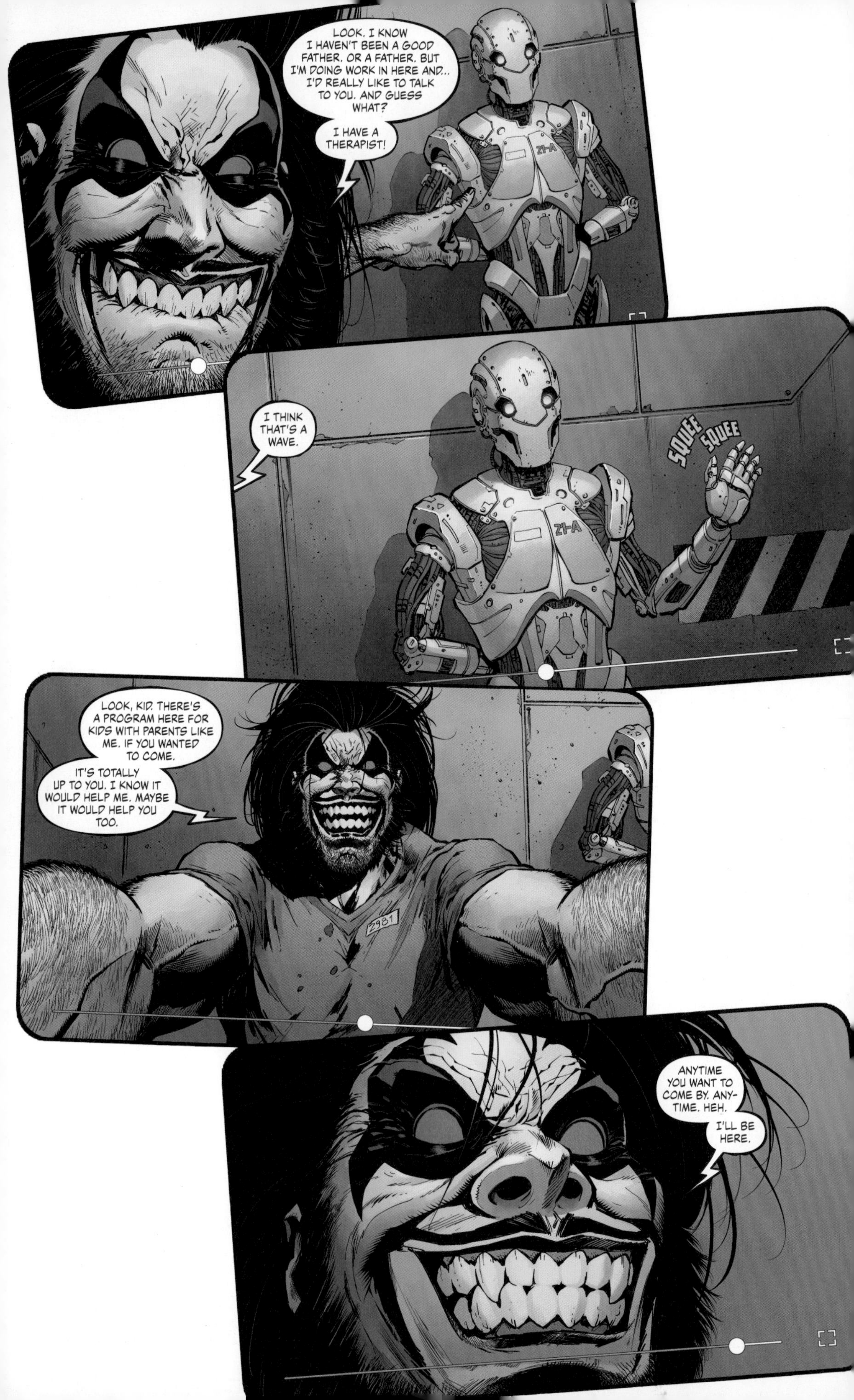
LOOK. I KNOW I HAVEN'T BEEN A GOOD FATHER. OR A FATHER. BUT I'M DOING WORK IN HERE AND... I'D REALLY LIKE TO TALK TO YOU. AND GUESS WHAT?
I HAVE A THERAPIST!
21-A
I THINK THAT'S A WAVE.
SQUEE
SQUEE
21-A
LOOK, KID. THERE'S A PROGRAM HERE FOR KIDS WITH PARENTS LIKE ME. IF YOU WANTED TO COME.
IT'S TOTALLY UP TO YOU. I KNOW IT WOULD HELP ME. MAYBE IT WOULD HELP YOU TOO.
2981
ANYTIME YOU WANT TO COME BY. ANY-TIME. HEH.
I'LL BE HERE.

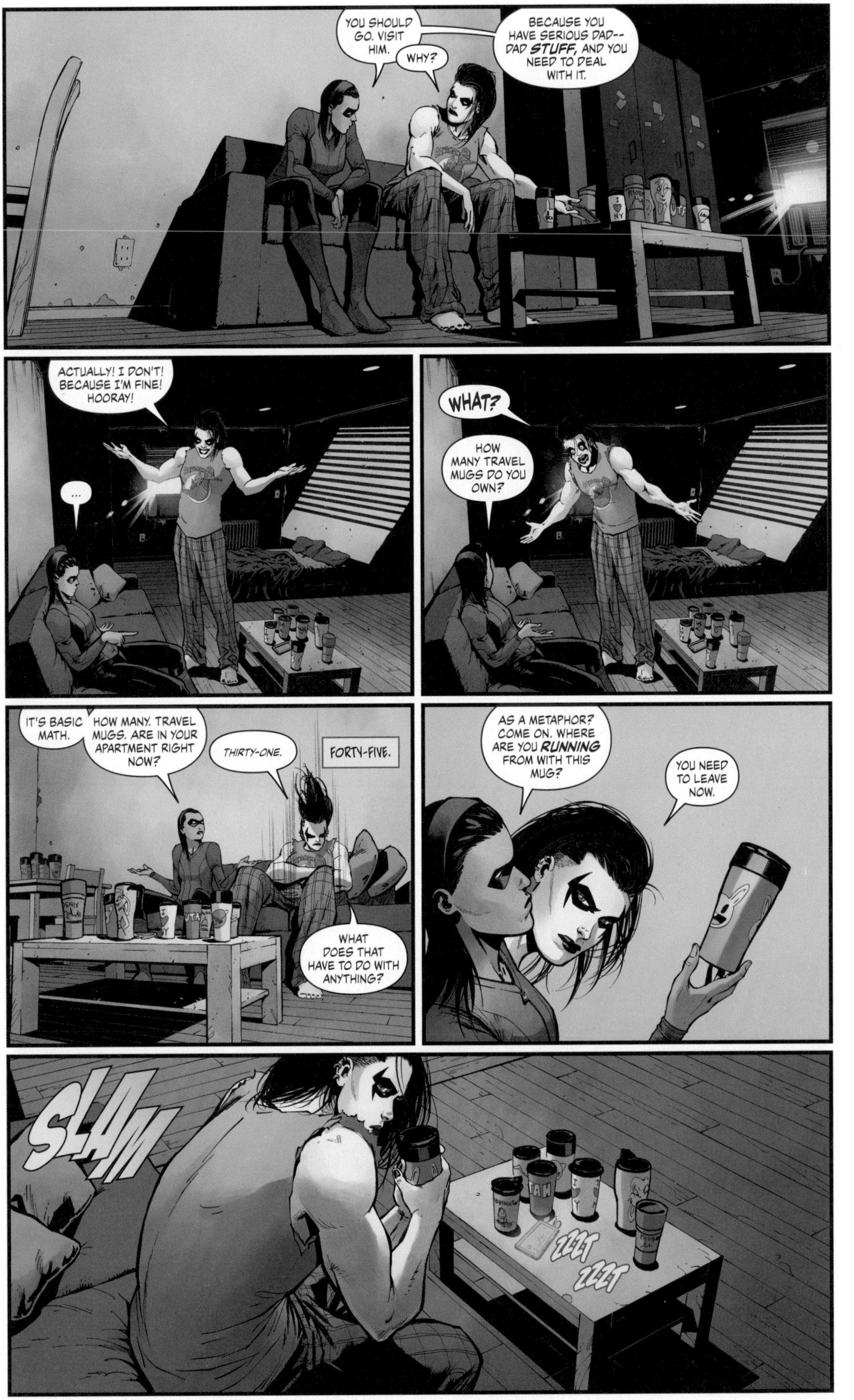
YOU SHOULD GO. VISIT HIM.
WHY?
BECAUSE YOU HAVE SERIOUS DAD--DAD STUFF, AND YOU NEED TO DEAL WITH IT.
ACTUALLY! I DON'T! BECAUSE I'M FINE! HOORAY!
...
WHAT?
HOW MANY TRAVEL MUGS DO YOU OWN?
IT'S BASIC MATH.
HOW MANY. TRAVEL MUGS. ARE IN YOUR APARTMENT RIGHT NOW?
THIRTY-ONE.
FORTY-FIVE.
WHAT DOES THAT HAVE TO DO WITH ANYTHING?
AS A METAPHOR? COME ON. WHERE ARE YOU RUNNING FROM WITH THIS MUG?
YOU NEED TO LEAVE NOW.
SLAM
ZZZT
ZZZT

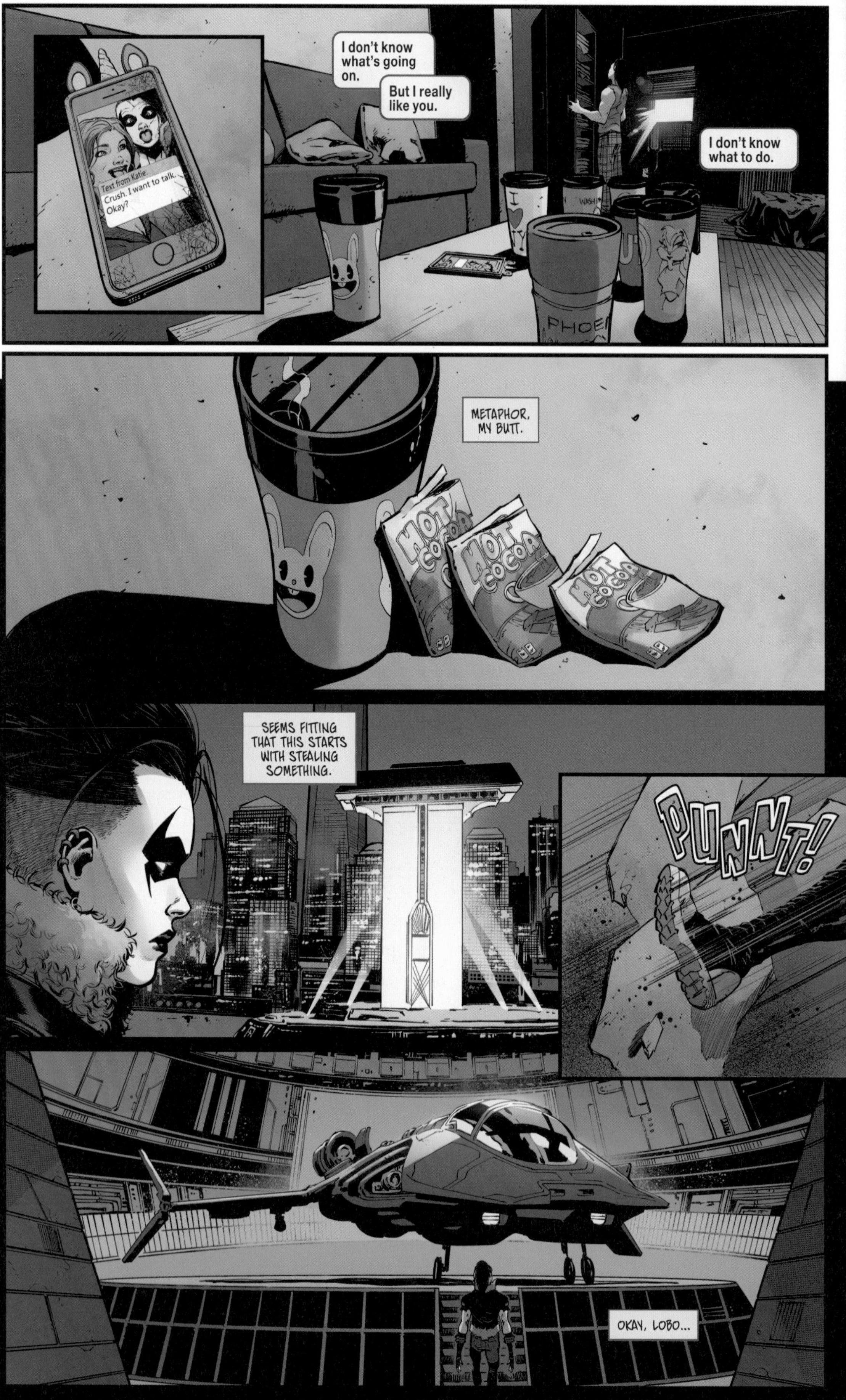
Text from Katie:
Crush. I want to talk. Okay?
I don't know what's going on.
But I really like you.
I don't know what to do.
METAPHOR, MY BUTT.
HOT COCOA
HOT COCOA
HOT COCOA
SEEMS FITTING THAT THIS STARTS WITH STEALING SOMETHING.
PUNNT!
OKAY, LOBO...

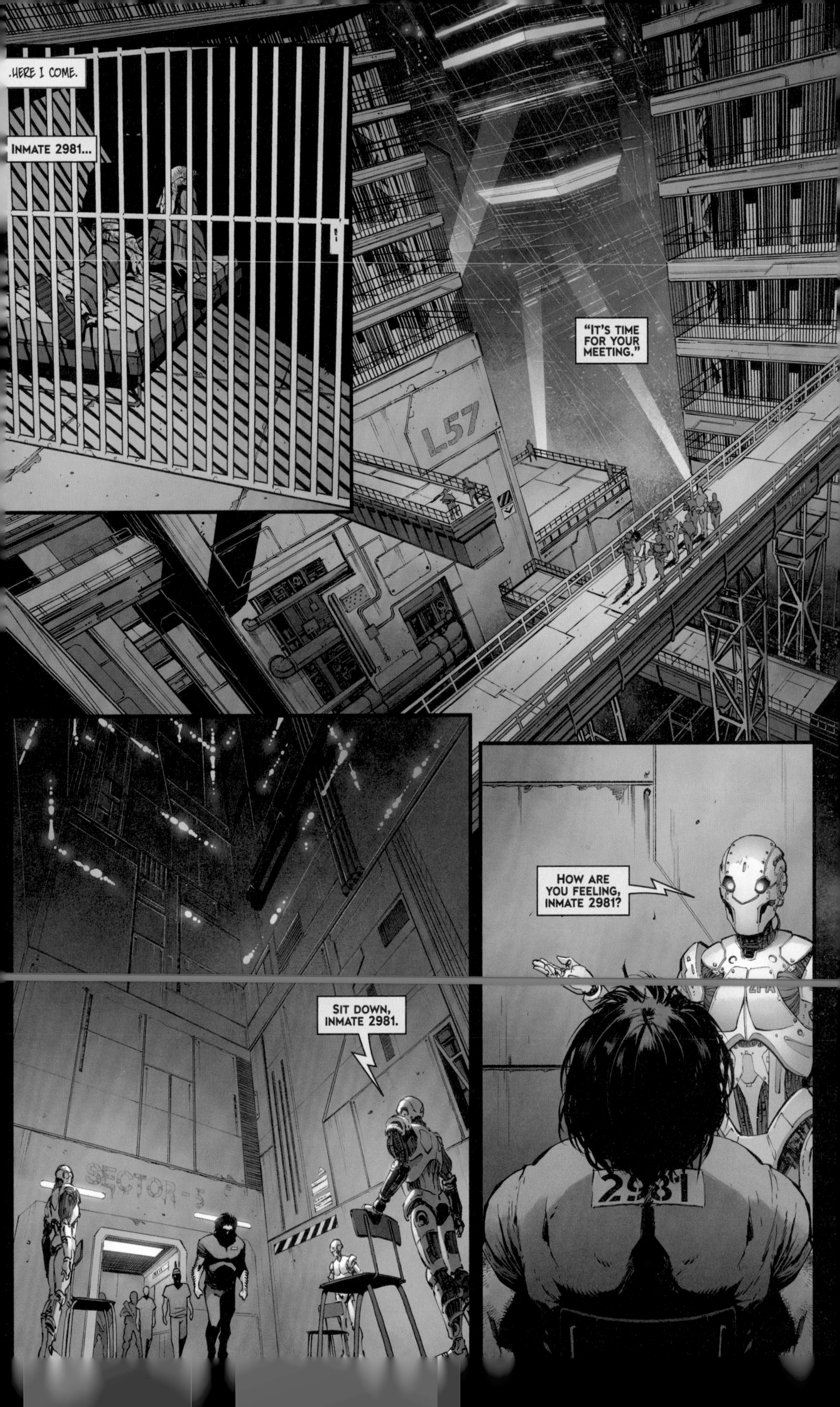
...HERE I COME.
INMATE 2981...
"IT'S TIME FOR YOUR MEETING."
L57
SIT DOWN, INMATE 2981.
SECTOR-5
HOW ARE YOU FEELING, INMATE 2981?
2981

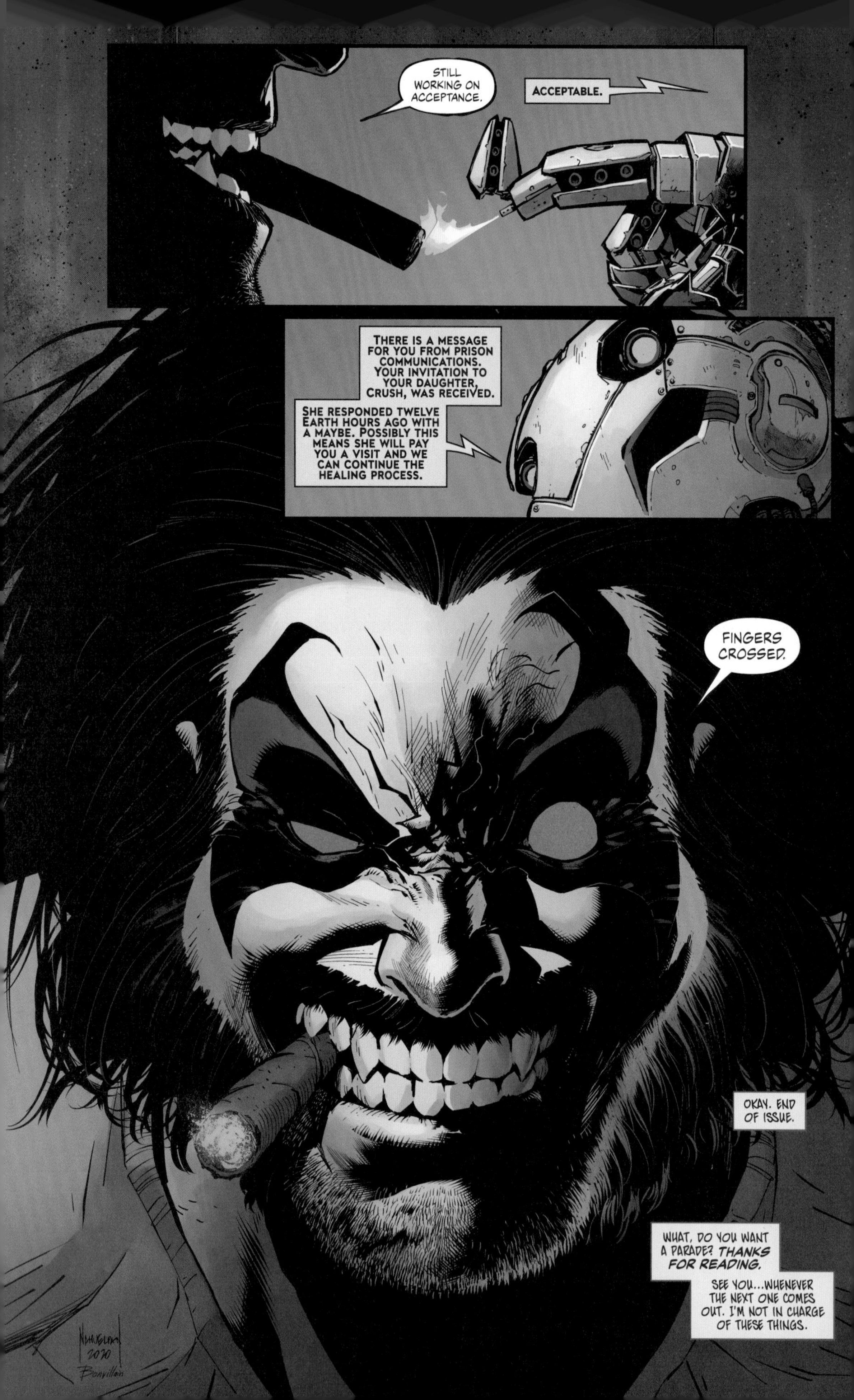
STILL WORKING ON ACCEPTANCE.
ACCEPTABLE.
THERE IS A MESSAGE FOR YOU FROM PRISON COMMUNICATIONS. YOUR INVITATION TO YOUR DAUGHTER, CRUSH, WAS RECEIVED.
SHE RESPONDED TWELVE EARTH HOURS AGO WITH A MAYBE. POSSIBLY THIS MEANS SHE WILL PAY YOU A VISIT AND WE CAN CONTINUE THE HEALING PROCESS.
FINGERS CROSSED.
OKAY. END OF ISSUE.
WHAT, DO YOU WANT A PARADE? THANKS FOR READING.
SEE YOU...WHENEVER THE NEXT ONE COMES OUT. I'M NOT IN CHARGE OF THESE THINGS.

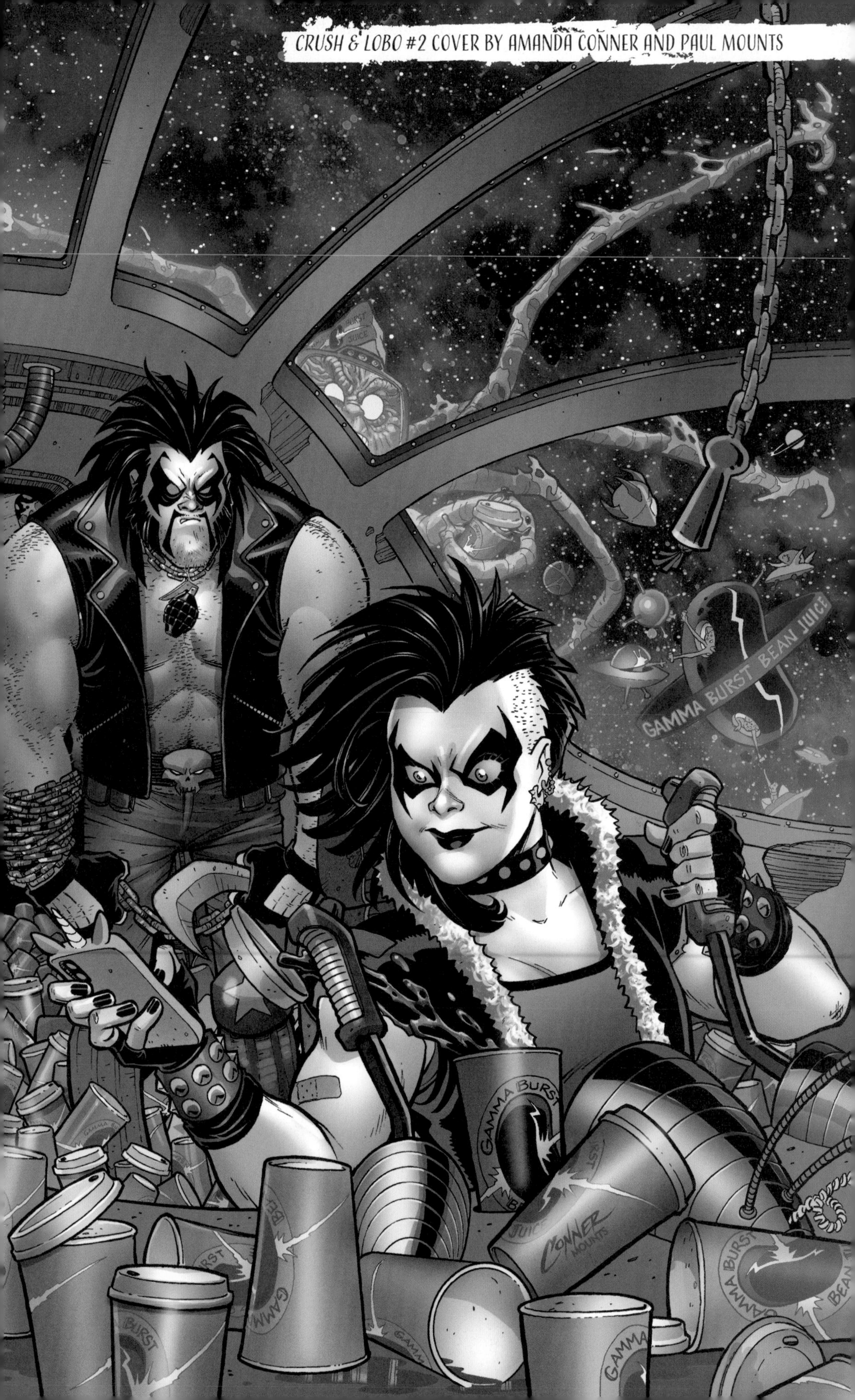
GAMMA BURST BEAN JUICE
GAMMA BURST
CONNER
MOUNTS
CRUSH & LOBO #2 COVER BY AMANDA CONNER AND PAUL MOUNTS

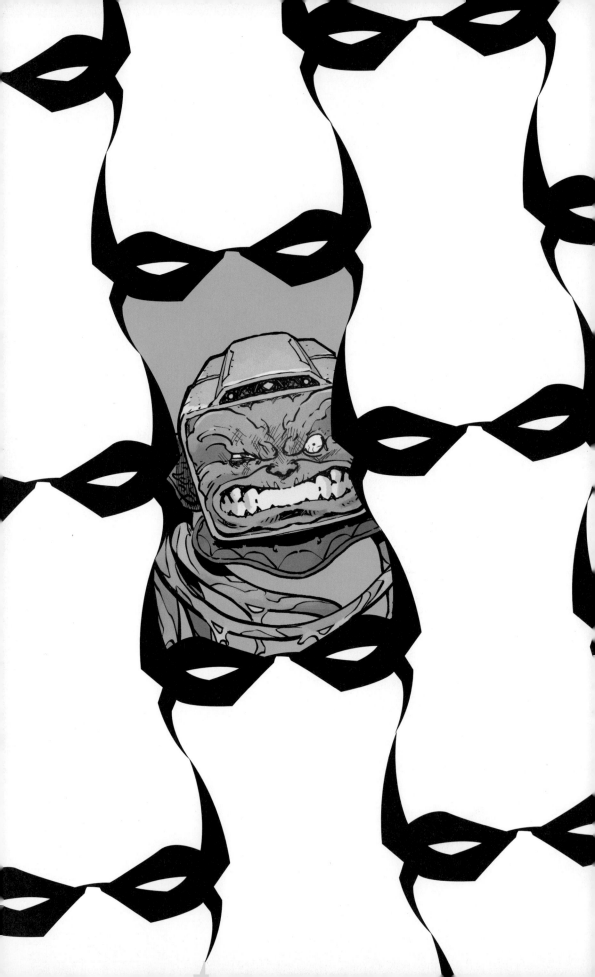

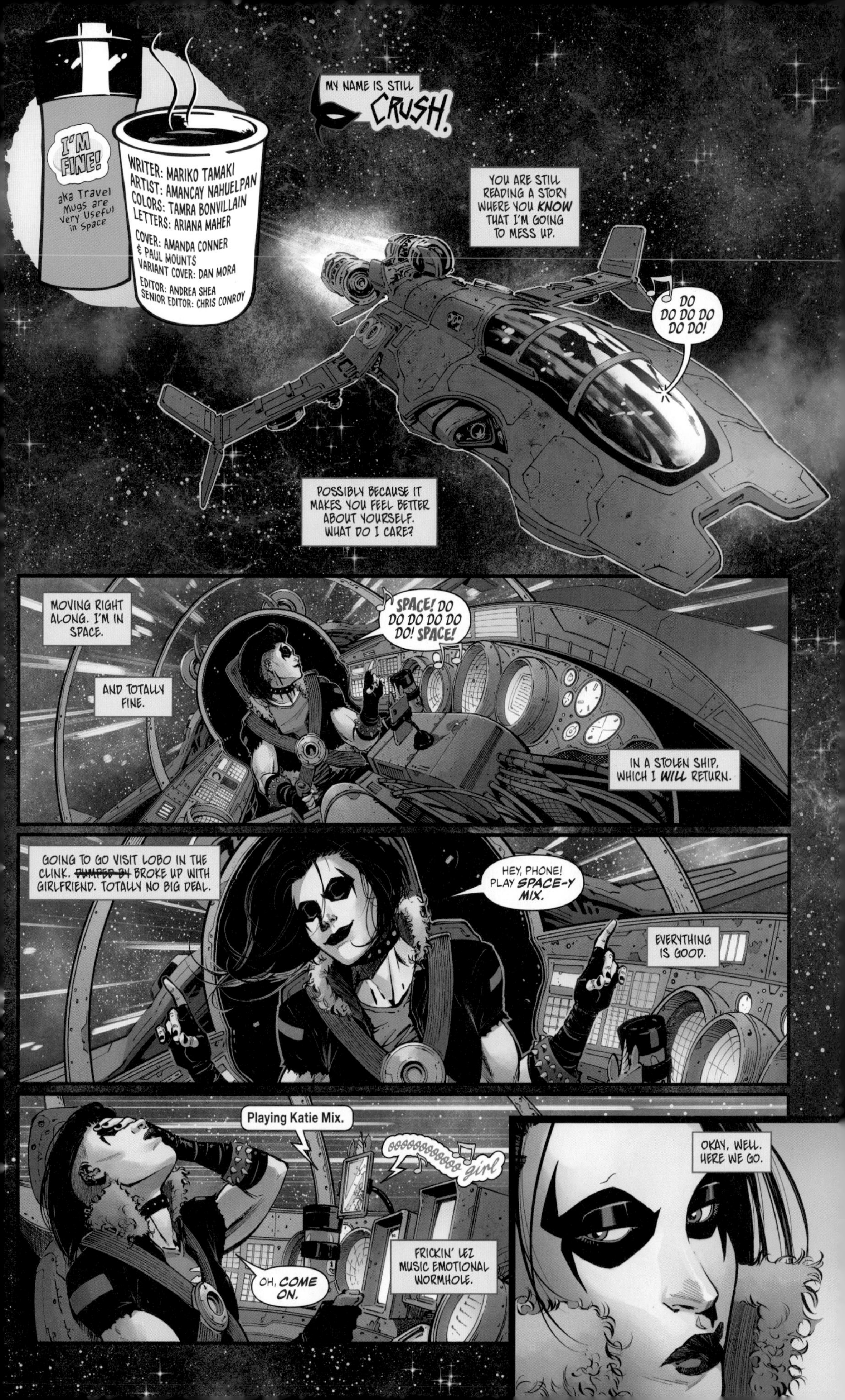
I'M FINE!
aka Travel Mugs are Very Useful in Space
WRITER: MARIKO TAMAKI
ARTIST: AMANCAY NAHUELPAN
COLORS: TAMRA BONVILLAIN
LETTERS: ARIANA MAHER
COVER: AMANDA CONNER & PAUL MOUNTS
VARIANT COVER: DAN MORA
EDITOR: ANDREA SHEA
SENIOR EDITOR: CHRIS CONROY
MY NAME IS STILL CRUSH.
YOU ARE STILL READING A STORY WHERE YOU KNOW THAT I'M GOING TO MESS UP.
DO DO DO DO DO DO!
POSSIBLY BECAUSE IT MAKES YOU FEEL BETTER ABOUT YOURSELF. WHAT DO I CARE?
MOVING RIGHT ALONG. I'M IN SPACE.
SPACE! DO DO DO DO DO DO! SPACE!
AND TOTALLY FINE.
IN A STOLEN SHIP, WHICH I WILL RETURN.
GOING TO GO VISIT LOBO IN THE CLINK. ~~DUMPED BY~~ BROKE UP WITH GIRLFRIEND. TOTALLY NO BIG DEAL.
HEY, PHONE! PLAY SPACE-Y MIX.
EVERYTHING IS GOOD.
Playing Katie Mix.
oooooooooooo girl
OH, COME ON.
FRICKIN' LEZ MUSIC EMOTIONAL WORMHOLE.
OKAY, WELL. HERE WE GO.

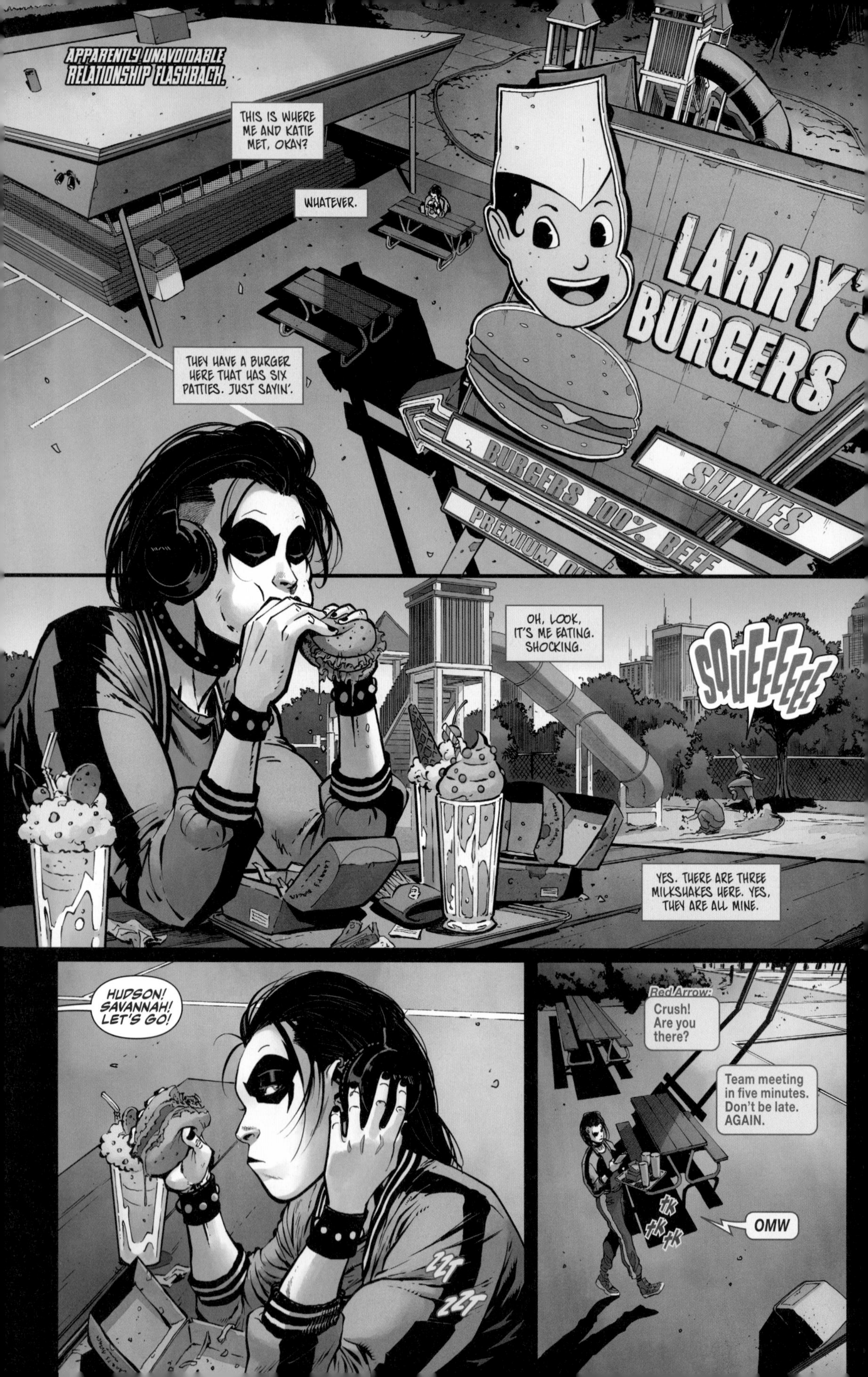

APPARENTLY UNAVOIDABLE RELATIONSHIP FLASHBACK.
THIS IS WHERE ME AND KATIE MET, OKAY?
WHATEVER.
LARRY'S BURGERS
THEY HAVE A BURGER HERE THAT HAS SIX PATTIES. JUST SAYIN'.
BURGERS 100% BEEF
SHAKES
OH, LOOK, IT'S ME EATING. SHOCKING.
SQUEEEEEE
YES. THERE ARE THREE MILKSHAKES HERE. YES, THEY ARE ALL MINE.
HUDSON! SAVANNAH! LET'S GO!
ZZZT
ZZZT
Red Arrow:
Crush! Are you there?
Team meeting in five minutes. Don't be late. AGAIN.
tk tk tk
OMW

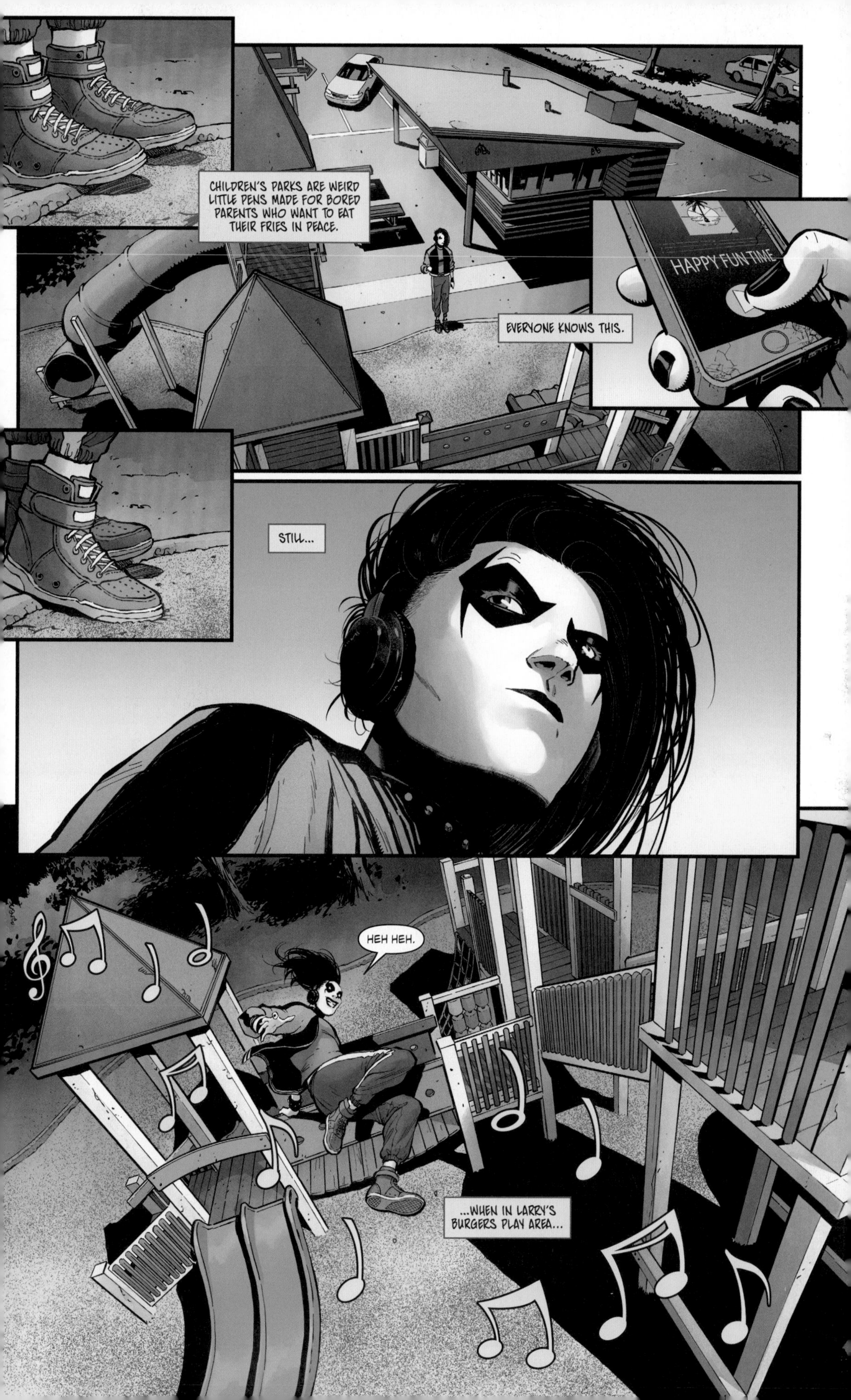
CHILDREN'S PARKS ARE WEIRD LITTLE PENS MADE FOR BORED PARENTS WHO WANT TO EAT THEIR FRIES IN PEACE.
HAPPY FUN TIME
EVERYONE KNOWS THIS.
STILL...
HEH HEH.
...WHEN IN LARRY'S BURGERS PLAY AREA...

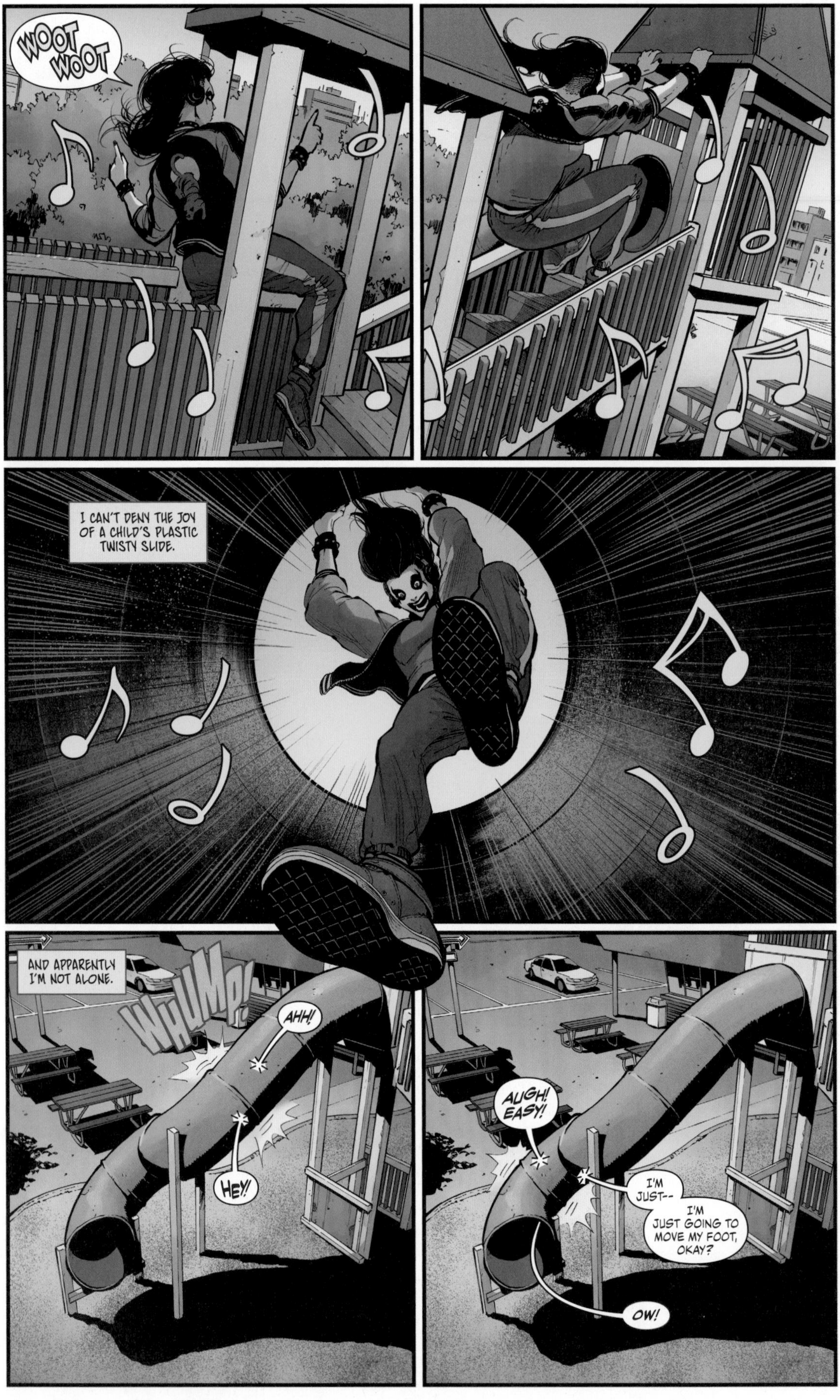
WOOT WOOT
I CAN'T DENY THE JOY OF A CHILD'S PLASTIC TWISTY SLIDE.
AND APPARENTLY I'M NOT ALONE.
WHUMP!
AHH!
HEY!
AUGH! EASY!
I'M JUST--
I'M JUST GOING TO MOVE MY FOOT, OKAY?
OW!

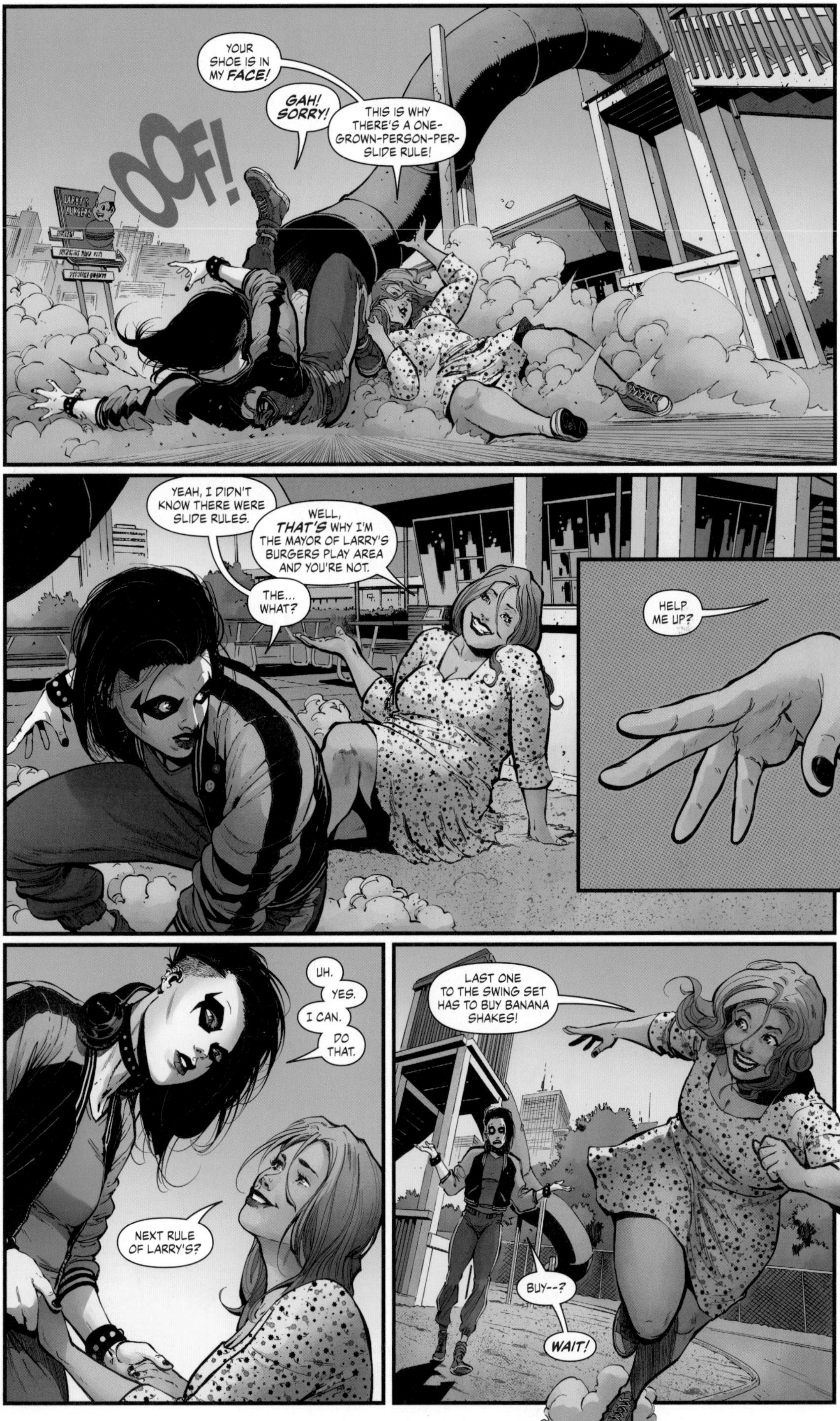
OOF!
YOUR SHOE IS IN MY *FACE!*
GAH! SORRY!
THIS IS WHY THERE'S A ONE-GROWN-PERSON-PER-SLIDE RULE!
YEAH, I DIDN'T KNOW THERE WERE SLIDE RULES.
WELL, *THAT'S* WHY I'M THE MAYOR OF LARRY'S BURGERS PLAY AREA AND YOU'RE NOT.
THE... WHAT?
HELP ME UP?
UH.
YES.
I CAN.
DO THAT.
NEXT RULE OF LARRY'S?
LAST ONE TO THE SWING SET HAS TO BUY BANANA SHAKES!
BUY--?
WAIT!

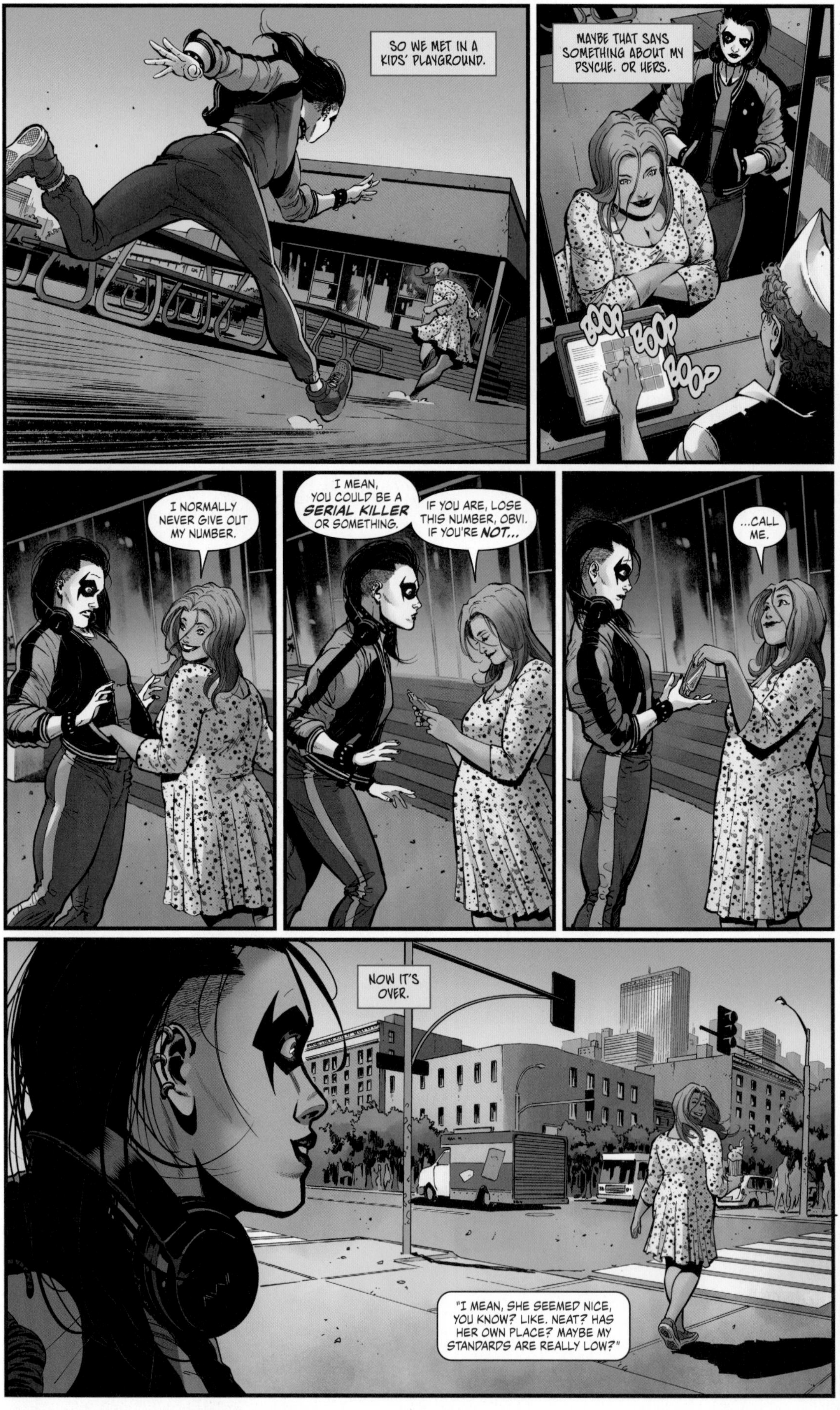
SO WE MET IN A KIDS' PLAYGROUND.
MAYBE THAT SAYS SOMETHING ABOUT MY PSYCHE. OR HERS.
BOOP BOOP BOOP
I NORMALLY NEVER GIVE OUT MY NUMBER.
I MEAN, YOU COULD BE A SERIAL KILLER OR SOMETHING.
IF YOU ARE, LOSE THIS NUMBER, OBVI. IF YOU'RE NOT...
...CALL ME.
NOW IT'S OVER.
"I MEAN, SHE SEEMED NICE, YOU KNOW? LIKE. NEAT? HAS HER OWN PLACE? MAYBE MY STANDARDS ARE REALLY LOW?"

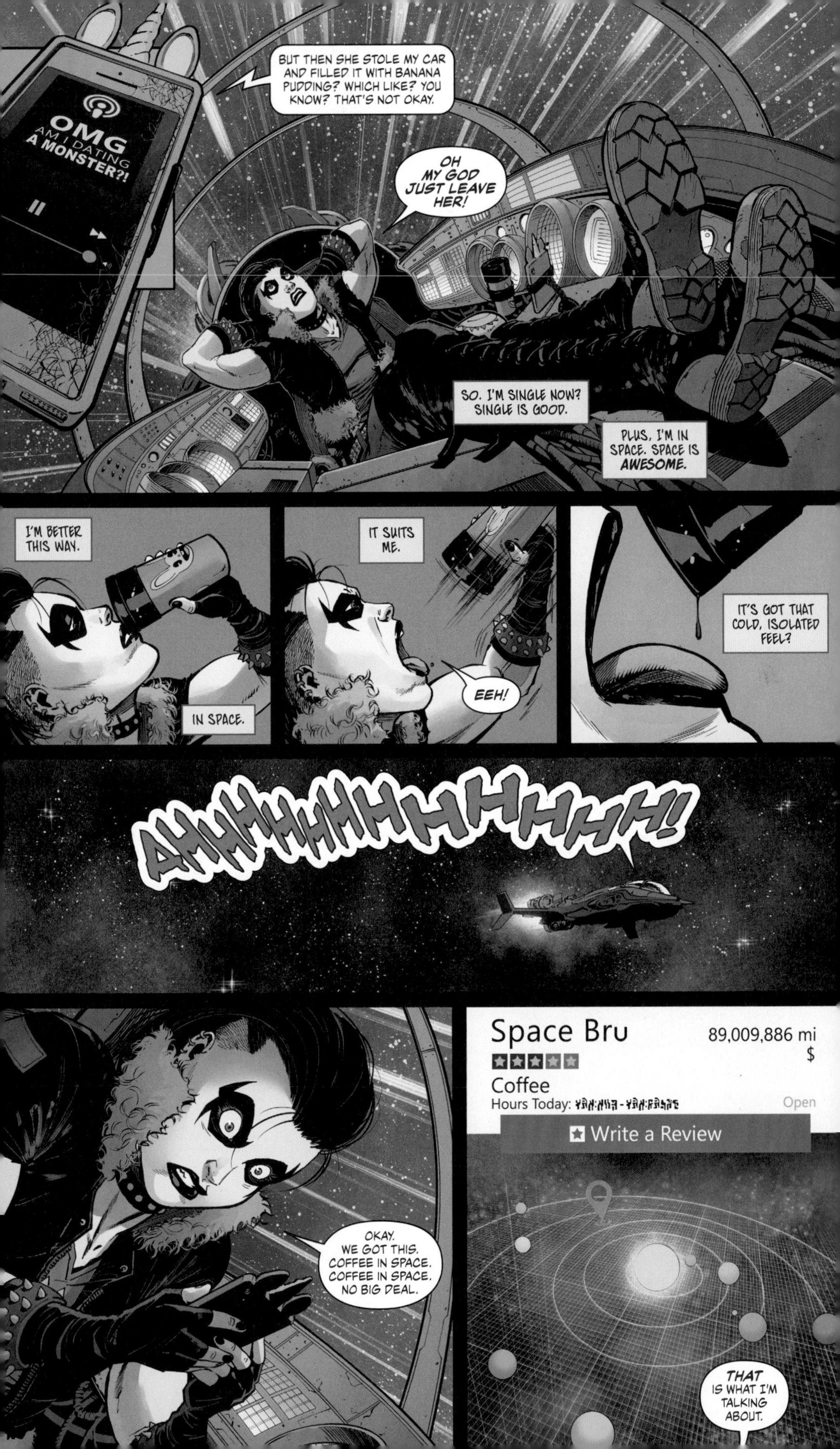
OMG
AM I DATING
A MONSTER?!
BUT THEN SHE STOLE MY CAR AND FILLED IT WITH BANANA PUDDING? WHICH LIKE? YOU KNOW? THAT'S NOT OKAY.
OH MY GOD JUST LEAVE HER!
SO. I'M SINGLE NOW? SINGLE IS GOOD.
PLUS, I'M IN SPACE. SPACE IS AWESOME.
I'M BETTER THIS WAY.
IN SPACE.
IT SUITS ME.
EEH!
IT'S GOT THAT COLD, ISOLATED FEEL?
AHHHHHHHHHHHH!
OKAY. WE GOT THIS. COFFEE IN SPACE. COFFEE IN SPACE. NO BIG DEAL.
Space Bru
89,009,886 mi
$
Coffee
Hours Today:
Open
Write a Review
THAT IS WHAT I'M TALKING ABOUT.

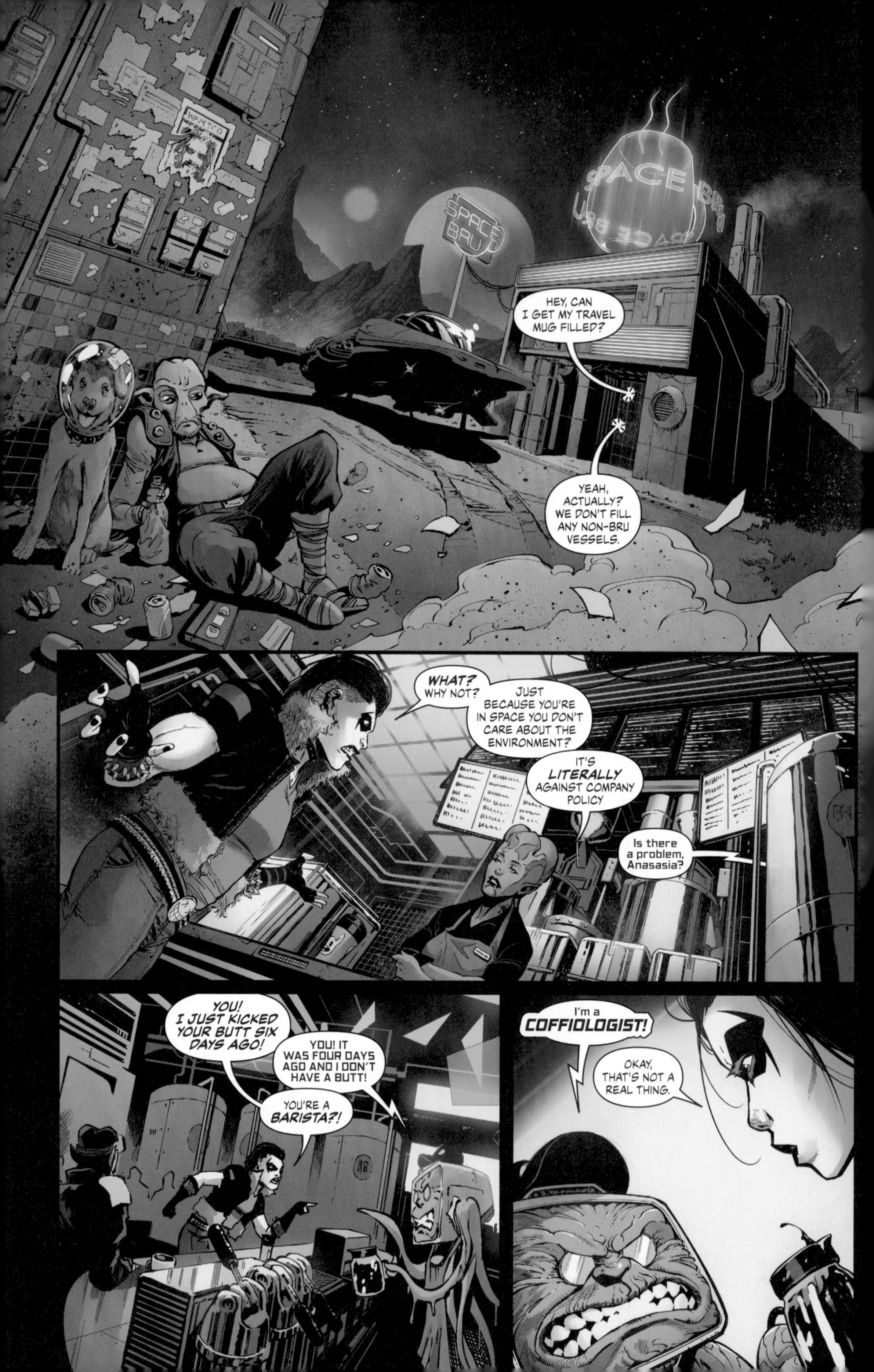
SPACE BRU
SPACE BRU
HEY, CAN I GET MY TRAVEL MUG FILLED?
YEAH, ACTUALLY? WE DON'T FILL ANY NON-BRU VESSELS.
WHAT? WHY NOT?
JUST BECAUSE YOU'RE IN SPACE YOU DON'T CARE ABOUT THE ENVIRONMENT?
IT'S LITERALLY AGAINST COMPANY POLICY
Is there a problem, Anasasia?
YOU! I JUST KICKED YOUR BUTT SIX DAYS AGO!
YOU! IT WAS FOUR DAYS AGO AND I DON'T HAVE A BUTT!
YOU'RE A BARISTA?!
I'm a COFFIOLOGIST!
OKAY, THAT'S NOT A REAL THING.

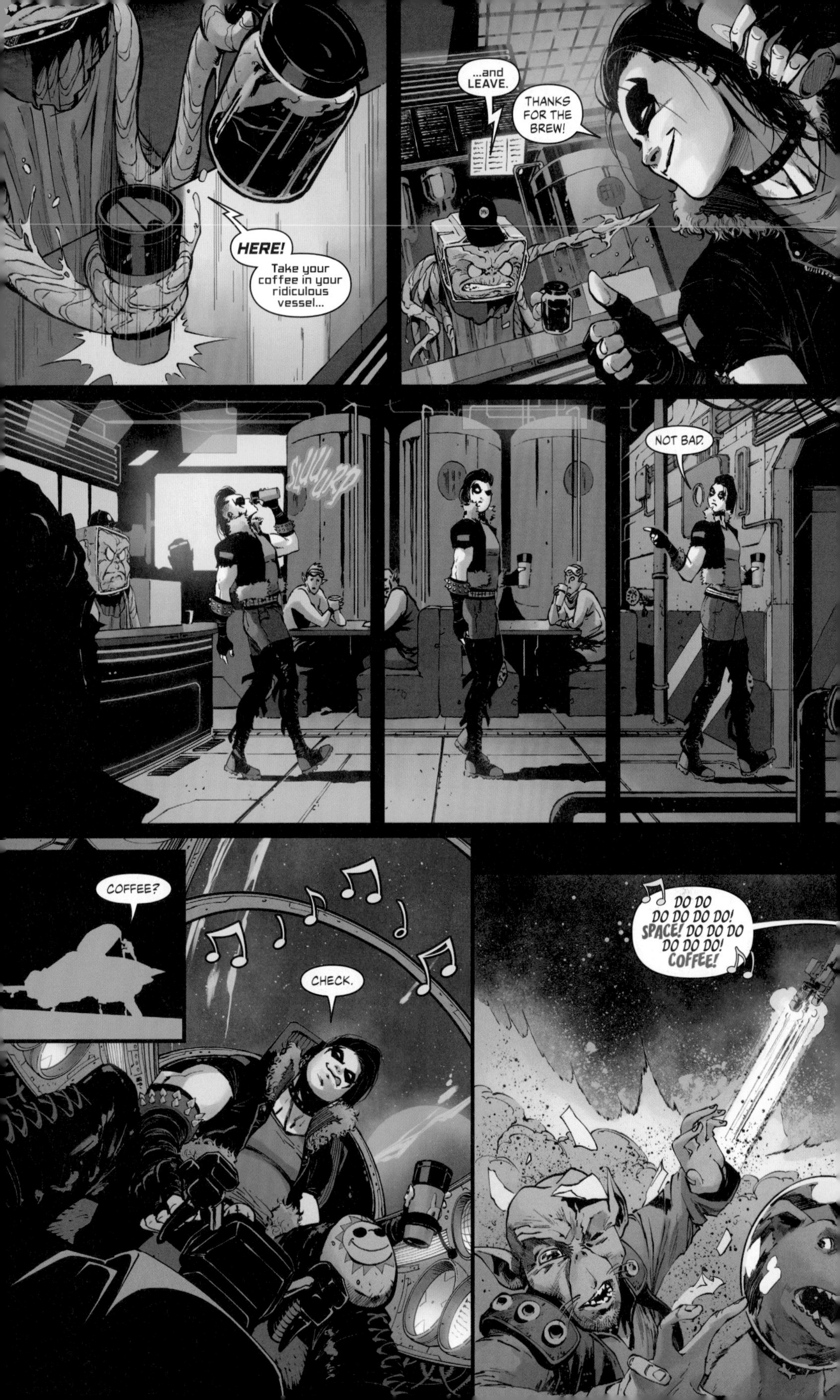
HERE!
Take your coffee in your ridiculous vessel...
...and LEAVE.
THANKS FOR THE BREW!
SLUUURP
NOT BAD.
COFFEE?
CHECK.
DO DO DO DO DO DO! SPACE! DO DO DO DO DO DO! COFFEE!

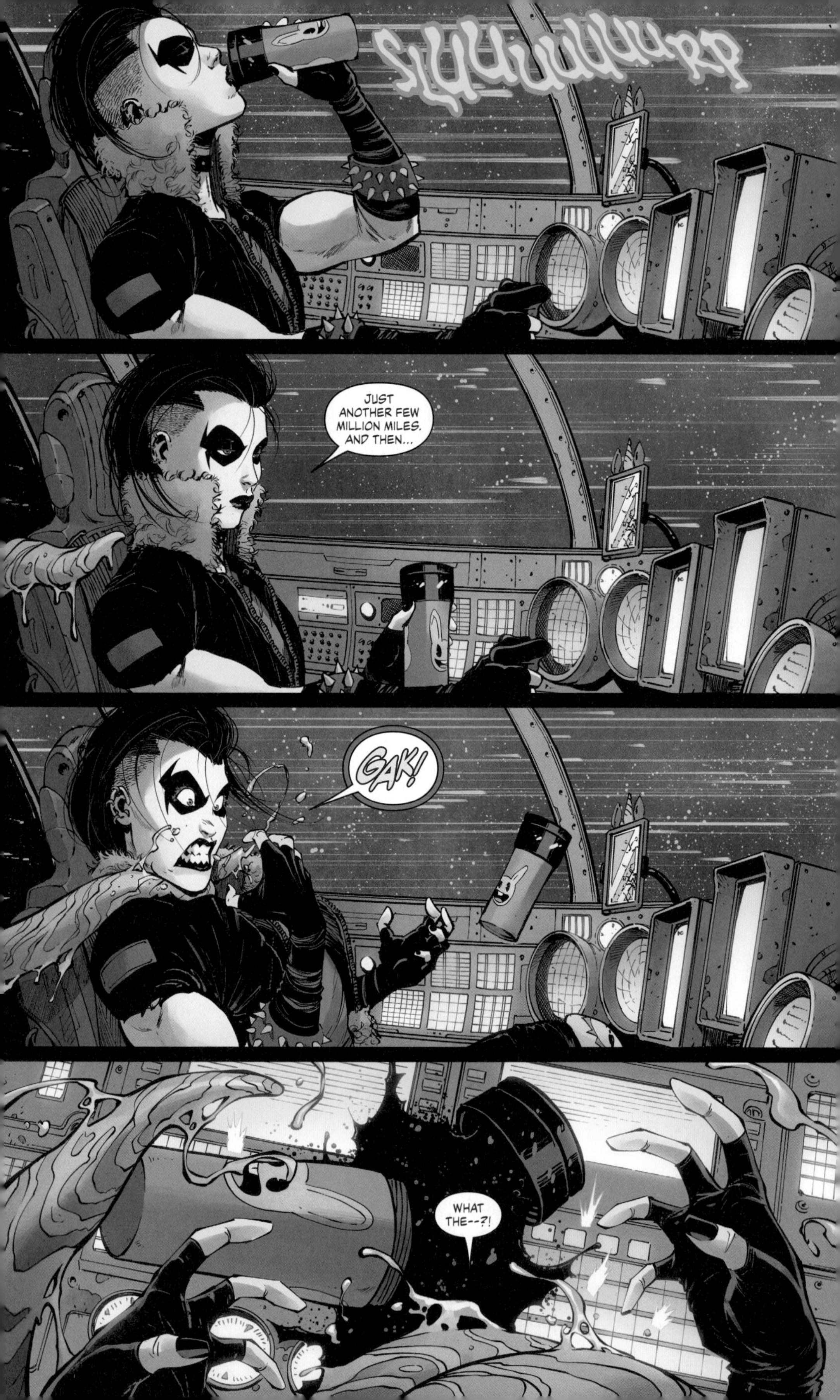
SLLLURRRRRRURRP
JUST ANOTHER FEW MILLION MILES, AND THEN...
GAK!
WHAT THE--?!

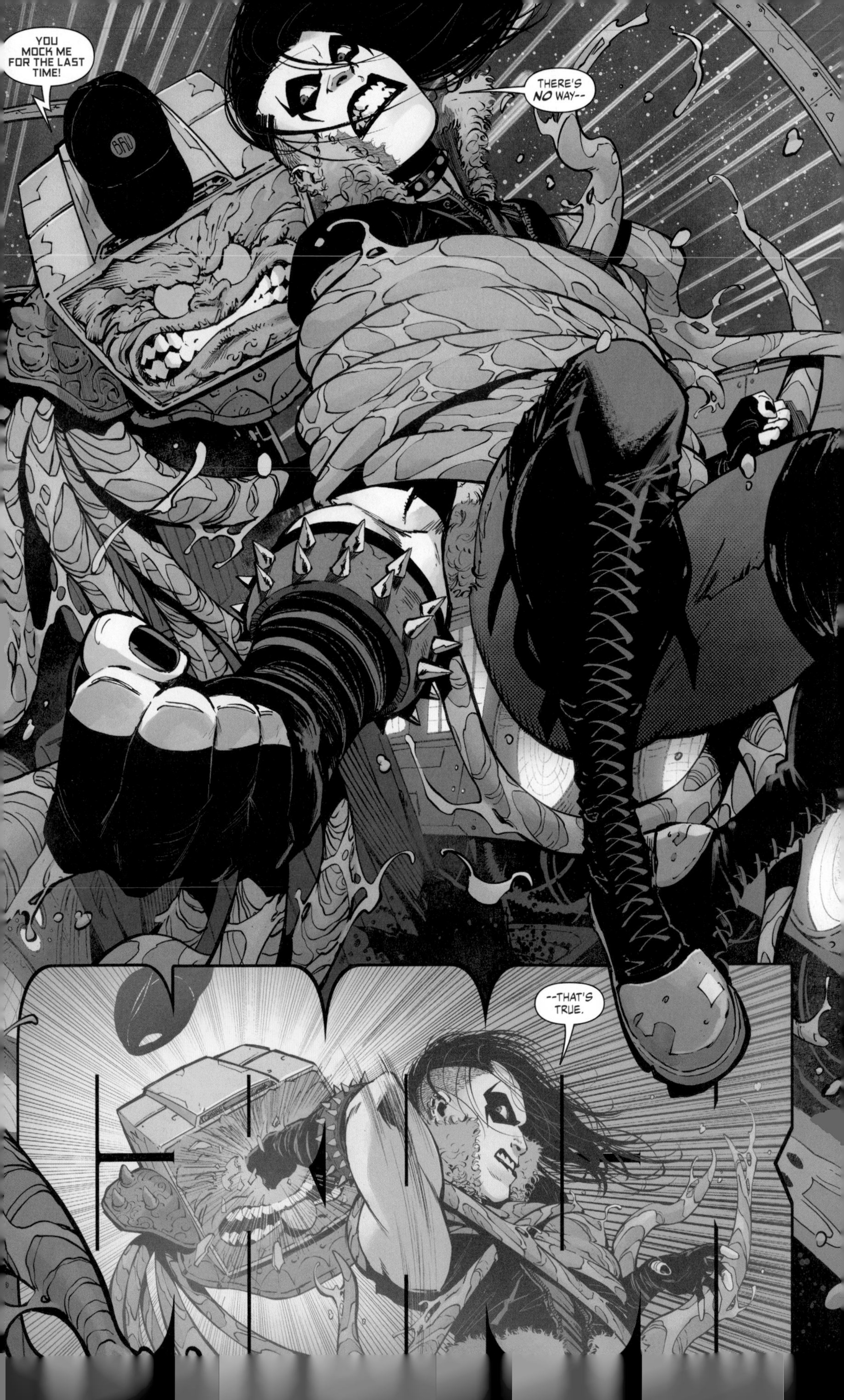

YOU MOCK ME FOR THE LAST TIME!
THERE'S NO WAY--
--THAT'S TRUE.

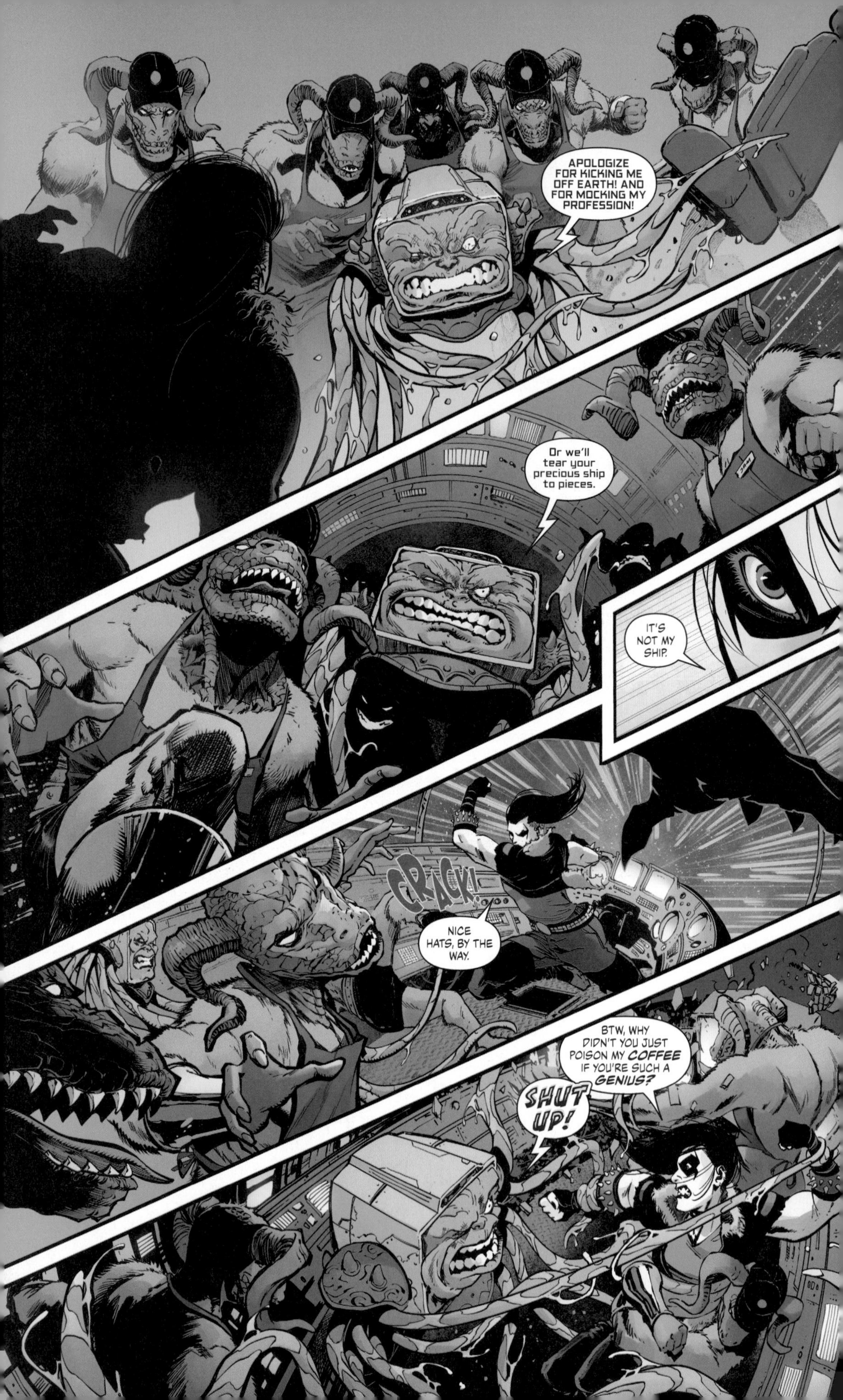
APOLOGIZE FOR KICKING ME OFF EARTH! AND FOR MOCKING MY PROFESSION!
Or we'll tear your precious ship to pieces.
IT'S NOT MY SHIP.
CRACK!
NICE HATS, BY THE WAY.
BTW, WHY DIDN'T YOU JUST POISON MY COFFEE IF YOU'RE SUCH A GENIUS?
SHUT UP!

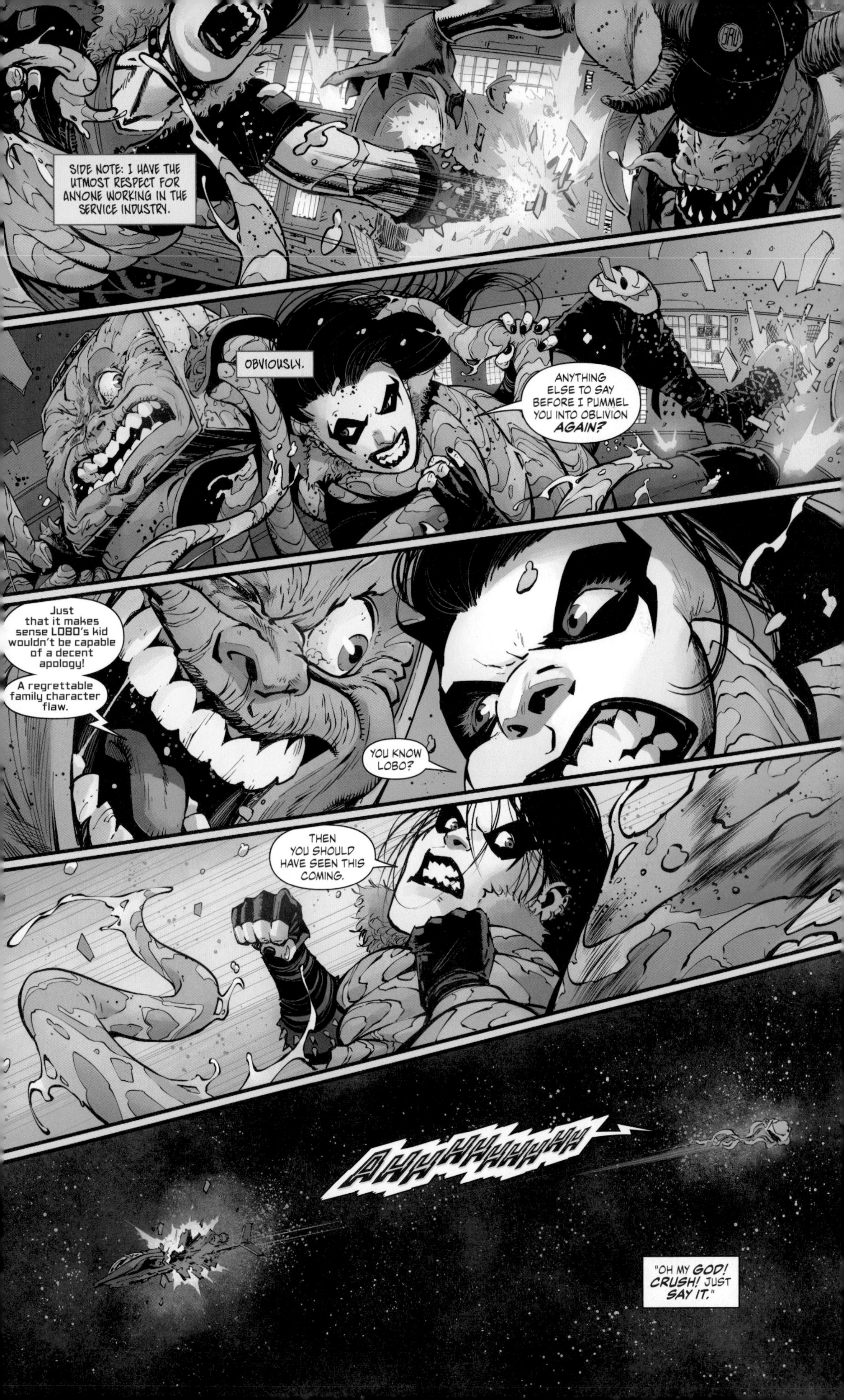
SIDE NOTE: I HAVE THE UTMOST RESPECT FOR ANYONE WORKING IN THE SERVICE INDUSTRY.
OBVIOUSLY.
ANYTHING ELSE TO SAY BEFORE I PUMMEL YOU INTO OBLIVION AGAIN?
Just that it makes sense LOBO's kid wouldn't be capable of a decent apology!
A regrettable family character flaw.
YOU KNOW LOBO?
THEN YOU SHOULD HAVE SEEN THIS COMING.
AHHHHHHHHH
"OH MY GOD! CRUSH! JUST SAY IT."

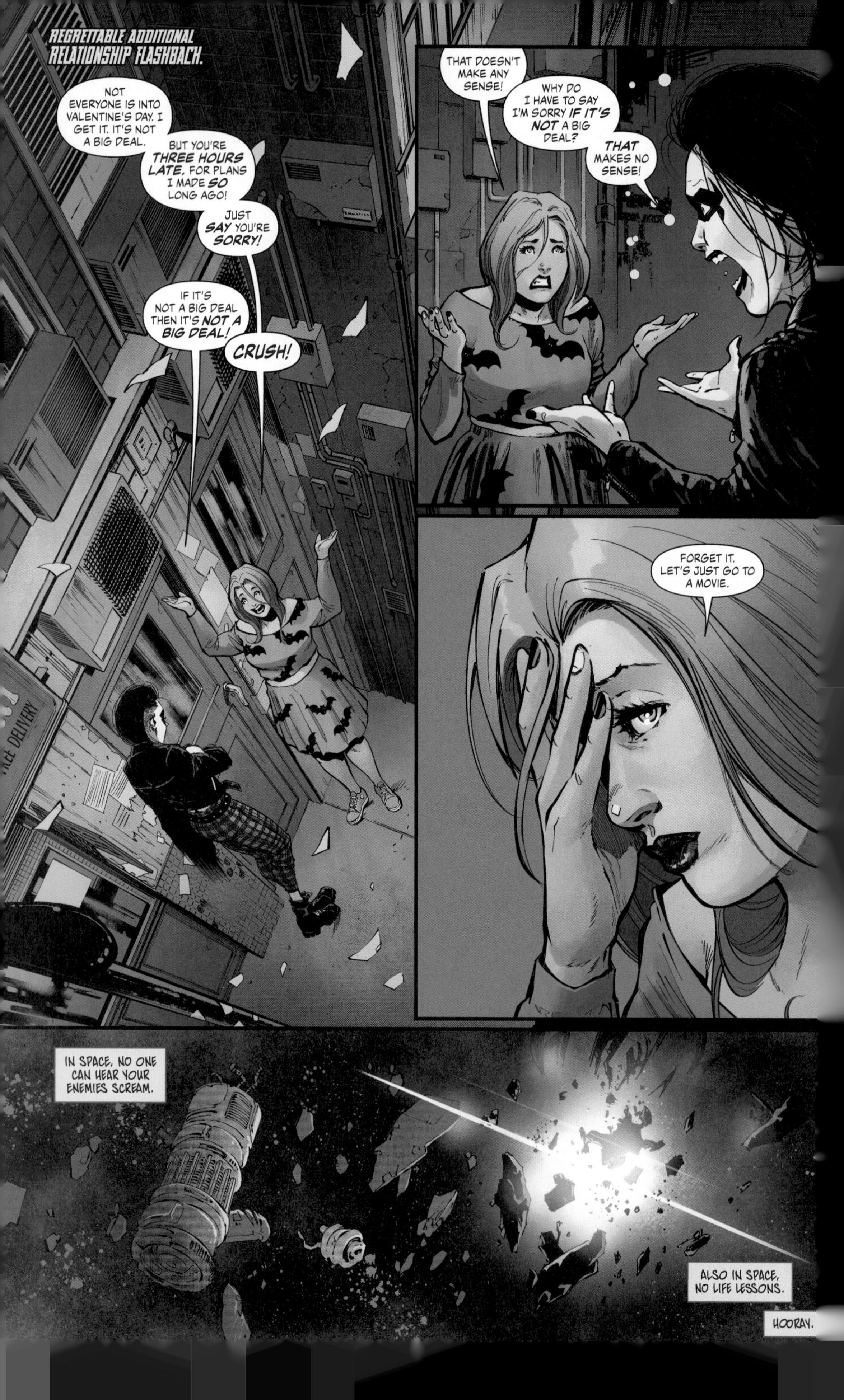

REGRETTABLE ADDITIONAL RELATIONSHIP FLASHBACK.
NOT EVERYONE IS INTO VALENTINE'S DAY. I GET IT. IT'S NOT A BIG DEAL.
BUT YOU'RE THREE HOURS LATE. FOR PLANS I MADE SO LONG AGO!
JUST SAY YOU'RE SORRY!
IF IT'S NOT A BIG DEAL THEN IT'S NOT A BIG DEAL!
CRUSH!
THAT DOESN'T MAKE ANY SENSE!
WHY DO I HAVE TO SAY I'M SORRY IF IT'S NOT A BIG DEAL?
THAT MAKES NO SENSE!
FORGET IT. LET'S JUST GO TO A MOVIE.
IN SPACE, NO ONE CAN HEAR YOUR ENEMIES SCREAM.
ALSO IN SPACE, NO LIFE LESSONS.
HOORAY.

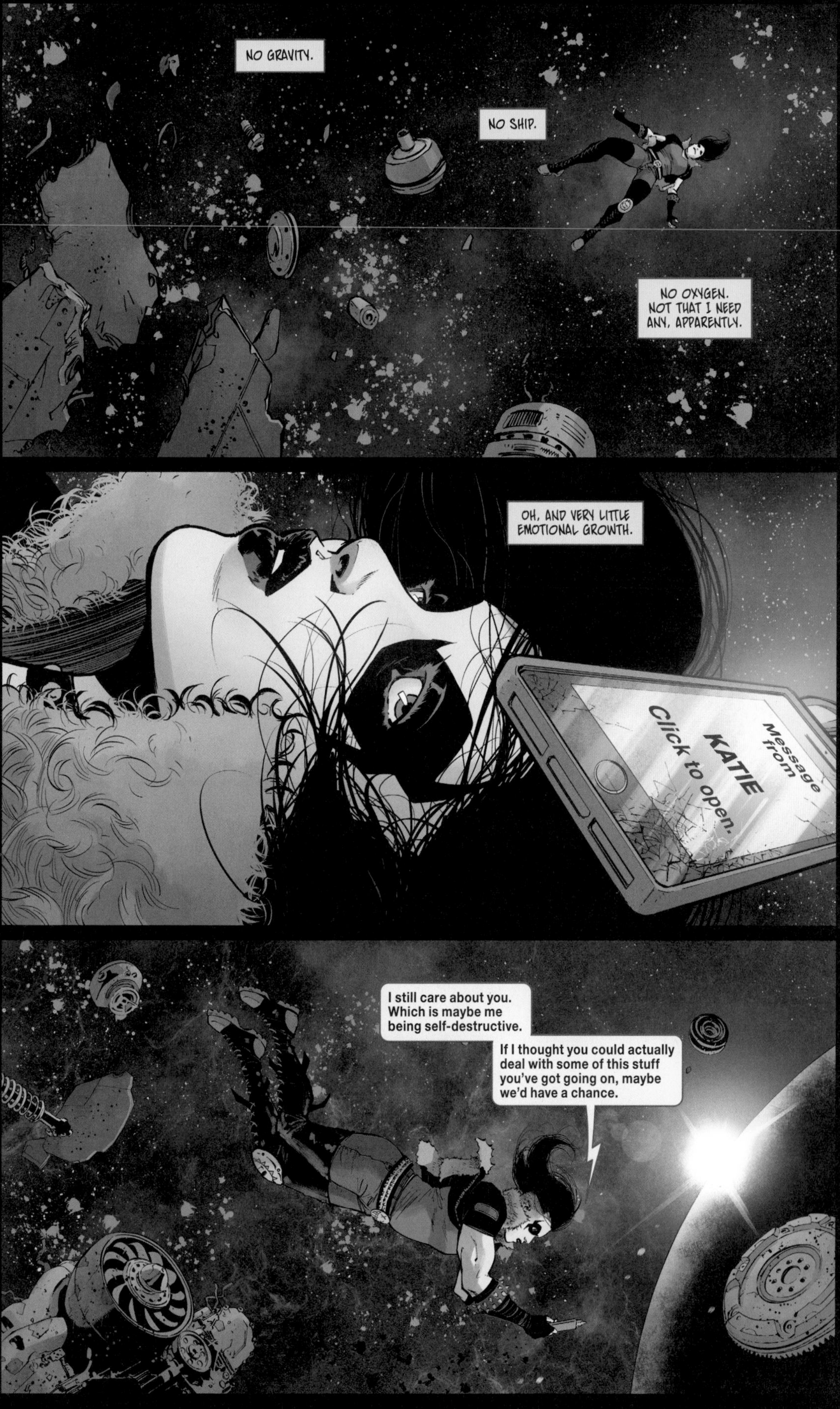
NO GRAVITY.
NO SHIP.
NO OXYGEN. NOT THAT I NEED ANY, APPARENTLY.
OH, AND VERY LITTLE EMOTIONAL GROWTH.
Message from
KATIE
Click to open.
I still care about you. Which is maybe me being self-destructive.
If I thought you could actually deal with some of this stuff you've got going on, maybe we'd have a chance.

SO MAYBE THIS
WAS A BAD IDEA.

AND JUST WHEN YOUR
FAVORITE ALIEN CATASTROPHE
WAS CONSIDERING SWIMMING
HOME THROUGH SPACE (IF
YOU CAN DO THAT?)...

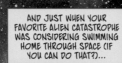

WHAT
THE--

RUMBLE RUMBLE

I MEAN THERE'S
SIGNS AND
THERE'S *SIGNS.*

PROPERTY OF INTERGALACTIC

PRISON

CORRECTIONAL FACILITY

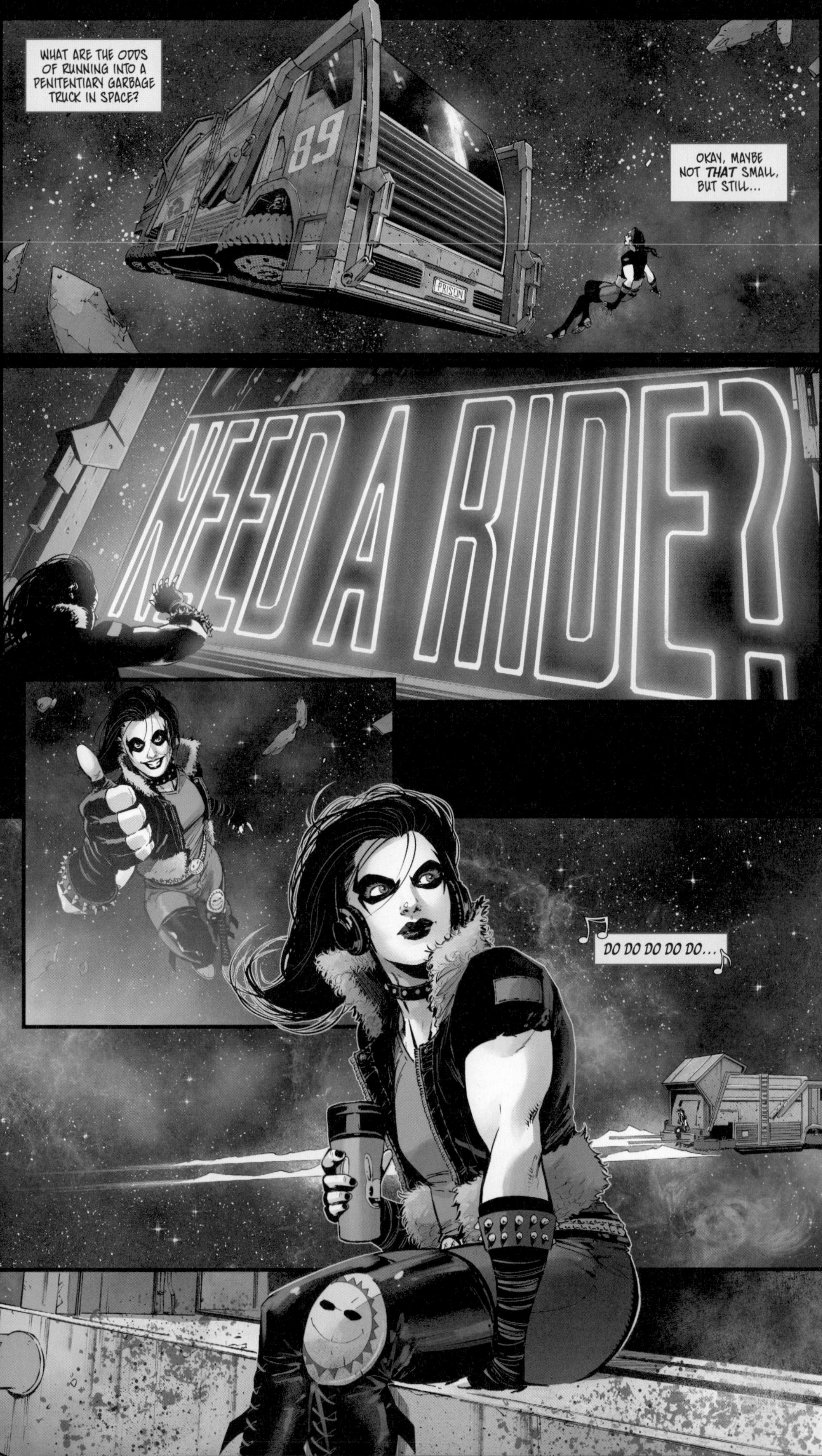
WHAT ARE THE ODDS OF RUNNING INTO A PENITENTIARY GARBAGE TRUCK IN SPACE?
OKAY, MAYBE NOT **THAT** SMALL, BUT STILL...
89
PRISON
NEED A RIDE?
DO DO DO DO DO...
89

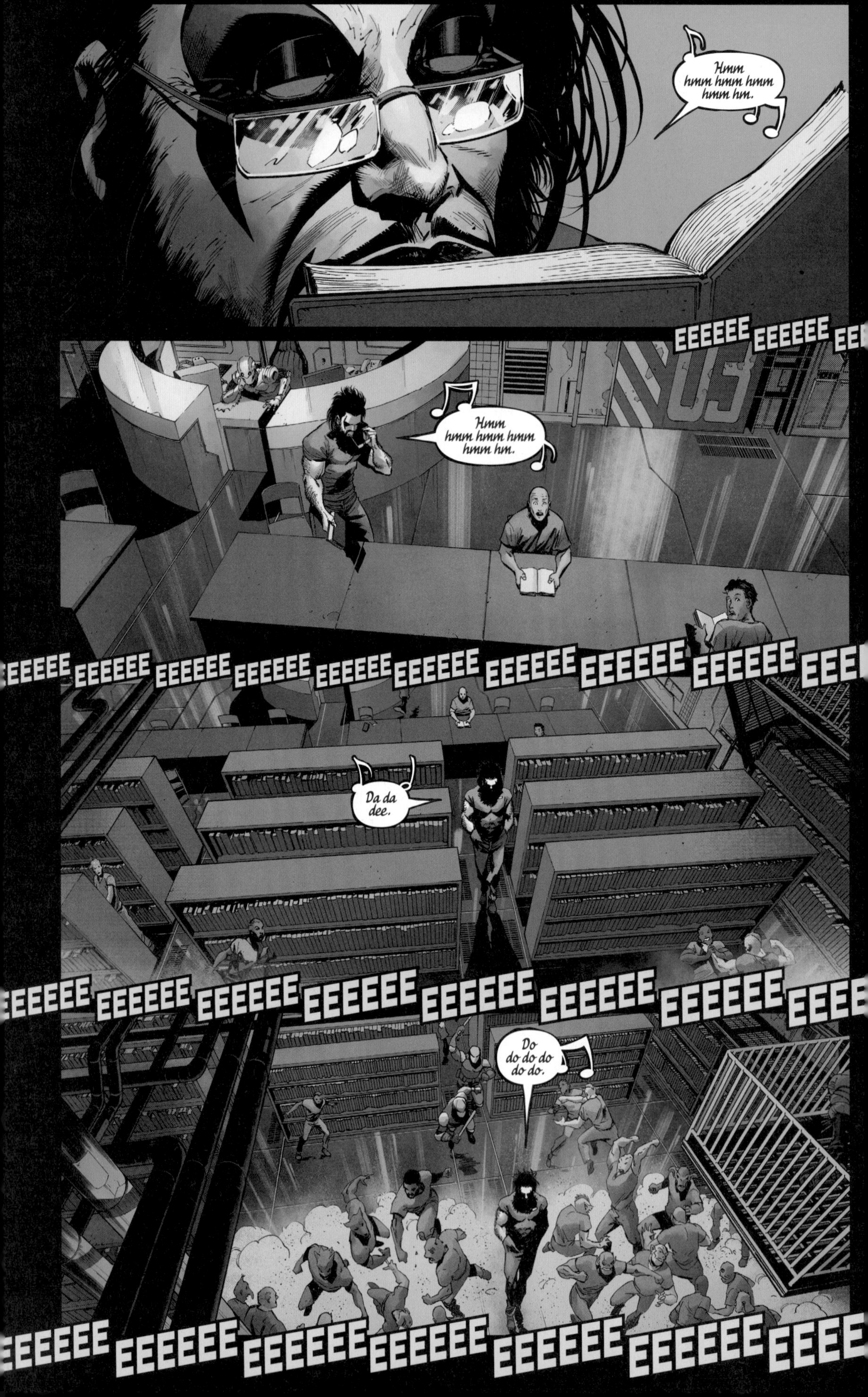
Hmm hmm hmm hmm hmm hm.
EEEEEE EEEEEE
Hmm hmm hmm hmm hmm hm.
EEEEEE EEEEEE EEEEEE EEEEEE EEEEEE EEEEEE EEEEEE EEEEEE EEEEEE
Da da dee.
EEEEEE EEEEEE EEEEEE EEEEEE EEEEEE EEEEEE EEEEEE
Do do do do do do.
EEEEEE EEEEEE EEEEEE EEEEEE EEEEEE EEEEEE

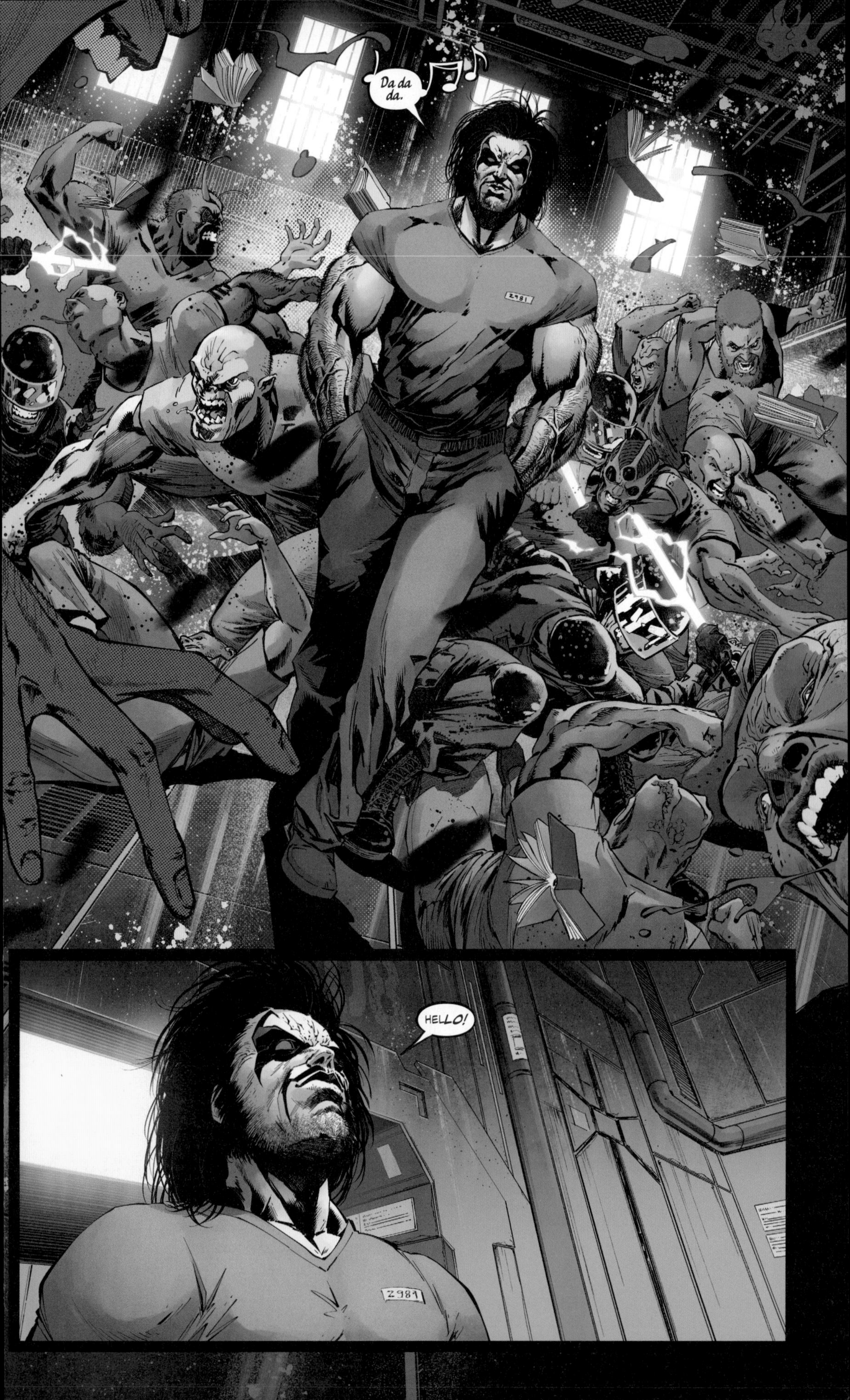
Da da da.
HELLO!

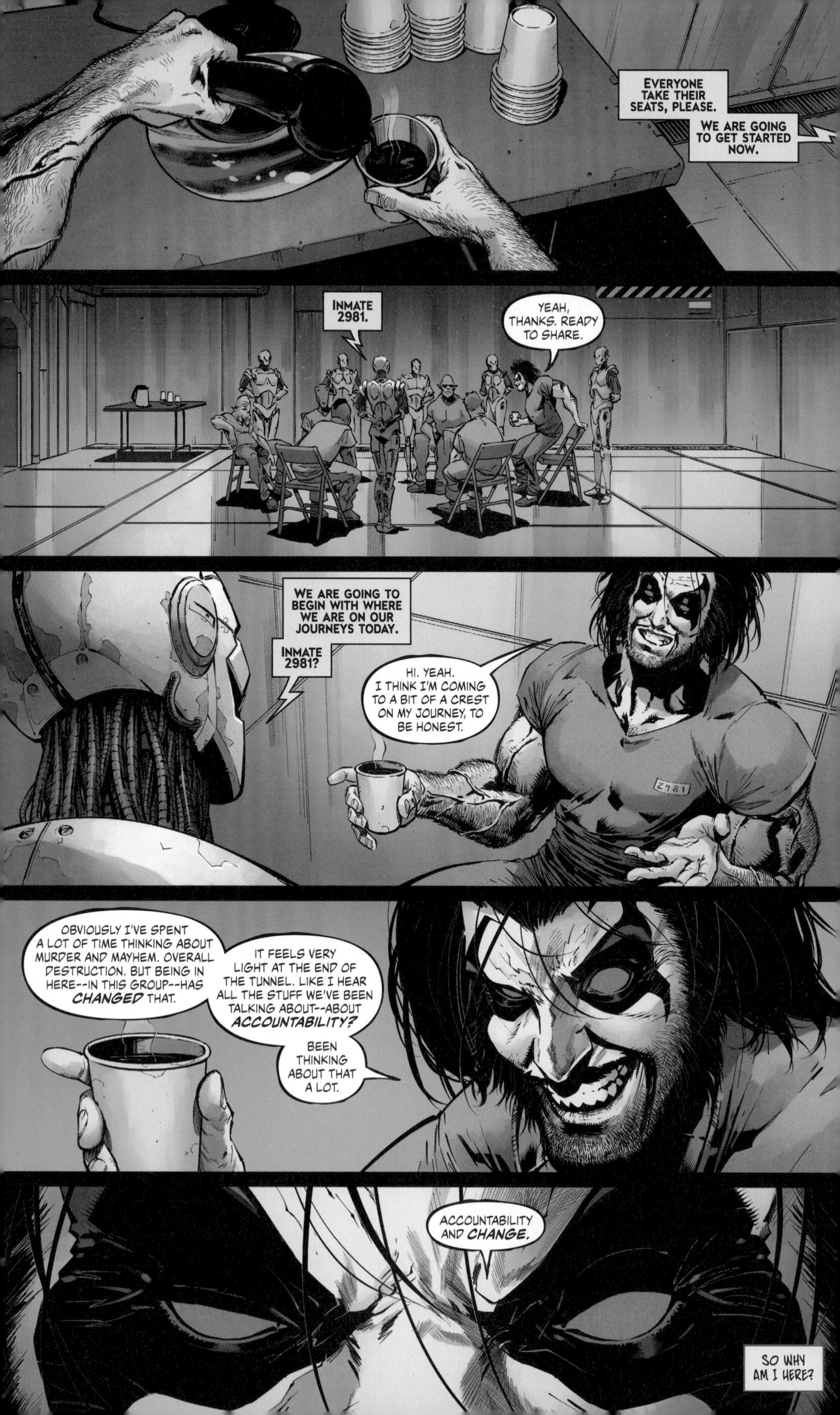
EVERYONE TAKE THEIR SEATS, PLEASE.
WE ARE GOING TO GET STARTED NOW.
INMATE 2981.
YEAH, THANKS. READY TO SHARE.
WE ARE GOING TO BEGIN WITH WHERE WE ARE ON OUR JOURNEYS TODAY.
INMATE 2981?
HI. YEAH. I THINK I'M COMING TO A BIT OF A CREST ON MY JOURNEY, TO BE HONEST.
2981
OBVIOUSLY I'VE SPENT A LOT OF TIME THINKING ABOUT MURDER AND MAYHEM. OVERALL DESTRUCTION. BUT BEING IN HERE--IN THIS GROUP--HAS *CHANGED* THAT.
IT FEELS VERY LIGHT AT THE END OF THE TUNNEL. LIKE I HEAR ALL THE STUFF WE'VE BEEN TALKING ABOUT--ABOUT *ACCOUNTABILITY?*
BEEN THINKING ABOUT THAT A LOT.
ACCOUNTABILITY AND *CHANGE.*
SO WHY AM I HERE?

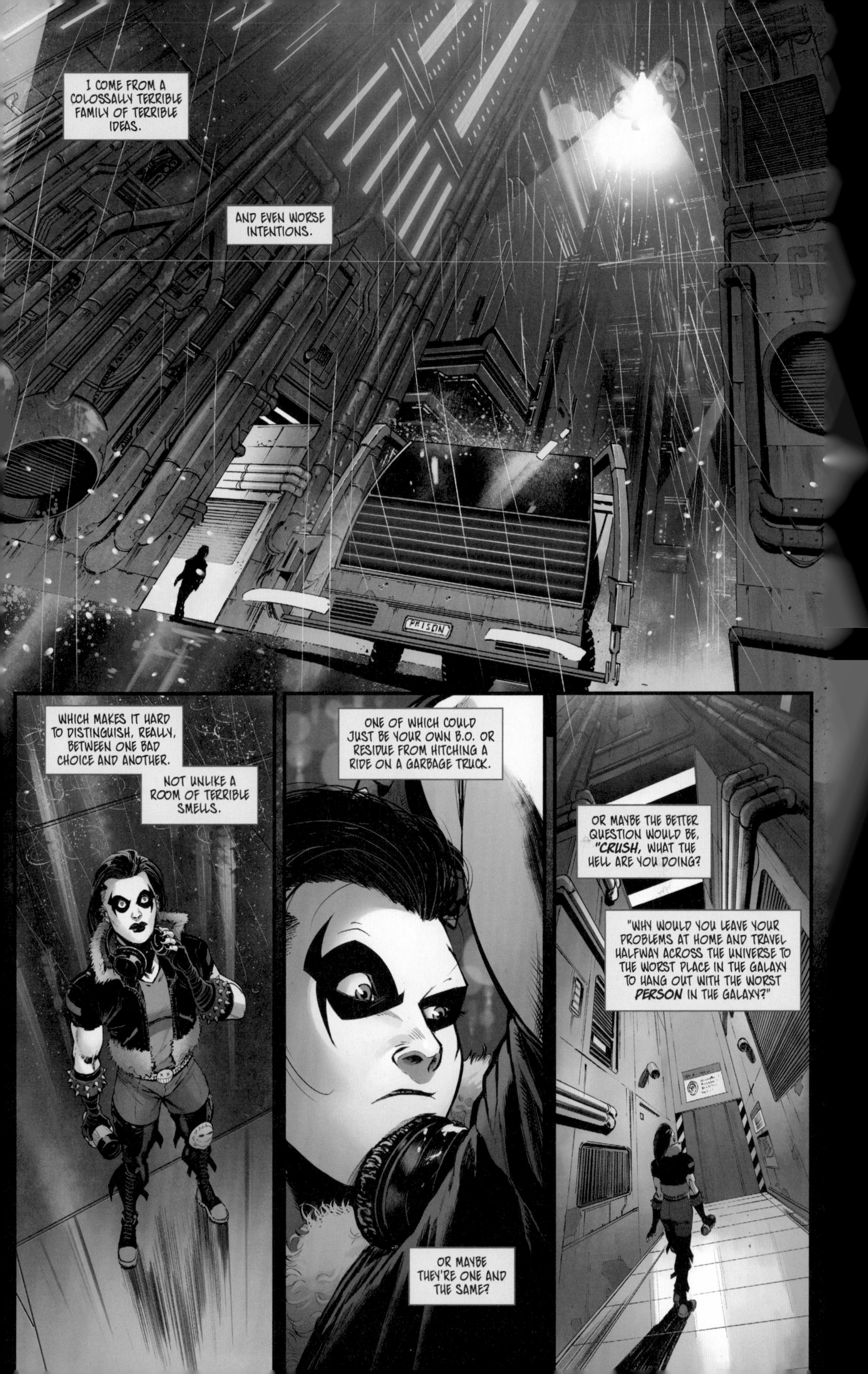
I COME FROM A COLOSSALLY TERRIBLE FAMILY OF TERRIBLE IDEAS.
AND EVEN WORSE INTENTIONS.
PRISON
WHICH MAKES IT HARD TO DISTINGUISH, REALLY, BETWEEN ONE BAD CHOICE AND ANOTHER.
NOT UNLIKE A ROOM OF TERRIBLE SMELLS.
ONE OF WHICH COULD JUST BE YOUR OWN B.O. OR RESIDUE FROM HITCHING A RIDE ON A GARBAGE TRUCK.
OR MAYBE THEY'RE ONE AND THE SAME?
OR MAYBE THE BETTER QUESTION WOULD BE, "CRUSH, WHAT THE HELL ARE YOU DOING?
"WHY WOULD YOU LEAVE YOUR PROBLEMS AT HOME AND TRAVEL HALFWAY ACROSS THE UNIVERSE TO THE WORST PLACE IN THE GALAXY TO HANG OUT WITH THE WORST PERSON IN THE GALAXY?"

MAYBE BECAUSE THERE'S NOT EXACTLY A LINEUP OF PEOPLE READY TO DEAL WITH ME AND MY @#$%.

HUMANOID FORM DETECTED.

PLACE HAND ON SCANNER.

CLEARLY, I NEED TO DEAL WITH MY @#$%, AND MY @#$%...

...IS HIM.

NOTICE

NYONE PROCEE
BEYOND THIS
PLIES THEIR P
TO A SEARCH
PERSONAL PRO

IDENTIFY YOURSELF.

I'M HERE TO SEE LOBO.

I'M HIS KID.

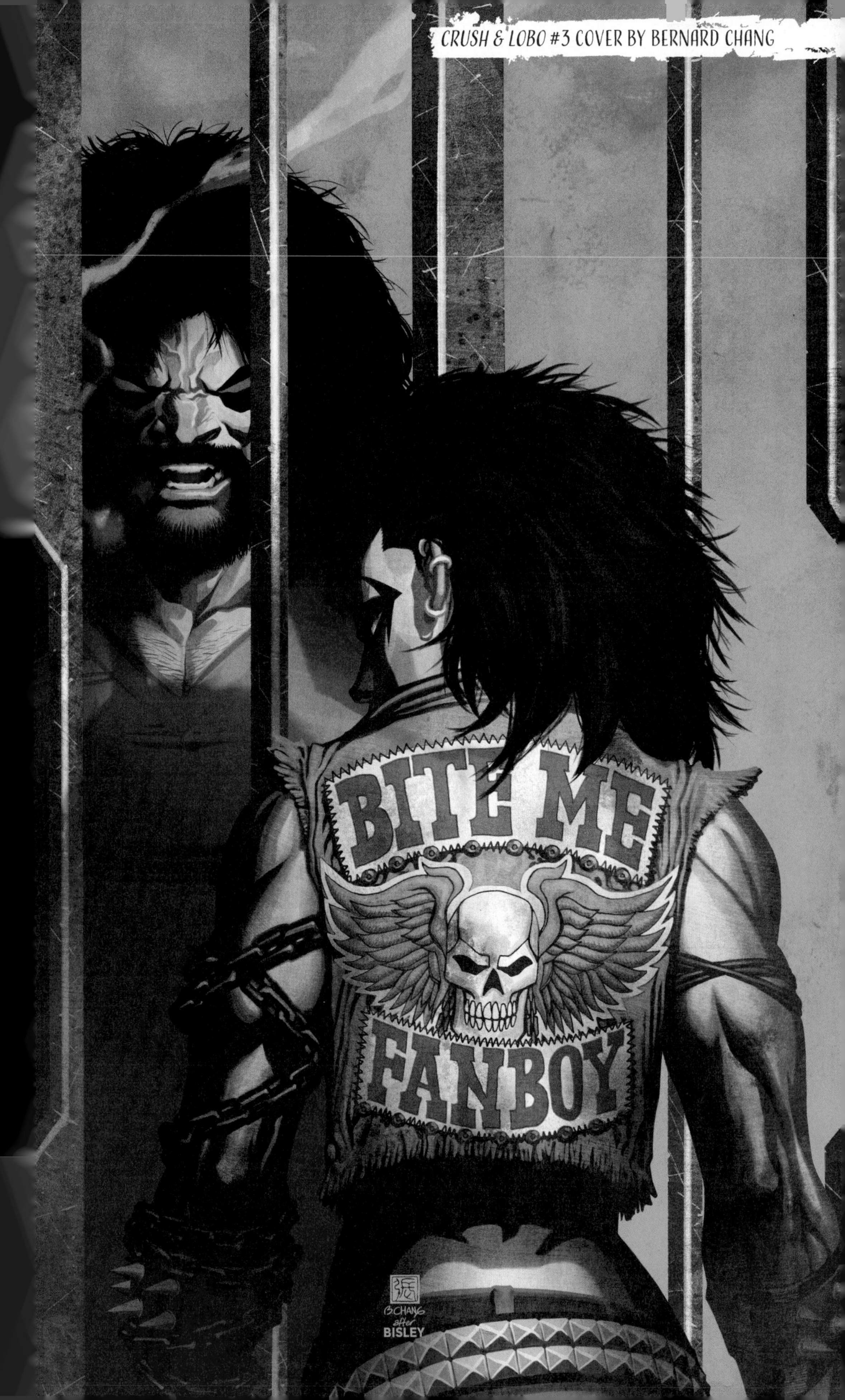
BITE ME
FANBOY
BCHANG
after
BISLEY

CRUSH & LOBO #3 COVER BY BERNARD CHANG

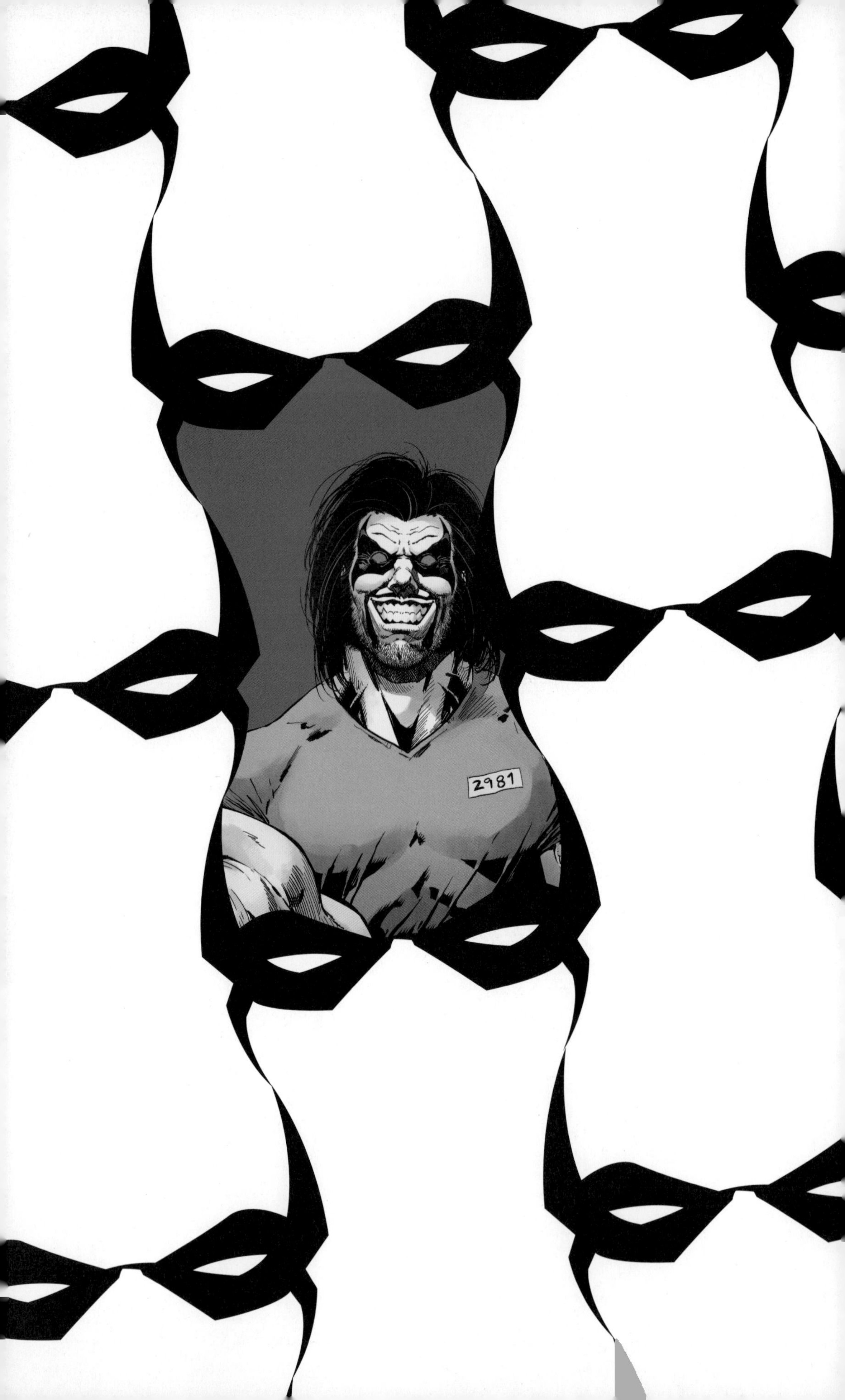
2981

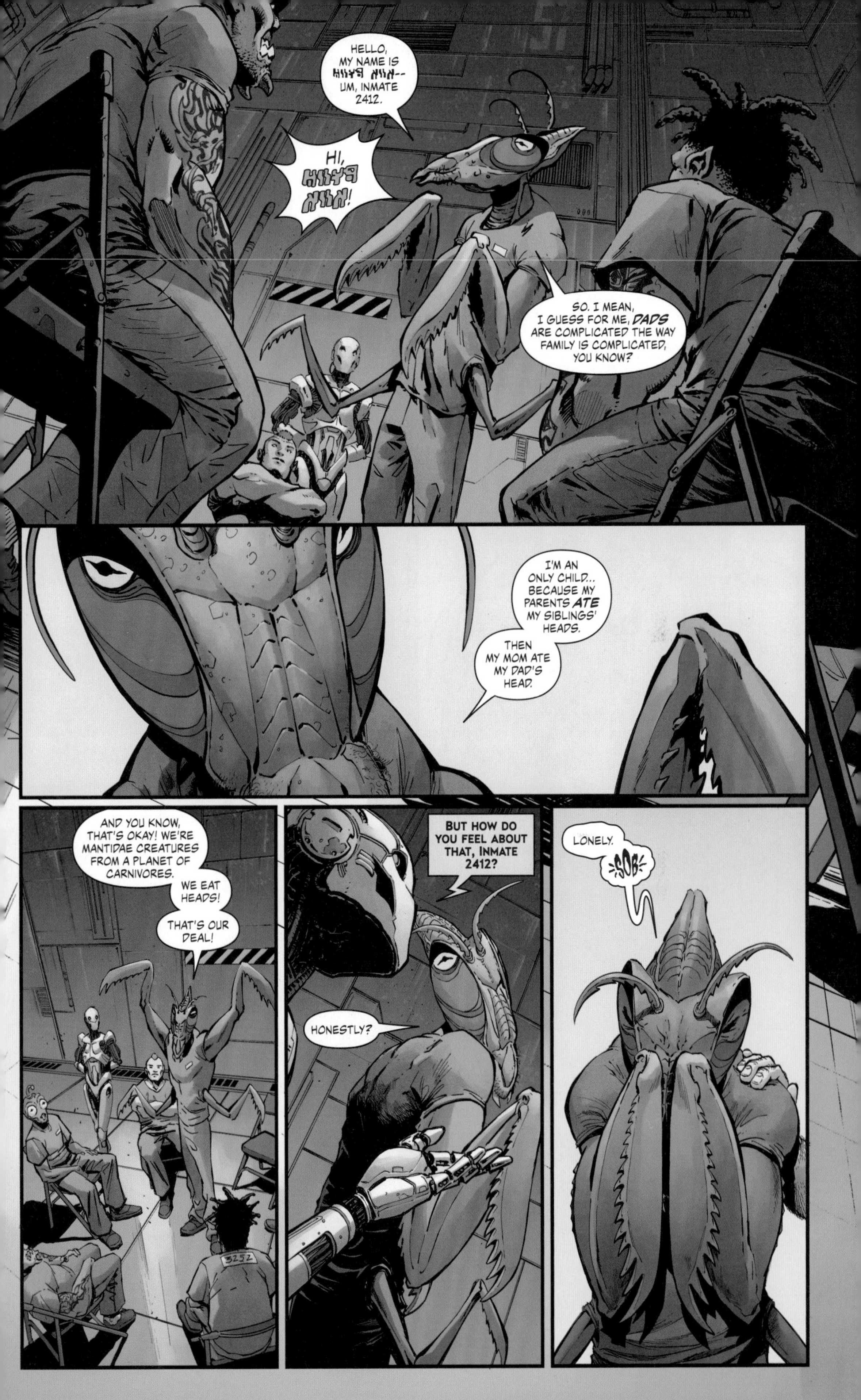
HELLO, MY NAME IS
UM, INMATE 2412.
HI,
SO. I MEAN, I GUESS FOR ME, DADS ARE COMPLICATED THE WAY FAMILY IS COMPLICATED, YOU KNOW?
I'M AN ONLY CHILD... BECAUSE MY PARENTS ATE MY SIBLINGS' HEADS.
THEN MY MOM ATE MY DAD'S HEAD.
AND YOU KNOW, THAT'S OKAY! WE'RE MANTIDAE CREATURES FROM A PLANET OF CARNIVORES.
WE EAT HEADS!
THAT'S OUR DEAL!
3252
BUT HOW DO YOU FEEL ABOUT THAT, INMATE 2412?
HONESTLY?
LONELY.
SOB

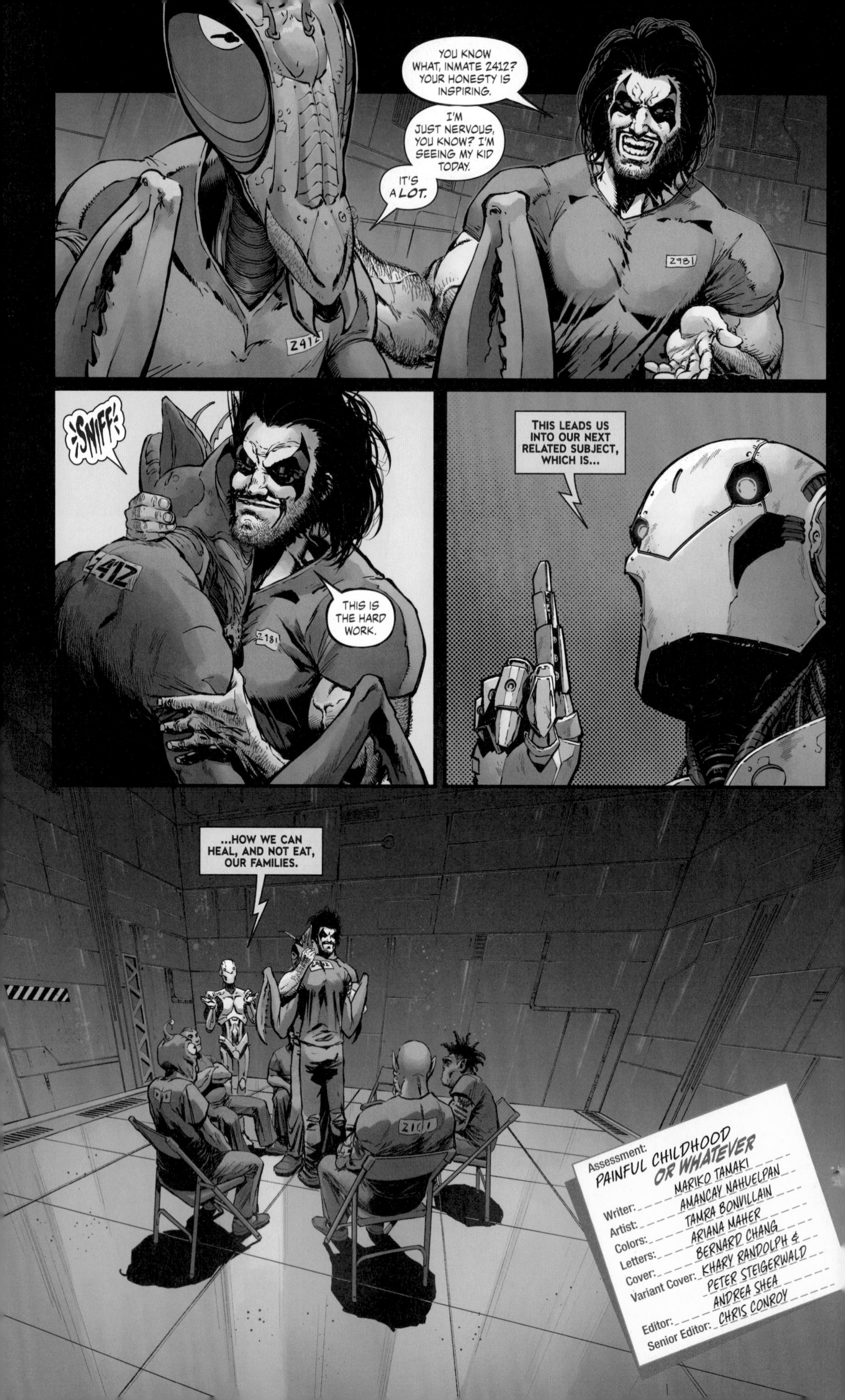
YOU KNOW WHAT, INMATE 2412? YOUR HONESTY IS INSPIRING.
I'M JUST NERVOUS, YOU KNOW? I'M SEEING MY KID TODAY.
IT'S A LOT.
SNIFF
THIS IS THE HARD WORK.
THIS LEADS US INTO OUR NEXT RELATED SUBJECT, WHICH IS...
...HOW WE CAN HEAL, AND NOT EAT, OUR FAMILIES.
Assessment: PAINFUL CHILDHOOD OR WHATEVER
Writer: MARIKO TAMAKI
Artist: AMANCAY NAHUELPAN
Colors: TAMRA BONVILLAIN
Letters: ARIANA MAHER
Cover: BERNARD CHANG
Variant Cover: KHARY RANDOLPH & PETER STEIGERWALD
Editor: ANDREA SHEA
Senior Editor: CHRIS CONROY

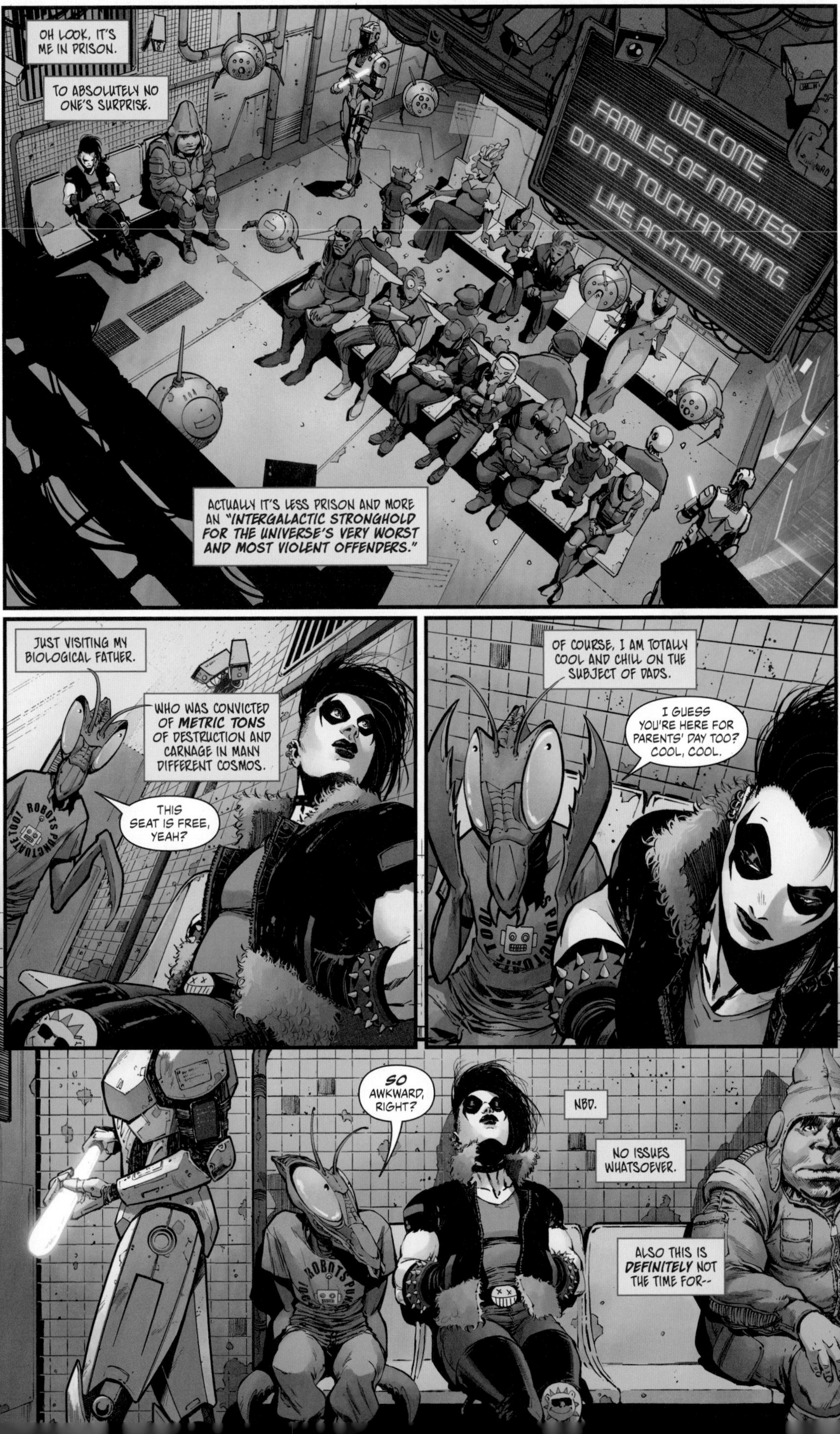
OH LOOK, IT'S ME IN PRISON.
TO ABSOLUTELY NO ONE'S SURPRISE.
WELCOME, FAMILIES OF INMATES! DO NOT TOUCH ANYTHING. LIKE, ANYTHING.
ACTUALLY IT'S LESS PRISON AND MORE AN "INTERGALACTIC STRONGHOLD FOR THE UNIVERSE'S VERY WORST AND MOST VIOLENT OFFENDERS."
JUST VISITING MY BIOLOGICAL FATHER.
WHO WAS CONVICTED OF METRIC TONS OF DESTRUCTION AND CARNAGE IN MANY DIFFERENT COSMOS.
THIS SEAT IS FREE, YEAH?
ROBOTS PUNCTUATE TOO!
OF COURSE, I AM TOTALLY COOL AND CHILL ON THE SUBJECT OF DADS.
I GUESS YOU'RE HERE FOR PARENTS' DAY TOO? COOL, COOL.
SO AWKWARD, RIGHT?
NBD.
NO ISSUES WHATSOEVER.
ALSO THIS IS DEFINITELY NOT THE TIME FOR--

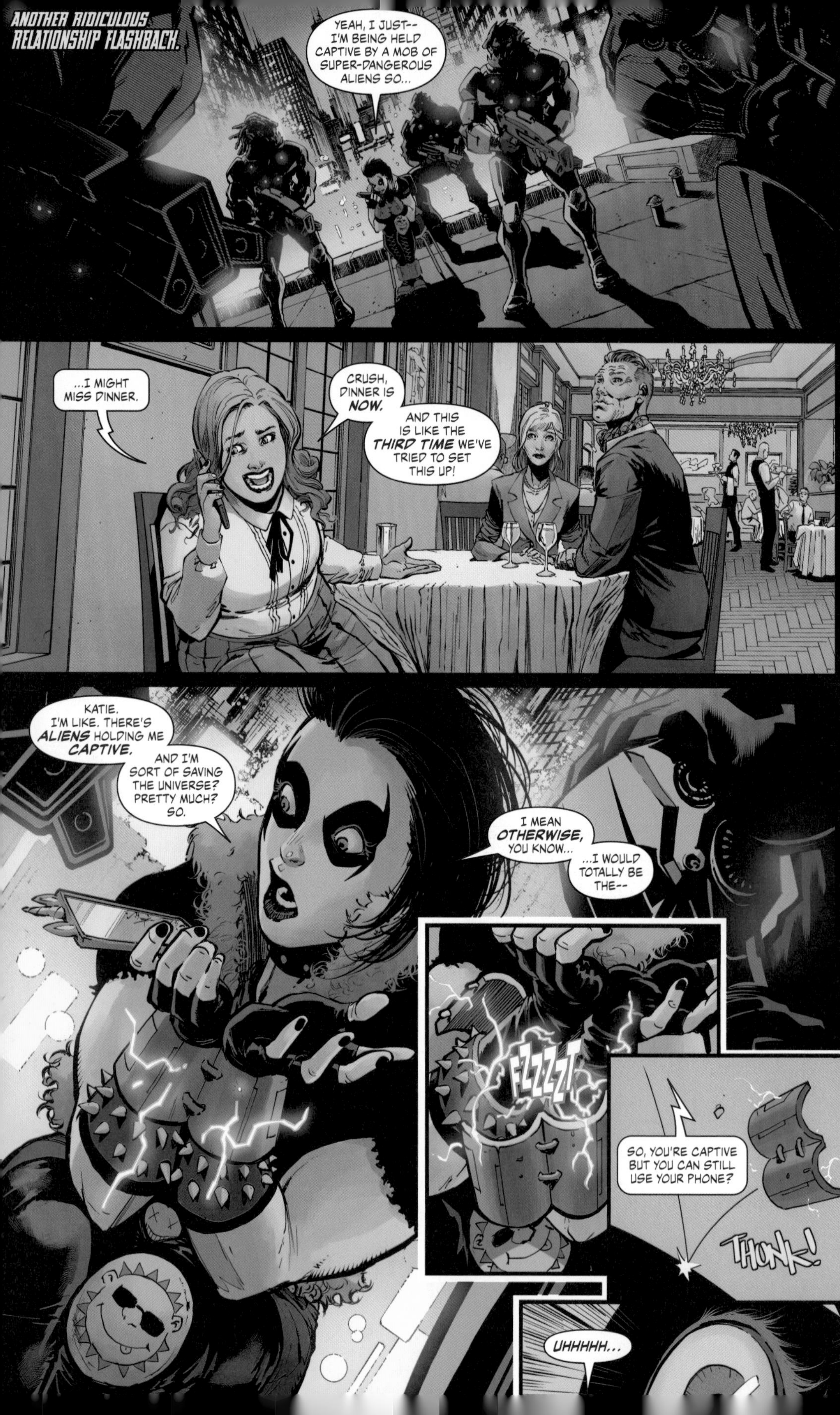

ANOTHER RIDICULOUS RELATIONSHIP FLASHBACK.
YEAH, I JUST-- I'M BEING HELD CAPTIVE BY A MOB OF SUPER-DANGEROUS ALIENS SO...
...I MIGHT MISS DINNER.
CRUSH, DINNER IS NOW.
AND THIS IS LIKE THE THIRD TIME WE'VE TRIED TO SET THIS UP!
KATIE. I'M LIKE. THERE'S ALIENS HOLDING ME CAPTIVE.
AND I'M SORT OF SAVING THE UNIVERSE? PRETTY MUCH? SO.
I MEAN OTHERWISE, YOU KNOW...
...I WOULD TOTALLY BE THE--
FZZZZT
SO, YOU'RE CAPTIVE BUT YOU CAN STILL USE YOUR PHONE?
THONK!
UHHHHH...

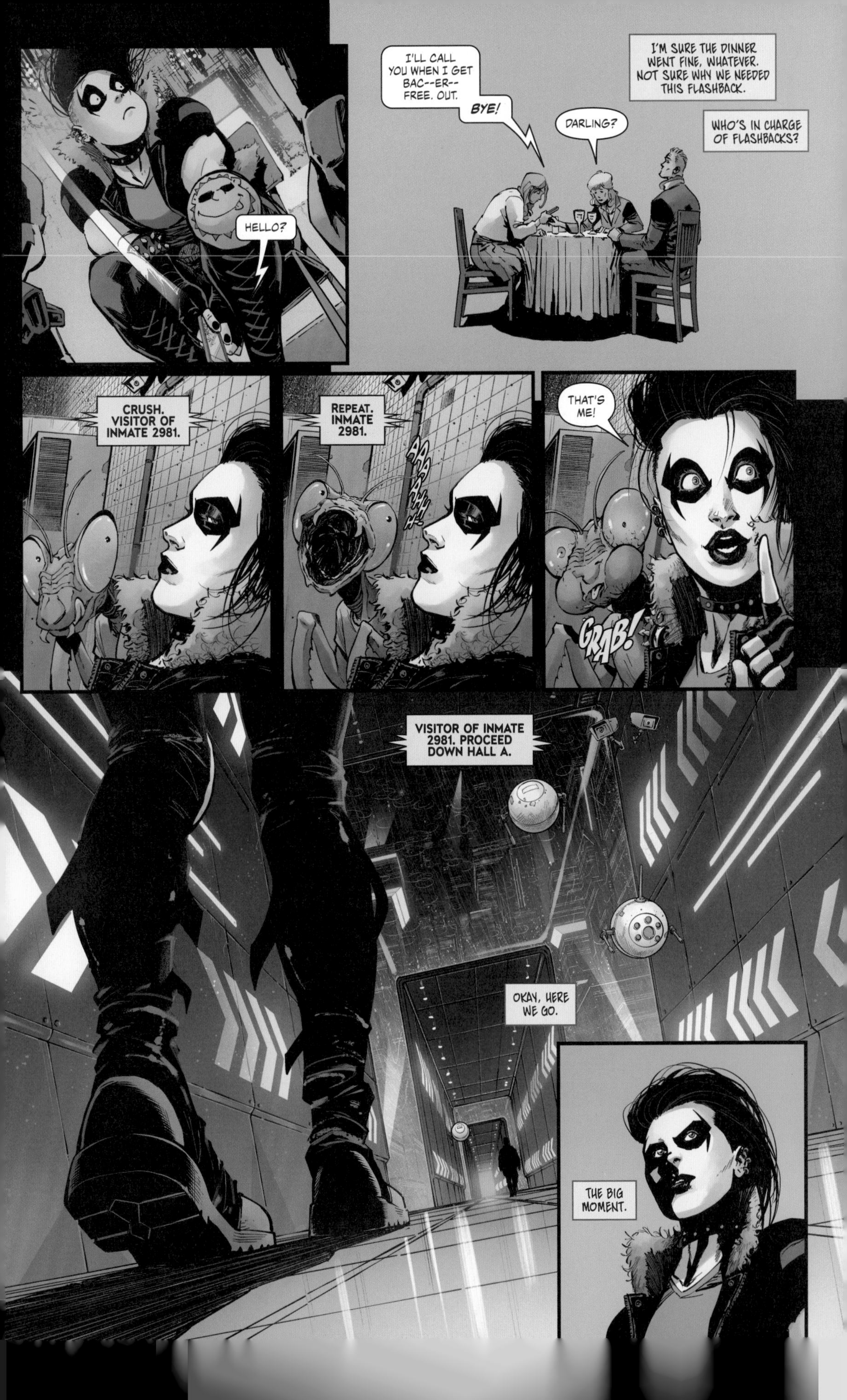
HELLO?
I'LL CALL YOU WHEN I GET BAC--ER-- FREE. OUT.
BYE!
DARLING?
I'M SURE THE DINNER WENT FINE, WHATEVER. NOT SURE WHY WE NEEDED THIS FLASHBACK.
WHO'S IN CHARGE OF FLASHBACKS?
CRUSH. VISITOR OF INMATE 2981.
REPEAT. INMATE 2981.
AAAAAHH
THAT'S ME!
GRAB!
VISITOR OF INMATE 2981. PROCEED DOWN HALL A.
OKAY, HERE WE GO.
THE BIG MOMENT.

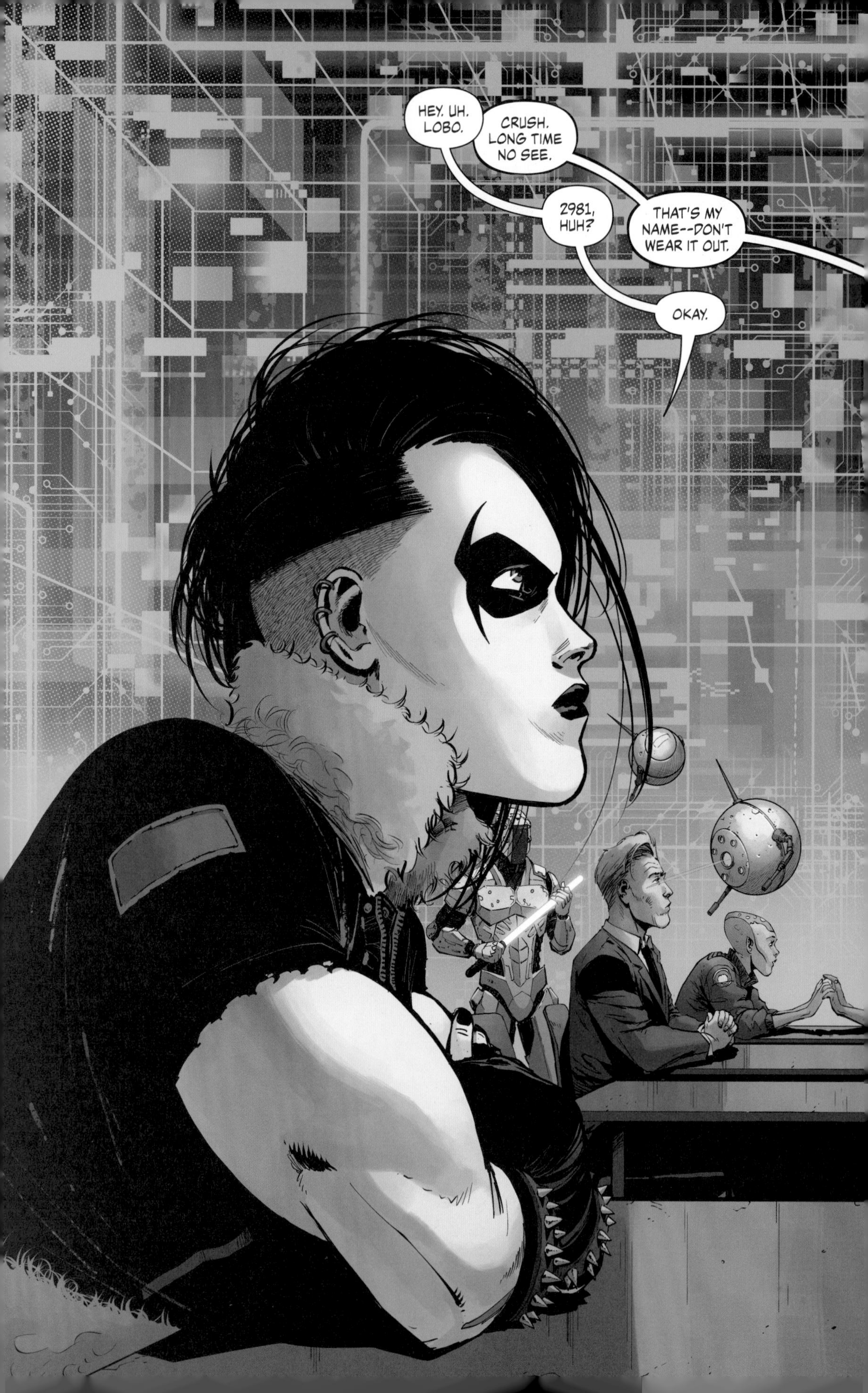
HEY. UH. LOBO.
CRUSH. LONG TIME NO SEE.
2981, HUH?
THAT'S MY NAME--DON'T WEAR IT OUT.
OKAY.

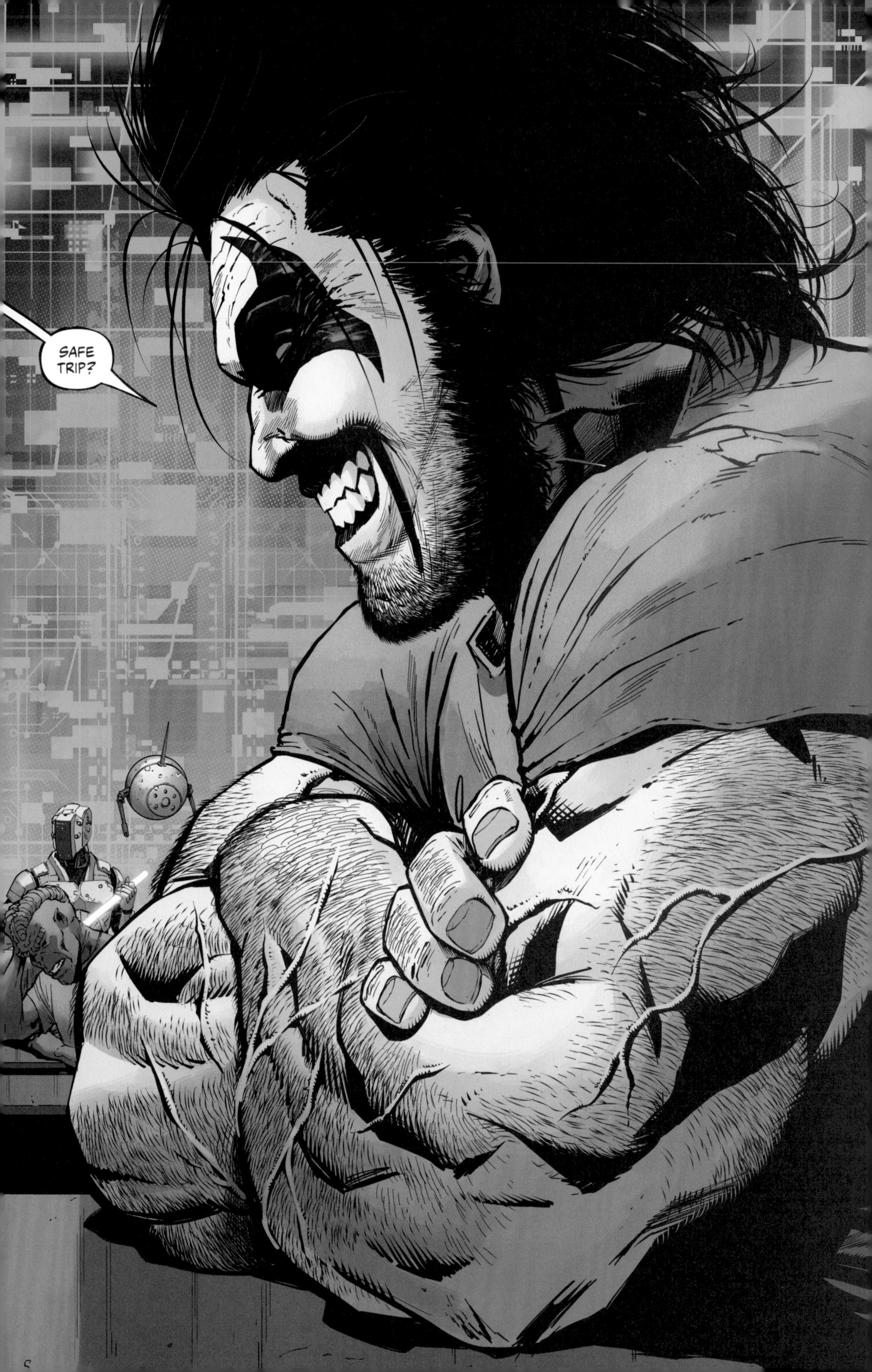
SAFE TRIP?

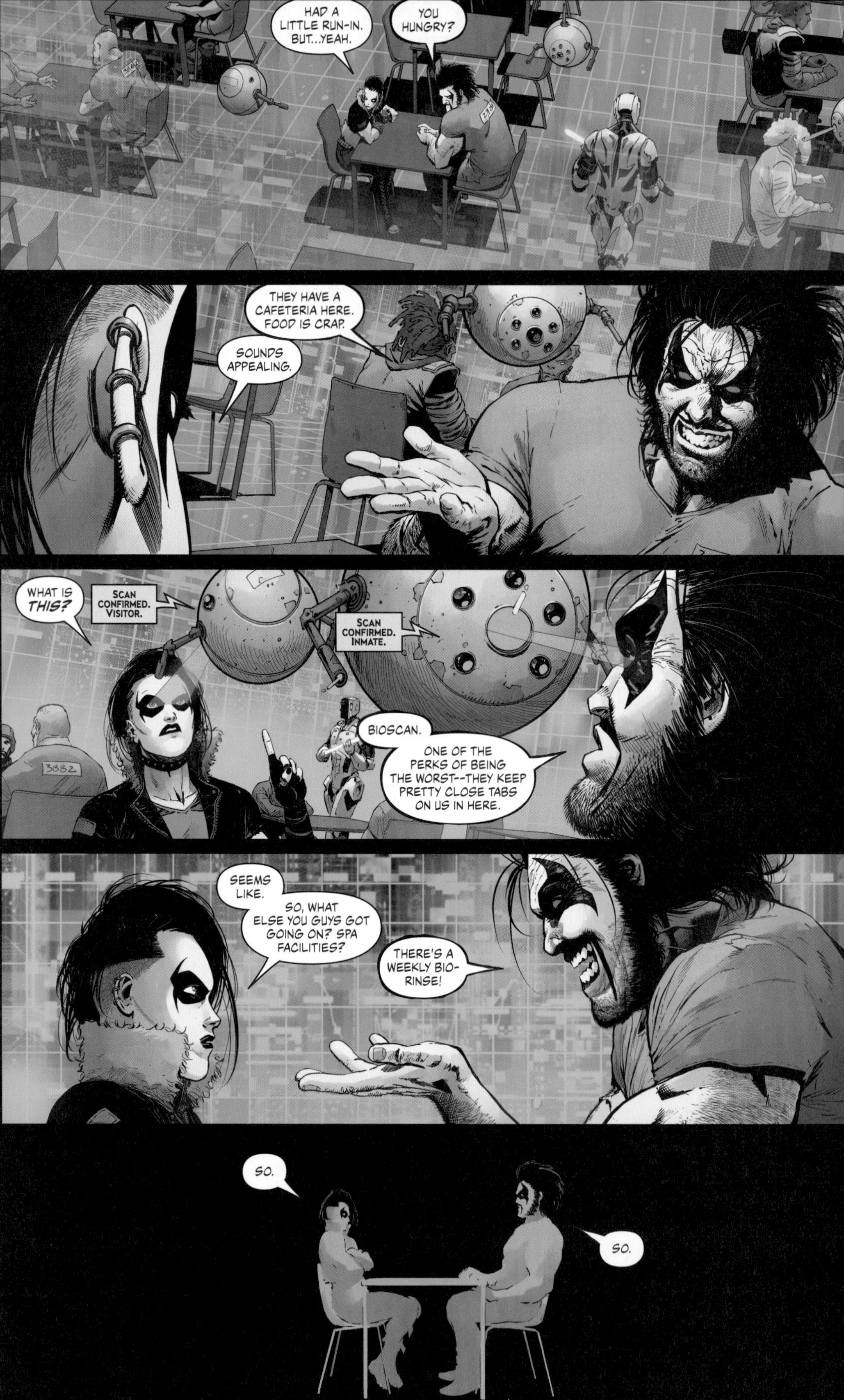
HAD A LITTLE RUN-IN. BUT...YEAH.
YOU HUNGRY?
THEY HAVE A CAFETERIA HERE. FOOD IS CRAP.
SOUNDS APPEALING.
WHAT IS *THIS?*
SCAN CONFIRMED. VISITOR.
SCAN CONFIRMED. INMATE.
3882
BIOSCAN.
ONE OF THE PERKS OF BEING THE WORST--THEY KEEP PRETTY CLOSE TABS ON US IN HERE.
SEEMS LIKE.
SO, WHAT ELSE YOU GUYS GOT GOING ON? SPA FACILITIES?
THERE'S A WEEKLY BIO-RINSE!
SO.
SO.

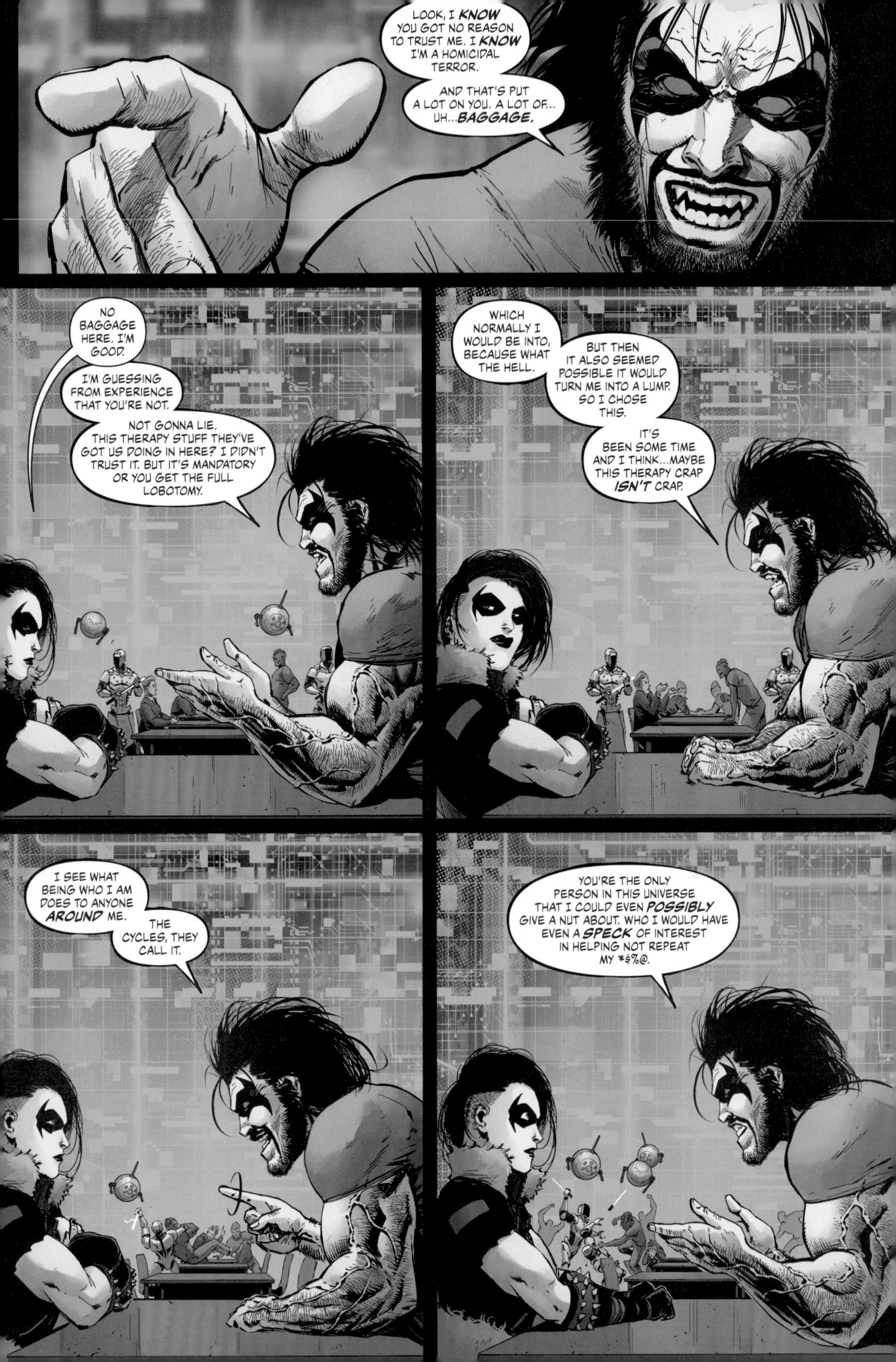
LOOK, I KNOW YOU GOT NO REASON TO TRUST ME. I KNOW I'M A HOMICIDAL TERROR.
AND THAT'S PUT A LOT ON YOU. A LOT OF... UH...BAGGAGE.
NO BAGGAGE HERE. I'M GOOD.
I'M GUESSING FROM EXPERIENCE THAT YOU'RE NOT.
NOT GONNA LIE. THIS THERAPY STUFF THEY'VE GOT US DOING IN HERE? I DIDN'T TRUST IT. BUT IT'S MANDATORY OR YOU GET THE FULL LOBOTOMY.
WHICH NORMALLY I WOULD BE INTO, BECAUSE WHAT THE HELL.
BUT THEN IT ALSO SEEMED POSSIBLE IT WOULD TURN ME INTO A LUMP. SO I CHOSE THIS.
IT'S BEEN SOME TIME AND I THINK...MAYBE THIS THERAPY CRAP ISN'T CRAP.
I SEE WHAT BEING WHO I AM DOES TO ANYONE AROUND ME.
THE CYCLES, THEY CALL IT.
YOU'RE THE ONLY PERSON IN THIS UNIVERSE THAT I COULD EVEN POSSIBLY GIVE A NUT ABOUT. WHO I WOULD HAVE EVEN A SPECK OF INTEREST IN HELPING NOT REPEAT MY *$%@.

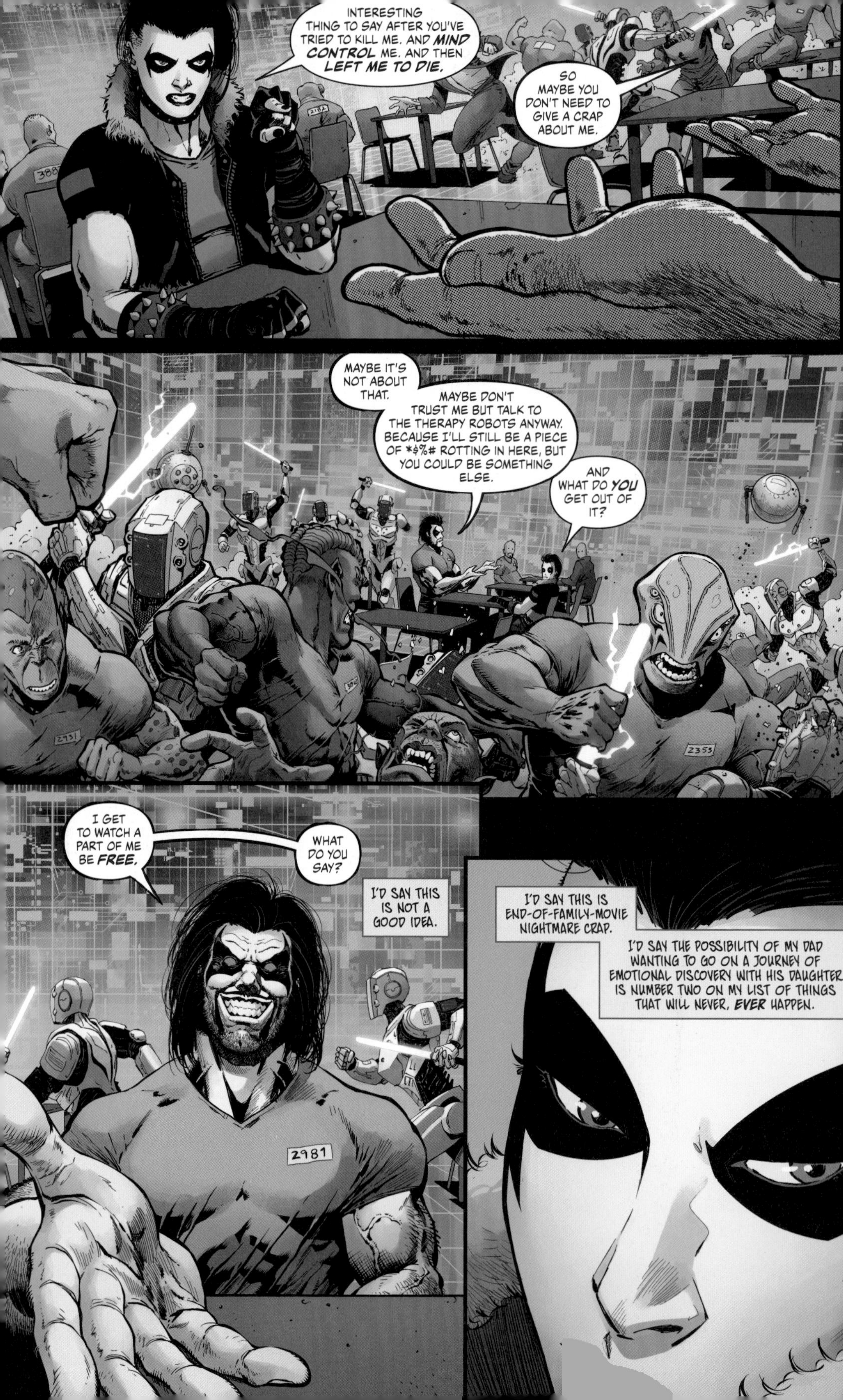

INTERESTING THING TO SAY AFTER YOU'VE TRIED TO KILL ME. AND MIND CONTROL ME. AND THEN LEFT ME TO DIE.
SO MAYBE YOU DON'T NEED TO GIVE A CRAP ABOUT ME.
MAYBE IT'S NOT ABOUT THAT.
MAYBE DON'T TRUST ME BUT TALK TO THE THERAPY ROBOTS ANYWAY. BECAUSE I'LL STILL BE A PIECE OF *$%# ROTTING IN HERE, BUT YOU COULD BE SOMETHING ELSE.
AND WHAT DO YOU GET OUT OF IT?
I GET TO WATCH A PART OF ME BE FREE.
WHAT DO YOU SAY?
I'D SAY THIS IS NOT A GOOD IDEA.
I'D SAY THIS IS END-OF-FAMILY-MOVIE NIGHTMARE CRAP.
I'D SAY THE POSSIBILITY OF MY DAD WANTING TO GO ON A JOURNEY OF EMOTIONAL DISCOVERY WITH HIS DAUGHTER IS NUMBER TWO ON MY LIST OF THINGS THAT WILL NEVER, EVER HAPPEN.

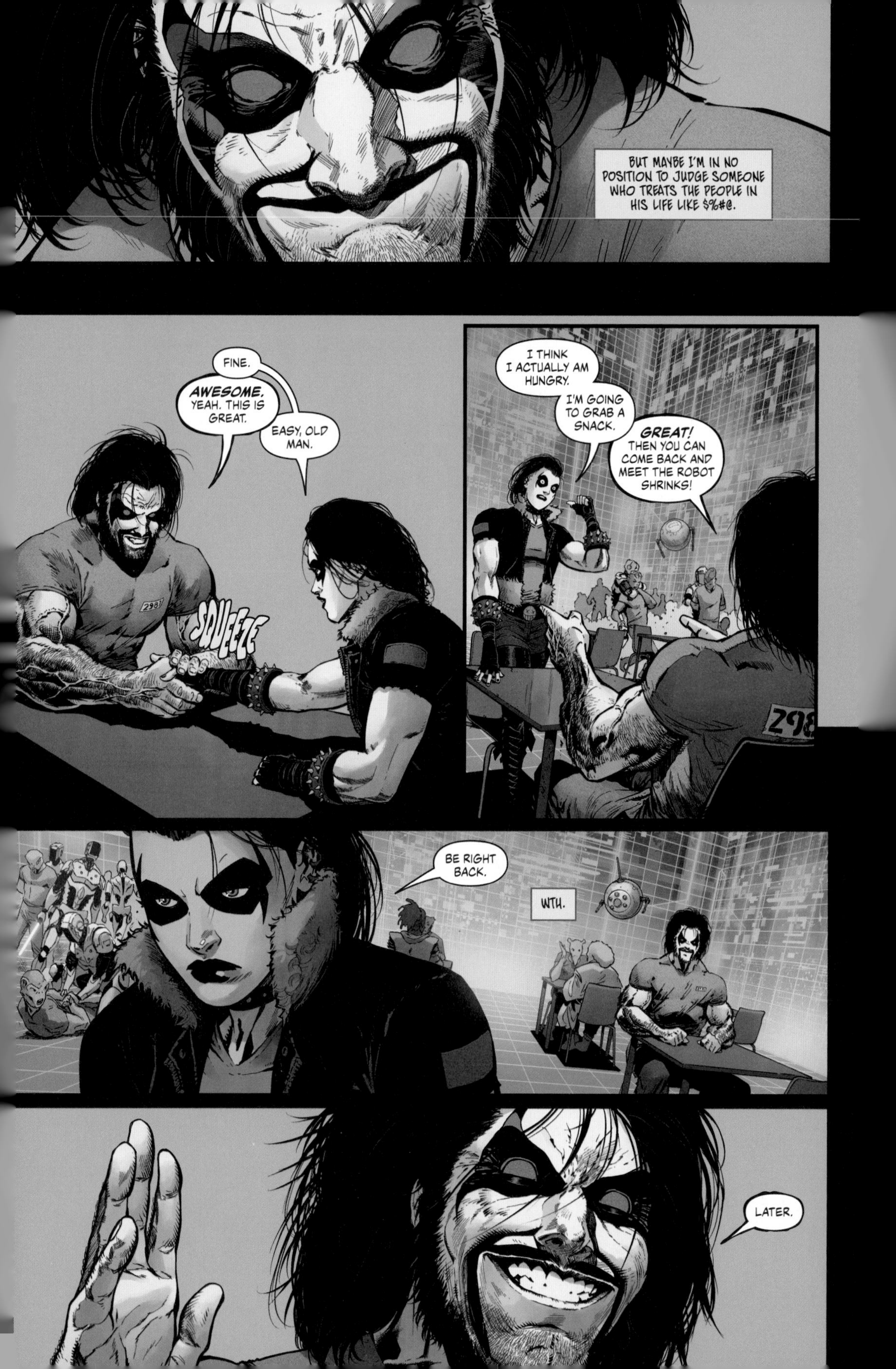
BUT MAYBE I'M IN NO POSITION TO JUDGE SOMEONE WHO TREATS THE PEOPLE IN HIS LIFE LIKE $%#@.
FINE.
AWESOME. YEAH. THIS IS GREAT.
EASY, OLD MAN.
SQUEEZE
I THINK I ACTUALLY AM HUNGRY.
I'M GOING TO GRAB A SNACK.
GREAT! THEN YOU CAN COME BACK AND MEET THE ROBOT SHRINKS!
BE RIGHT BACK.
WTH.
LATER.

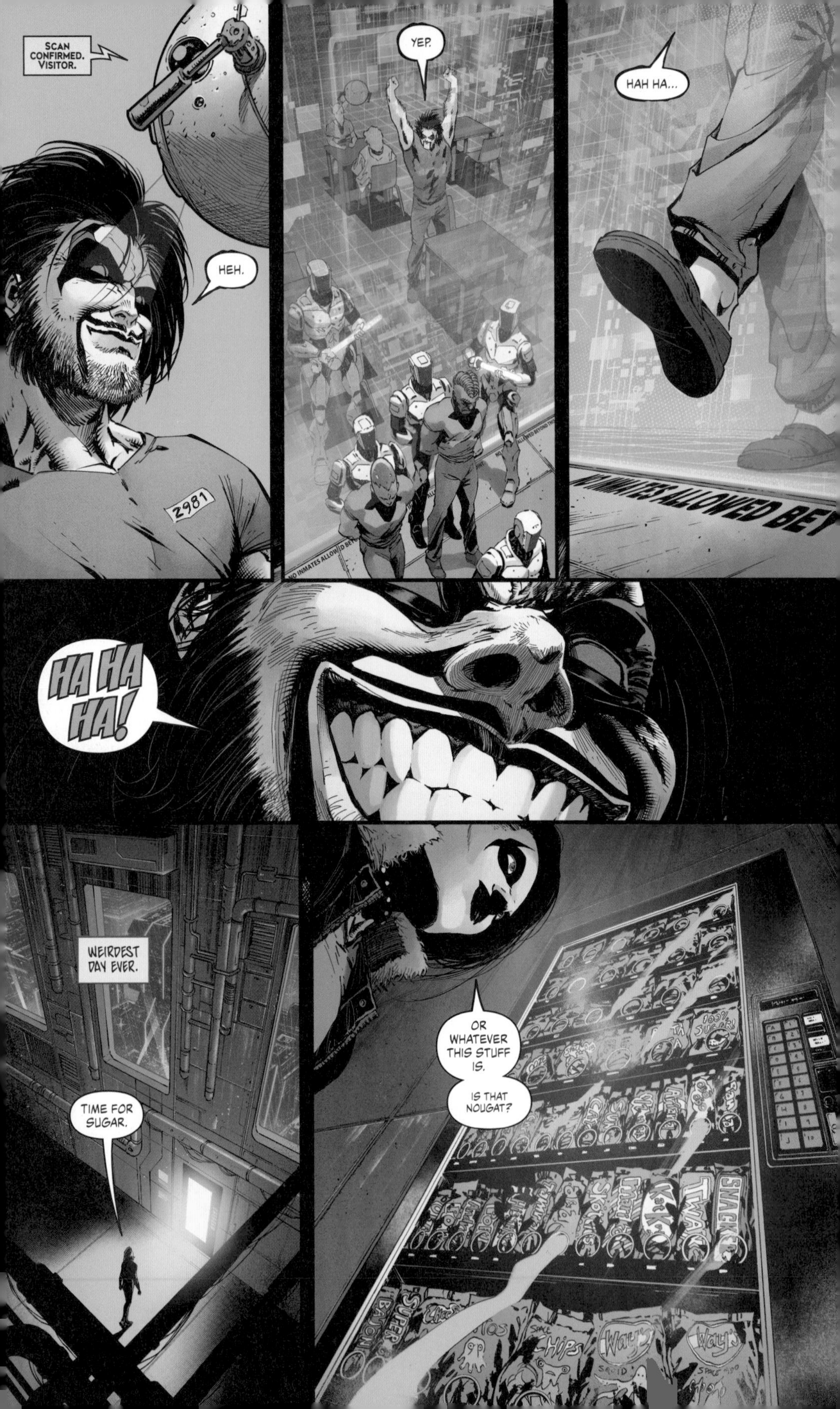
SCAN CONFIRMED. VISITOR.
HEH.
2981
YEP.
HAH HA...
HA HA HA!
WEIRDEST DAY EVER.
TIME FOR SUGAR.
OR WHATEVER THIS STUFF IS.
IS THAT NOUGAT?

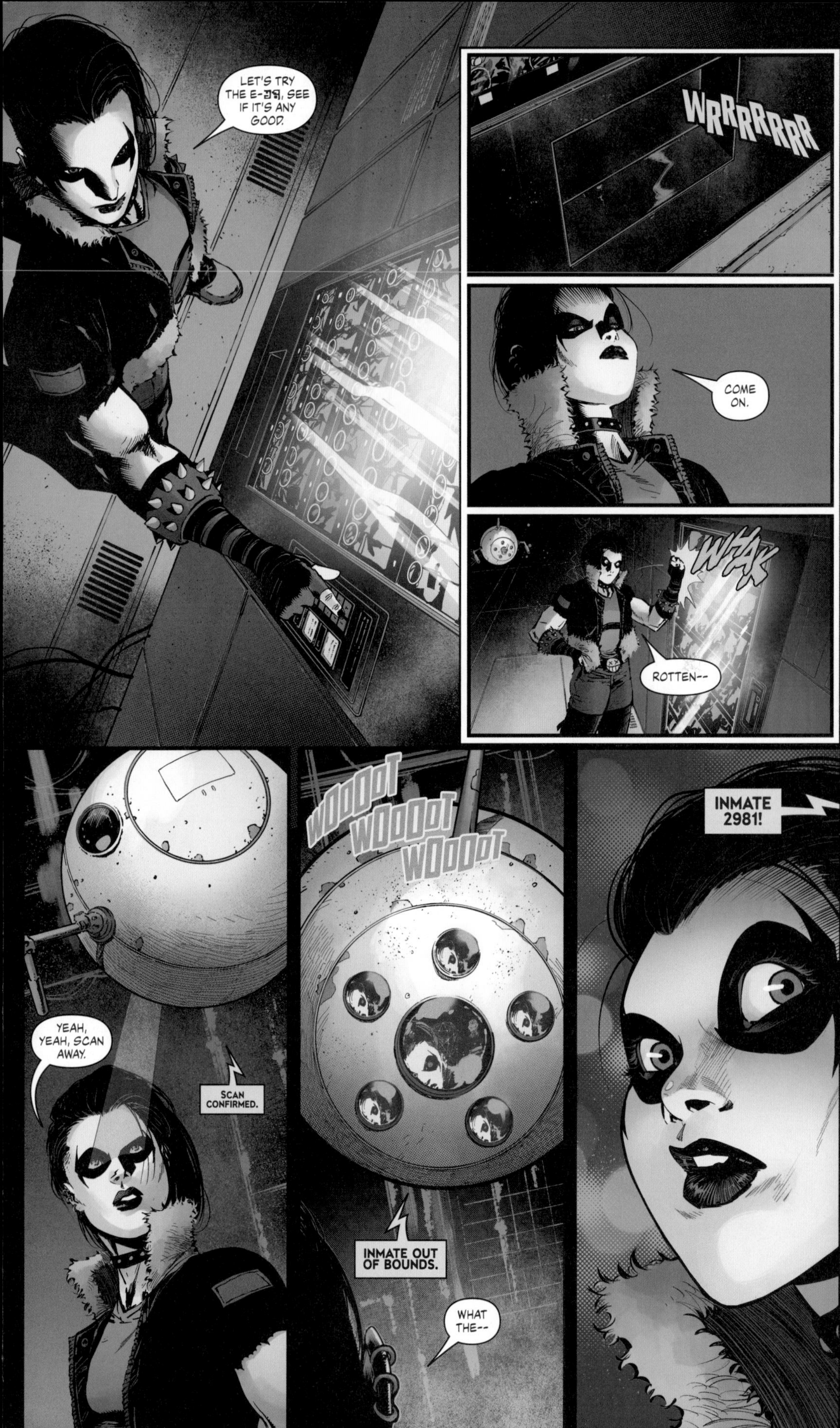
LET'S TRY THE E-, SEE IF IT'S ANY GOOD.
WRRRRRRR
COME ON.
WHAK
ROTTEN--
YEAH, YEAH, SCAN AWAY.
SCAN CONFIRMED.
WOOOOT WOOOOT WOOOOT
INMATE OUT OF BOUNDS.
WHAT THE--
INMATE 2981!

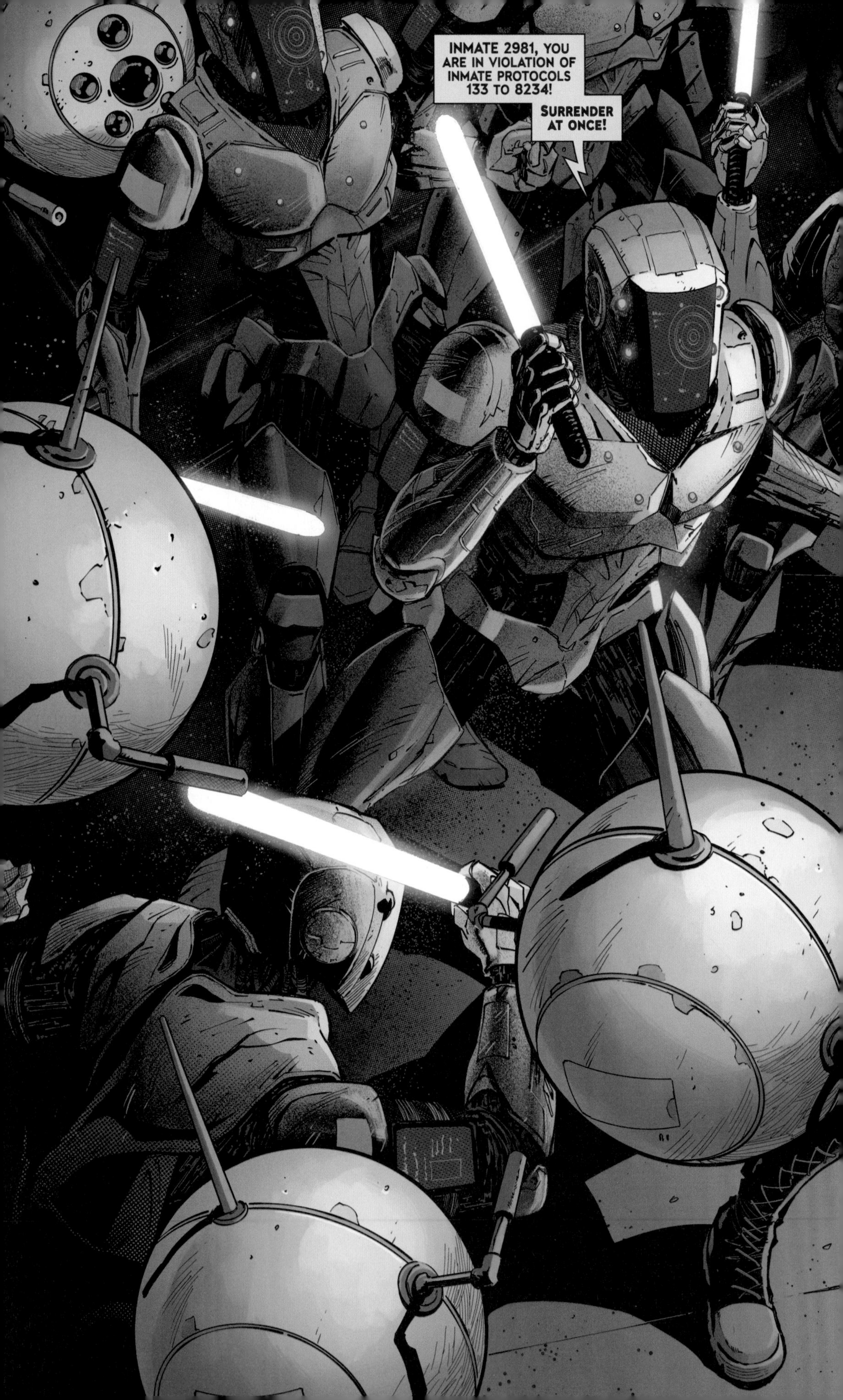
INMATE 2981, YOU ARE IN VIOLATION OF INMATE PROTOCOLS 133 TO 8234!
SURRENDER AT ONCE!

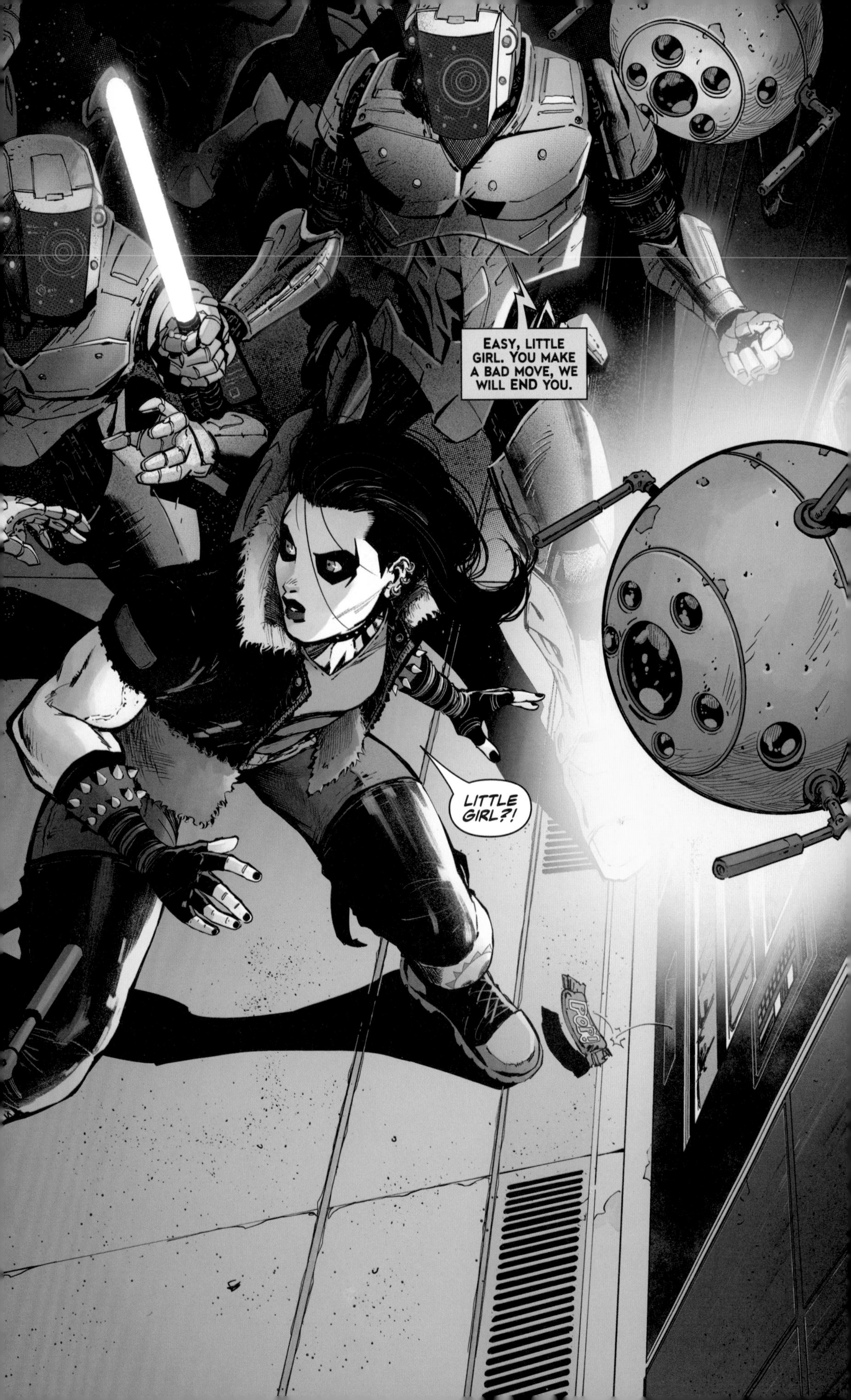
EASY, LITTLE GIRL. YOU MAKE A BAD MOVE, WE WILL END YOU.
LITTLE GIRL?!
POP!

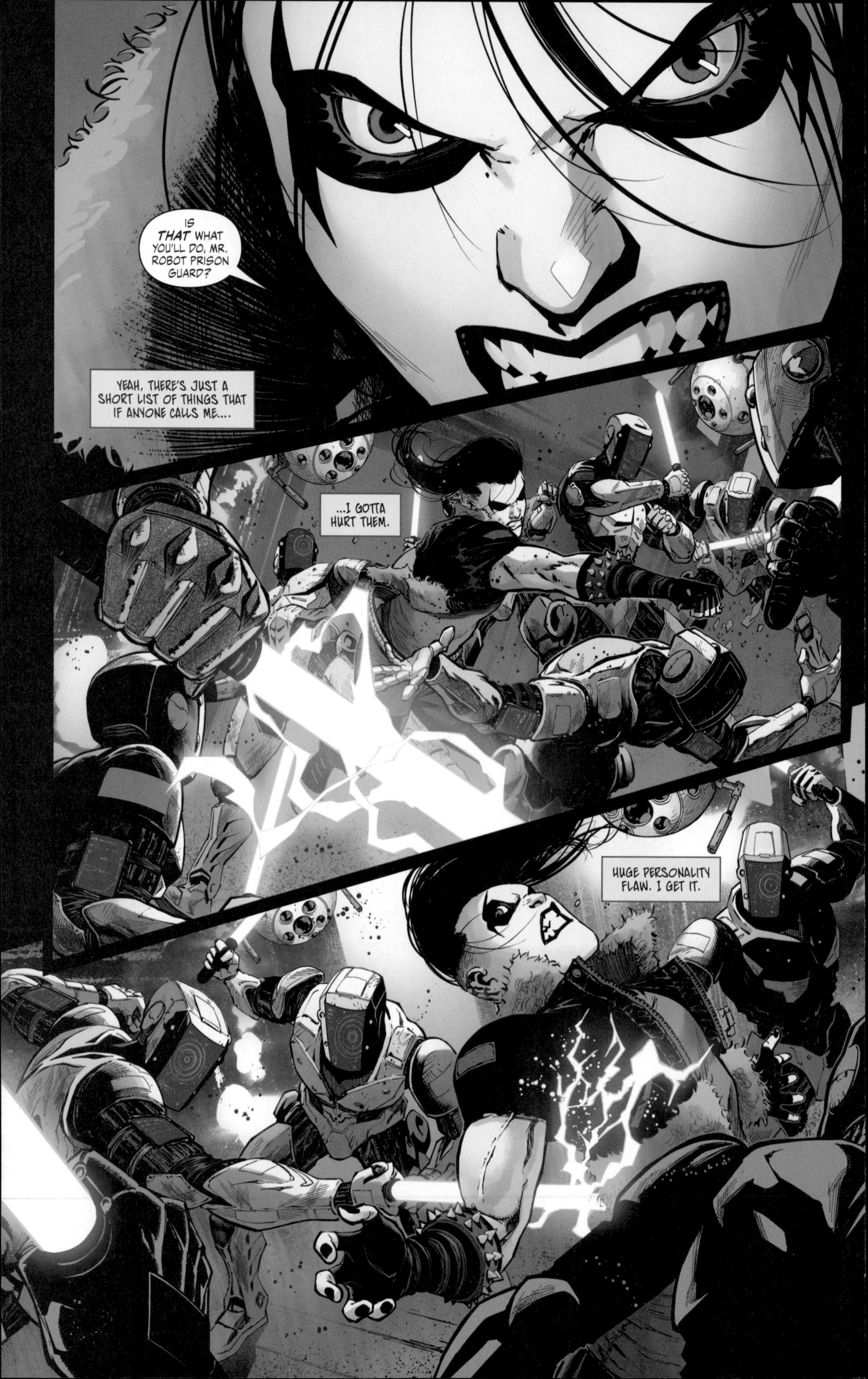
IS *THAT* WHAT YOU'LL DO, MR. ROBOT PRISON GUARD?
YEAH, THERE'S JUST A SHORT LIST OF THINGS THAT IF ANYONE CALLS ME....
...I GOTTA HURT THEM.
HUGE PERSONALITY FLAW. I GET IT.

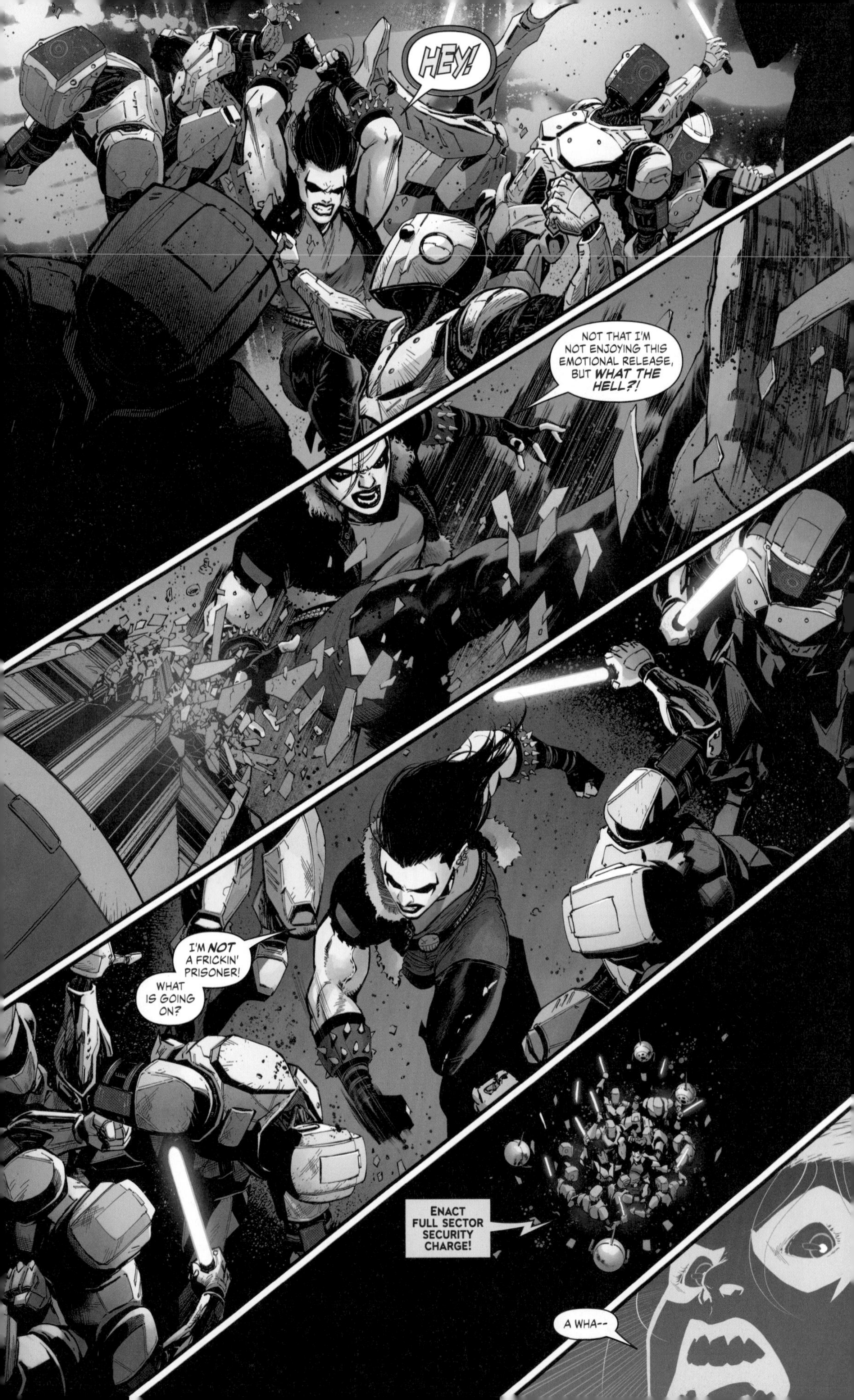
HEY!
NOT THAT I'M NOT ENJOYING THIS EMOTIONAL RELEASE, BUT WHAT THE HELL?!
I'M NOT A FRICKIN' PRISONER!
WHAT IS GOING ON?
ENACT FULL SECTOR SECURITY CHARGE!
A WHA--

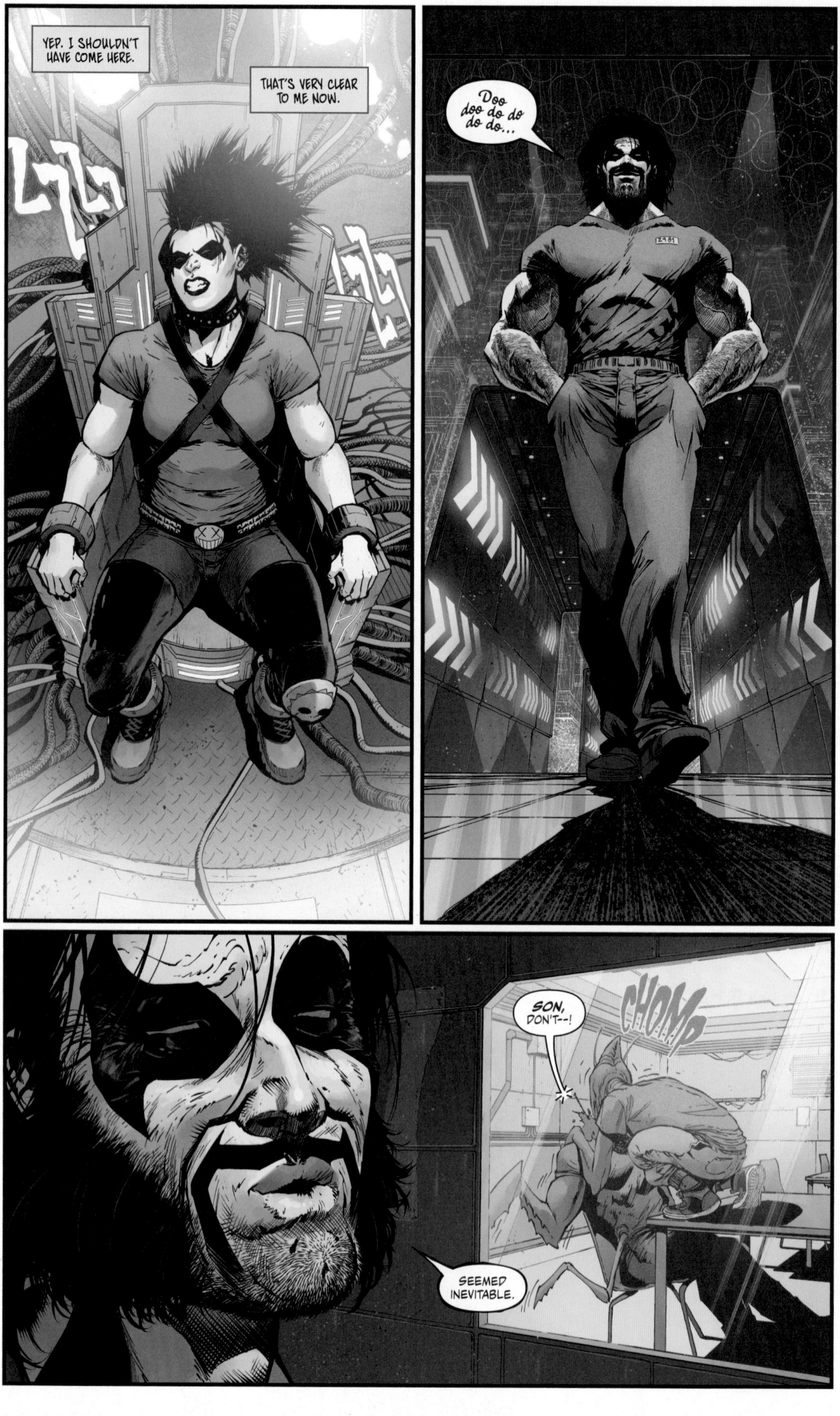
YEP. I SHOULDN'T HAVE COME HERE.
THAT'S VERY CLEAR TO ME NOW.
Doo doo do do do do...
SON, DON'T--!
CHOMP
SEEMED INEVITABLE.

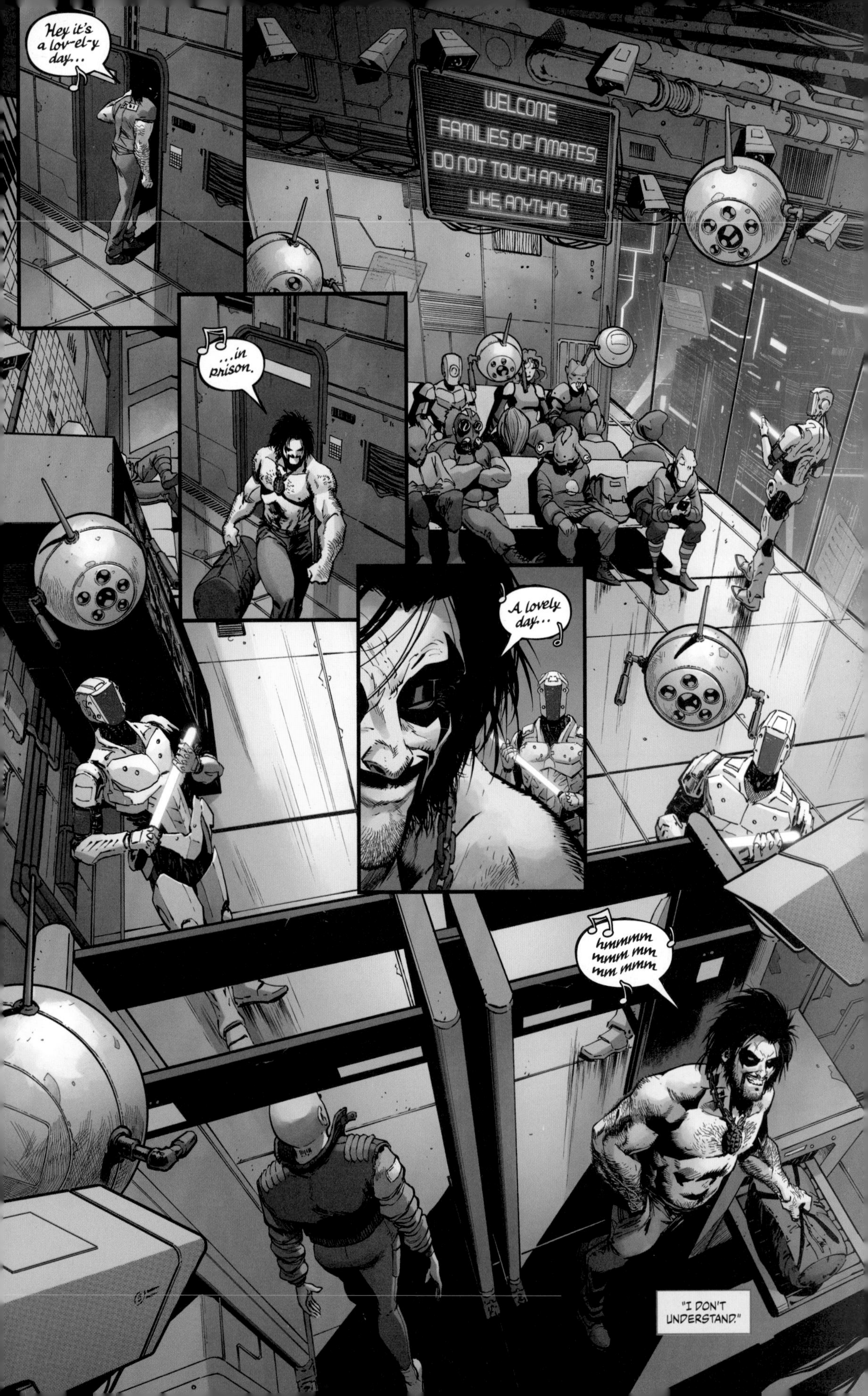
Hey it's a lov-el-y day...
WELCOME, FAMILIES OF INMATES! DO NOT TOUCH ANYTHING. LIKE, ANYTHING.
...in prison.
A lovely day...
hmmmm mmmm mm mm mmm
"I DON'T UNDERSTAND."

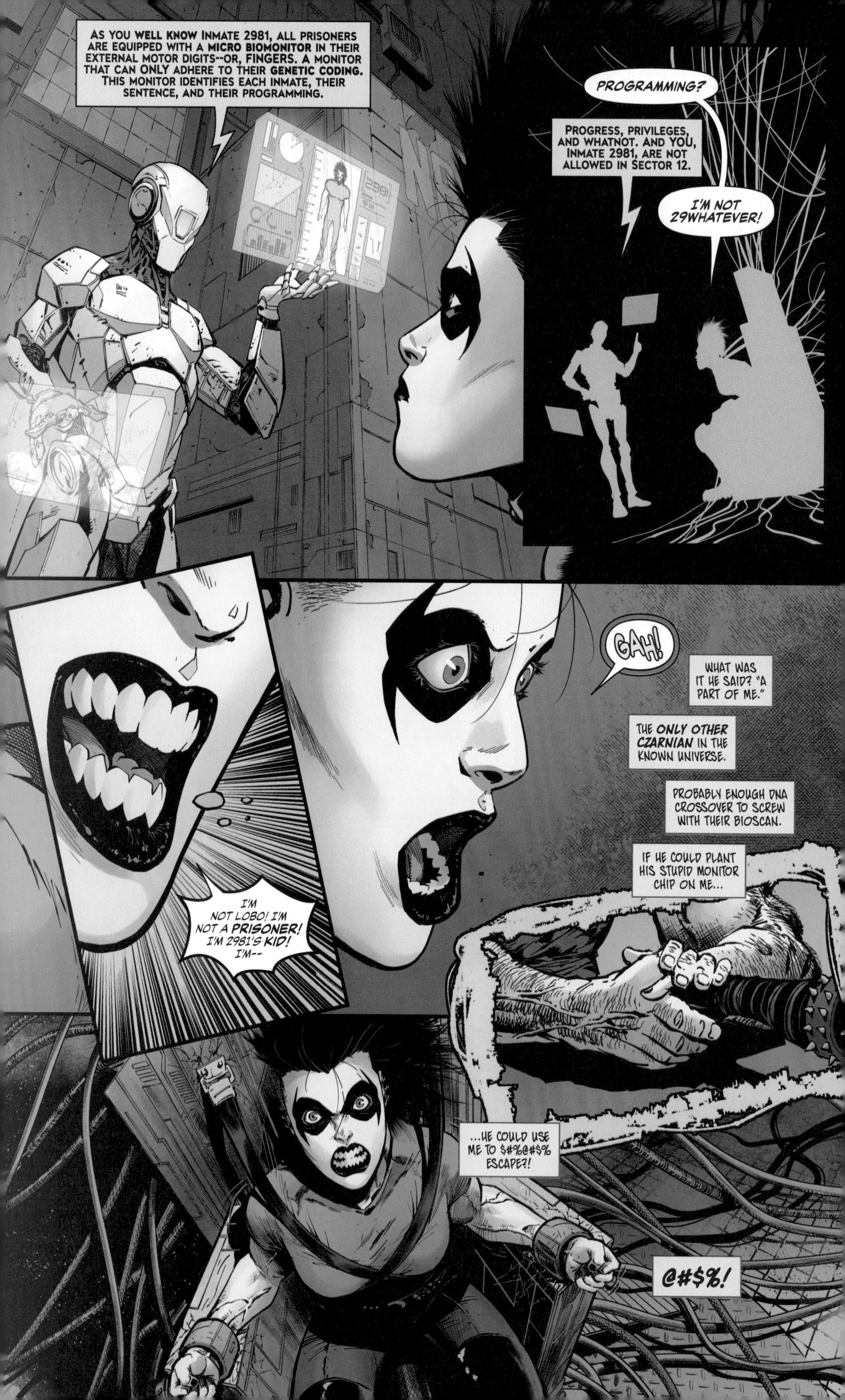
AS YOU WELL KNOW INMATE 2981, ALL PRISONERS ARE EQUIPPED WITH A MICRO BIOMONITOR IN THEIR EXTERNAL MOTOR DIGITS--OR, FINGERS. A MONITOR THAT CAN ONLY ADHERE TO THEIR GENETIC CODING. THIS MONITOR IDENTIFIES EACH INMATE, THEIR SENTENCE, AND THEIR PROGRAMMING.
PROGRAMMING?
PROGRESS, PRIVILEGES, AND WHATNOT. AND YOU, INMATE 2981, ARE NOT ALLOWED IN SECTOR 12.
I'M NOT 29WHATEVER!
I'M NOT LOBO! I'M NOT A PRISONER! I'M 2981'S KID! I'M--
GAH!
WHAT WAS IT HE SAID? "A PART OF ME."
THE ONLY OTHER CZARNIAN IN THE KNOWN UNIVERSE.
PROBABLY ENOUGH DNA CROSSOVER TO SCREW WITH THEIR BIOSCAN.
IF HE COULD PLANT HIS STUPID MONITOR CHIP ON ME...
...HE COULD USE ME TO $#%@#$% ESCAPE?!
@#$%!

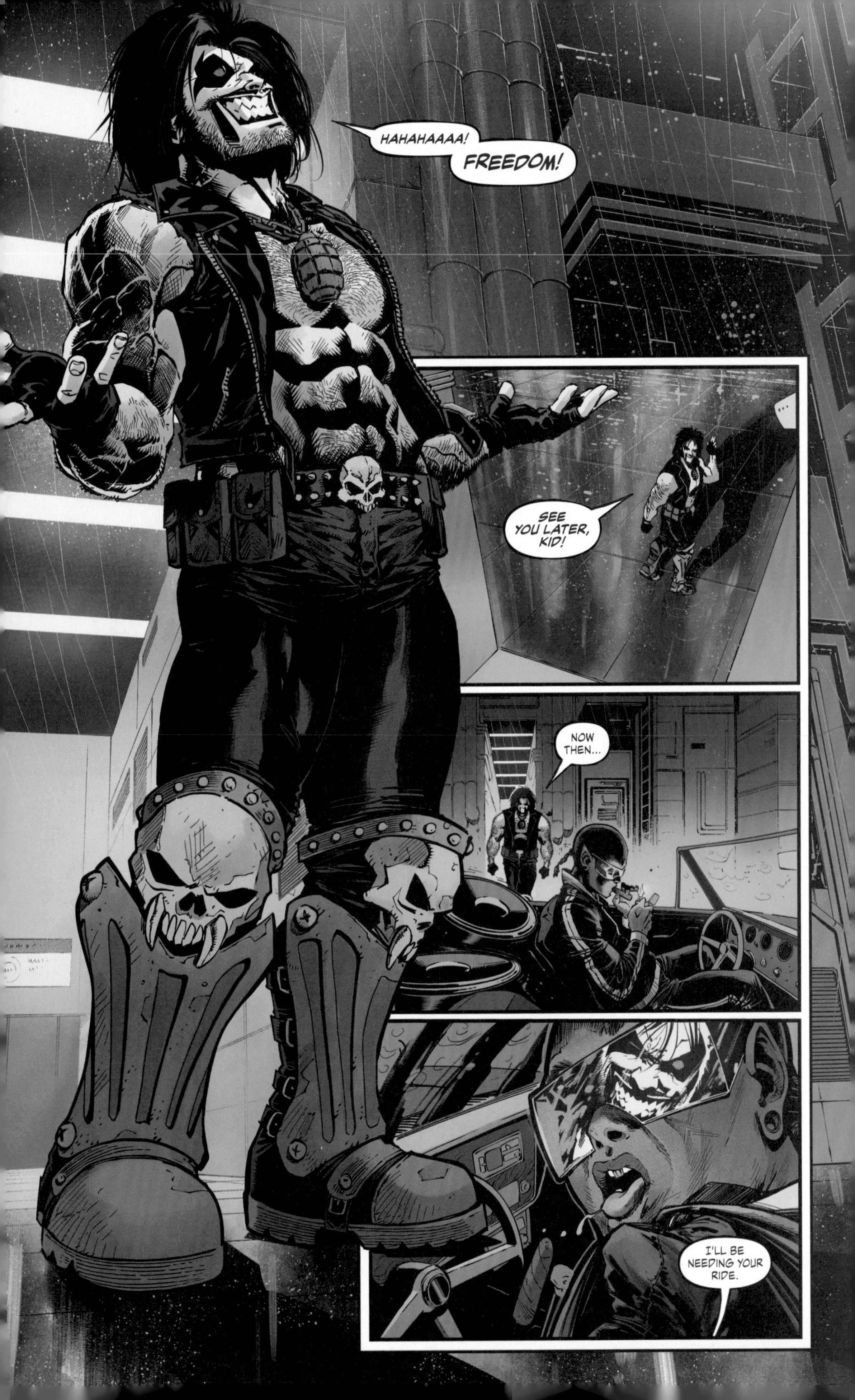
HAHAHAAAA!
FREEDOM!
SEE YOU LATER, KID!
NOW THEN...
I'LL BE NEEDING YOUR RIDE.

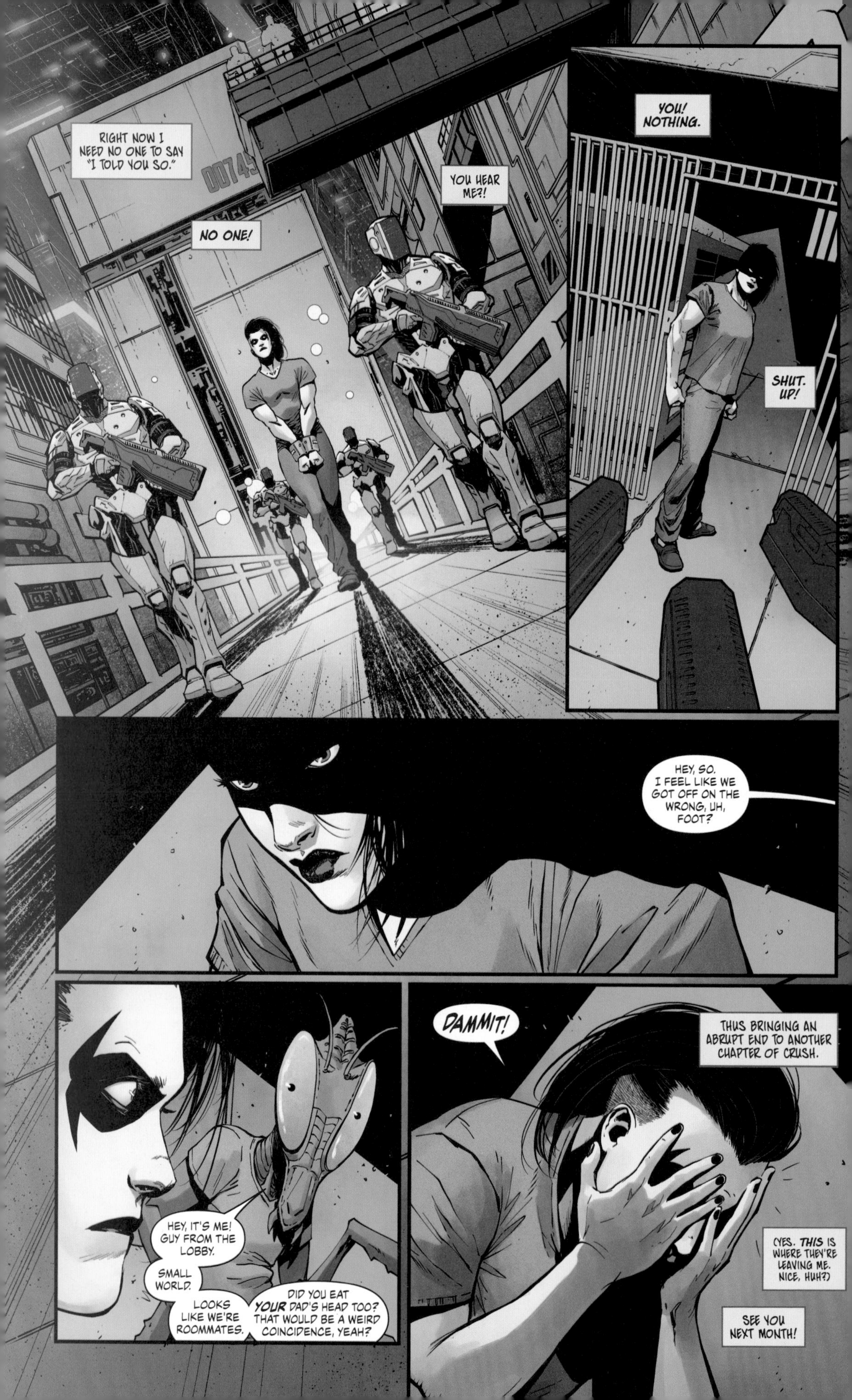
RIGHT NOW I NEED NO ONE TO SAY "I TOLD YOU SO."
NO ONE!
YOU HEAR ME?!
YOU! NOTHING.
SHUT. UP!
HEY, SO. I FEEL LIKE WE GOT OFF ON THE WRONG, UH, FOOT?
HEY, IT'S ME! GUY FROM THE LOBBY.
SMALL WORLD.
LOOKS LIKE WE'RE ROOMMATES.
DID YOU EAT YOUR DAD'S HEAD TOO? THAT WOULD BE A WEIRD COINCIDENCE, YEAH?
DAMMIT!
THUS BRINGING AN ABRUPT END TO ANOTHER CHAPTER OF CRUSH.
(YES. THIS IS WHERE THEY'RE LEAVING ME. NICE, HUH?)
SEE YOU NEXT MONTH!

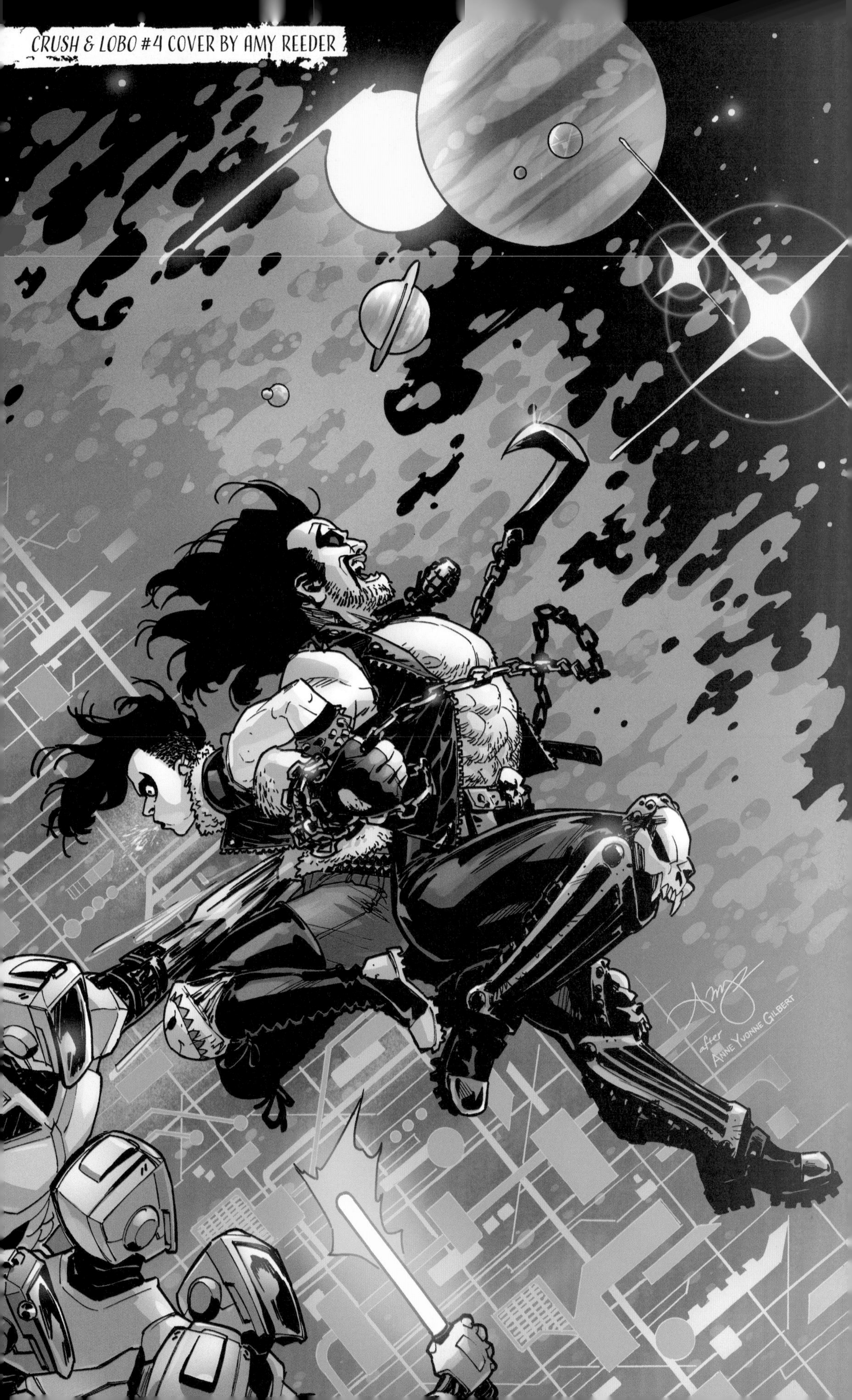
after Anne Yvonne Gilbert
CRUSH & LOBO #4 COVER BY AMY REEDER

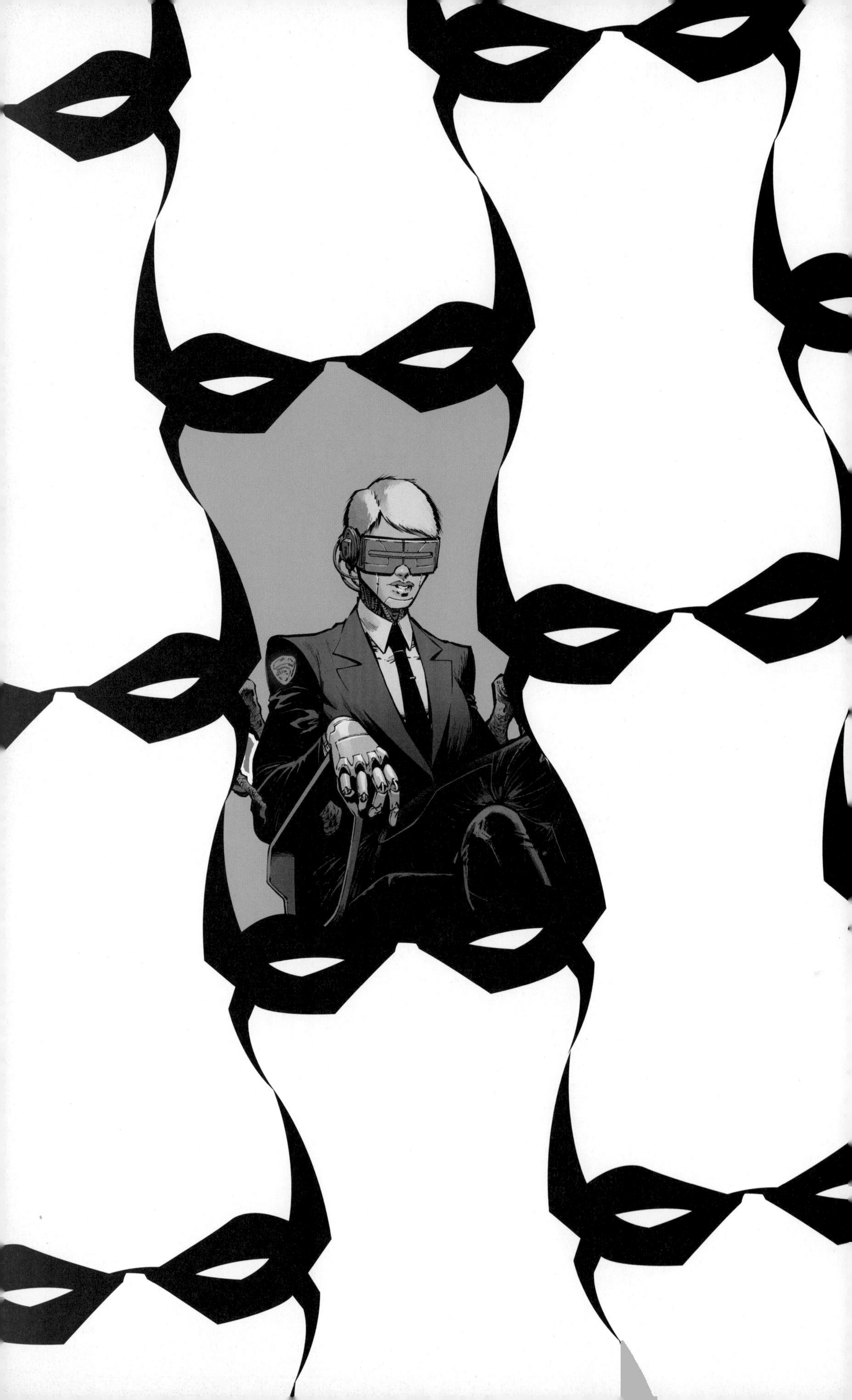

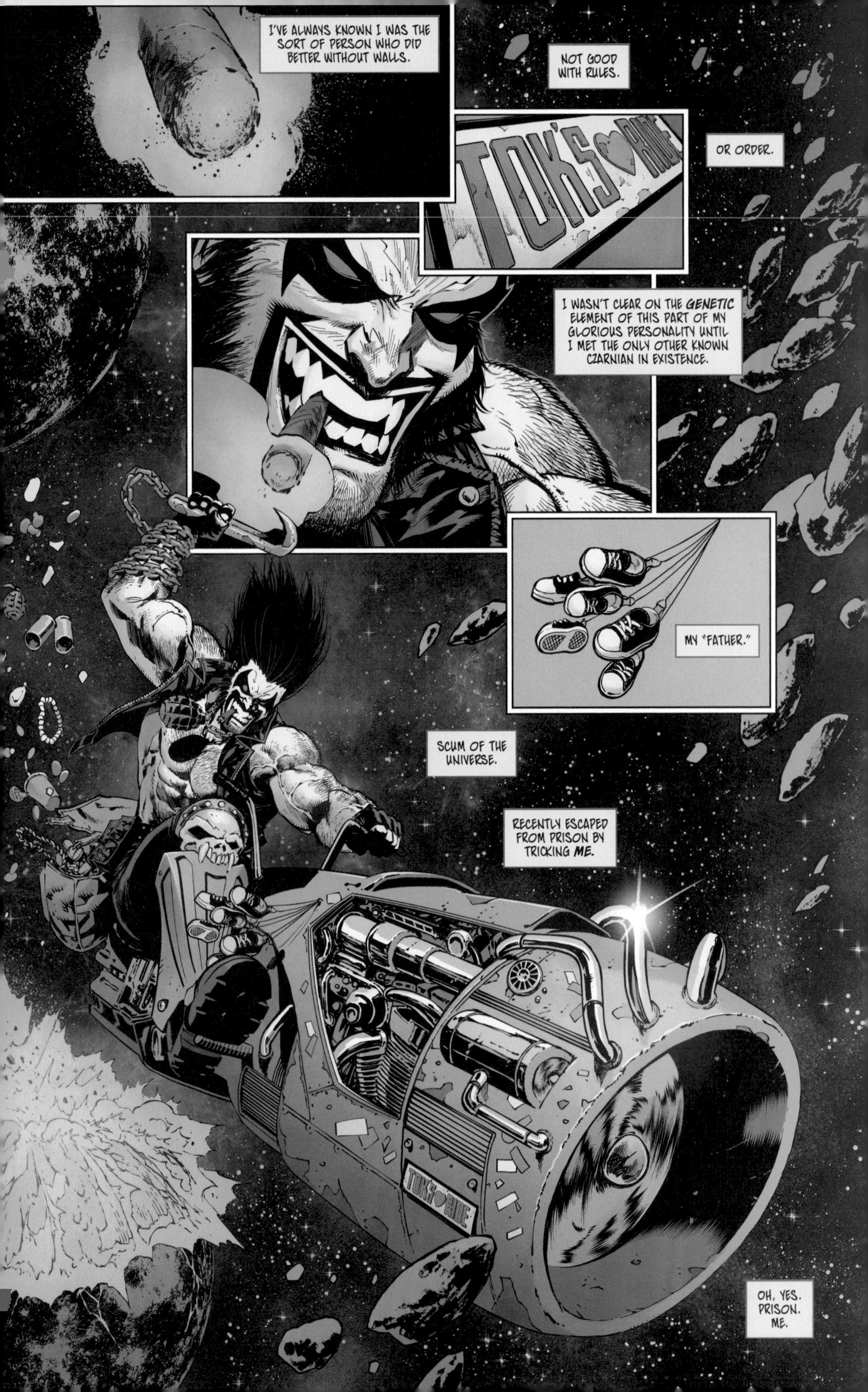
I'VE ALWAYS KNOWN I WAS THE SORT OF PERSON WHO DID BETTER WITHOUT WALLS.
NOT GOOD WITH RULES.
TOK'S RIDE
OR ORDER.
I WASN'T CLEAR ON THE GENETIC ELEMENT OF THIS PART OF MY GLORIOUS PERSONALITY UNTIL I MET THE ONLY OTHER KNOWN CZARNIAN IN EXISTENCE.
MY "FATHER."
SCUM OF THE UNIVERSE.
RECENTLY ESCAPED FROM PRISON BY TRICKING ME.
TOK'S RIDE
OH, YES. PRISON. ME.

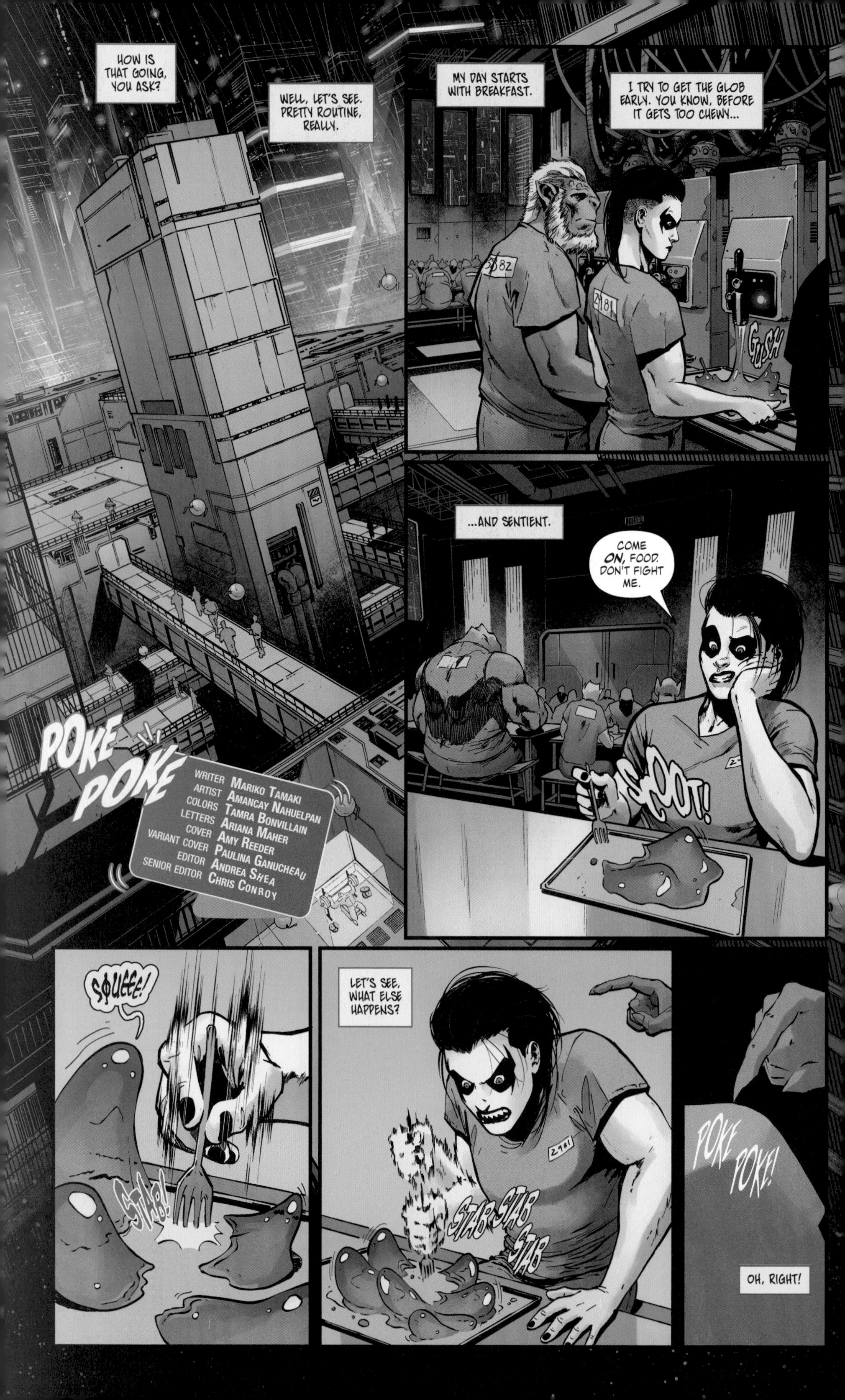
HOW IS THAT GOING, YOU ASK?
WELL, LET'S SEE. PRETTY ROUTINE, REALLY.
POKE POKE
WRITER MARIKO TAMAKI
ARTIST AMANCAY NAHUELPAN
COLORS TAMRA BONVILLAIN
LETTERS ARIANA MAHER
COVER AMY REEDER
VARIANT COVER PAULINA GANUCHEAU
EDITOR ANDREA SHEA
SENIOR EDITOR CHRIS CONROY
MY DAY STARTS WITH BREAKFAST.
I TRY TO GET THE GLOB EARLY. YOU KNOW, BEFORE IT GETS TOO CHEWY...
GUSH
...AND SENTIENT.
COME ON, FOOD. DON'T FIGHT ME.
SCOOT!
SQUEEE!
STAB!
LET'S SEE, WHAT ELSE HAPPENS?
STAB STAB STAB
POKE POKE!
OH, RIGHT!

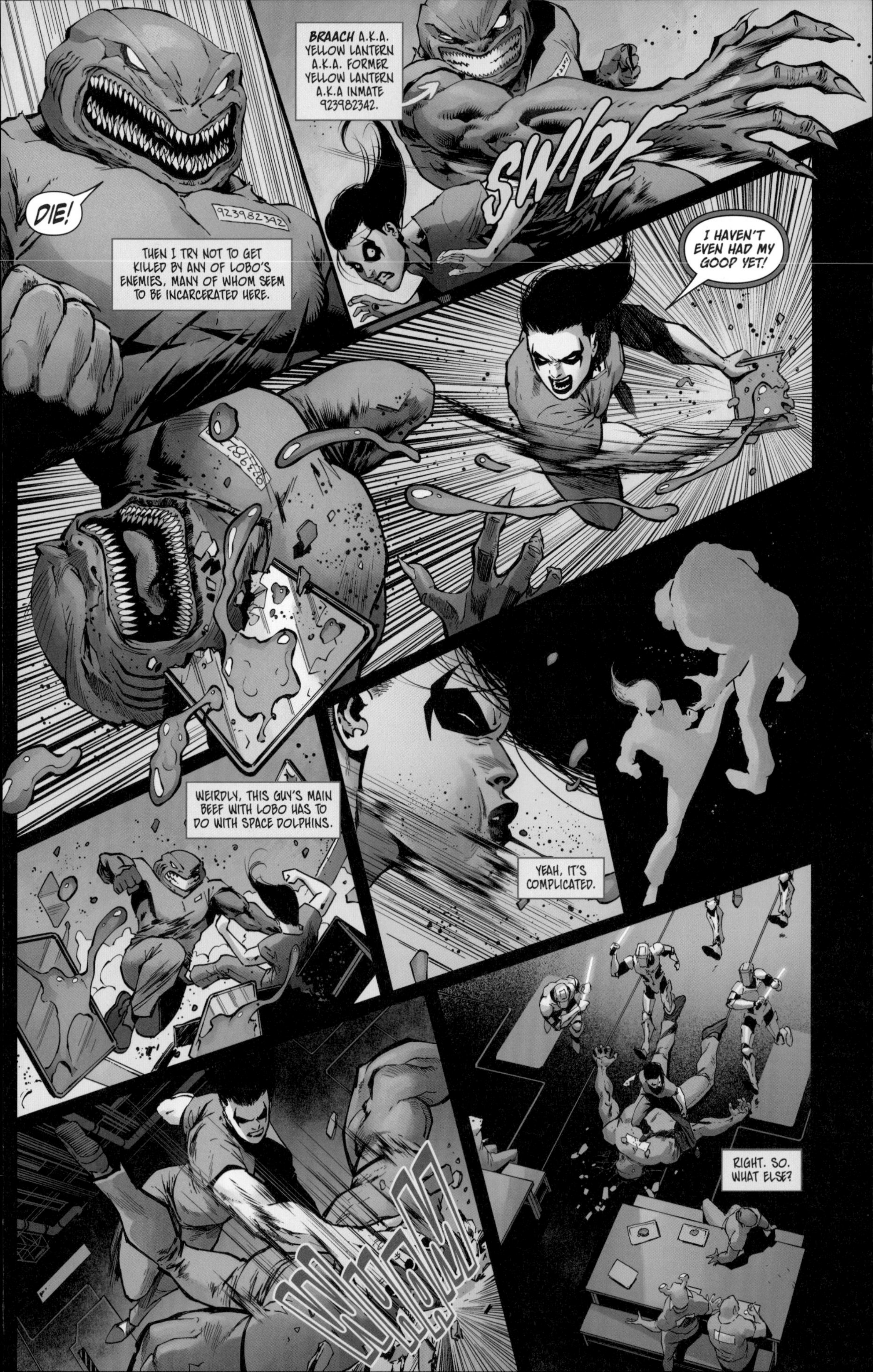
BRAACH A.K.A. YELLOW LANTERN A.K.A. FORMER YELLOW LANTERN A.K.A INMATE 923982342.
DIE!
923982342
SWIPE
THEN I TRY NOT TO GET KILLED BY ANY OF LOBO'S ENEMIES, MANY OF WHOM SEEM TO BE INCARCERATED HERE.
I HAVEN'T EVEN HAD MY GOOP YET!
WEIRDLY, THIS GUY'S MAIN BEEF WITH LOBO HAS TO DO WITH SPACE DOLPHINS.
YEAH, IT'S COMPLICATED.
RIGHT. SO. WHAT ELSE?

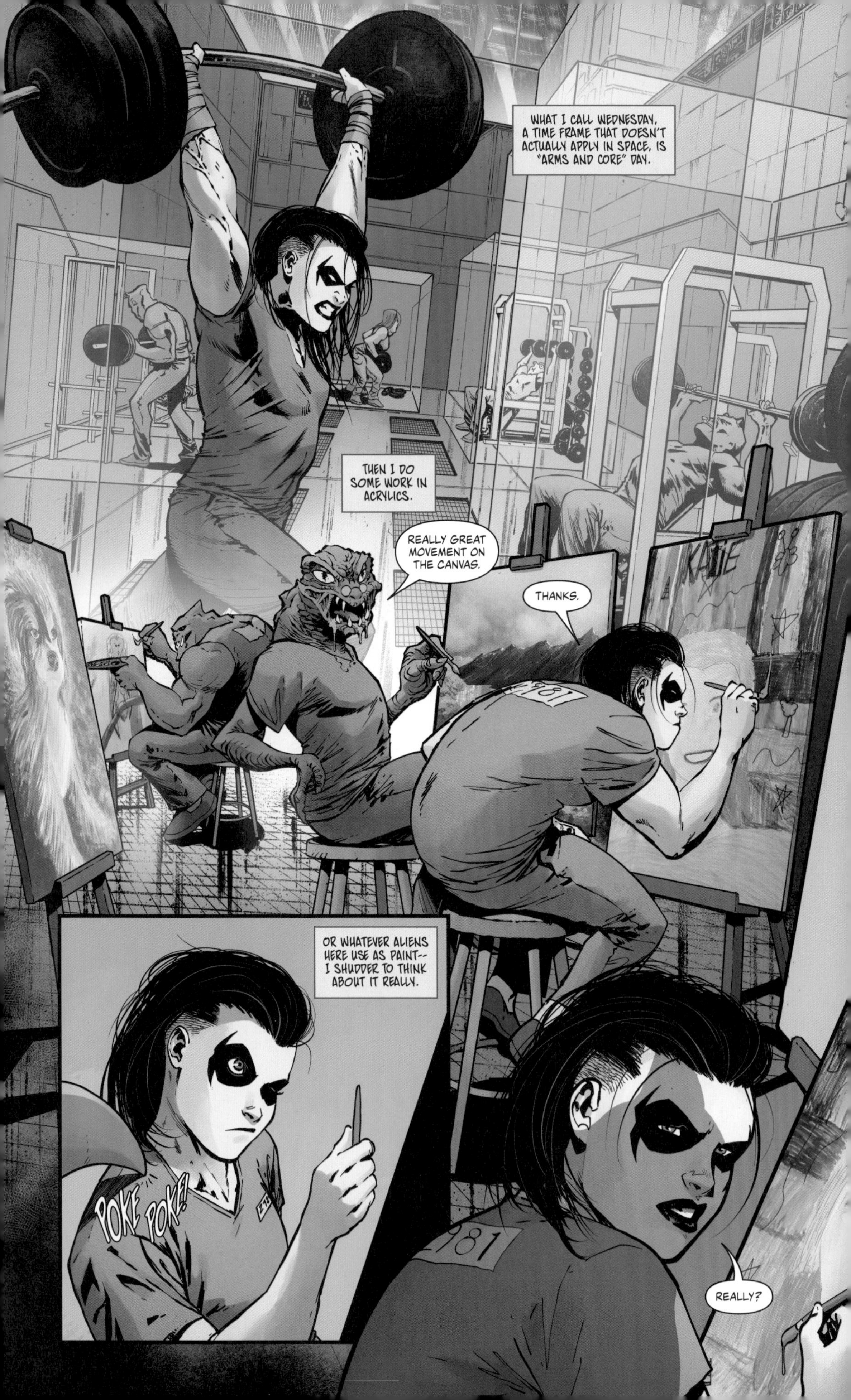
WHAT I CALL WEDNESDAY, A TIME FRAME THAT DOESN'T ACTUALLY APPLY IN SPACE, IS "ARMS AND CORE" DAY.
THEN I DO SOME WORK IN ACRYLICS.
REALLY GREAT MOVEMENT ON THE CANVAS.
THANKS.
KATE
OR WHATEVER ALIENS HERE USE AS PAINT-- I SHUDDER TO THINK ABOUT IT REALLY.
POKE POKE!
REALLY?

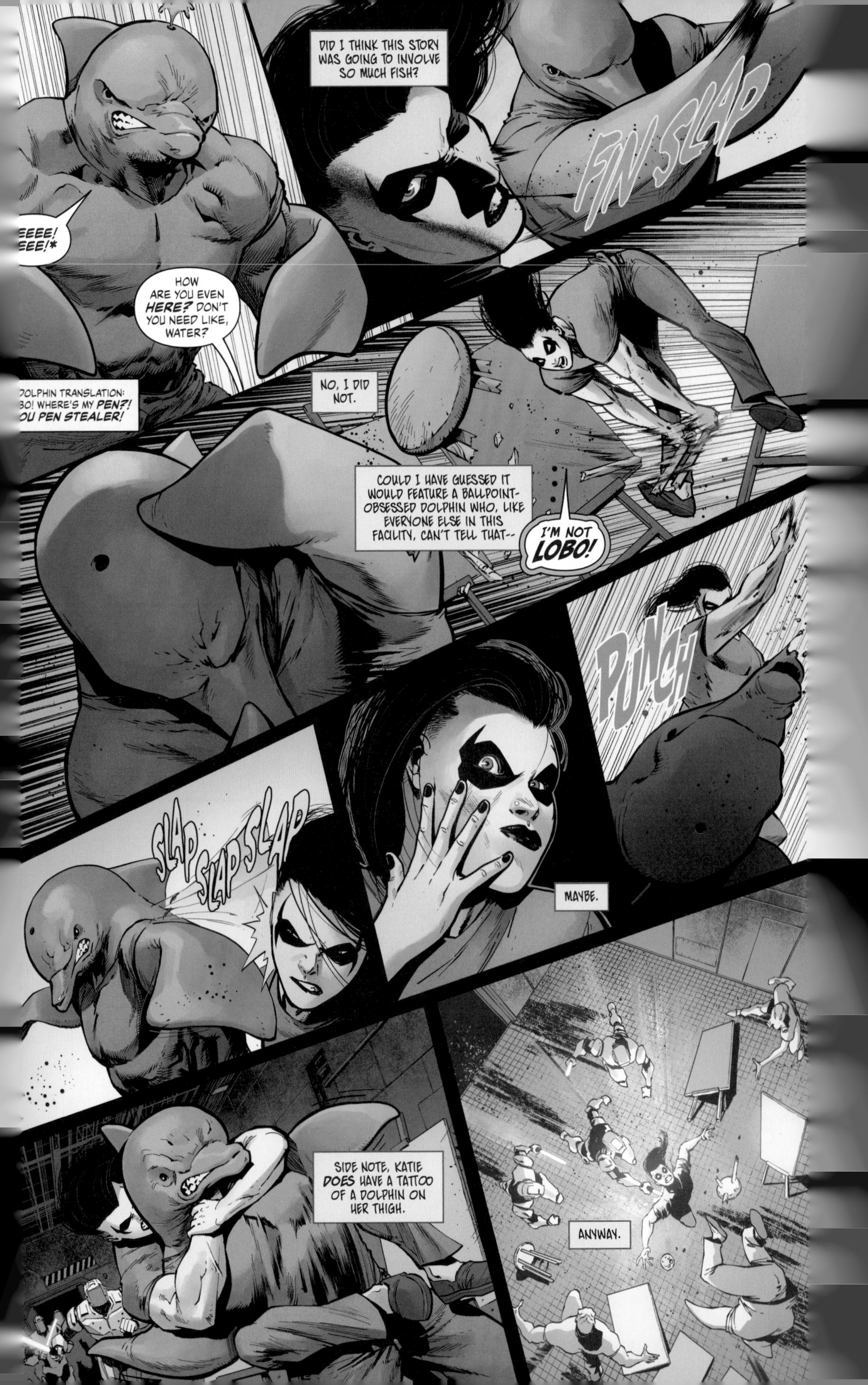
DID I THINK THIS STORY WAS GOING TO INVOLVE SO MUCH FISH?
EEEE! EEE!*
HOW ARE YOU EVEN HERE? DON'T YOU NEED LIKE, WATER?
FIN SLAP
NO, I DID NOT.
DOLPHIN TRANSLATION: BO! WHERE'S MY PEN?! OU PEN STEALER!
COULD I HAVE GUESSED IT WOULD FEATURE A BALLPOINT-OBSESSED DOLPHIN WHO, LIKE EVERYONE ELSE IN THIS FACILITY, CAN'T TELL THAT--
I'M NOT LOBO!
PUNCH
SLAP SLAP SLAP
MAYBE.
SIDE NOTE, KATIE DOES HAVE A TATTOO OF A DOLPHIN ON HER THIGH.
ANYWAY.

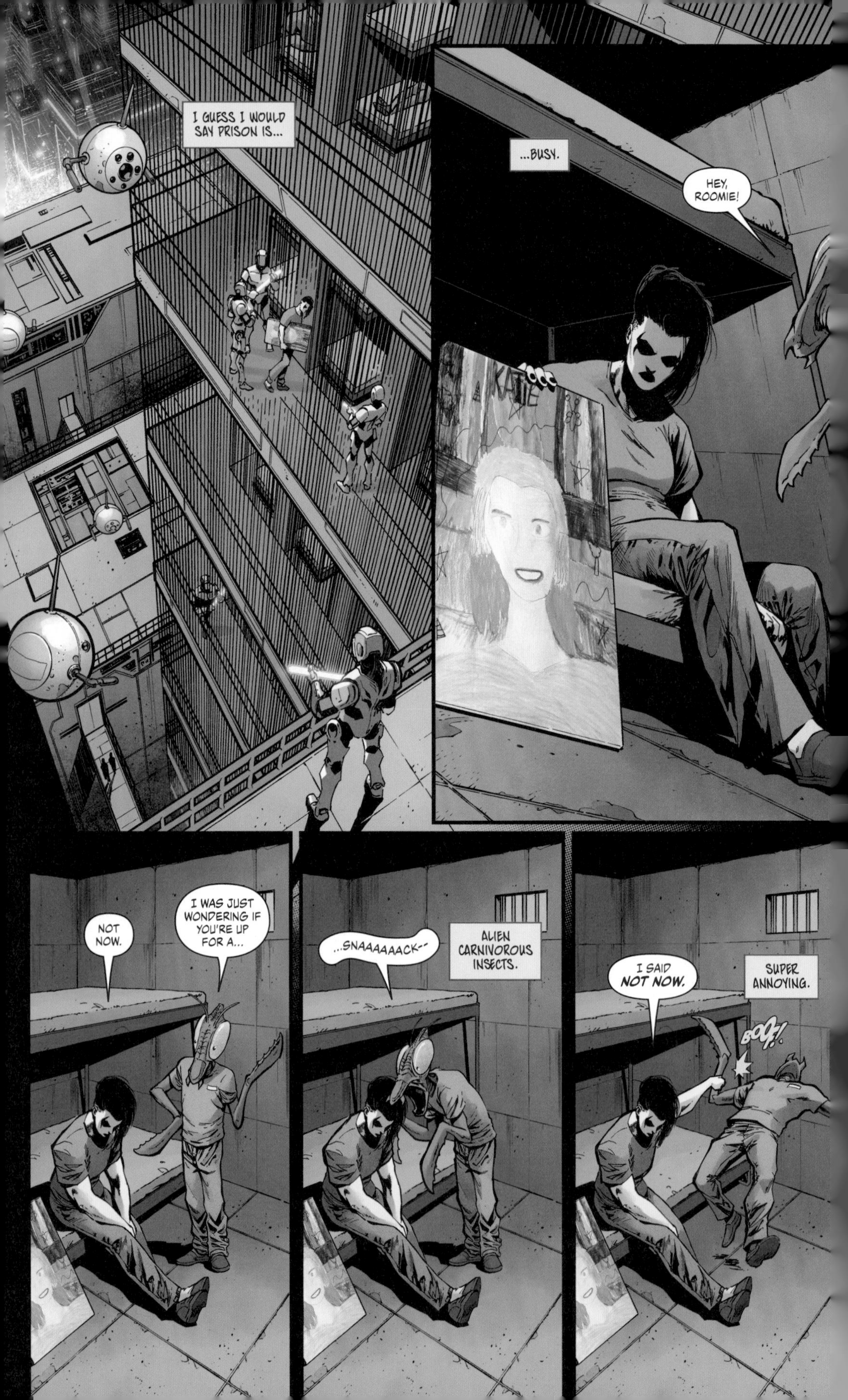
I GUESS I WOULD SAY PRISON IS...
...BUSY.
HEY, ROOMIE!
KATIE
NOT NOW.
I WAS JUST WONDERING IF YOU'RE UP FOR A...
...SNAAAAAACK--
ALIEN CARNIVOROUS INSECTS.
I SAID NOT NOW.
SUPER ANNOYING.
BOOF!

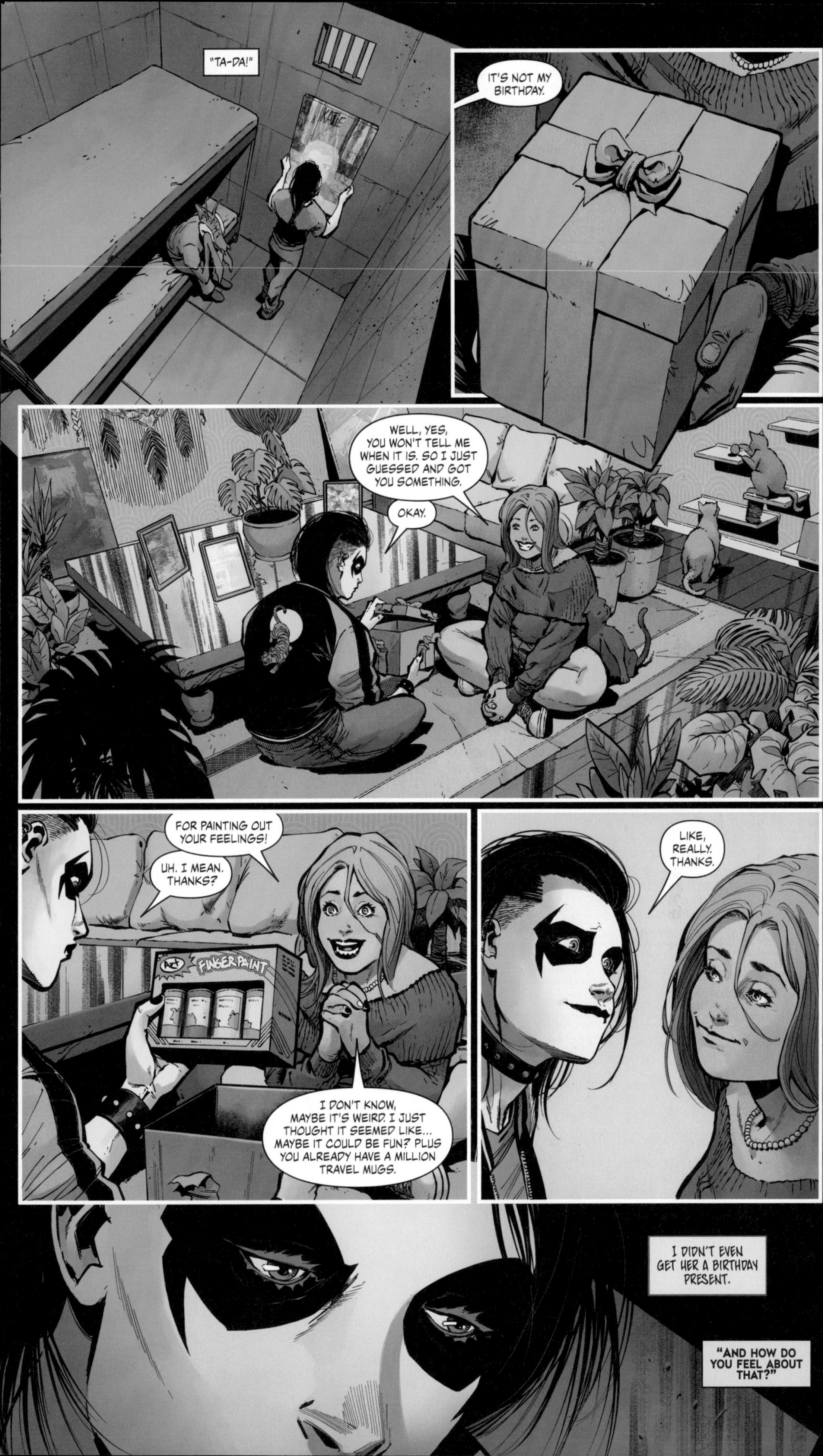
"TA-DA!"
IT'S NOT MY BIRTHDAY.
WELL, YES, YOU WON'T TELL ME WHEN IT IS. SO I JUST GUESSED AND GOT YOU SOMETHING.
OKAY.
FOR PAINTING OUT YOUR FEELINGS!
UH. I MEAN. THANKS?
FINGER PAINT
I DON'T KNOW, MAYBE IT'S WEIRD. I JUST THOUGHT IT SEEMED LIKE... MAYBE IT COULD BE FUN? PLUS YOU ALREADY HAVE A MILLION TRAVEL MUGS.
LIKE, REALLY. THANKS.
I DIDN'T EVEN GET HER A BIRTHDAY PRESENT.
"AND HOW DO YOU FEEL ABOUT THAT?"

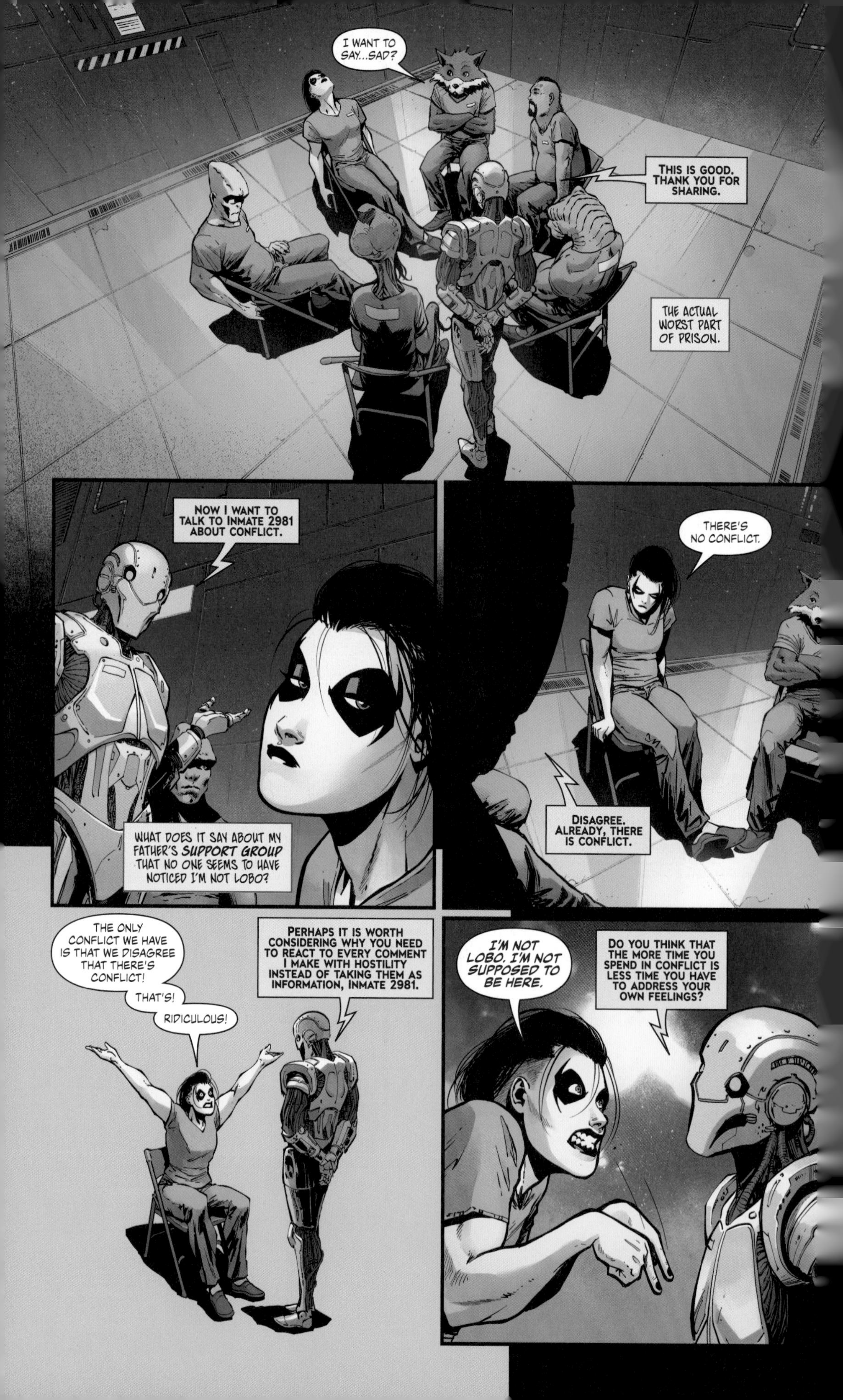
I WANT TO SAY...SAD?
THIS IS GOOD. THANK YOU FOR SHARING.
THE ACTUAL WORST PART OF PRISON.
NOW I WANT TO TALK TO INMATE 2981 ABOUT CONFLICT.
WHAT DOES IT SAY ABOUT MY FATHER'S *SUPPORT GROUP* THAT NO ONE SEEMS TO HAVE NOTICED I'M NOT LOBO?
THERE'S NO CONFLICT.
DISAGREE. ALREADY, THERE IS CONFLICT.
THE ONLY CONFLICT WE HAVE IS THAT WE DISAGREE THAT THERE'S CONFLICT!
THAT'S!
RIDICULOUS!
PERHAPS IT IS WORTH CONSIDERING WHY YOU NEED TO REACT TO EVERY COMMENT I MAKE WITH HOSTILITY INSTEAD OF TAKING THEM AS INFORMATION, INMATE 2981.
I'M NOT LOBO. I'M NOT SUPPOSED TO BE HERE.
DO YOU THINK THAT THE MORE TIME YOU SPEND IN CONFLICT IS LESS TIME YOU HAVE TO ADDRESS YOUR OWN FEELINGS?

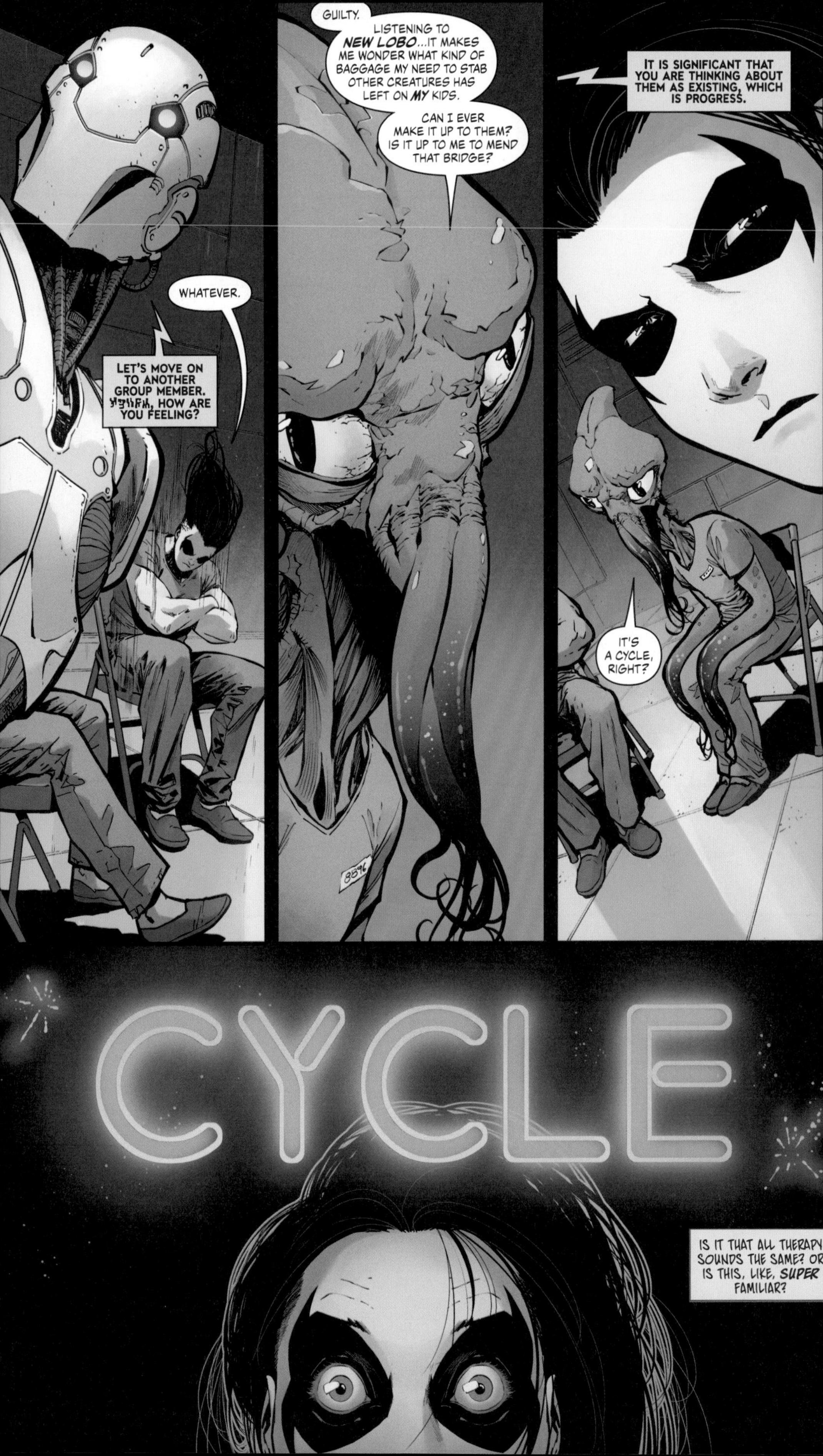

LET'S MOVE ON TO ANOTHER GROUP MEMBER. , HOW ARE YOU FEELING?
WHATEVER.
GUILTY.
LISTENING TO NEW LOBO...IT MAKES ME WONDER WHAT KIND OF BAGGAGE MY NEED TO STAB OTHER CREATURES HAS LEFT ON MY KIDS.
CAN I EVER MAKE IT UP TO THEM? IS IT UP TO ME TO MEND THAT BRIDGE?
8896
IT IS SIGNIFICANT THAT YOU ARE THINKING ABOUT THEM AS EXISTING, WHICH IS PROGRESS.
IT'S A CYCLE, RIGHT?
CYCLE
IS IT THAT ALL THERAPY SOUNDS THE SAME? OR IS THIS, LIKE, SUPER FAMILIAR?

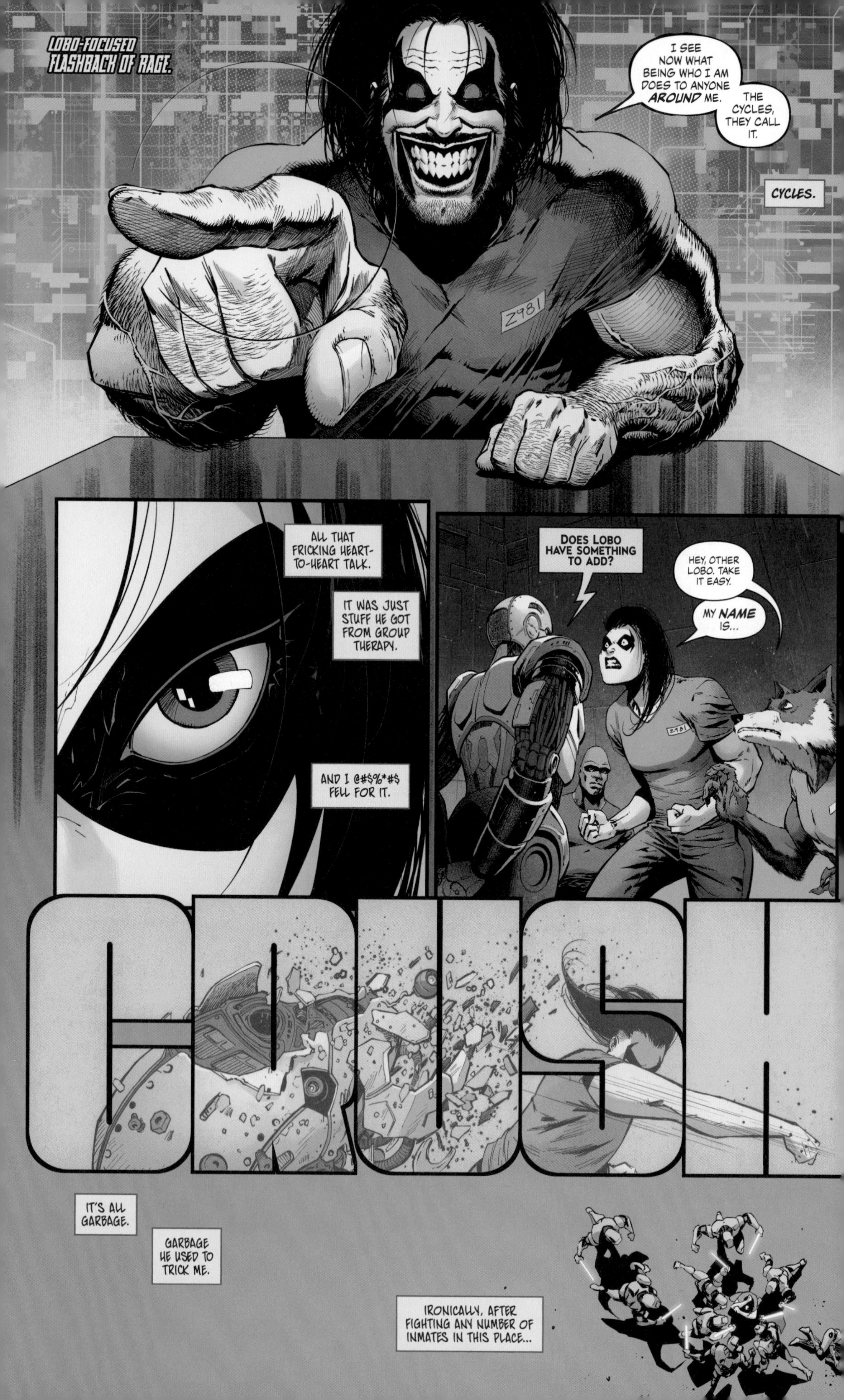
LOBO-FOCUSED FLASHBACK OF RAGE.
I SEE NOW WHAT BEING WHO I AM DOES TO ANYONE AROUND ME.
THE CYCLES, THEY CALL IT.
CYCLES.
Z981
ALL THAT FRICKING HEART-TO-HEART TALK.
IT WAS JUST STUFF HE GOT FROM GROUP THERAPY.
AND I @#$%*#$ FELL FOR IT.
DOES LOBO HAVE SOMETHING TO ADD?
HEY, OTHER LOBO. TAKE IT EASY.
MY NAME IS...
Z981
CRUSH
IT'S ALL GARBAGE.
GARBAGE HE USED TO TRICK ME.
IRONICALLY, AFTER FIGHTING ANY NUMBER OF INMATES IN THIS PLACE...

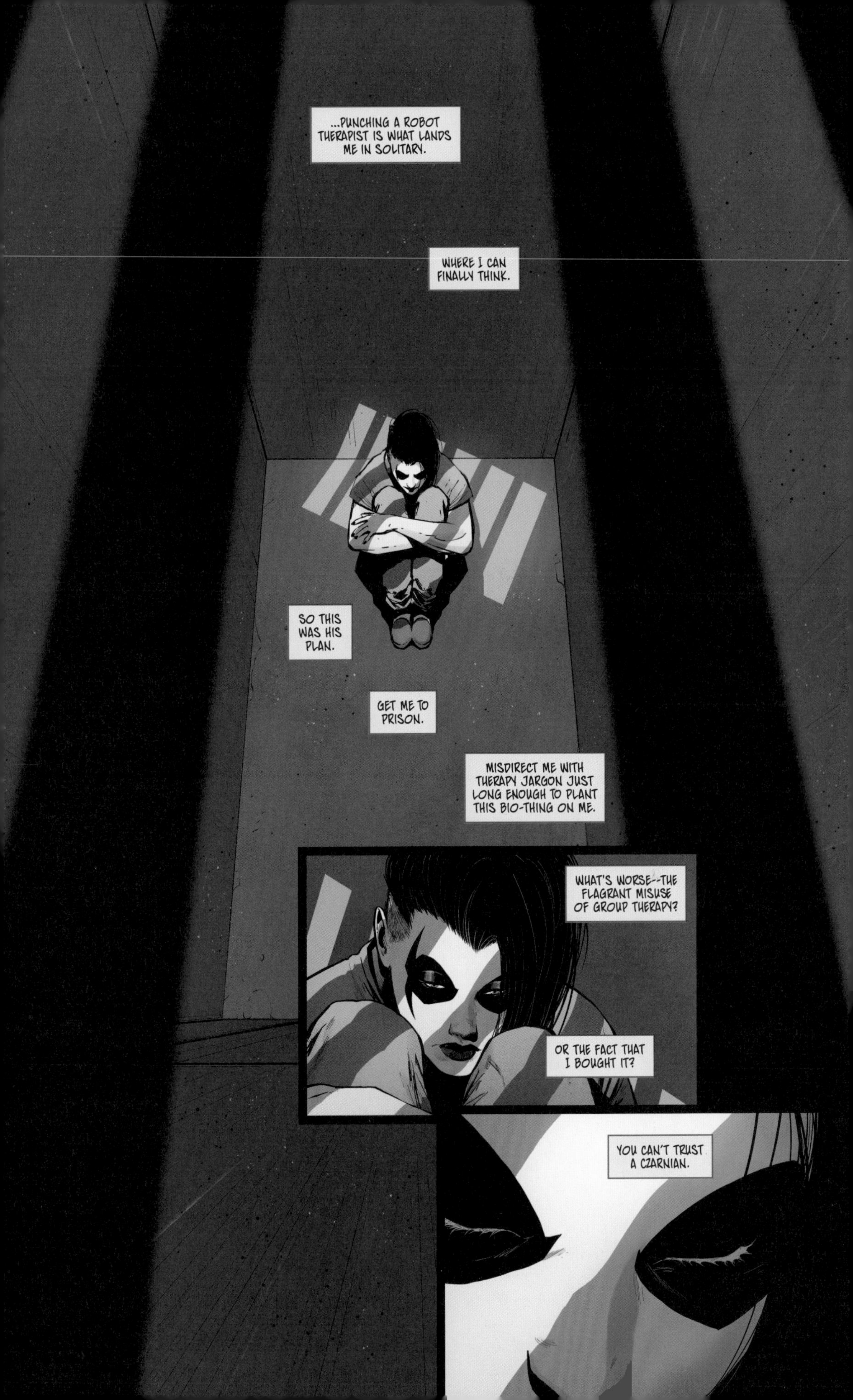
...PUNCHING A ROBOT THERAPIST IS WHAT LANDS ME IN SOLITARY.
WHERE I CAN FINALLY THINK.
SO THIS WAS HIS PLAN.
GET ME TO PRISON.
MISDIRECT ME WITH THERAPY JARGON JUST LONG ENOUGH TO PLANT THIS BIO-THING ON ME.
WHAT'S WORSE--THE FLAGRANT MISUSE OF GROUP THERAPY?
OR THE FACT THAT I BOUGHT IT?
YOU CAN'T TRUST A CZARNIAN.

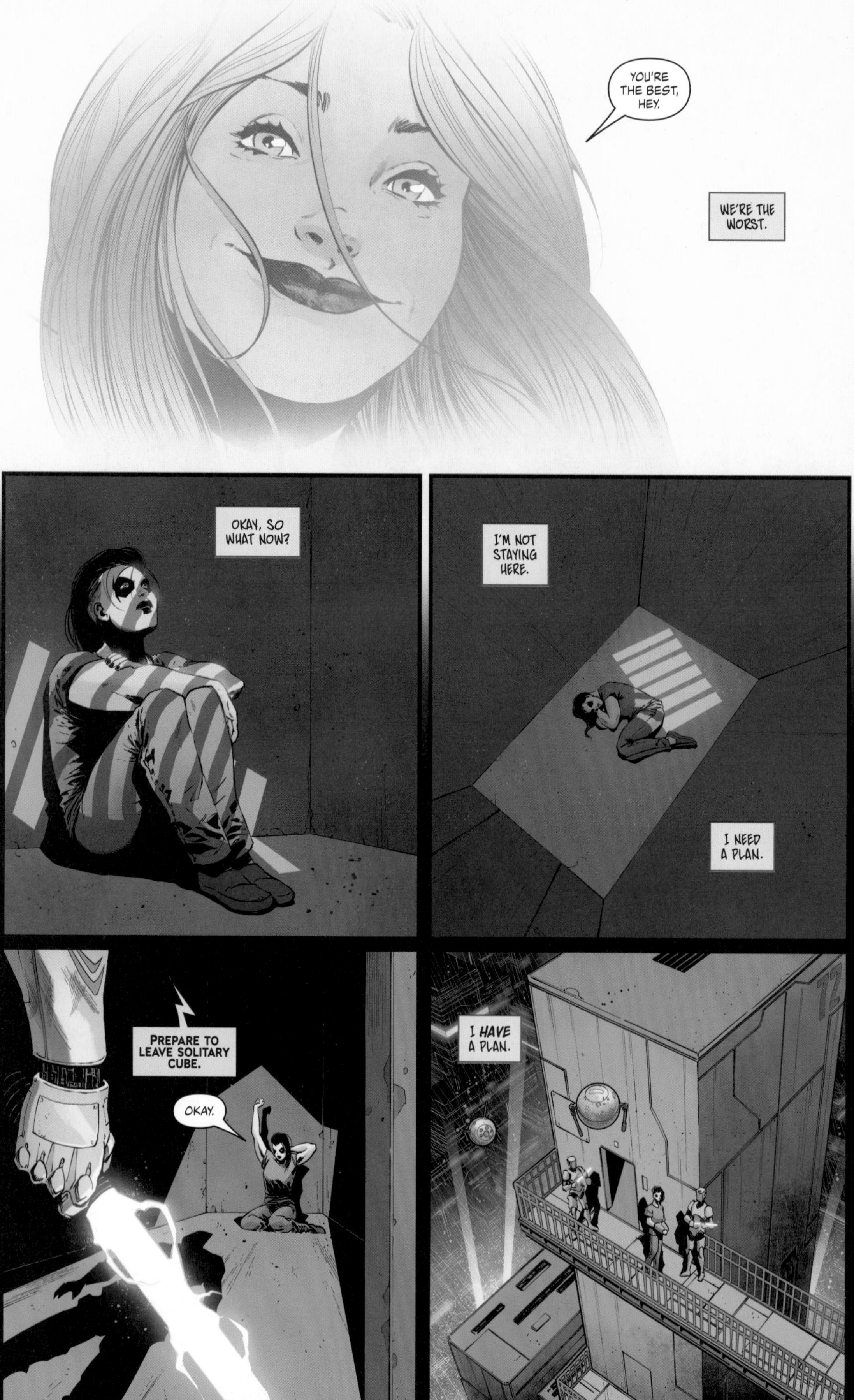
YOU'RE THE BEST, HEY.
WE'RE THE WORST.
OKAY, SO WHAT NOW?
I'M NOT STAYING HERE.
I NEED A PLAN.
PREPARE TO LEAVE SOLITARY CUBE.
OKAY.
I *HAVE* A PLAN.

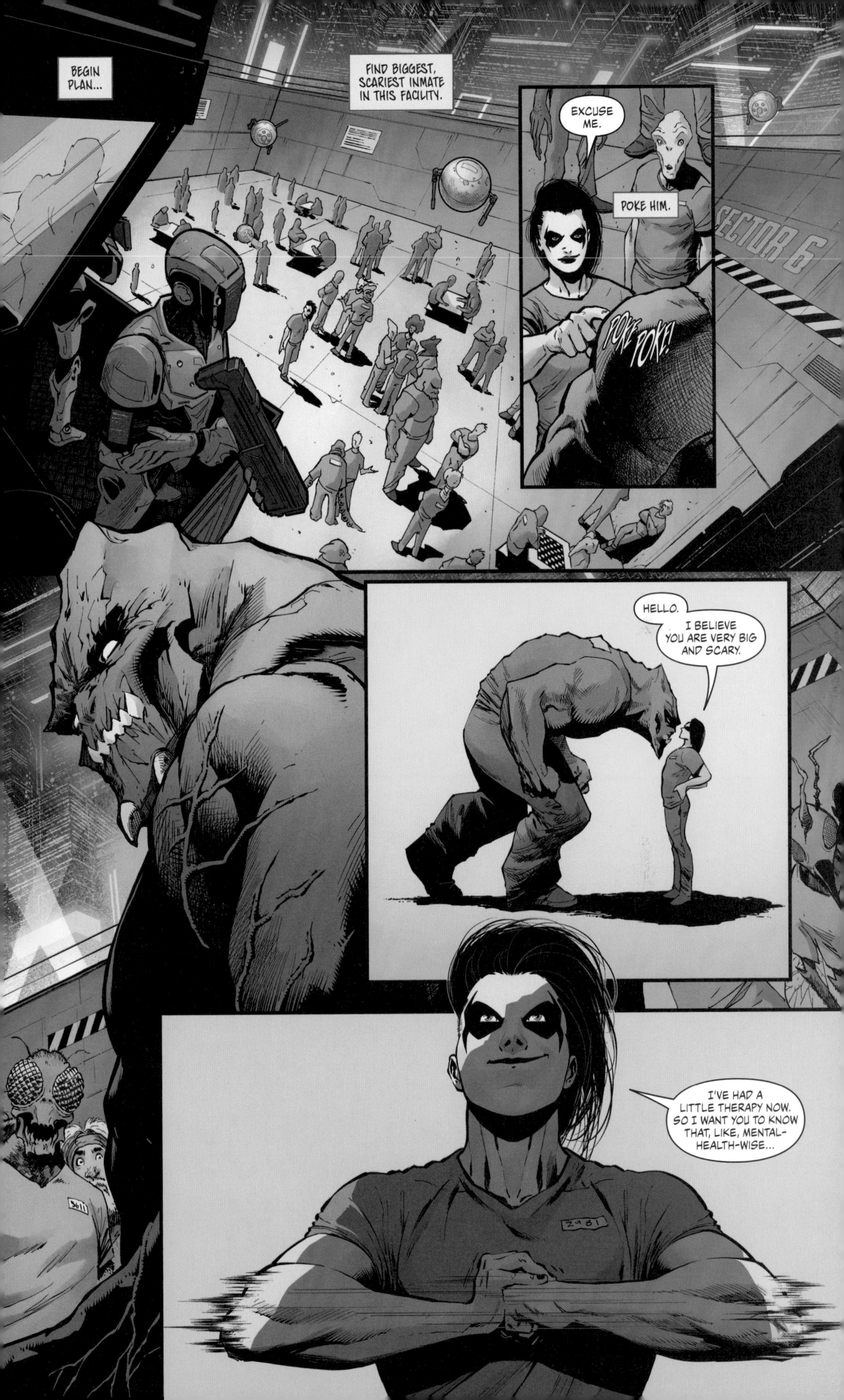
BEGIN PLAN...
FIND BIGGEST, SCARIEST INMATE IN THIS FACILITY.
EXCUSE ME.
POKE HIM.
POKE POKE!
SECTOR 6
HELLO.
I BELIEVE YOU ARE VERY BIG AND SCARY.
I'VE HAD A LITTLE THERAPY NOW. SO I WANT YOU TO KNOW THAT, LIKE, MENTAL-HEALTH-WISE...

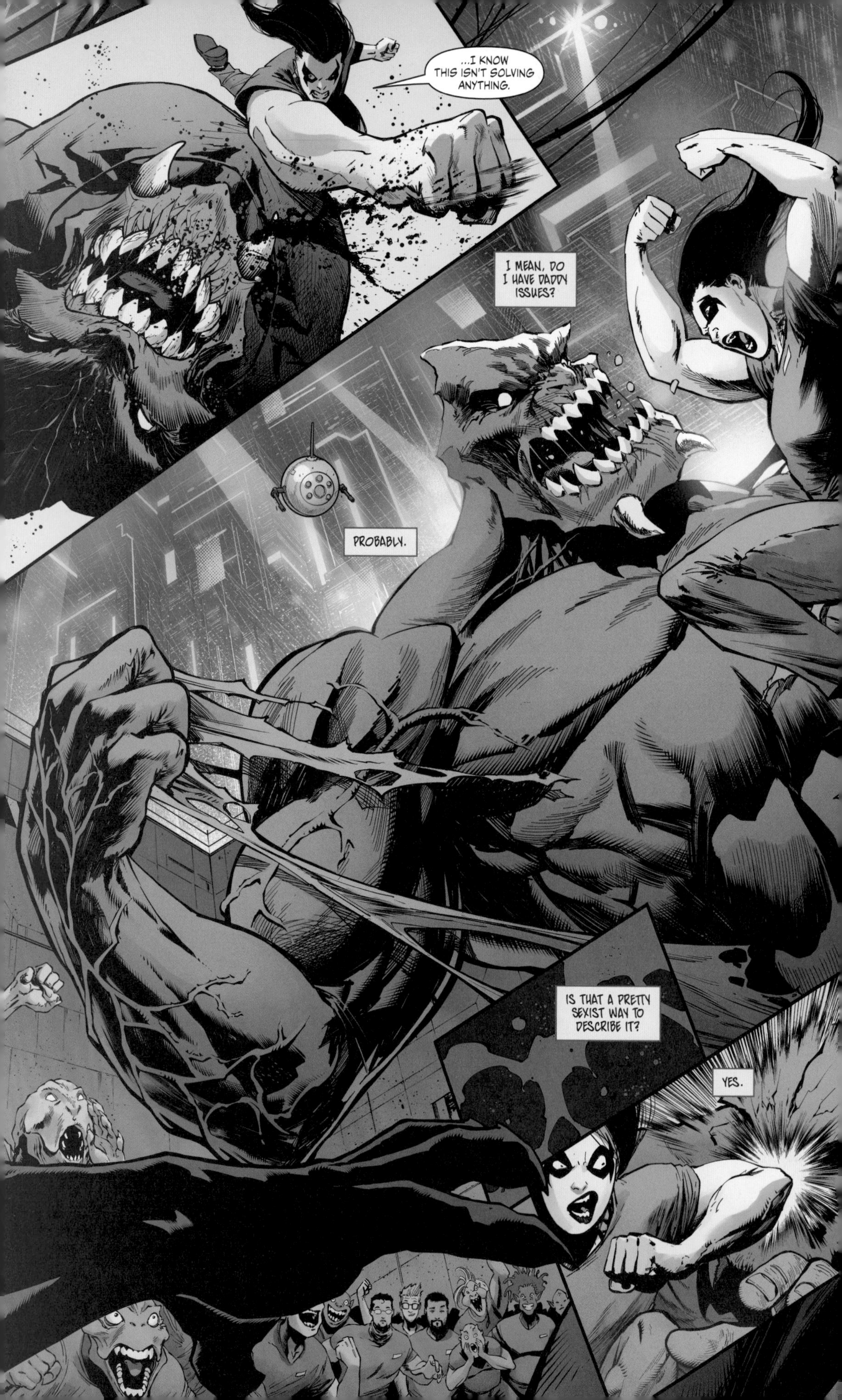

...I KNOW THIS ISN'T SOLVING ANYTHING.
I MEAN, DO I HAVE DADDY ISSUES?
PROBABLY.
IS THAT A PRETTY SEXIST WAY TO DESCRIBE IT?
YES.

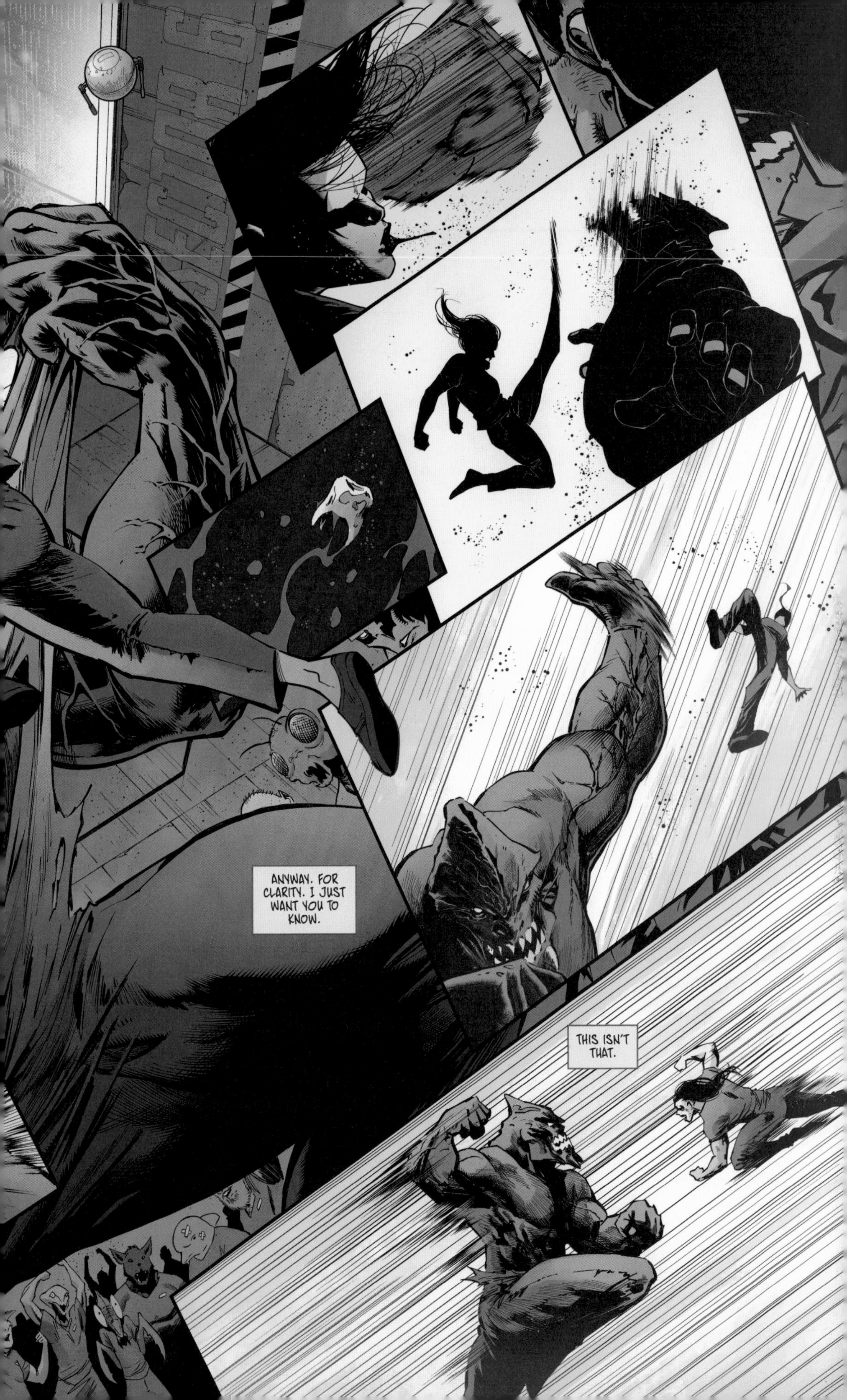
ANYWAY. FOR CLARITY. I JUST WANT YOU TO KNOW.
THIS ISN'T THAT.

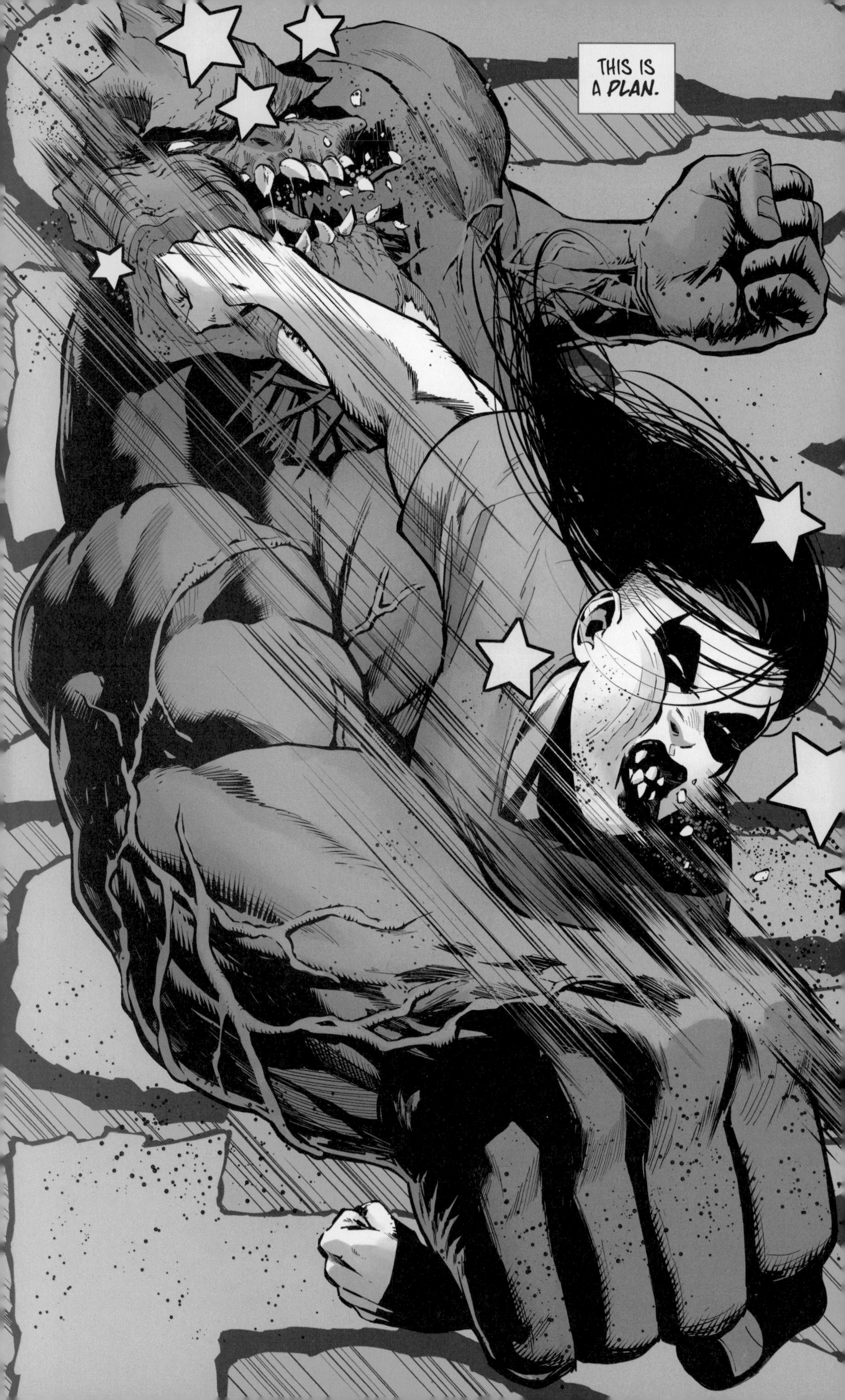
THIS IS A PLAN.

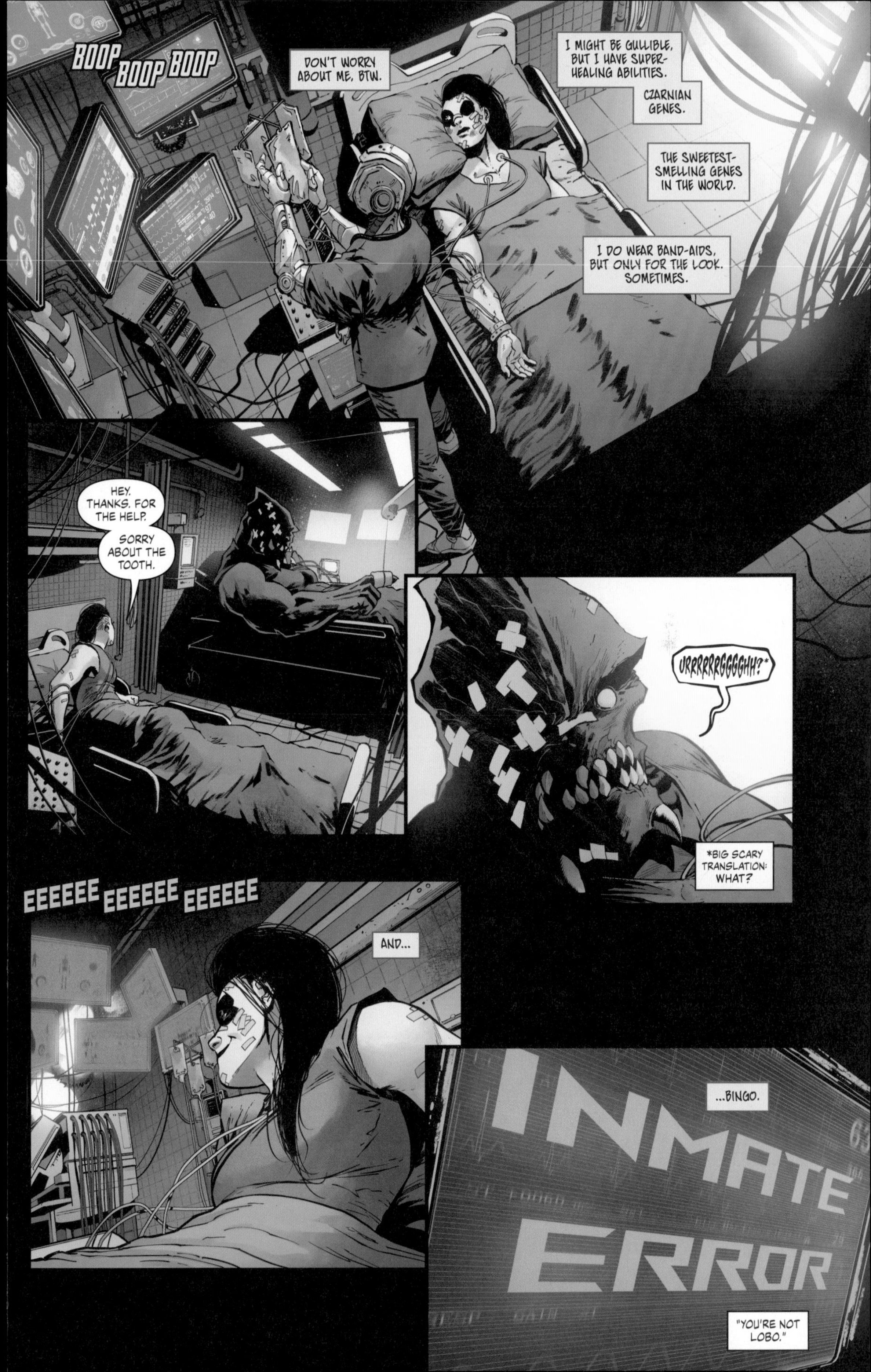
BOOP BOOP BOOP
DON'T WORRY ABOUT ME, BTW.
I MIGHT BE GULLIBLE, BUT I HAVE SUPER-HEALING ABILITIES.
CZARNIAN GENES.
THE SWEETEST-SMELLING GENES IN THE WORLD.
I DO WEAR BAND-AIDS, BUT ONLY FOR THE LOOK. SOMETIMES.
HEY. THANKS. FOR THE HELP.
SORRY ABOUT THE TOOTH.
URRRRRGGGGHH?*
*BIG SCARY TRANSLATION: WHAT?
EEEEEE EEEEEE EEEEEE
AND...
...BINGO.
INMATE ERROR
"YOU'RE NOT LOBO."

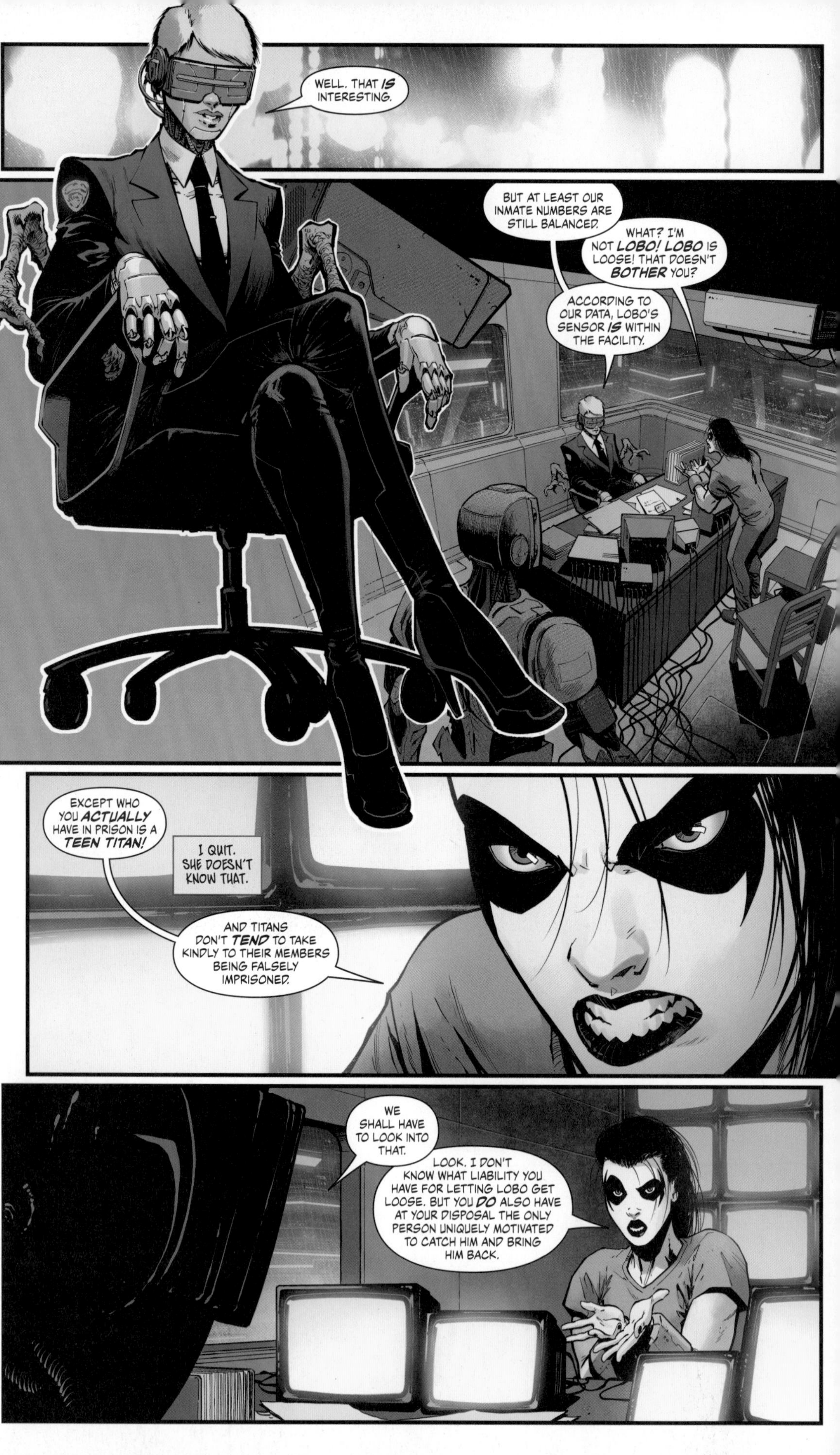
WELL. THAT *IS* INTERESTING.
BUT AT LEAST OUR INMATE NUMBERS ARE STILL BALANCED.
WHAT? I'M NOT *LOBO! LOBO* IS LOOSE! THAT DOESN'T *BOTHER* YOU?
ACCORDING TO OUR DATA, LOBO'S SENSOR *IS* WITHIN THE FACILITY.
EXCEPT WHO YOU *ACTUALLY* HAVE IN PRISON IS A *TEEN TITAN!*
I QUIT. SHE DOESN'T KNOW THAT.
AND TITANS DON'T *TEND* TO TAKE KINDLY TO THEIR MEMBERS BEING FALSELY IMPRISONED.
WE SHALL HAVE TO LOOK INTO THAT.
LOOK. I DON'T KNOW WHAT LIABILITY YOU HAVE FOR LETTING LOBO GET LOOSE. BUT YOU *DO* ALSO HAVE AT YOUR DISPOSAL THE ONLY PERSON UNIQUELY MOTIVATED TO CATCH HIM AND BRING HIM BACK.

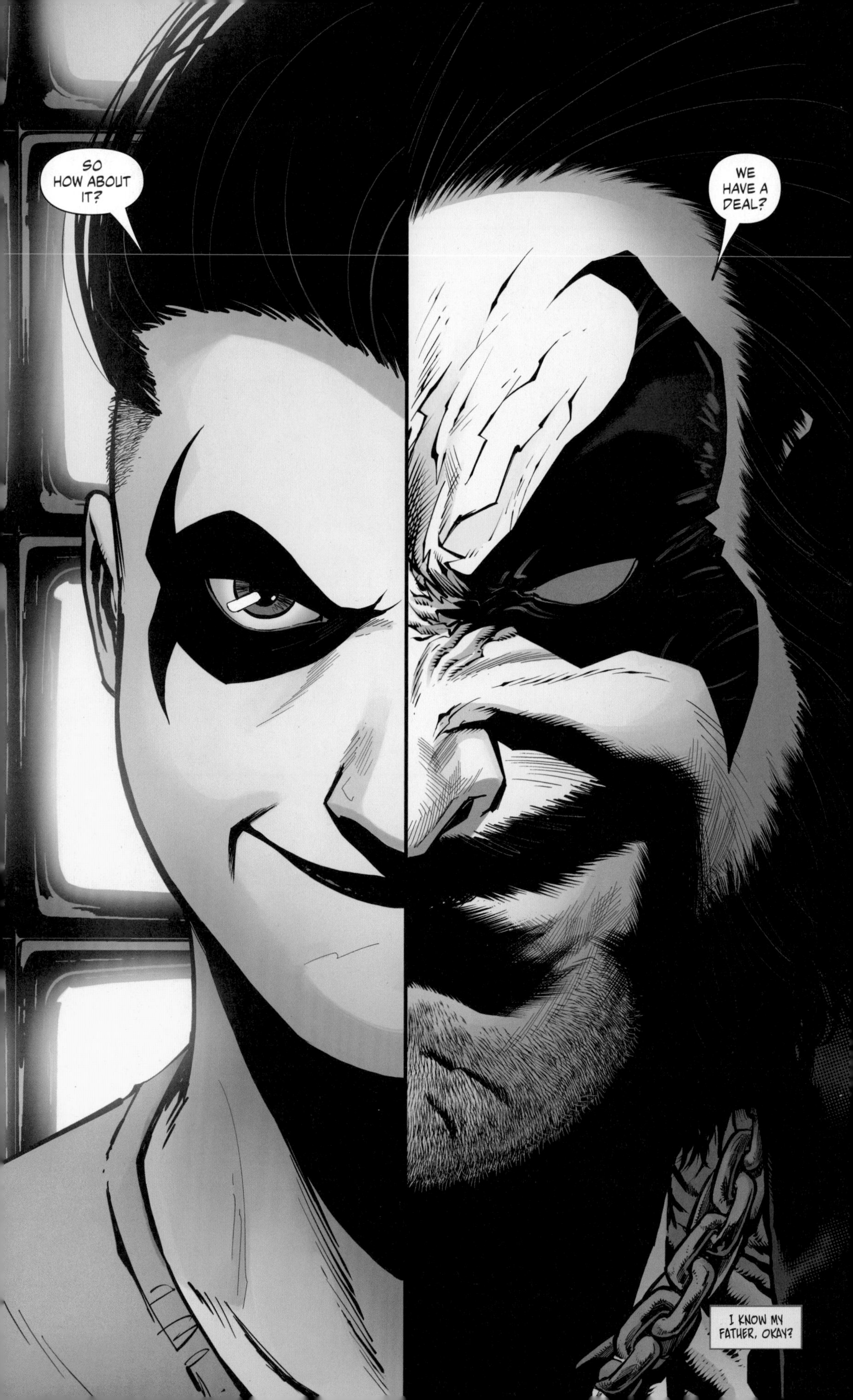
SO HOW ABOUT IT?
WE HAVE A DEAL?
I KNOW MY FATHER, OKAY?

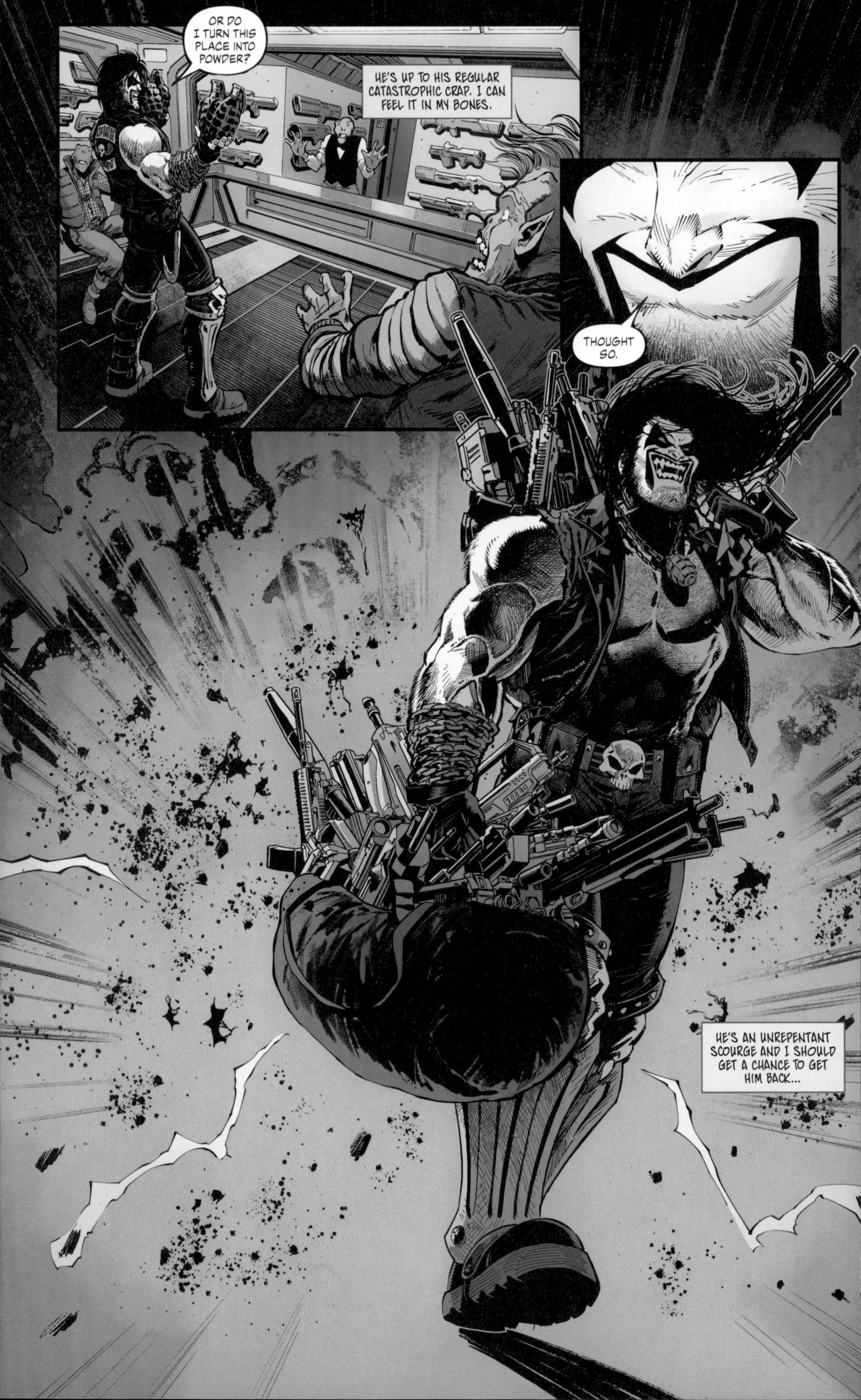
OR DO I TURN THIS PLACE INTO POWDER?
HE'S UP TO HIS REGULAR CATASTROPHIC CRAP. I CAN FEEL IT IN MY BONES.
THOUGHT SO.
HE'S AN UNREPENTANT SCOURGE AND I SHOULD GET A CHANCE TO GET HIM BACK...

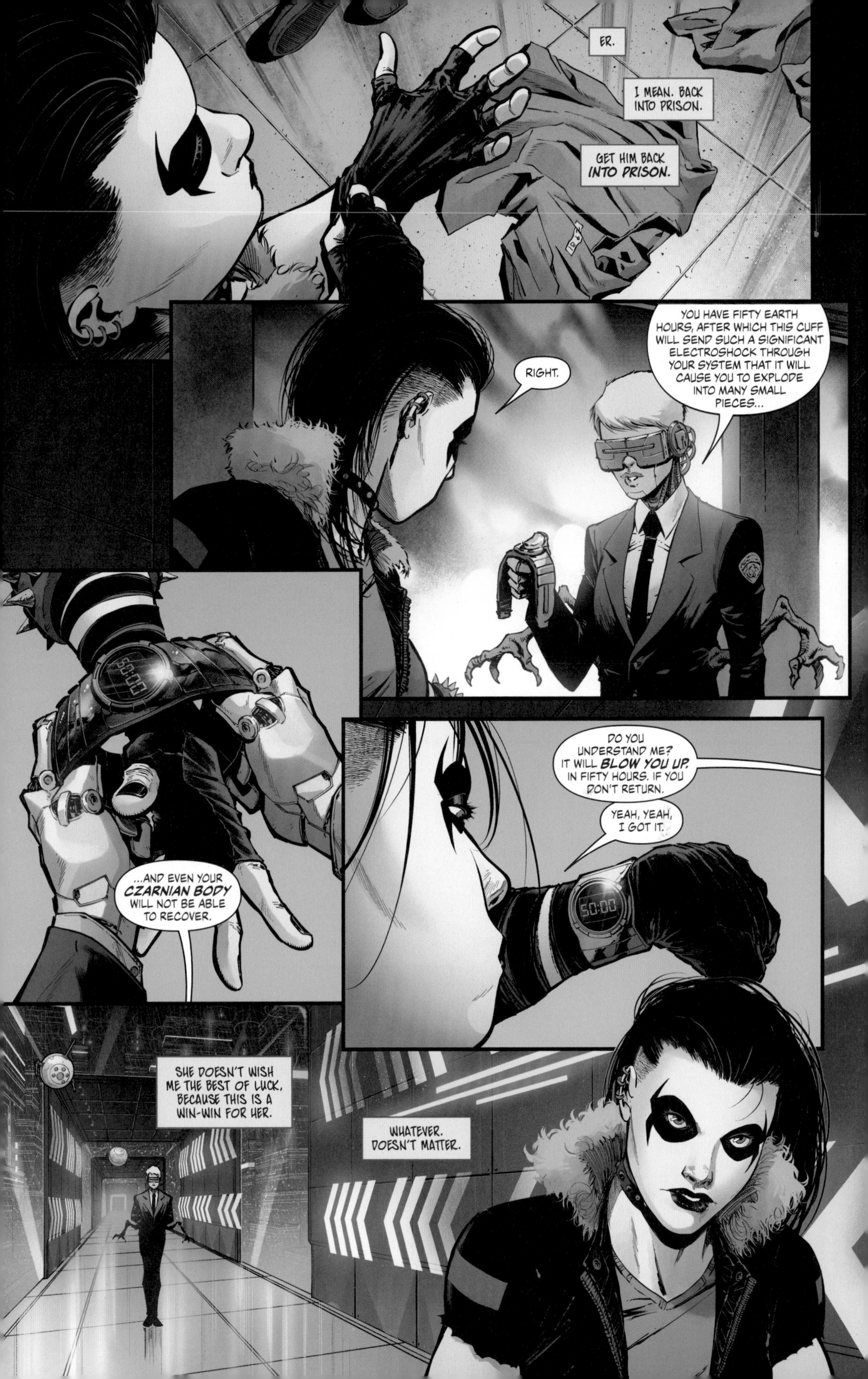

ER.
I MEAN. BACK INTO PRISON.
GET HIM BACK INTO PRISON.
RIGHT.
YOU HAVE FIFTY EARTH HOURS, AFTER WHICH THIS CUFF WILL SEND SUCH A SIGNIFICANT ELECTROSHOCK THROUGH YOUR SYSTEM THAT IT WILL CAUSE YOU TO EXPLODE INTO MANY SMALL PIECES...
50:00
...AND EVEN YOUR CZARNIAN BODY WILL NOT BE ABLE TO RECOVER.
DO YOU UNDERSTAND ME? IT WILL BLOW YOU UP. IN FIFTY HOURS. IF YOU DON'T RETURN.
YEAH, YEAH, I GOT IT.
50:00
SHE DOESN'T WISH ME THE BEST OF LUCK, BECAUSE THIS IS A WIN-WIN FOR HER.
WHATEVER. DOESN'T MATTER.

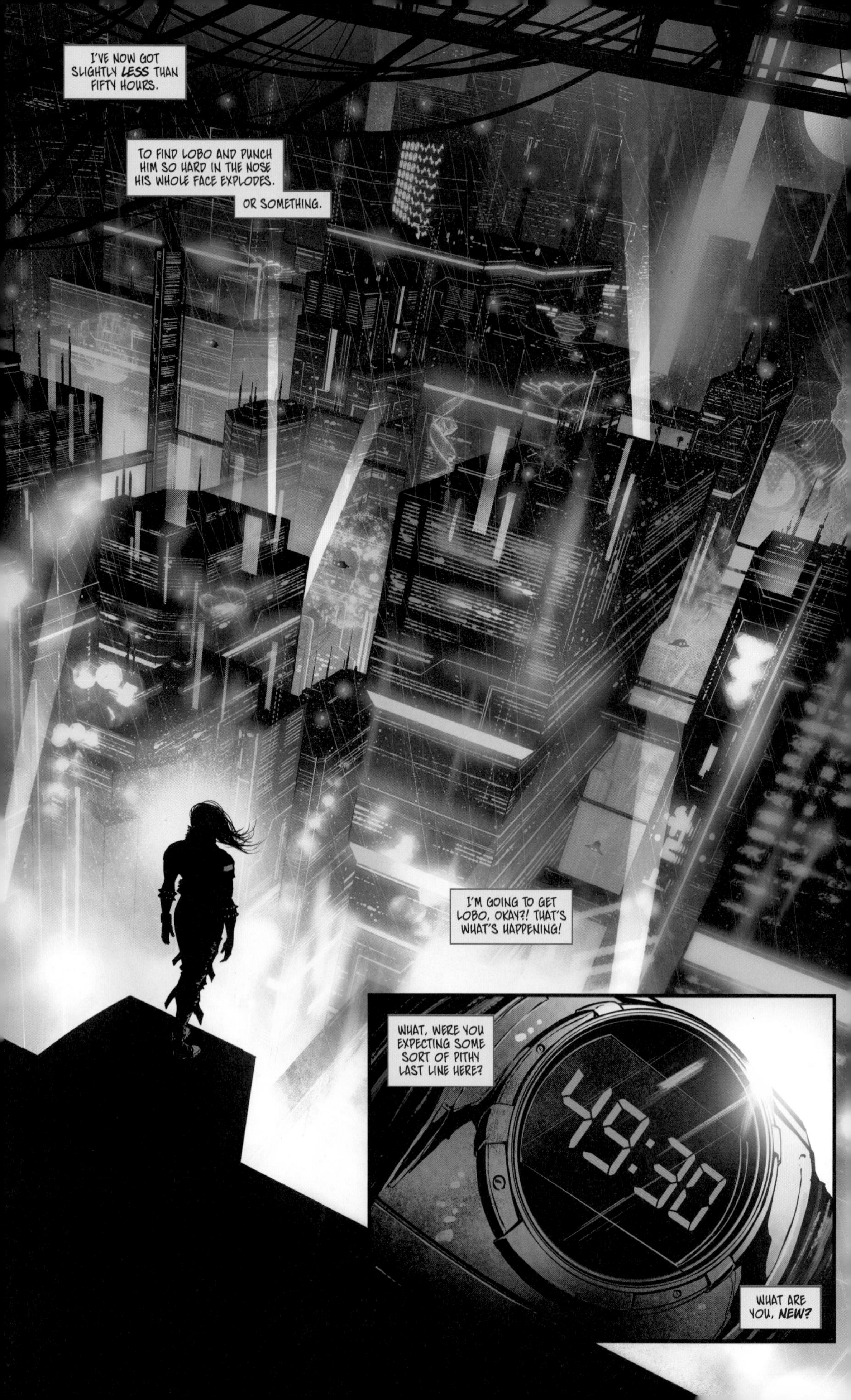
I'VE NOW GOT SLIGHTLY LESS THAN FIFTY HOURS.
TO FIND LOBO AND PUNCH HIM SO HARD IN THE NOSE HIS WHOLE FACE EXPLODES.
OR SOMETHING.
I'M GOING TO GET LOBO, OKAY?! THAT'S WHAT'S HAPPENING!
WHAT, WERE YOU EXPECTING SOME SORT OF PITHY LAST LINE HERE?
49:30
WHAT ARE YOU, NEW?

CRUSH & LOBO #5 COVER BY SWEENEY BOO

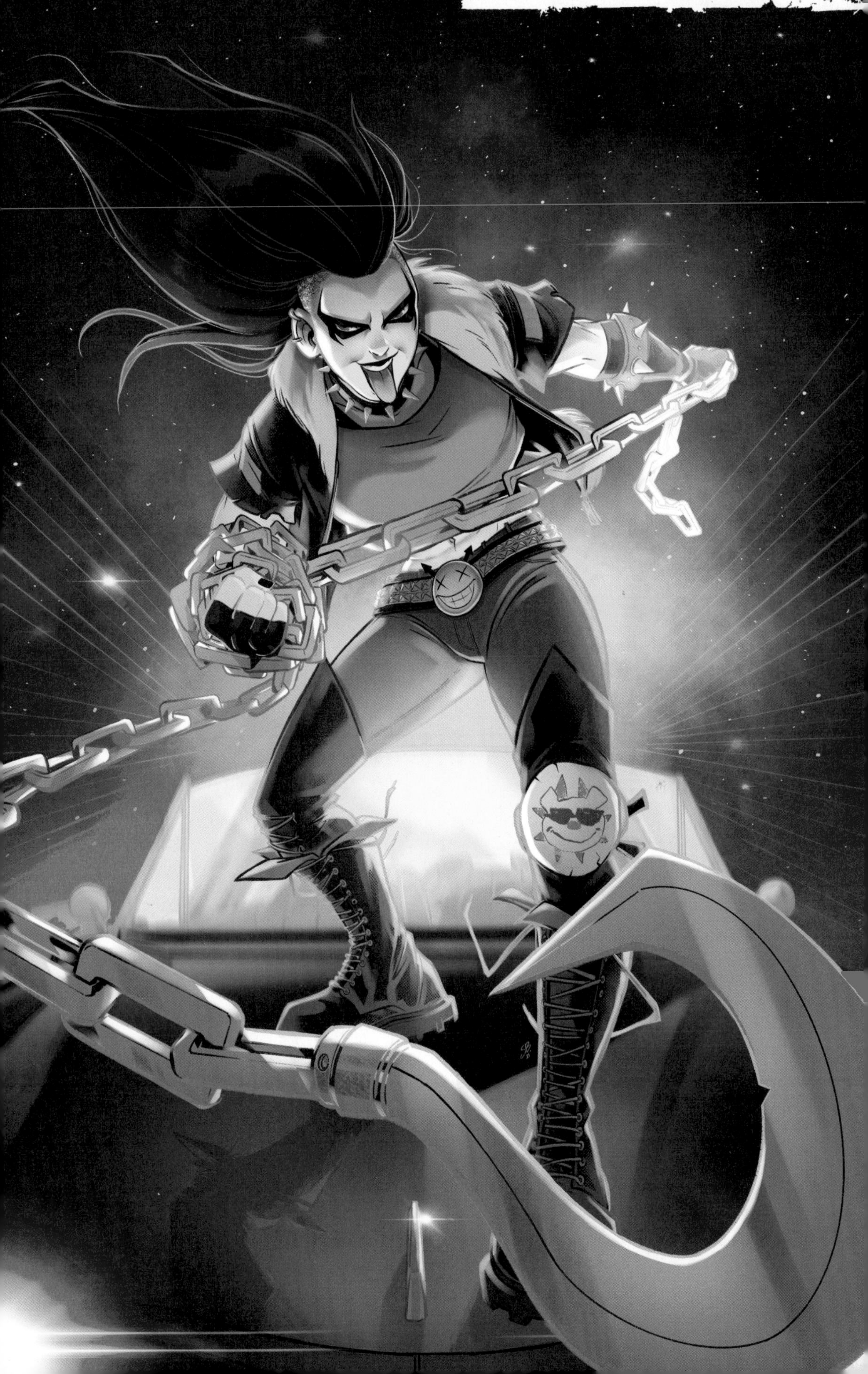

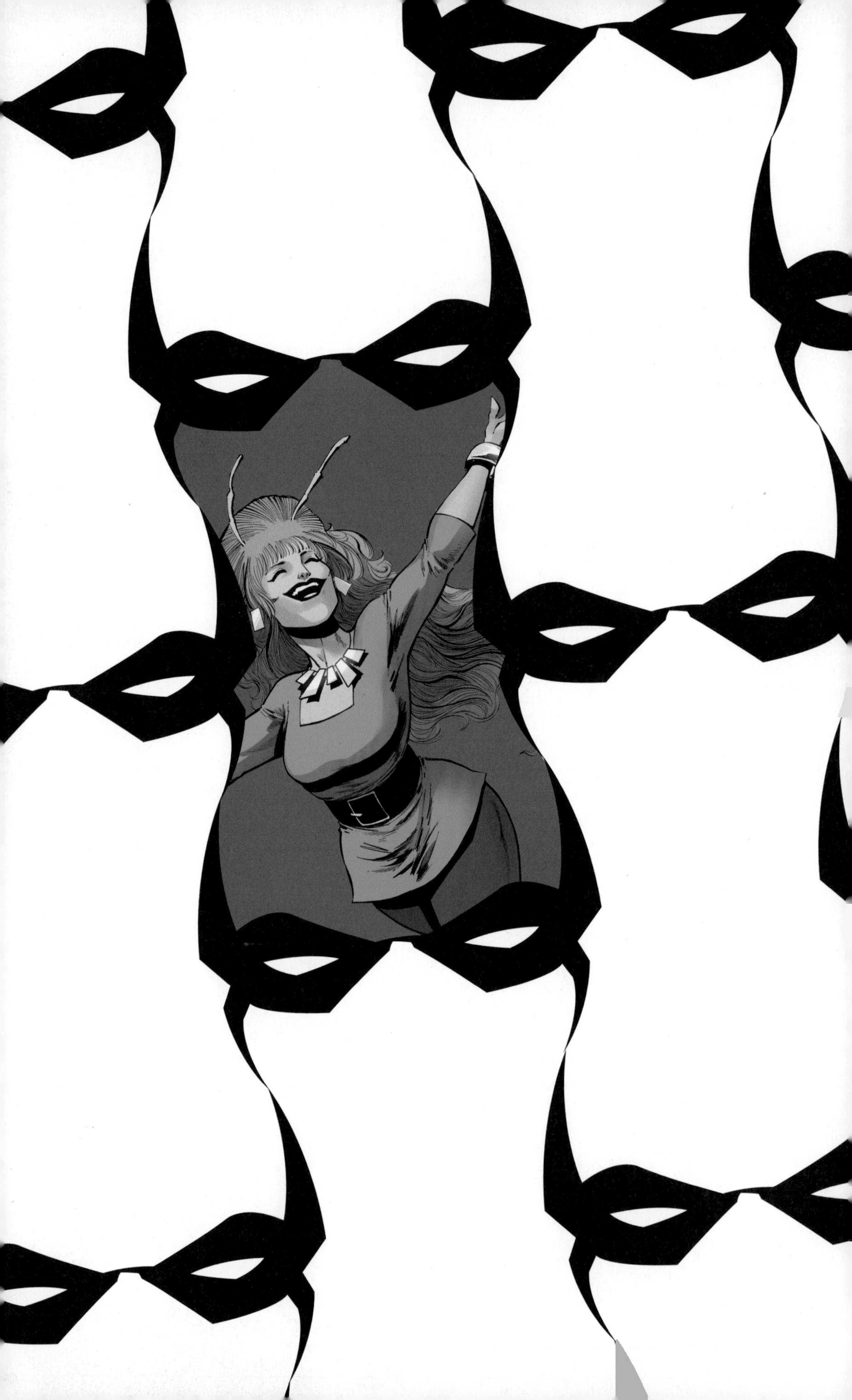

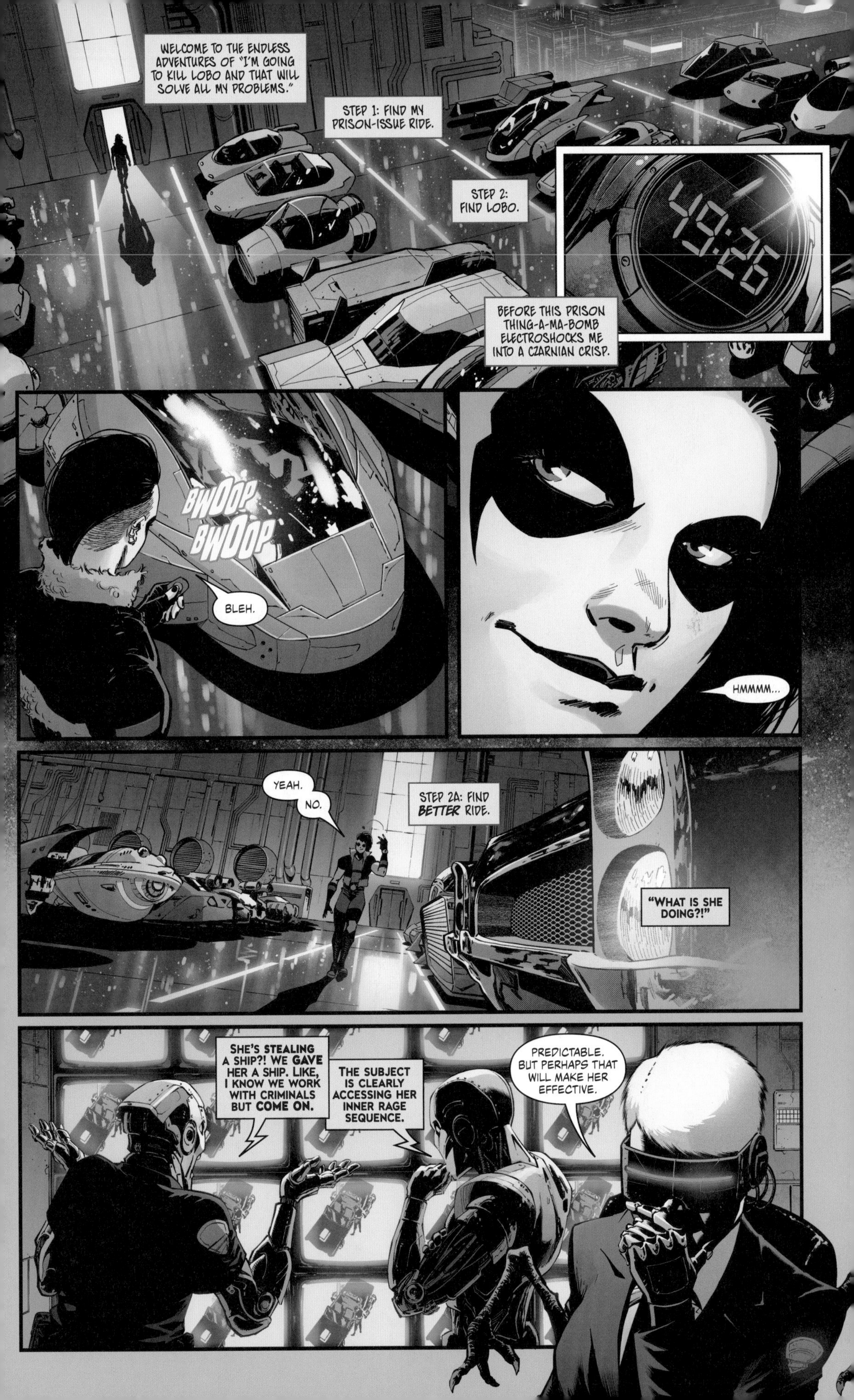

WELCOME TO THE ENDLESS ADVENTURES OF "I'M GOING TO KILL LOBO AND THAT WILL SOLVE ALL MY PROBLEMS."
STEP 1: FIND MY PRISON-ISSUE RIDE.
STEP 2: FIND LOBO.
49:26
BEFORE THIS PRISON THING-A-MA-BOMB ELECTROSHOCKS ME INTO A CZARNIAN CRISP.
BWOOP BWOOP
BLEH.
HMMMM...
YEAH.
NO.
STEP 2A: FIND BETTER RIDE.
"WHAT IS SHE DOING?!"
SHE'S STEALING A SHIP?! WE GAVE HER A SHIP. LIKE, I KNOW WE WORK WITH CRIMINALS BUT COME ON.
THE SUBJECT IS CLEARLY ACCESSING HER INNER RAGE SEQUENCE.
PREDICTABLE. BUT PERHAPS THAT WILL MAKE HER EFFECTIVE.

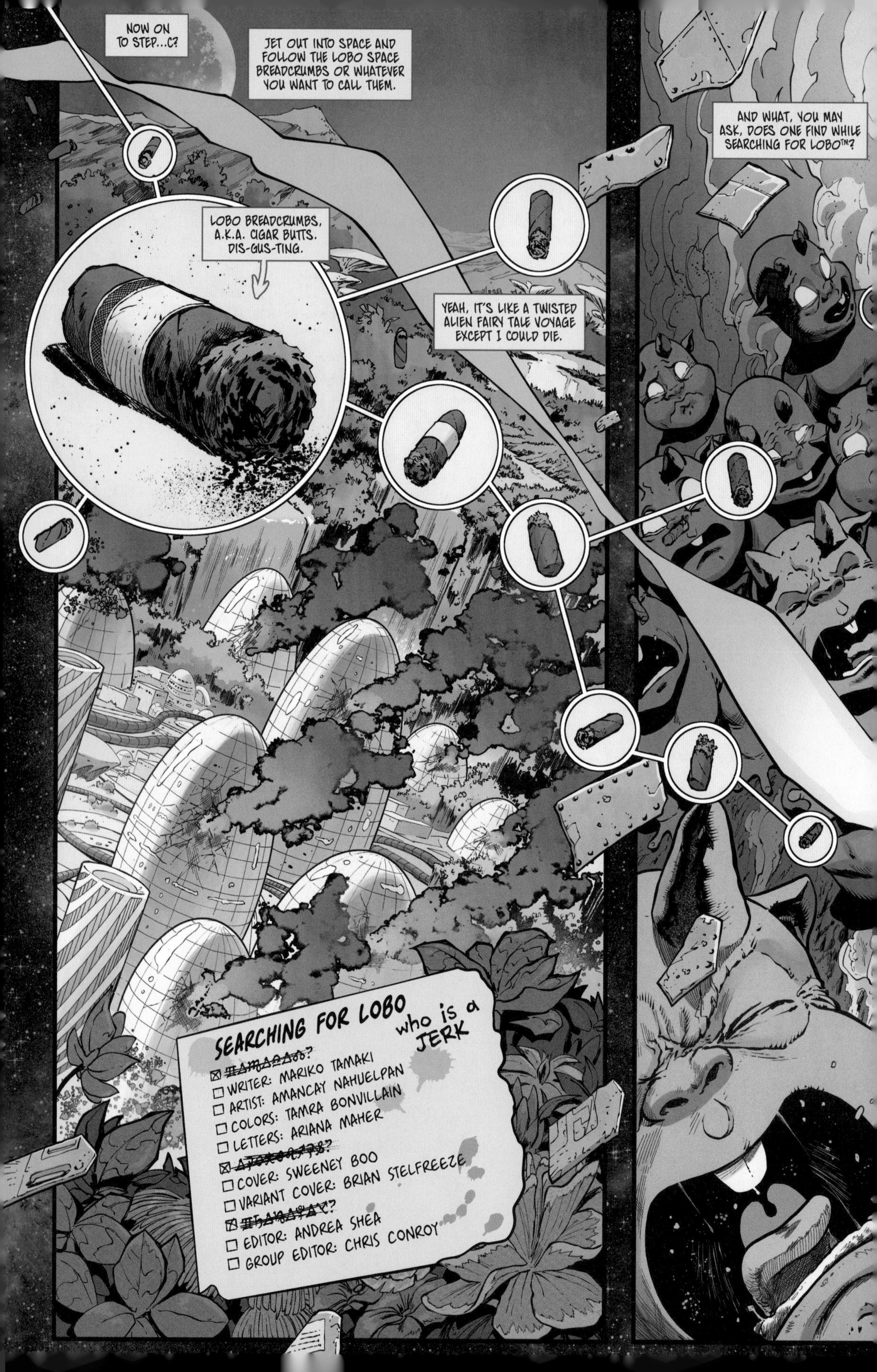
NOW ON TO STEP...C?
JET OUT INTO SPACE AND FOLLOW THE LOBO SPACE BREADCRUMBS OR WHATEVER YOU WANT TO CALL THEM.
LOBO BREADCRUMBS, A.K.A. CIGAR BUTTS. DIS-GUS-TING.
YEAH, IT'S LIKE A TWISTED ALIEN FAIRY TALE VOYAGE EXCEPT I COULD DIE.
SEARCHING FOR LOBO
who is a JERK
WRITER: MARIKO TAMAKI
ARTIST: AMANCAY NAHUELPAN
COLORS: TAMRA BONVILLAIN
LETTERS: ARIANA MAHER
COVER: SWEENEY BOO
VARIANT COVER: BRIAN STELFREEZE
EDITOR: ANDREA SHEA
GROUP EDITOR: CHRIS CONROY
AND WHAT, YOU MAY ASK, DOES ONE FIND WHILE SEARCHING FOR LOBO™?

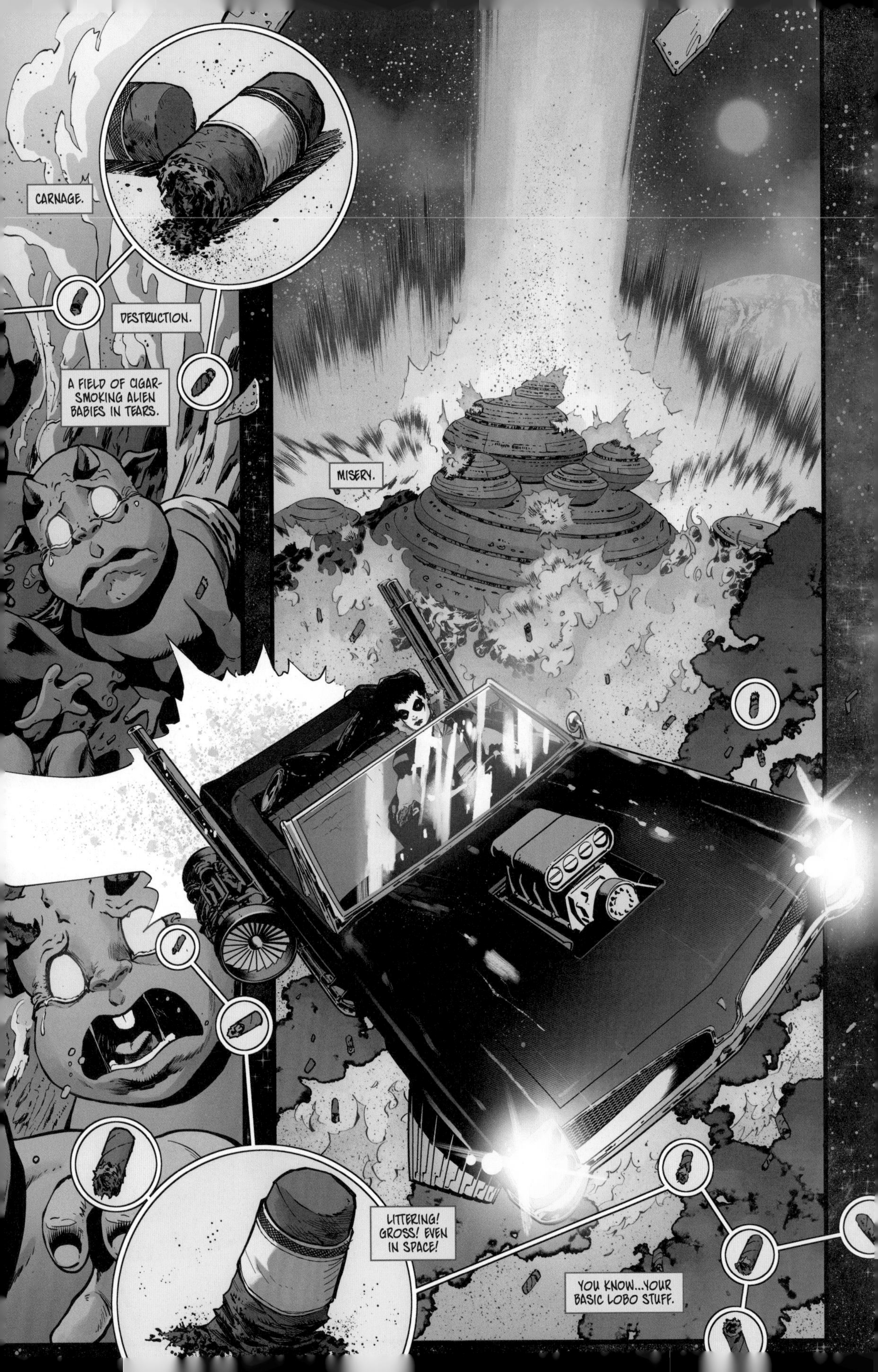
CARNAGE.
DESTRUCTION.
A FIELD OF CIGAR-SMOKING ALIEN BABIES IN TEARS.
MISERY.
LITTERING! GROSS! EVEN IN SPACE!
YOU KNOW...YOUR BASIC LOBO STUFF.

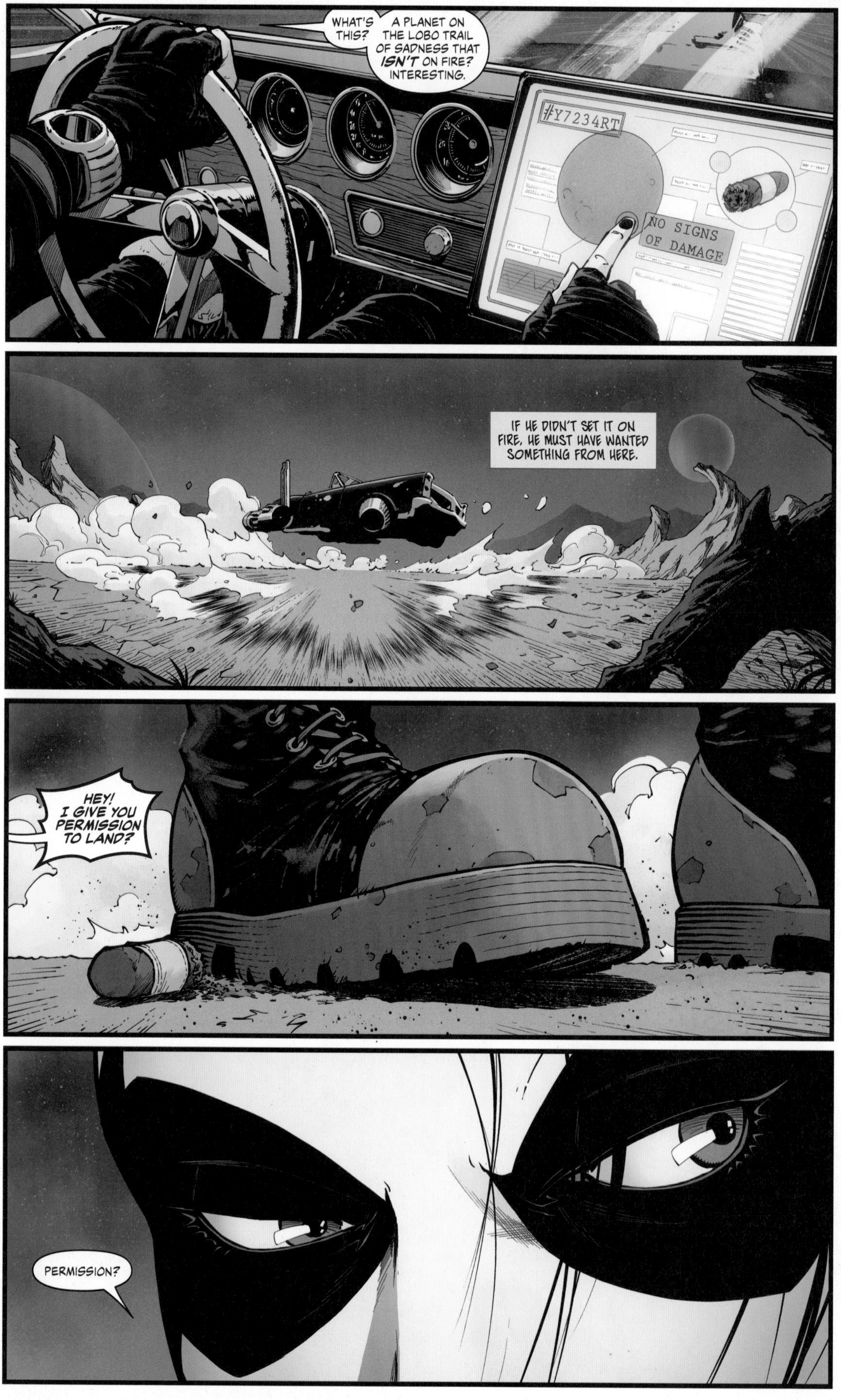
WHAT'S THIS?
A PLANET ON THE LOBO TRAIL OF SADNESS THAT ISN'T ON FIRE? INTERESTING.
#Y7234RT
NO SIGNS OF DAMAGE
IF HE DIDN'T SET IT ON FIRE, HE MUST HAVE WANTED SOMETHING FROM HERE.
HEY! I GIVE YOU PERMISSION TO LAND?
PERMISSION?

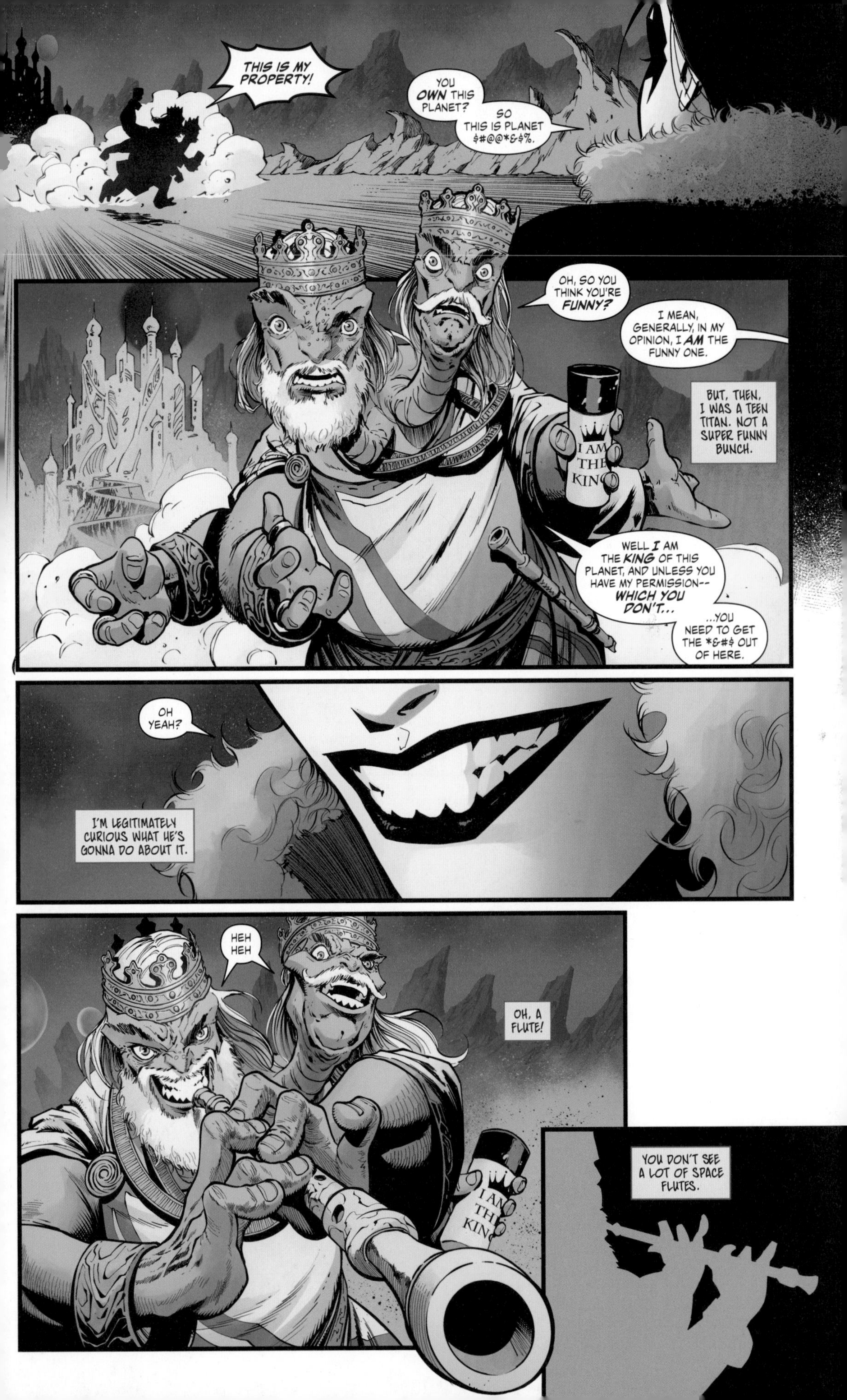
THIS IS MY PROPERTY!
YOU OWN THIS PLANET?
SO THIS IS PLANET $#@@*&$%.
OH, SO YOU THINK YOU'RE FUNNY?
I MEAN, GENERALLY, IN MY OPINION, I AM THE FUNNY ONE.
BUT, THEN, I WAS A TEEN TITAN. NOT A SUPER FUNNY BUNCH.
I AM THE KIN
WELL I AM THE KING OF THIS PLANET, AND UNLESS YOU HAVE MY PERMISSION-- WHICH YOU DON'T...
...YOU NEED TO GET THE *&#$ OUT OF HERE.
OH YEAH?
I'M LEGITIMATELY CURIOUS WHAT HE'S GONNA DO ABOUT IT.
HEH HEH
OH, A FLUTE!
YOU DON'T SEE A LOT OF SPACE FLUTES.

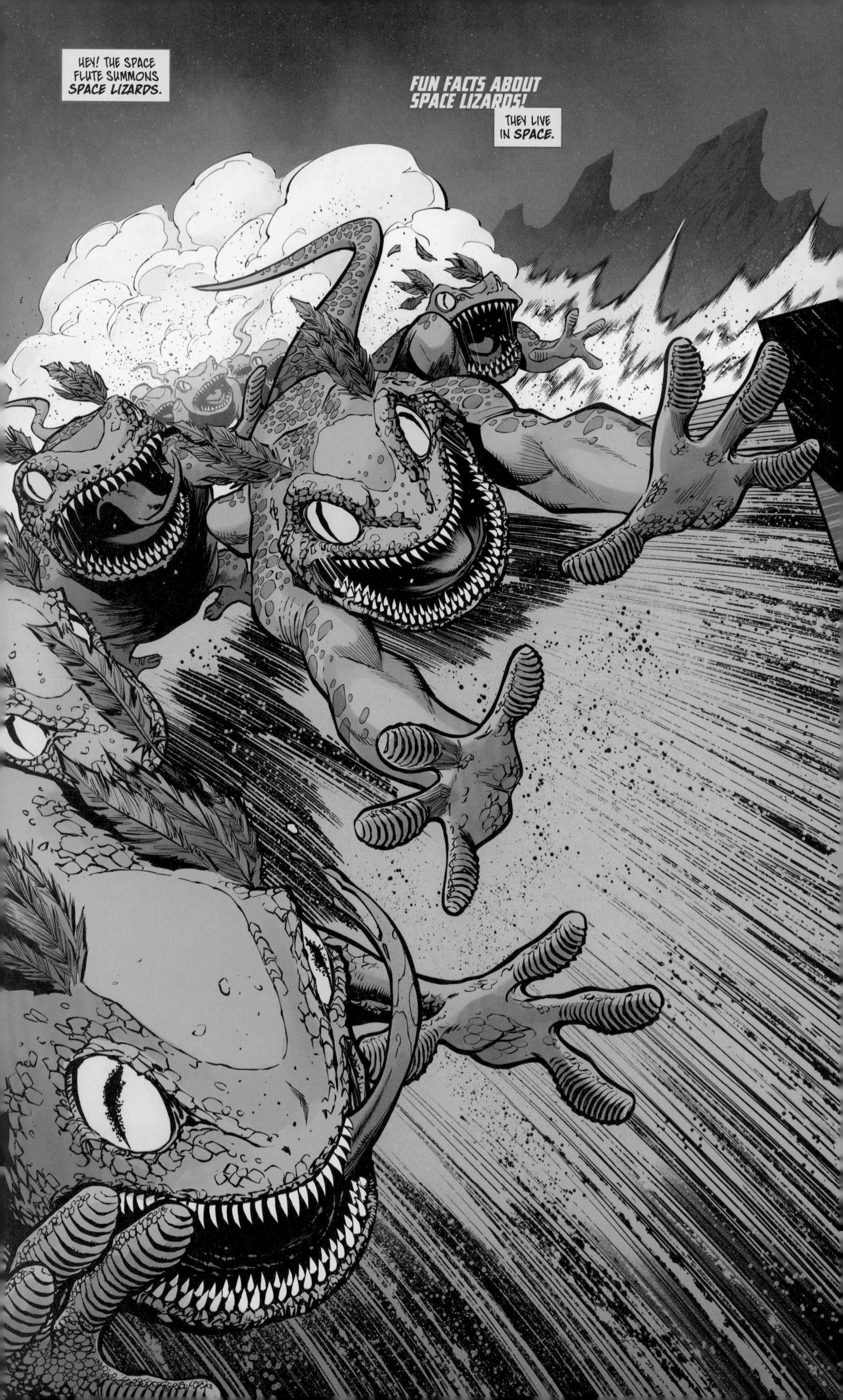
HEY! THE SPACE FLUTE SUMMONS SPACE LIZARDS.
FUN FACTS ABOUT SPACE LIZARDS!
THEY LIVE IN SPACE.

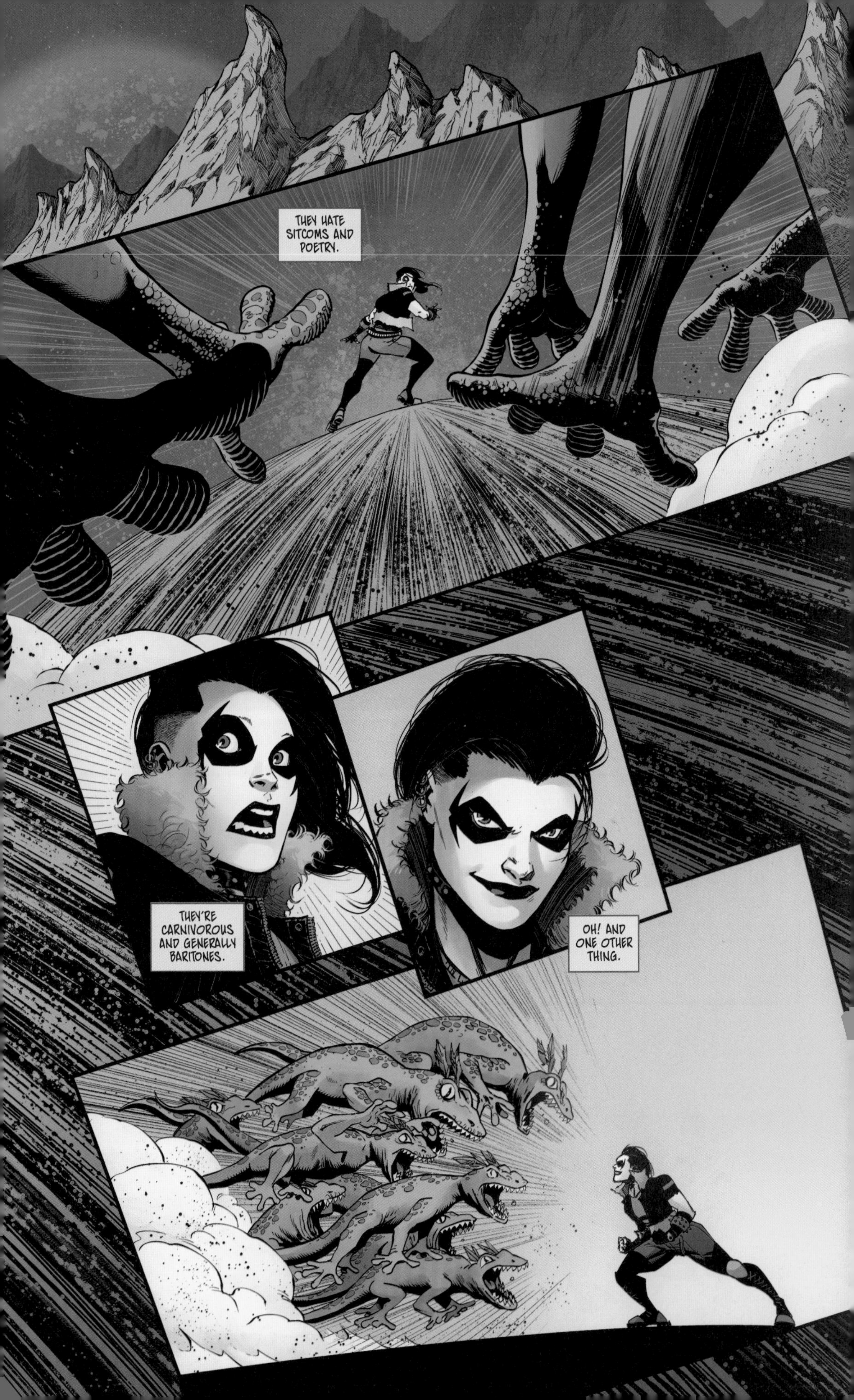
THEY HATE SITCOMS AND POETRY.
THEY'RE CARNIVOROUS AND GENERALLY BARITONES.
OH! AND ONE OTHER THING.

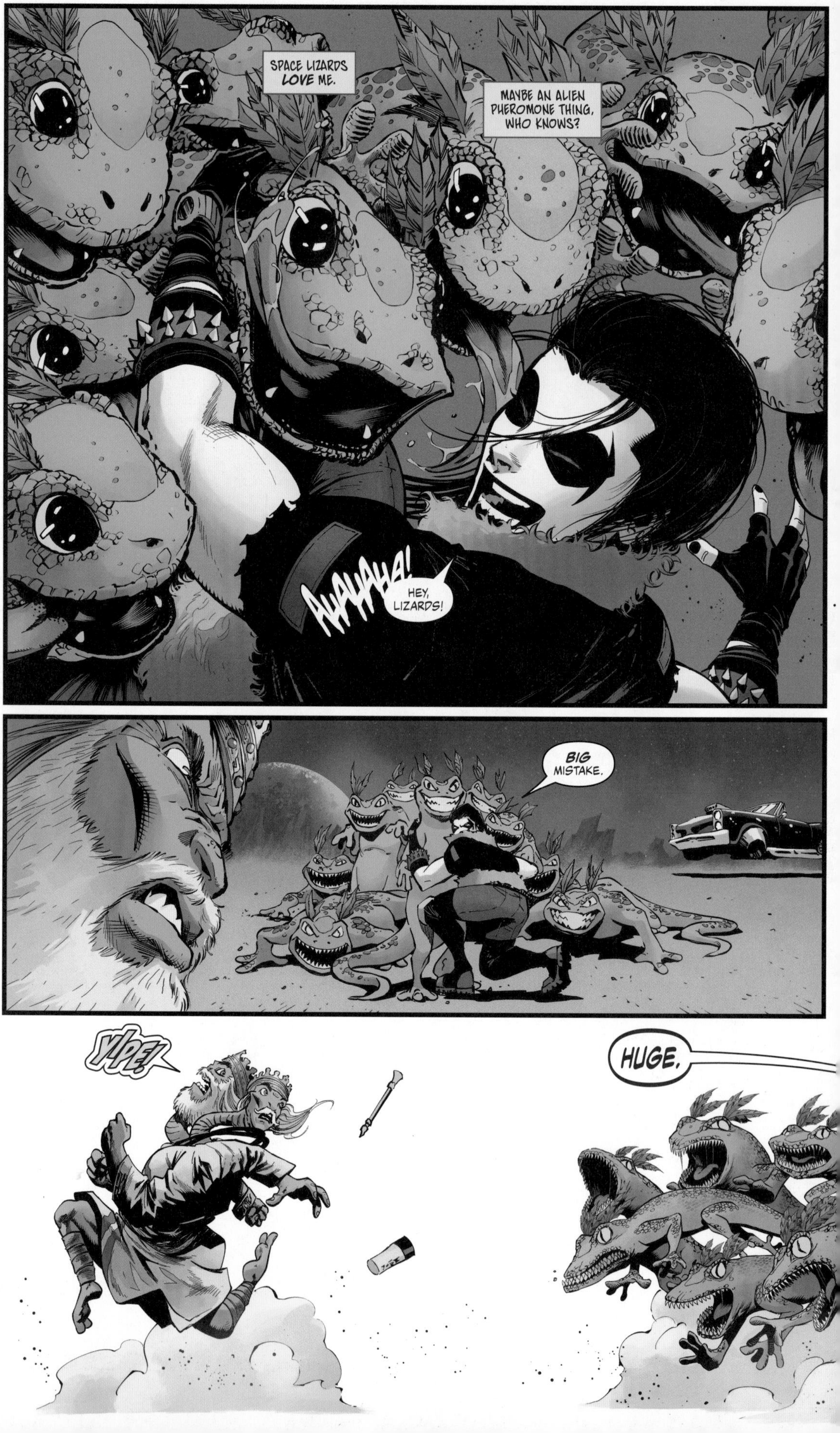

SPACE LIZARDS LOVE ME.
MAYBE AN ALIEN PHEROMONE THING, WHO KNOWS?
AHAHAHA!
HEY, LIZARDS!
BIG MISTAKE.
YIPE!
HUGE.

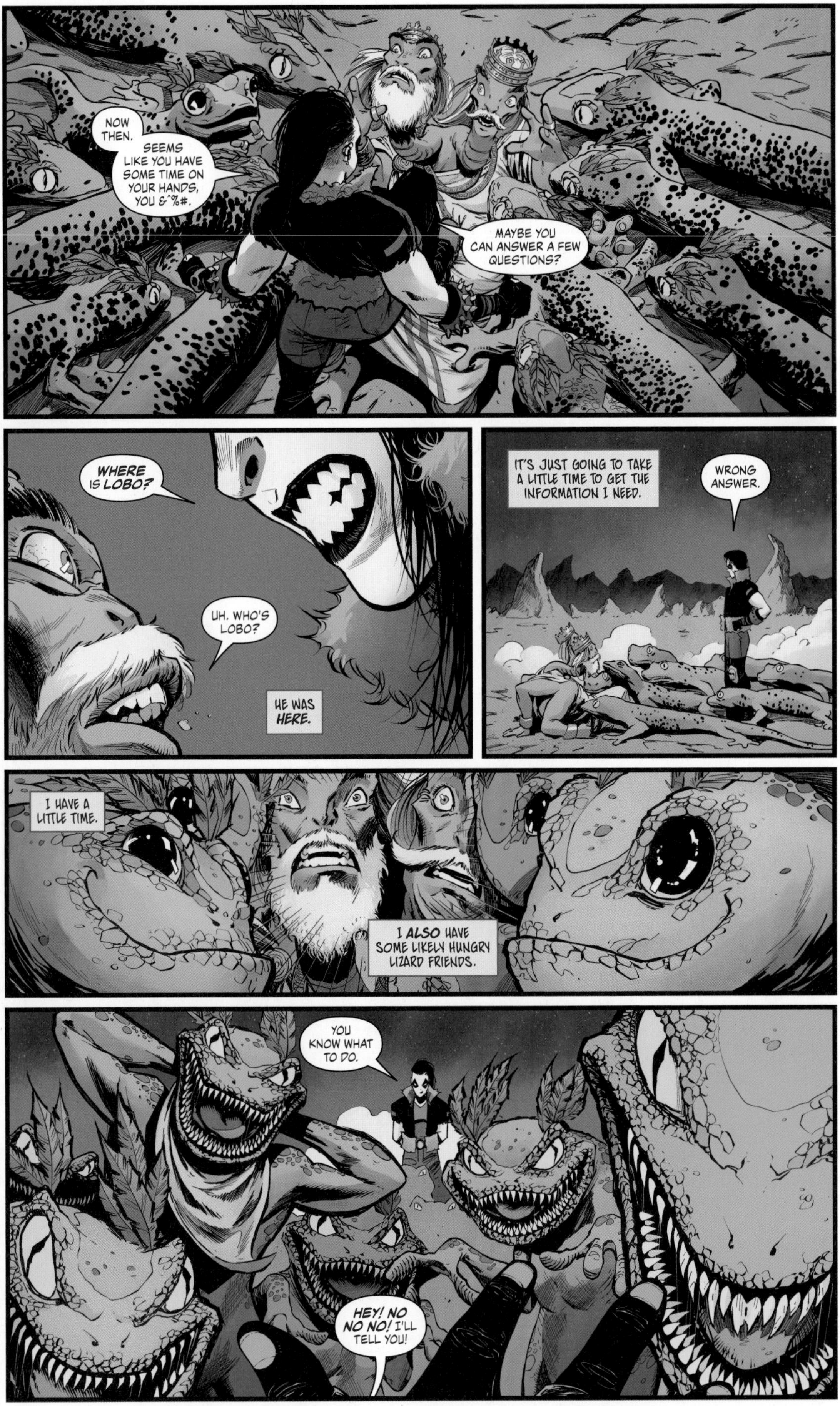
NOW THEN.
SEEMS LIKE YOU HAVE SOME TIME ON YOUR HANDS, YOU &^%#.
MAYBE YOU CAN ANSWER A FEW QUESTIONS?
WHERE IS LOBO?
UH. WHO'S LOBO?
HE WAS HERE.
IT'S JUST GOING TO TAKE A LITTLE TIME TO GET THE INFORMATION I NEED.
WRONG ANSWER.
I HAVE A LITTLE TIME.
I ALSO HAVE SOME LIKELY HUNGRY LIZARD FRIENDS.
YOU KNOW WHAT TO DO.
HEY! NO NO NO! I'LL TELL YOU!

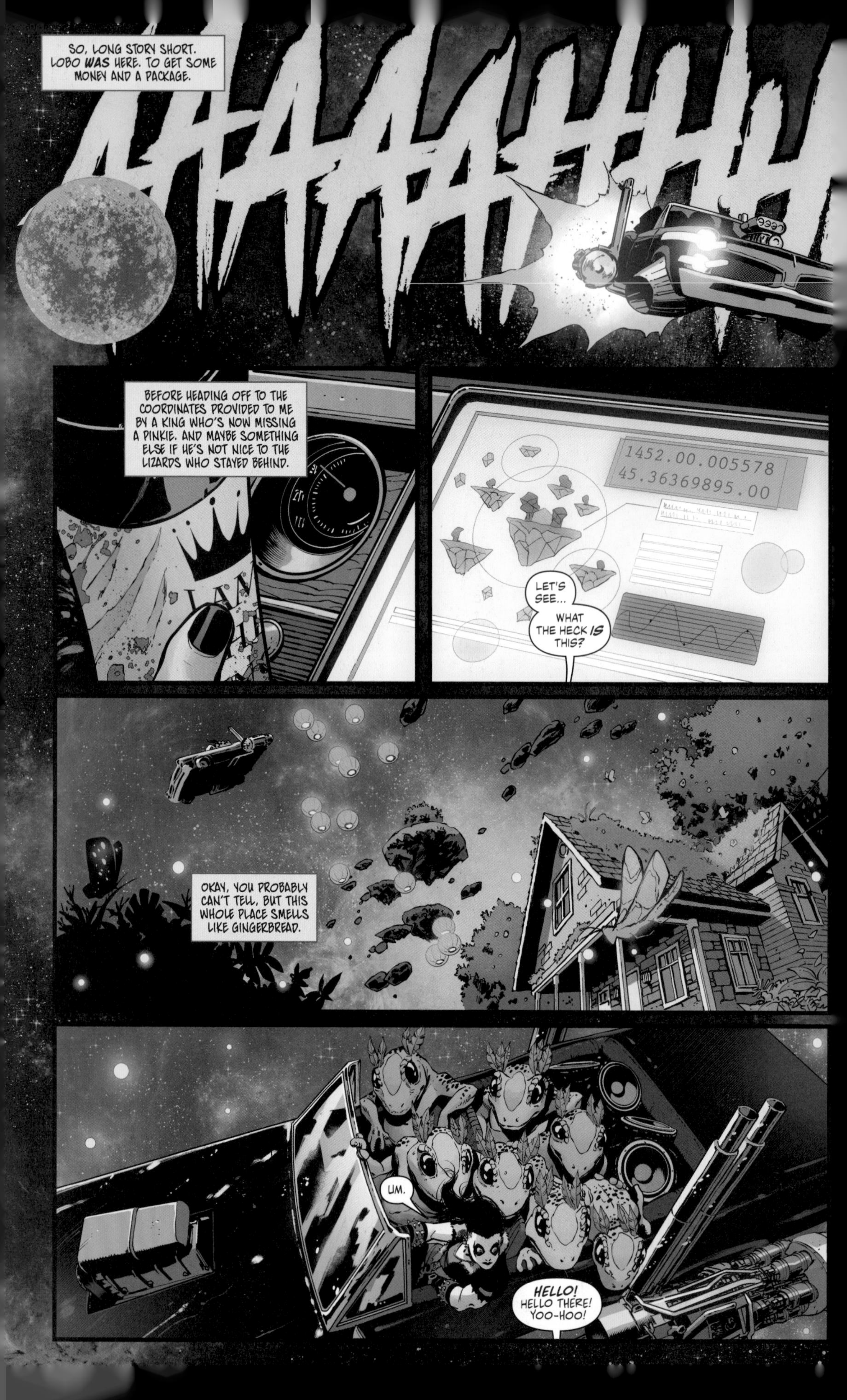

SO, LONG STORY SHORT. LOBO **WAS** HERE. TO GET SOME MONEY AND A PACKAGE.
BEFORE HEADING OFF TO THE COORDINATES PROVIDED TO ME BY A KING WHO'S NOW MISSING A PINKIE. AND MAYBE SOMETHING ELSE IF HE'S NOT NICE TO THE LIZARDS WHO STAYED BEHIND.
1452.00.005578
45.36369895.00
LET'S SEE...
WHAT THE HECK ***IS*** THIS?
OKAY, YOU PROBABLY CAN'T TELL, BUT THIS WHOLE PLACE SMELLS LIKE GINGERBREAD.
UM.
HELLO! HELLO THERE! YOO-HOO!

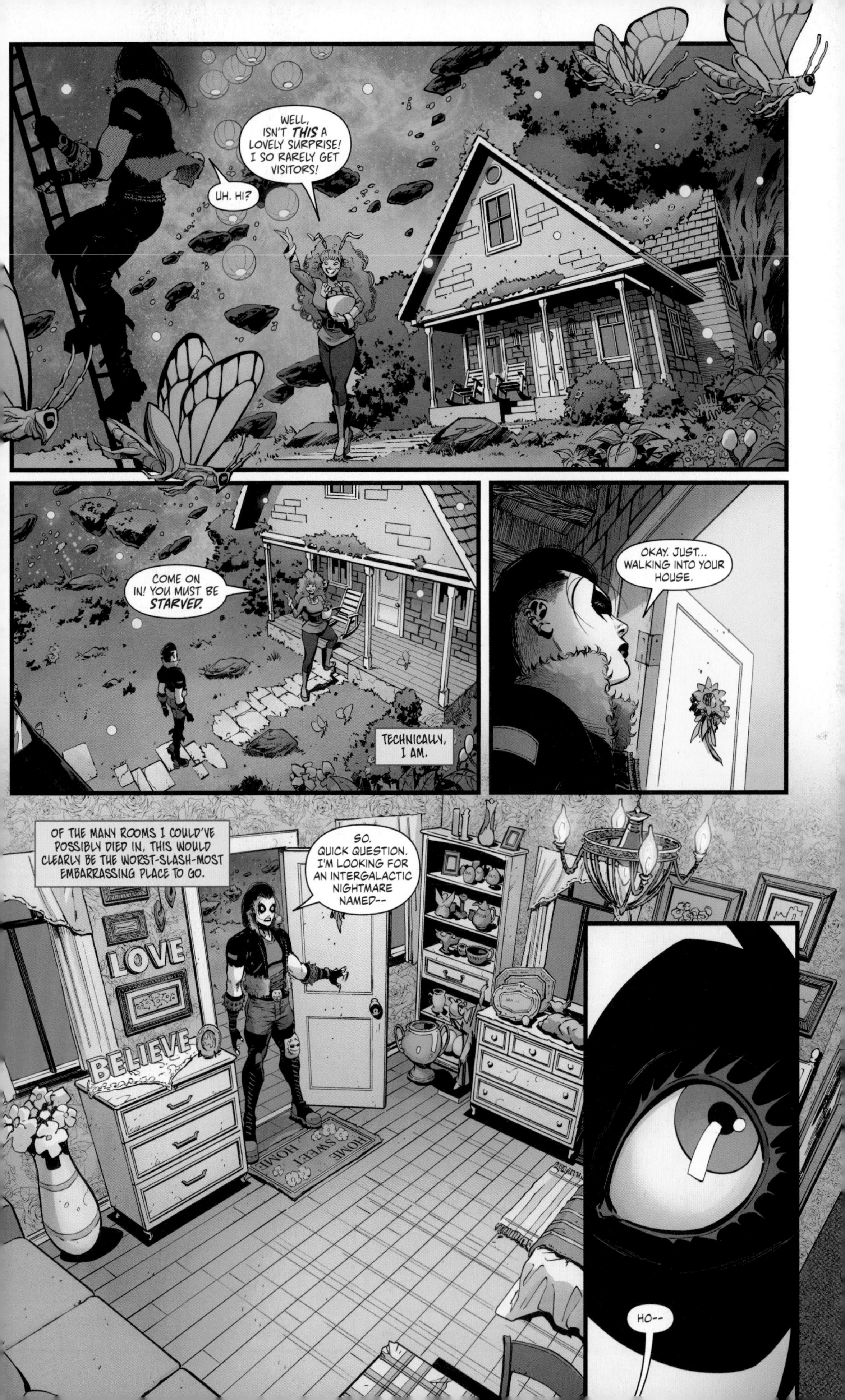
WELL, ISN'T THIS A LOVELY SURPRISE! I SO RARELY GET VISITORS!
UH. HI?
COME ON IN! YOU MUST BE STARVED.
TECHNICALLY, I AM.
OKAY. JUST... WALKING INTO YOUR HOUSE.
OF THE MANY ROOMS I COULD'VE POSSIBLY DIED IN, THIS WOULD CLEARLY BE THE WORST-SLASH-MOST EMBARRASSING PLACE TO GO.
SO. QUICK QUESTION. I'M LOOKING FOR AN INTERGALACTIC NIGHTMARE NAMED--
LOVE
BELIEVE
HOME SWEET HOME
HO--

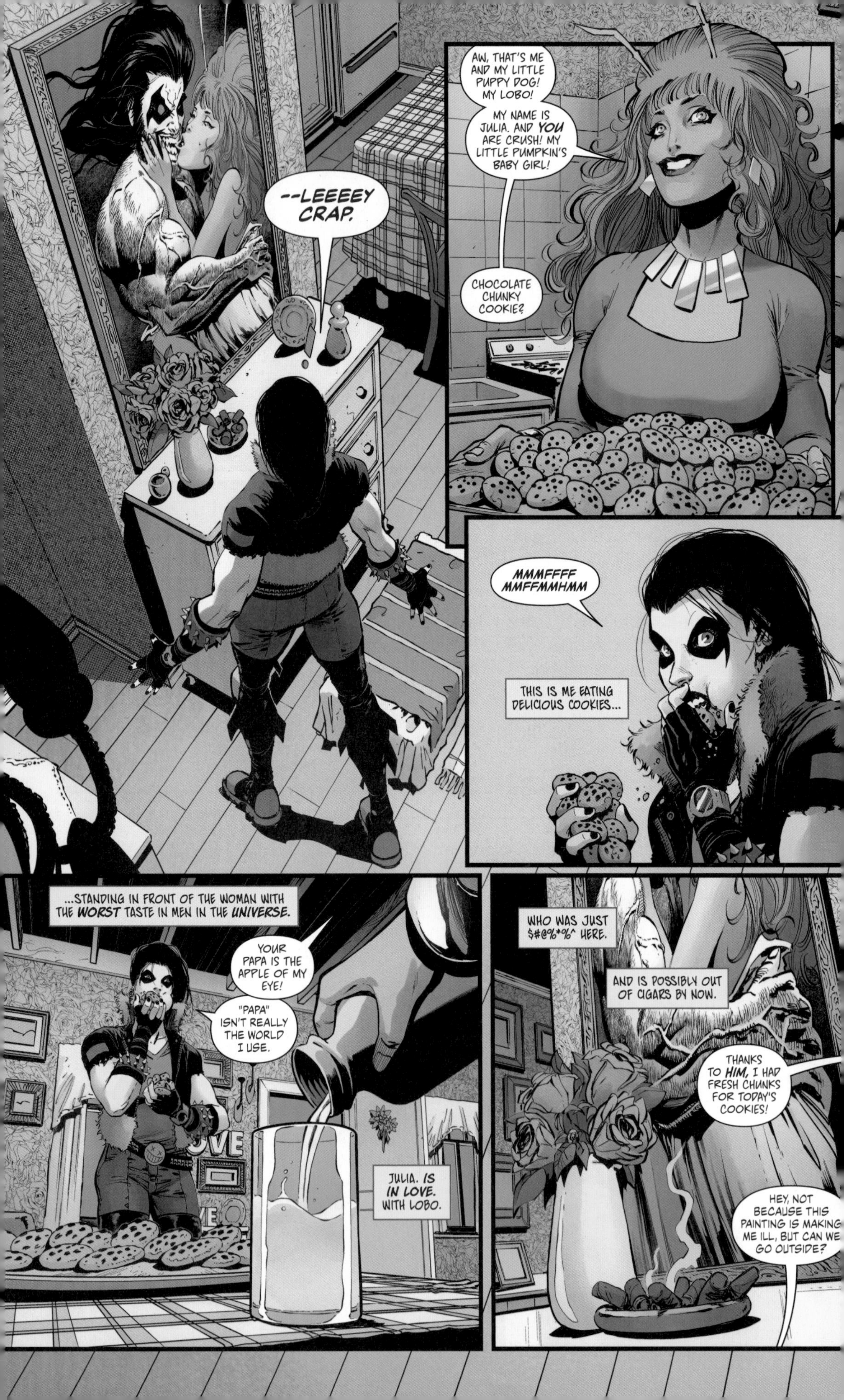
--LEEEEY CRAP.
AW, THAT'S ME AND MY LITTLE PUPPY DOG! MY LOBO!
MY NAME IS JULIA. AND YOU ARE CRUSH! MY LITTLE PUMPKIN'S BABY GIRL!
CHOCOLATE CHUNKY COOKIE?
MMMFFFF MMFFMMHMM
THIS IS ME EATING DELICIOUS COOKIES...
...STANDING IN FRONT OF THE WOMAN WITH THE WORST TASTE IN MEN IN THE UNIVERSE.
YOUR PAPA IS THE APPLE OF MY EYE!
"PAPA" ISN'T REALLY THE WORLD I USE.
JULIA. IS IN LOVE. WITH LOBO.
WHO WAS JUST $#@%*%^ HERE.
AND IS POSSIBLY OUT OF CIGARS BY NOW.
THANKS TO HIM, I HAD FRESH CHUNKS FOR TODAY'S COOKIES!
HEY, NOT BECAUSE THIS PAINTING IS MAKING ME ILL, BUT CAN WE GO OUTSIDE?

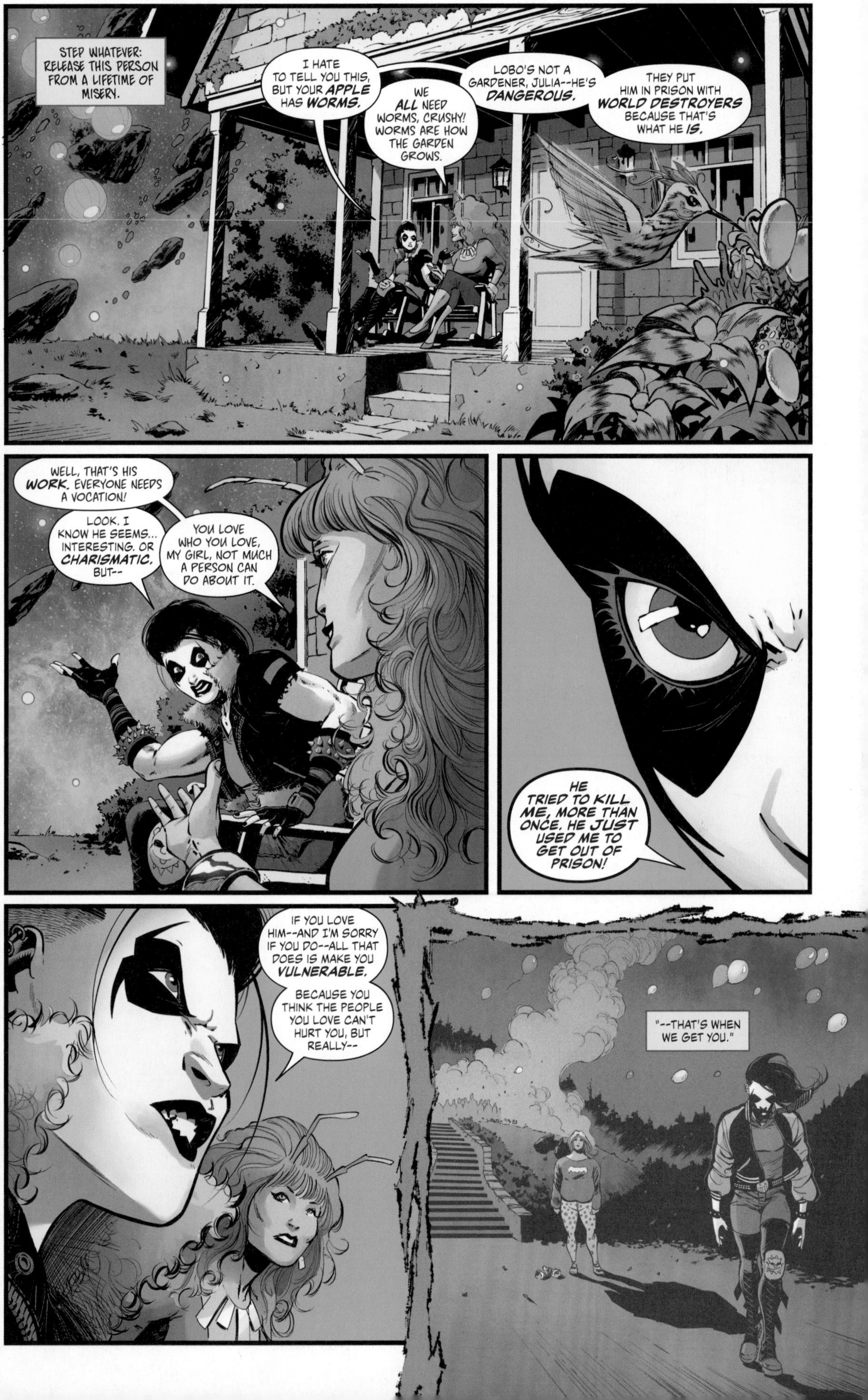
STEP WHATEVER: RELEASE THIS PERSON FROM A LIFETIME OF MISERY.
I HATE TO TELL YOU THIS, BUT YOUR APPLE HAS WORMS.
WE ALL NEED WORMS, CRUSHY! WORMS ARE HOW THE GARDEN GROWS.
LOBO'S NOT A GARDENER, JULIA--HE'S DANGEROUS.
THEY PUT HIM IN PRISON WITH WORLD DESTROYERS BECAUSE THAT'S WHAT HE IS.
WELL, THAT'S HIS WORK. EVERYONE NEEDS A VOCATION!
LOOK. I KNOW HE SEEMS... INTERESTING. OR CHARISMATIC. BUT--
YOU LOVE WHO YOU LOVE, MY GIRL, NOT MUCH A PERSON CAN DO ABOUT IT.
HE TRIED TO KILL ME, MORE THAN ONCE. HE JUST USED ME TO GET OUT OF PRISON!
IF YOU LOVE HIM--AND I'M SORRY IF YOU DO--ALL THAT DOES IS MAKE YOU VULNERABLE.
BECAUSE YOU THINK THE PEOPLE YOU LOVE CAN'T HURT YOU, BUT REALLY--
"--THAT'S WHEN WE GET YOU."

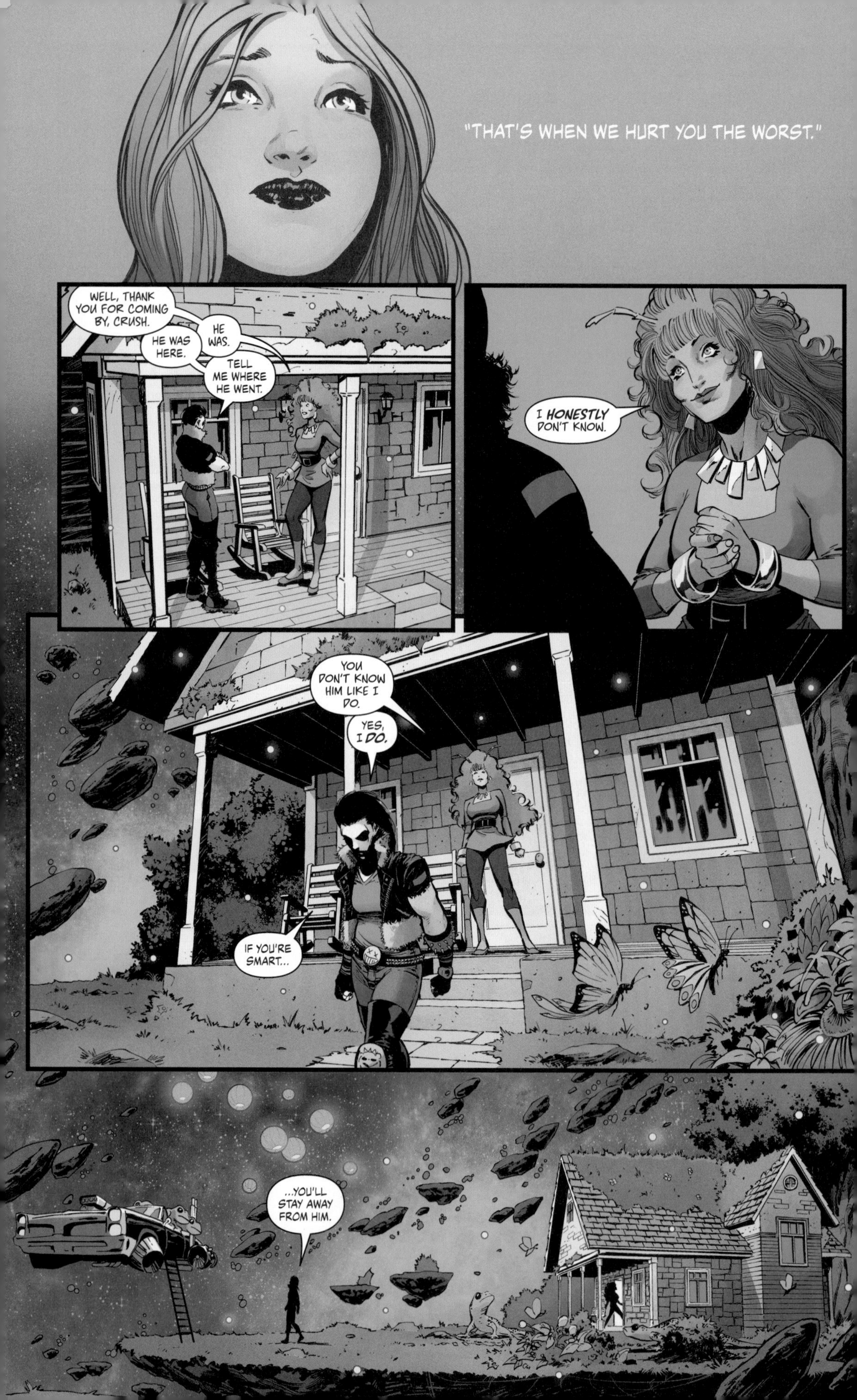
"THAT'S WHEN WE HURT YOU THE WORST."
WELL, THANK YOU FOR COMING BY, CRUSH.
HE WAS HERE.
HE WAS.
TELL ME WHERE HE WENT.
I HONESTLY DON'T KNOW.
YOU DON'T KNOW HIM LIKE I DO.
YES, I DO.
IF YOU'RE SMART...
...YOU'LL STAY AWAY FROM HIM.

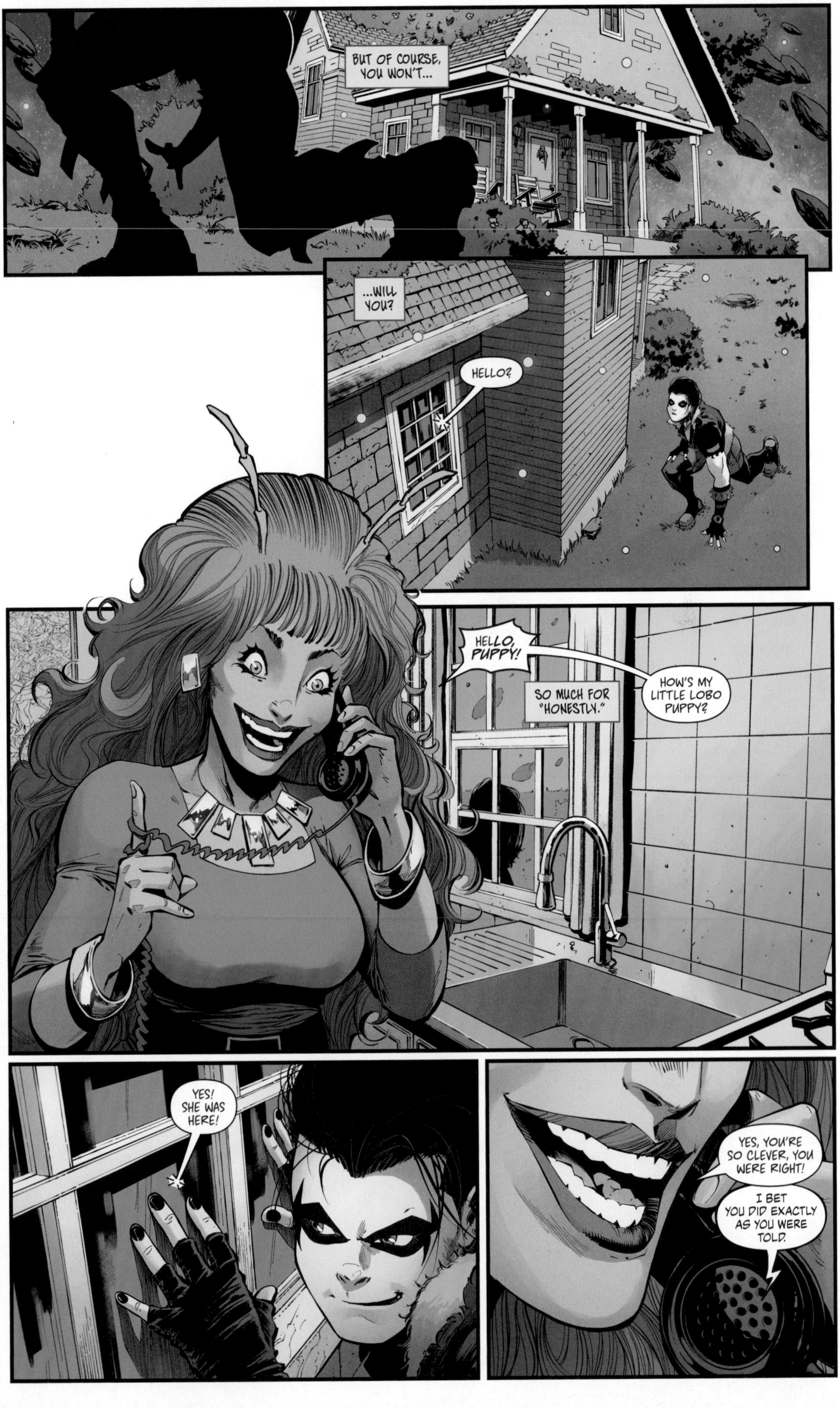
BUT OF COURSE, YOU WON'T...
...WILL YOU?
HELLO?
HELLO, PUPPY!
SO MUCH FOR "HONESTLY."
HOW'S MY LITTLE LOBO PUPPY?
YES! SHE WAS HERE!
YES, YOU'RE SO CLEVER, YOU WERE RIGHT!
I BET YOU DID EXACTLY AS YOU WERE TOLD.

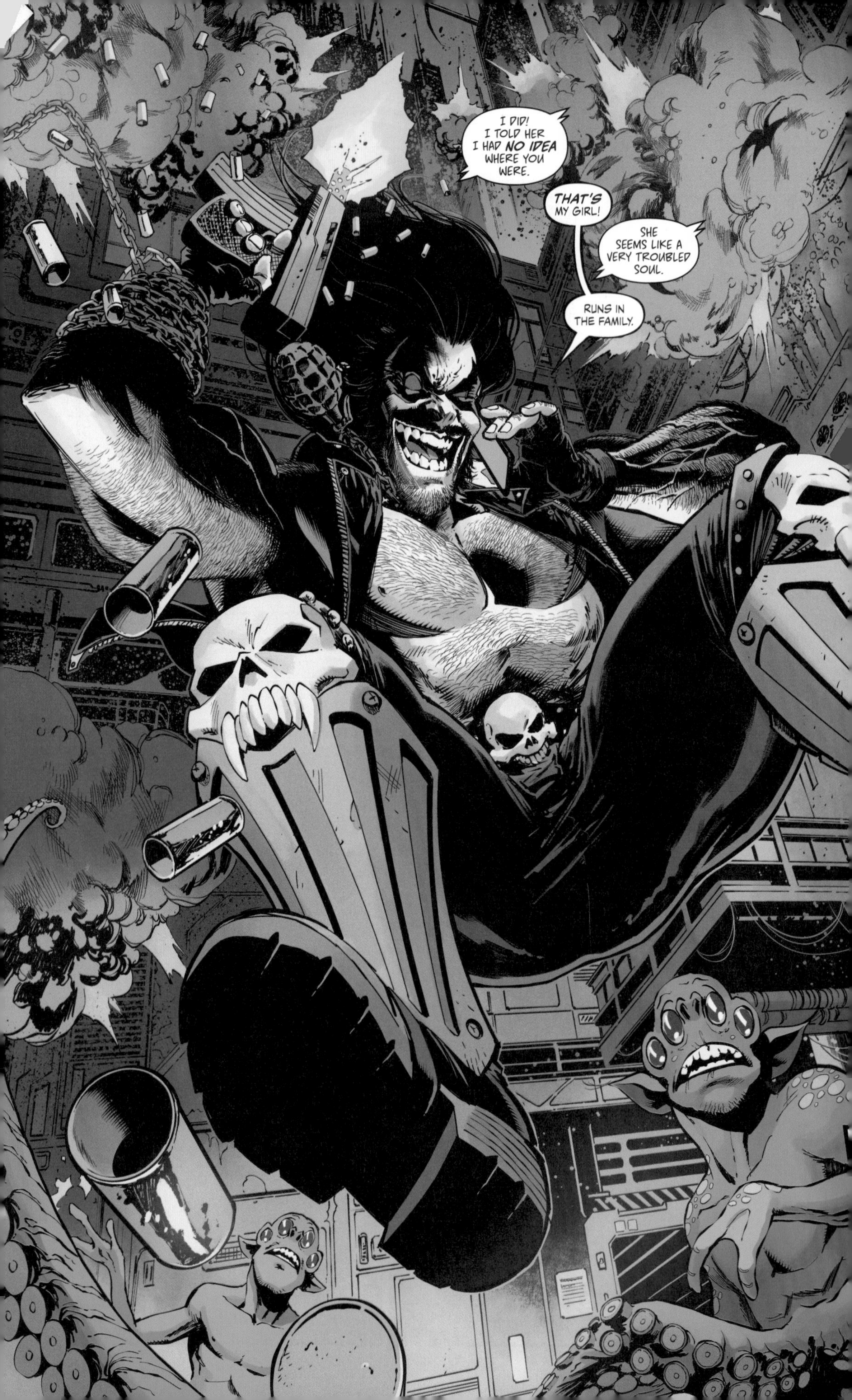
I DID! I TOLD HER I HAD **NO IDEA** WHERE YOU WERE.
THAT'S MY GIRL!
SHE SEEMS LIKE A VERY TROUBLED SOUL.
RUNS IN THE FAMILY.

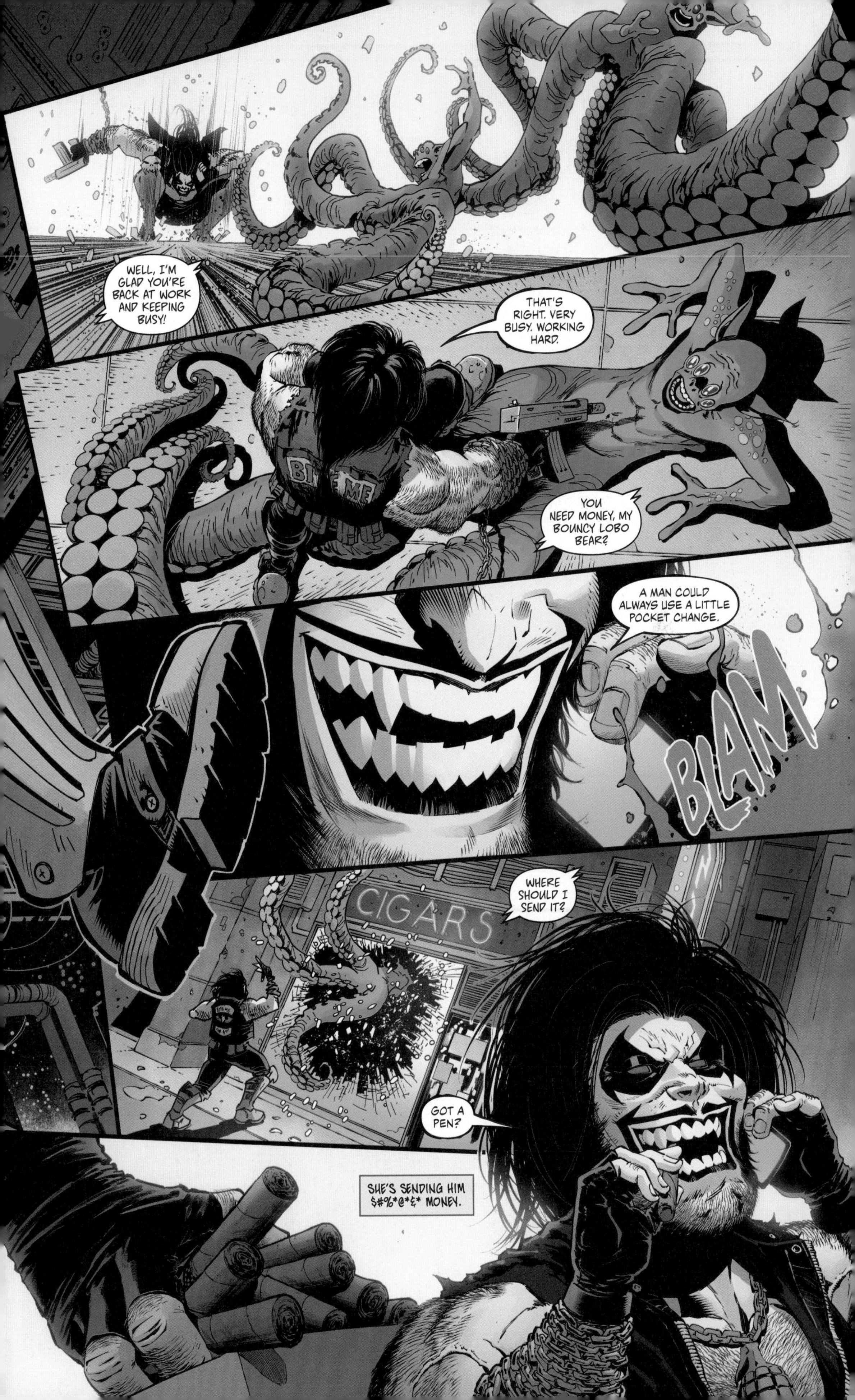

WELL, I'M GLAD YOU'RE BACK AT WORK AND KEEPING BUSY!
THAT'S RIGHT. VERY BUSY. WORKING HARD.
YOU NEED MONEY, MY BOUNCY LOBO BEAR?
A MAN COULD ALWAYS USE A LITTLE POCKET CHANGE.
BLAM
WHERE SHOULD I SEND IT?
CIGARS
GOT A PEN?
SHE'S SENDING HIM $#%*@*&* MONEY.

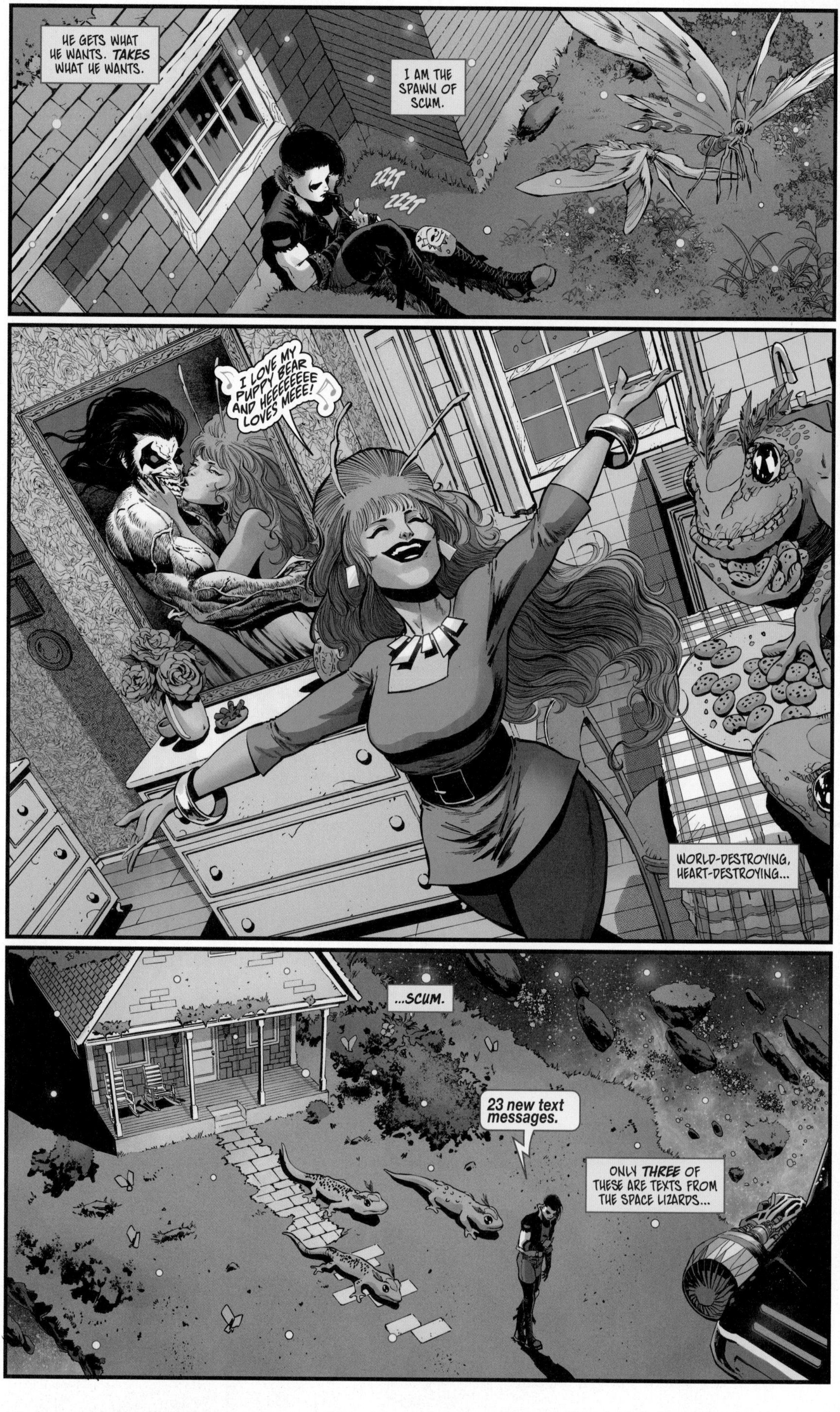
HE GETS WHAT HE WANTS. TAKES WHAT HE WANTS.
I AM THE SPAWN OF SCUM.
ZZZT ZZZT
I LOVE MY PUPPY BEAR AND HEEEEEEE LOVES MEEE!
WORLD-DESTROYING, HEART-DESTROYING...
...SCUM.
23 new text messages.
ONLY THREE OF THESE ARE TEXTS FROM THE SPACE LIZARDS...

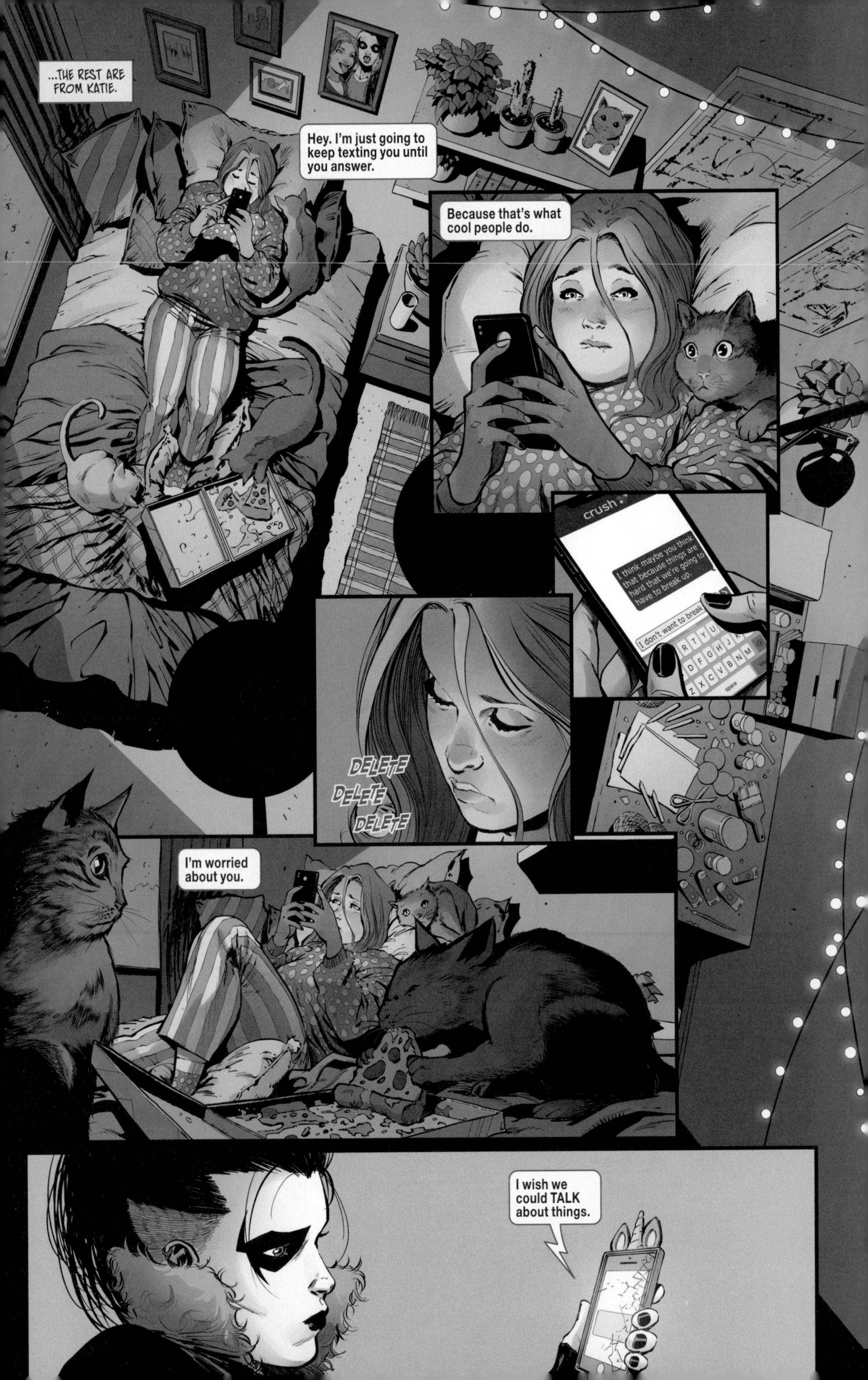
...THE REST ARE FROM KATIE.
Hey. I'm just going to keep texting you until you answer.
Because that's what cool people do.
crush
I think maybe you think that because things are hard that we're going to have to break up.
I don't want to break
DELETE
DELETE
DELETE
I'm worried about you.
I wish we could TALK about things.

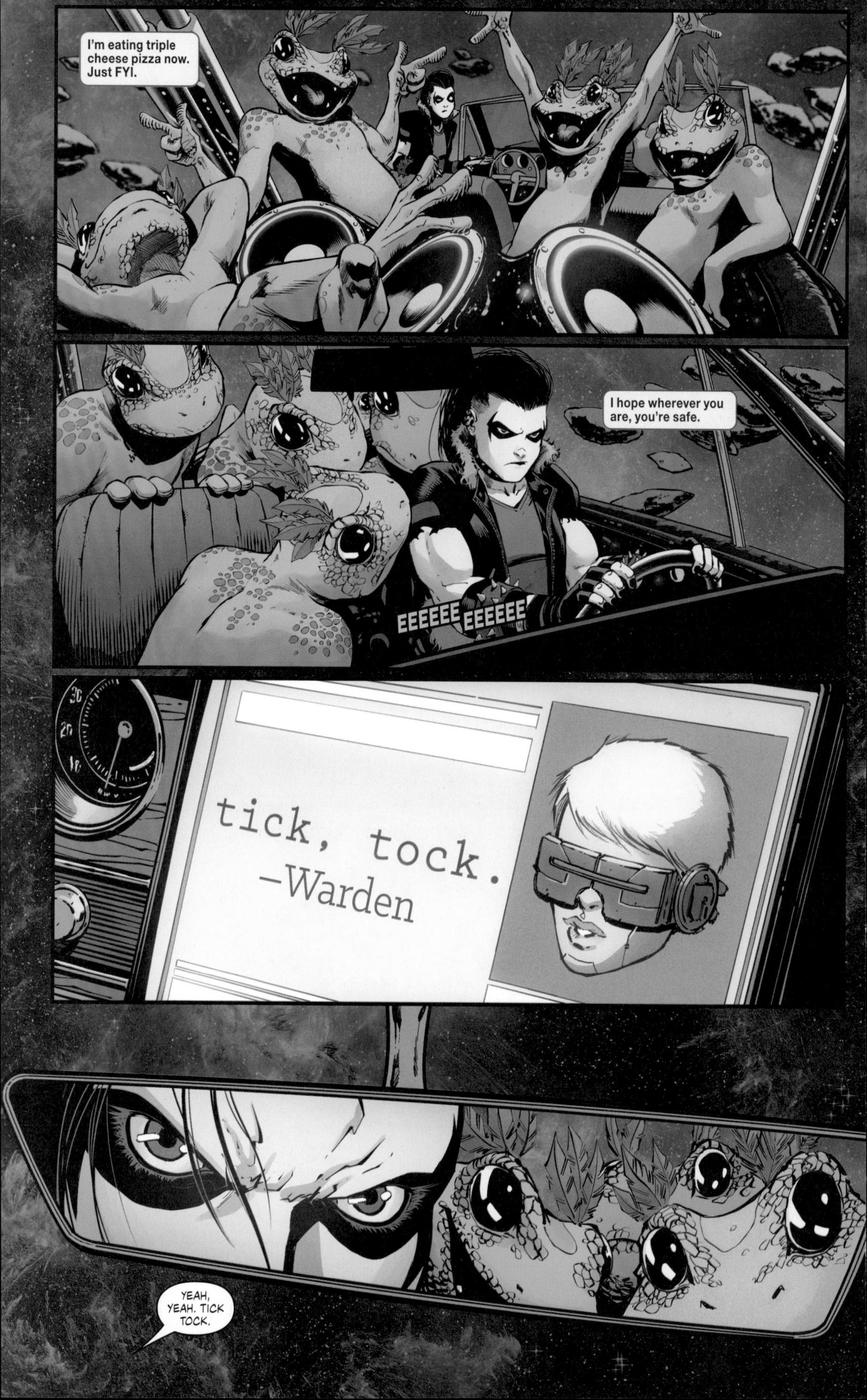

I'm eating triple cheese pizza now. Just FYI.
I hope wherever you are, you're safe.
EEEEEE EEEEEE
tick, tock.
—Warden
YEAH, YEAH. TICK TOCK.

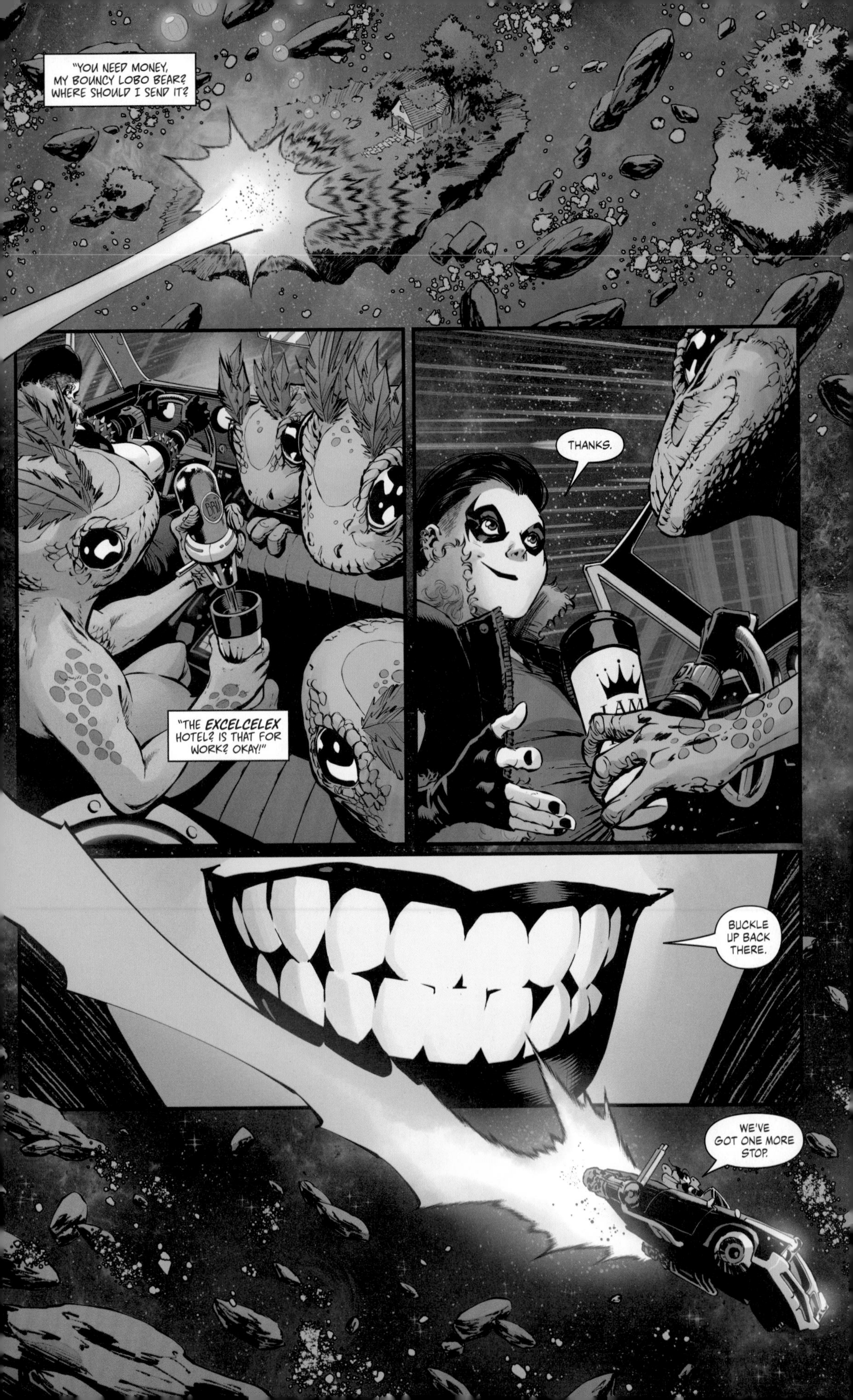
"YOU NEED MONEY, MY BOUNCY LOBO BEAR? WHERE SHOULD I SEND IT?
"THE EXCELCELEX HOTEL? IS THAT FOR WORK? OKAY!"
THANKS.
BUCKLE UP BACK THERE.
WE'VE GOT ONE MORE STOP.

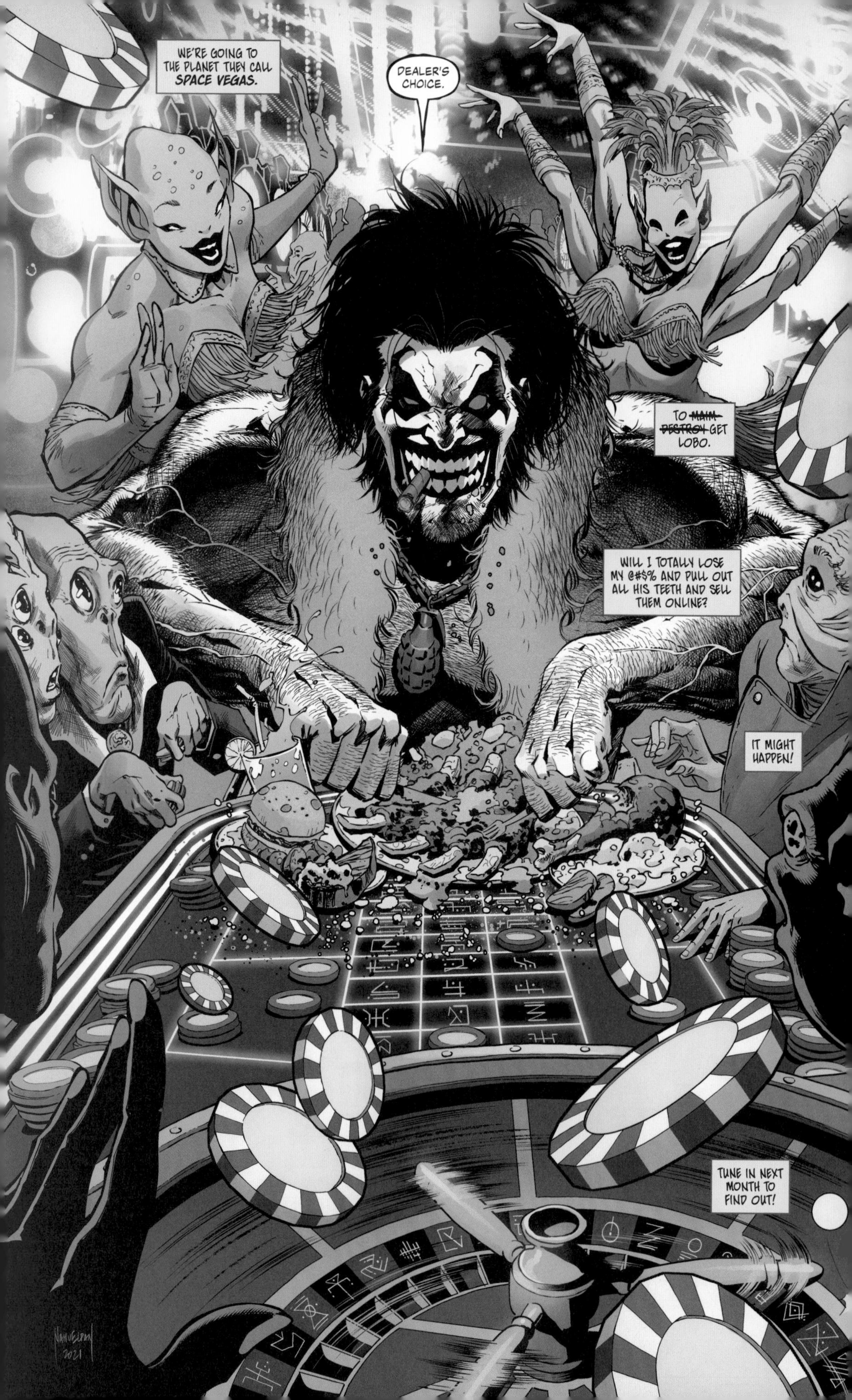
WE'RE GOING TO THE PLANET THEY CALL SPACE VEGAS.
DEALER'S CHOICE.
TO ~~MAIM~~ ~~DESTROY~~ GET LOBO.
WILL I TOTALLY LOSE MY @#$% AND PULL OUT ALL HIS TEETH AND SELL THEM ONLINE?
IT MIGHT HAPPEN!
TUNE IN NEXT MONTH TO FIND OUT!

CRUSH & LOBO #6 COVER BY NICK ROBLES

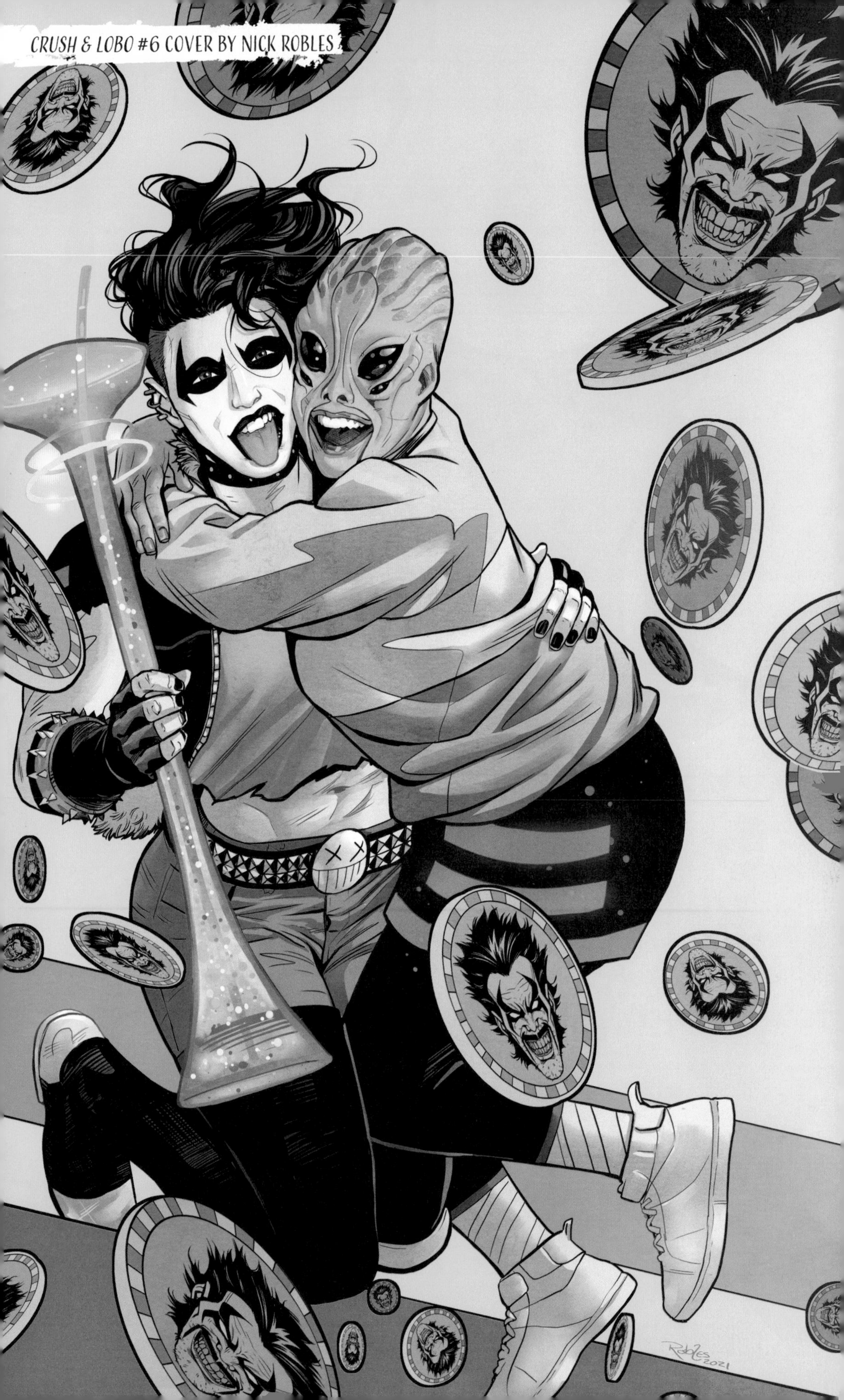

ROBLES 2021

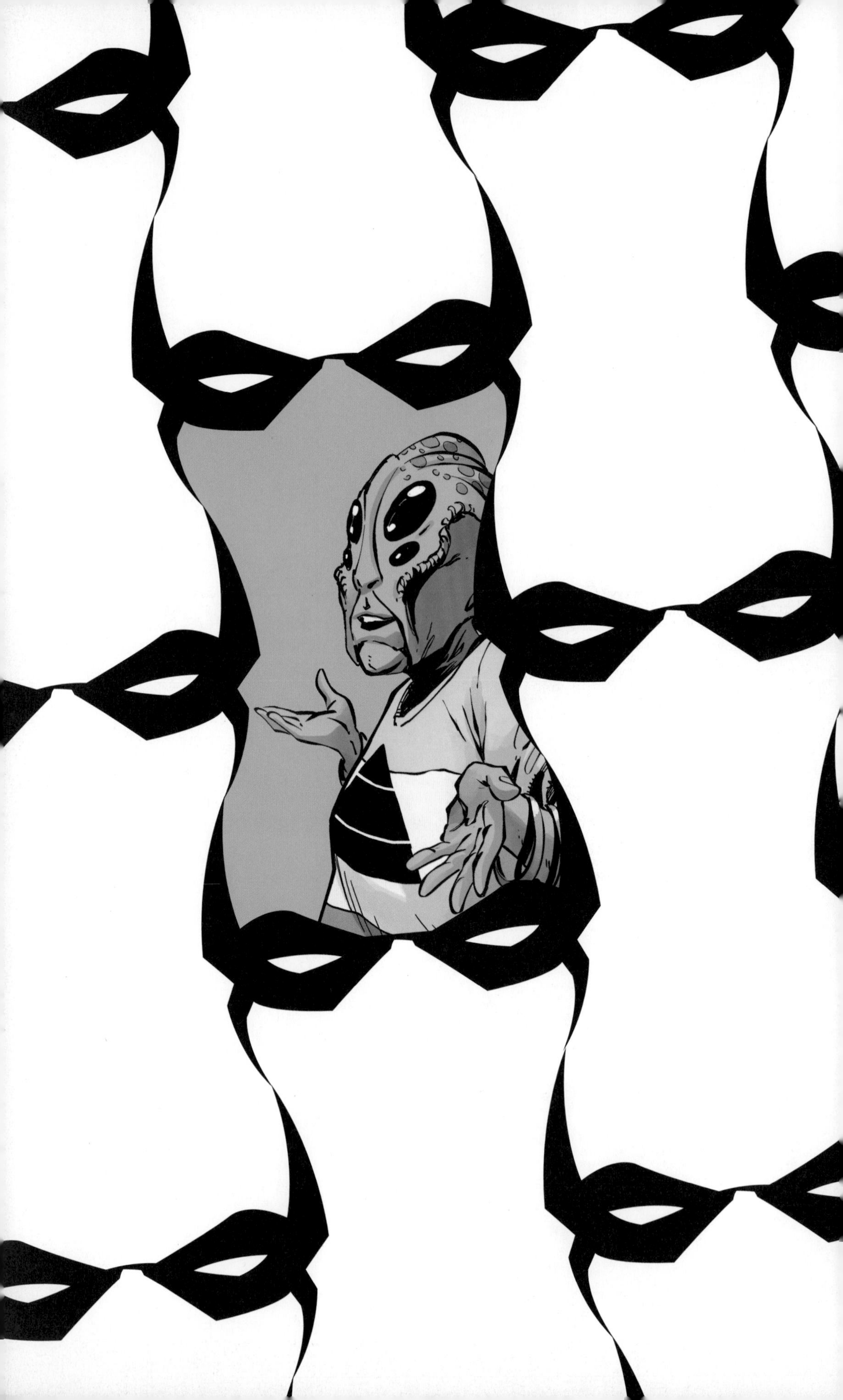

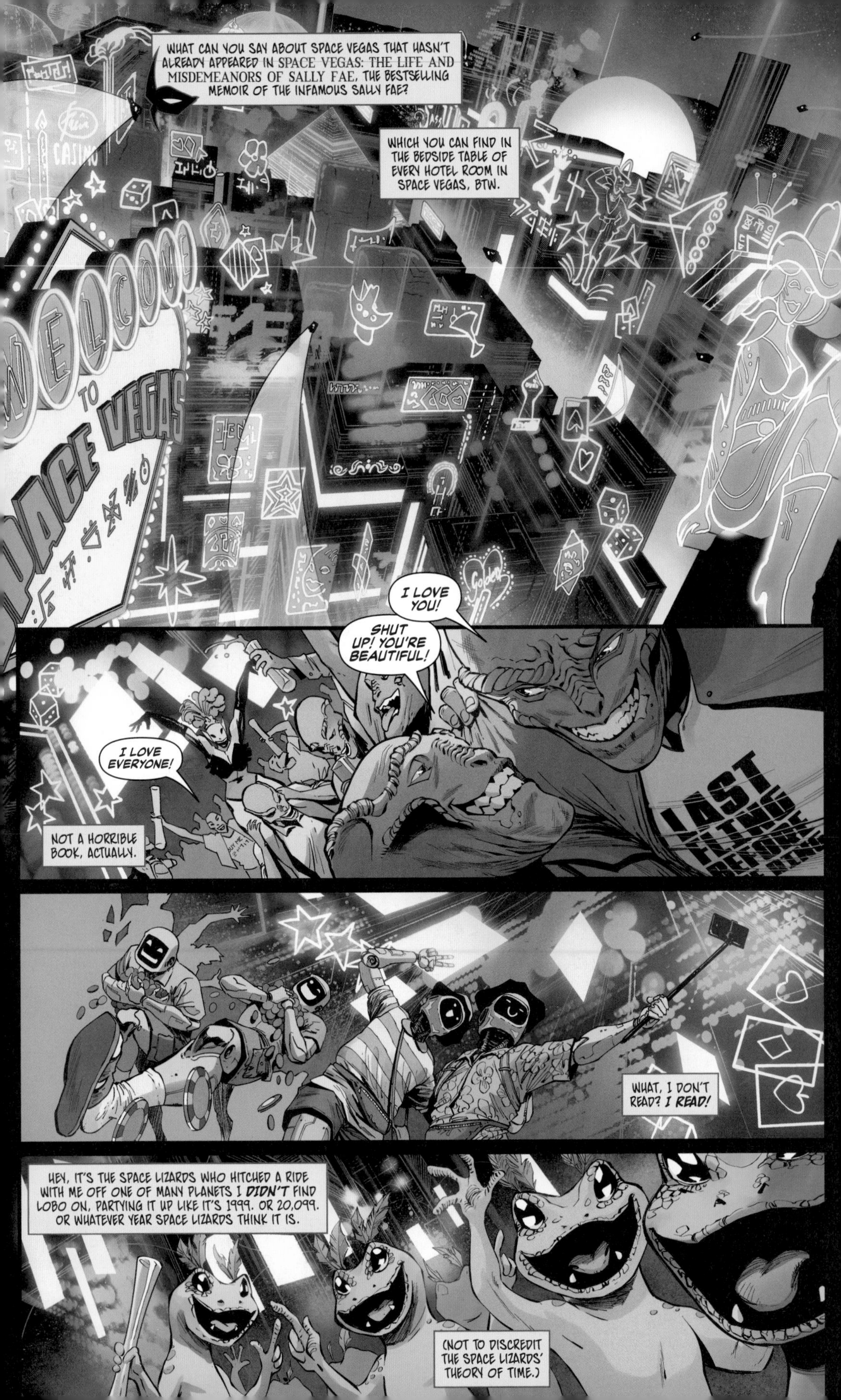
WHAT CAN YOU SAY ABOUT SPACE VEGAS THAT HASN'T ALREADY APPEARED IN SPACE VEGAS: THE LIFE AND MISDEMEANORS OF SALLY FAE, THE BESTSELLING MEMOIR OF THE INFAMOUS SALLY FAE?
WHICH YOU CAN FIND IN THE BEDSIDE TABLE OF EVERY HOTEL ROOM IN SPACE VEGAS, BTW.
WELCOME TO SPACE VEGAS
CASINO
I LOVE YOU!
SHUT UP! YOU'RE BEAUTIFUL!
I LOVE EVERYONE!
NOT A HORRIBLE BOOK, ACTUALLY.
WHAT, I DON'T READ? I READ!
HEY, IT'S THE SPACE LIZARDS WHO HITCHED A RIDE WITH ME OFF ONE OF MANY PLANETS I DIDN'T FIND LOBO ON, PARTYING IT UP LIKE IT'S 1999. OR 20,099. OR WHATEVER YEAR SPACE LIZARDS THINK IT IS.
(NOT TO DISCREDIT THE SPACE LIZARDS' THEORY OF TIME.)

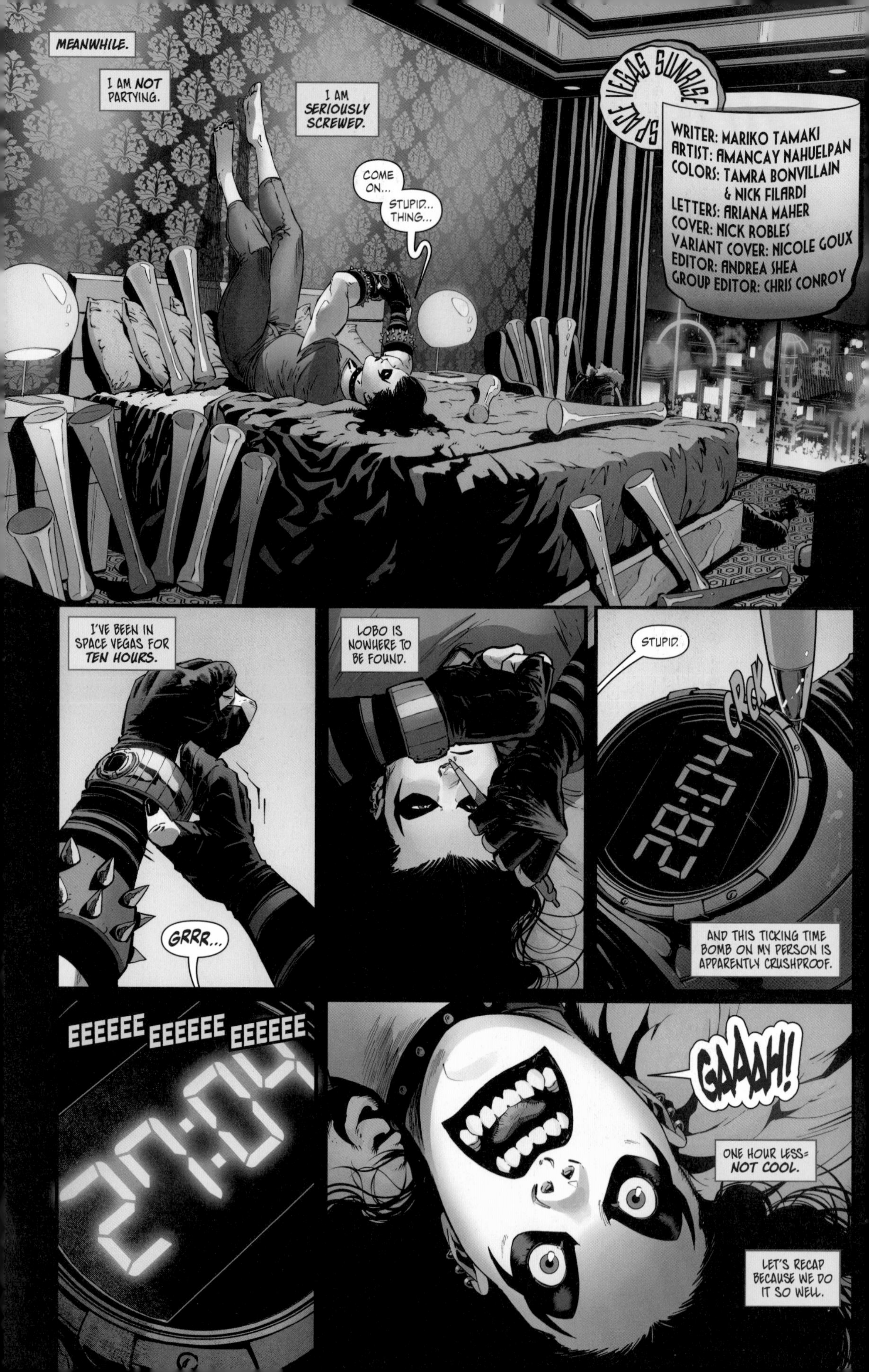
MEANWHILE.
I AM NOT PARTYING.
I AM SERIOUSLY SCREWED.
COME ON...
STUPID... THING...
SPACE VEGAS SUNRISE
WRITER: MARIKO TAMAKI
ARTIST: AMANCAY NAHUELPAN
COLORS: TAMRA BONVILLAIN & NICK FILARDI
LETTERS: ARIANA MAHER
COVER: NICK ROBLES
VARIANT COVER: NICOLE GOUX
EDITOR: ANDREA SHEA
GROUP EDITOR: CHRIS CONROY
I'VE BEEN IN SPACE VEGAS FOR TEN HOURS.
GRRR...
LOBO IS NOWHERE TO BE FOUND.
STUPID.
CRCK
AND THIS TICKING TIME BOMB ON MY PERSON IS APPARENTLY CRUSHPROOF.
EEEEEE EEEEEE EEEEEE
GAAAH!
ONE HOUR LESS= NOT COOL.
LET'S RECAP BECAUSE WE DO IT SO WELL.

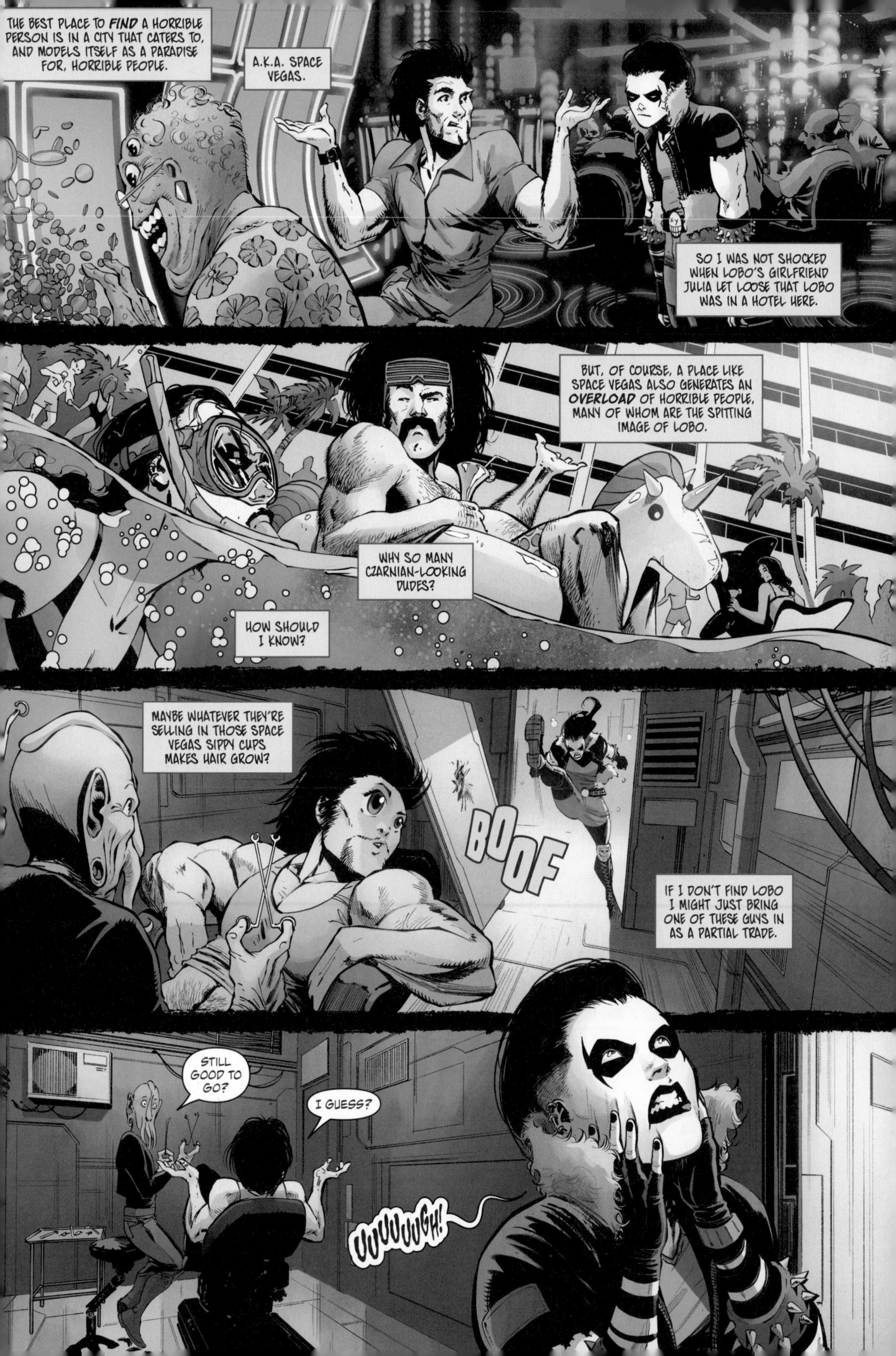
THE BEST PLACE TO FIND A HORRIBLE PERSON IS IN A CITY THAT CATERS TO, AND MODELS ITSELF AS A PARADISE FOR, HORRIBLE PEOPLE.
A.K.A. SPACE VEGAS.
SO I WAS NOT SHOCKED WHEN LOBO'S GIRLFRIEND JULIA LET LOOSE THAT LOBO WAS IN A HOTEL HERE.
BUT, OF COURSE, A PLACE LIKE SPACE VEGAS ALSO GENERATES AN OVERLOAD OF HORRIBLE PEOPLE, MANY OF WHOM ARE THE SPITTING IMAGE OF LOBO.
WHY SO MANY CZARNIAN-LOOKING DUDES?
HOW SHOULD I KNOW?
MAYBE WHATEVER THEY'RE SELLING IN THOSE SPACE VEGAS SIPPY CUPS MAKES HAIR GROW?
BOOF
IF I DON'T FIND LOBO I MIGHT JUST BRING ONE OF THESE GUYS IN AS A PARTIAL TRADE.
STILL GOOD TO GO?
I GUESS?
UUUUUUGH!

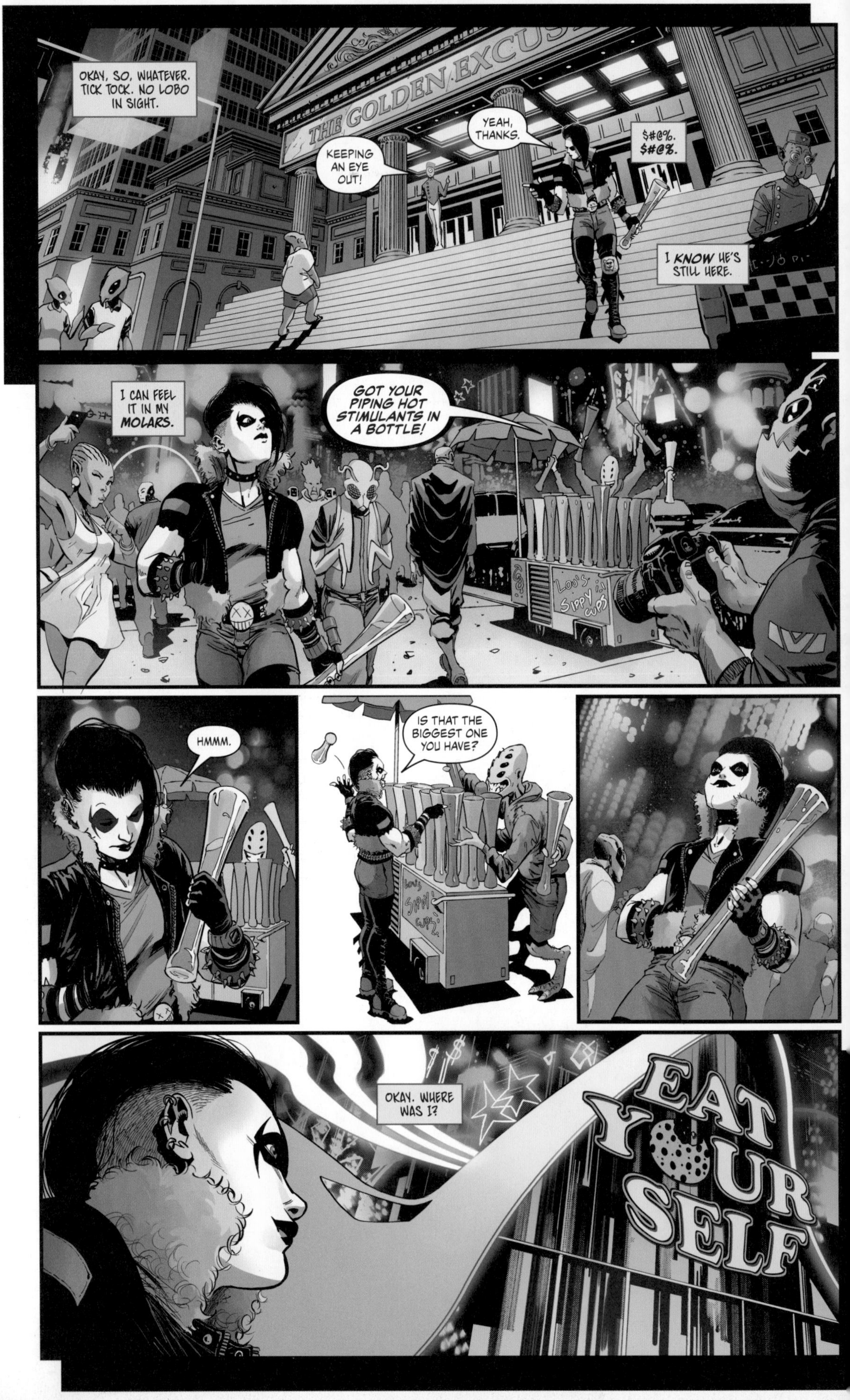

THE GOLDEN EXCUS
OKAY, SO, WHATEVER. TICK TOCK. NO LOBO IN SIGHT.
KEEPING AN EYE OUT!
YEAH, THANKS.
$#@%. $#@%.
I KNOW HE'S STILL HERE.
I CAN FEEL IT IN MY MOLARS.
GOT YOUR PIPING HOT STIMULANTS IN A BOTTLE!
LOU'S SIPPY CUPS
HMMM.
IS THAT THE BIGGEST ONE YOU HAVE?
OKAY. WHERE WAS I?
EAT YOUR SELF

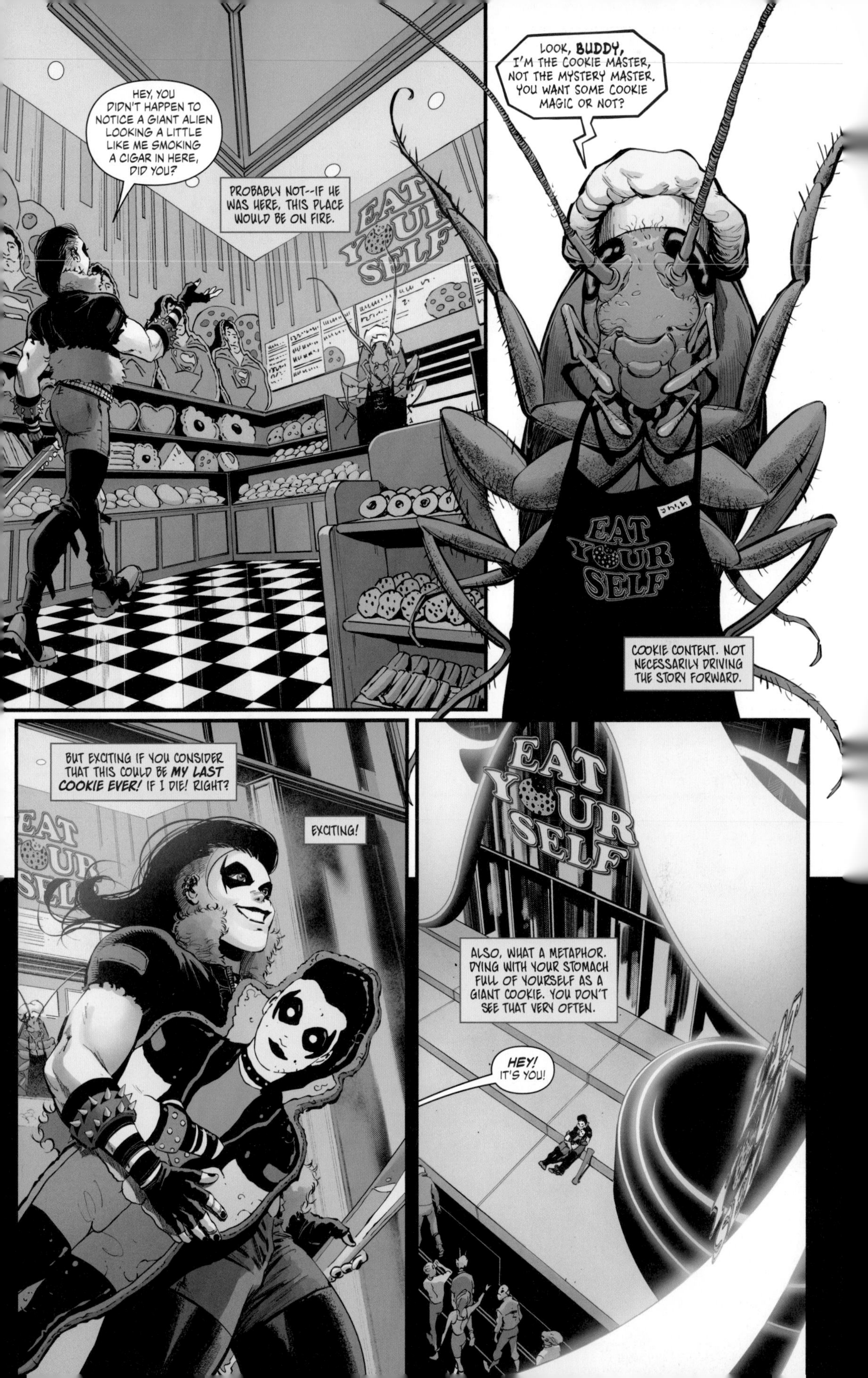
HEY, YOU DIDN'T HAPPEN TO NOTICE A GIANT ALIEN LOOKING A LITTLE LIKE ME SMOKING A CIGAR IN HERE, DID YOU?
PROBABLY NOT--IF HE WAS HERE, THIS PLACE WOULD BE ON FIRE.
EAT YOUR SELF
LOOK, BUDDY, I'M THE COOKIE MASTER, NOT THE MYSTERY MASTER. YOU WANT SOME COOKIE MAGIC OR NOT?
EAT YOUR SELF
COOKIE CONTENT. NOT NECESSARILY DRIVING THE STORY FORWARD.
BUT EXCITING IF YOU CONSIDER THAT THIS COULD BE MY LAST COOKIE EVER! IF I DIE! RIGHT?
EXCITING!
EAT YOUR SELF
EAT YOUR SELF
ALSO, WHAT A METAPHOR. DYING WITH YOUR STOMACH FULL OF YOURSELF AS A GIANT COOKIE. YOU DON'T SEE THAT VERY OFTEN.
HEY! IT'S YOU!

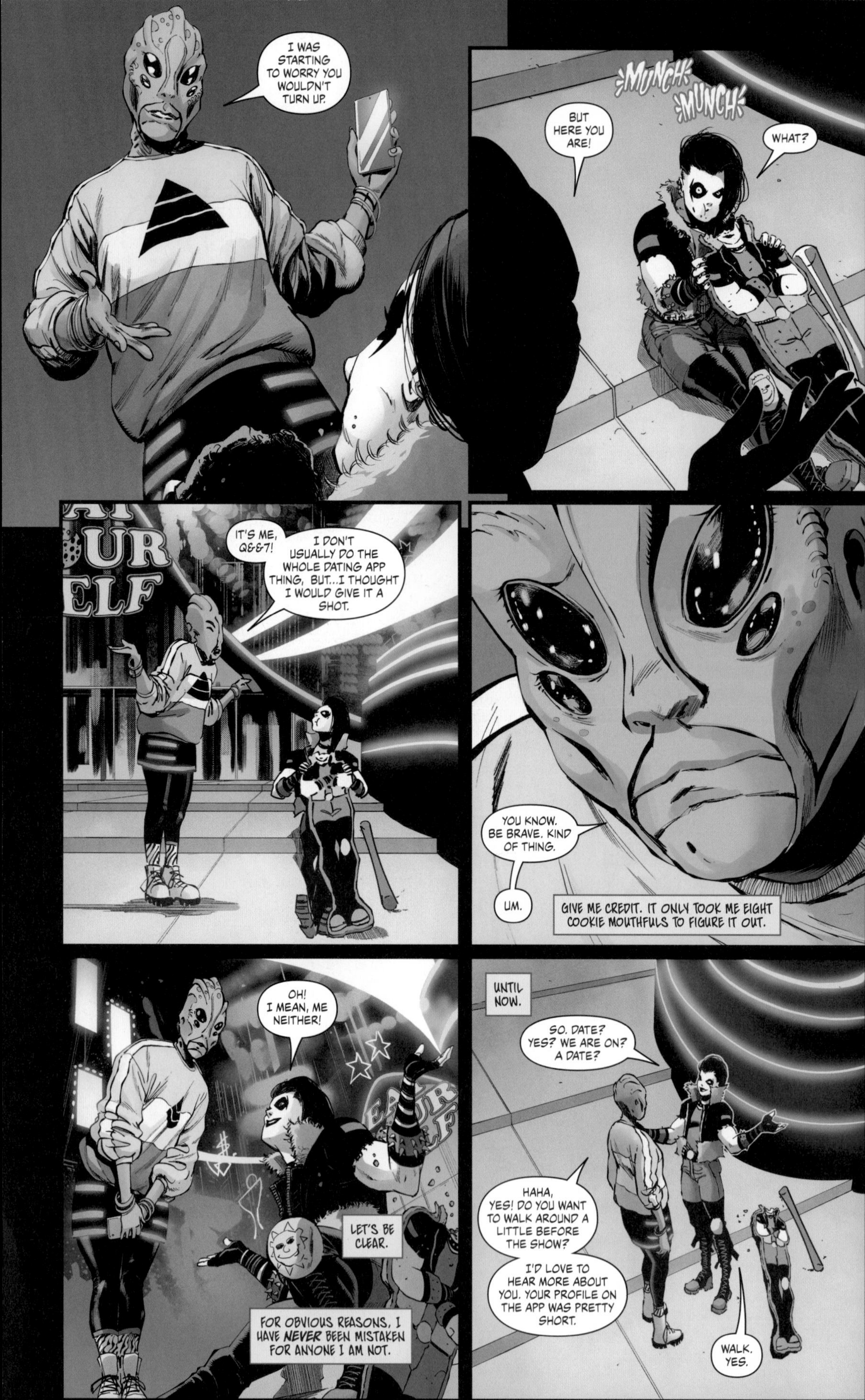
I WAS STARTING TO WORRY YOU WOULDN'T TURN UP.
MUNCH MUNCH
BUT HERE YOU ARE!
WHAT?
IT'S ME, Q&&7!
I DON'T USUALLY DO THE WHOLE DATING APP THING, BUT...I THOUGHT I WOULD GIVE IT A SHOT.
YOU KNOW. BE BRAVE. KIND OF THING.
UM.
GIVE ME CREDIT. IT ONLY TOOK ME EIGHT COOKIE MOUTHFULS TO FIGURE IT OUT.
OH! I MEAN, ME NEITHER!
LET'S BE CLEAR.
FOR OBVIOUS REASONS, I HAVE *NEVER* BEEN MISTAKEN FOR ANYONE I AM NOT.
UNTIL NOW.
SO. DATE? YES? WE ARE ON? A DATE?
HAHA, YES! DO YOU WANT TO WALK AROUND A LITTLE BEFORE THE SHOW?
I'D LOVE TO HEAR MORE ABOUT YOU. YOUR PROFILE ON THE APP WAS PRETTY SHORT.
WALK. YES.

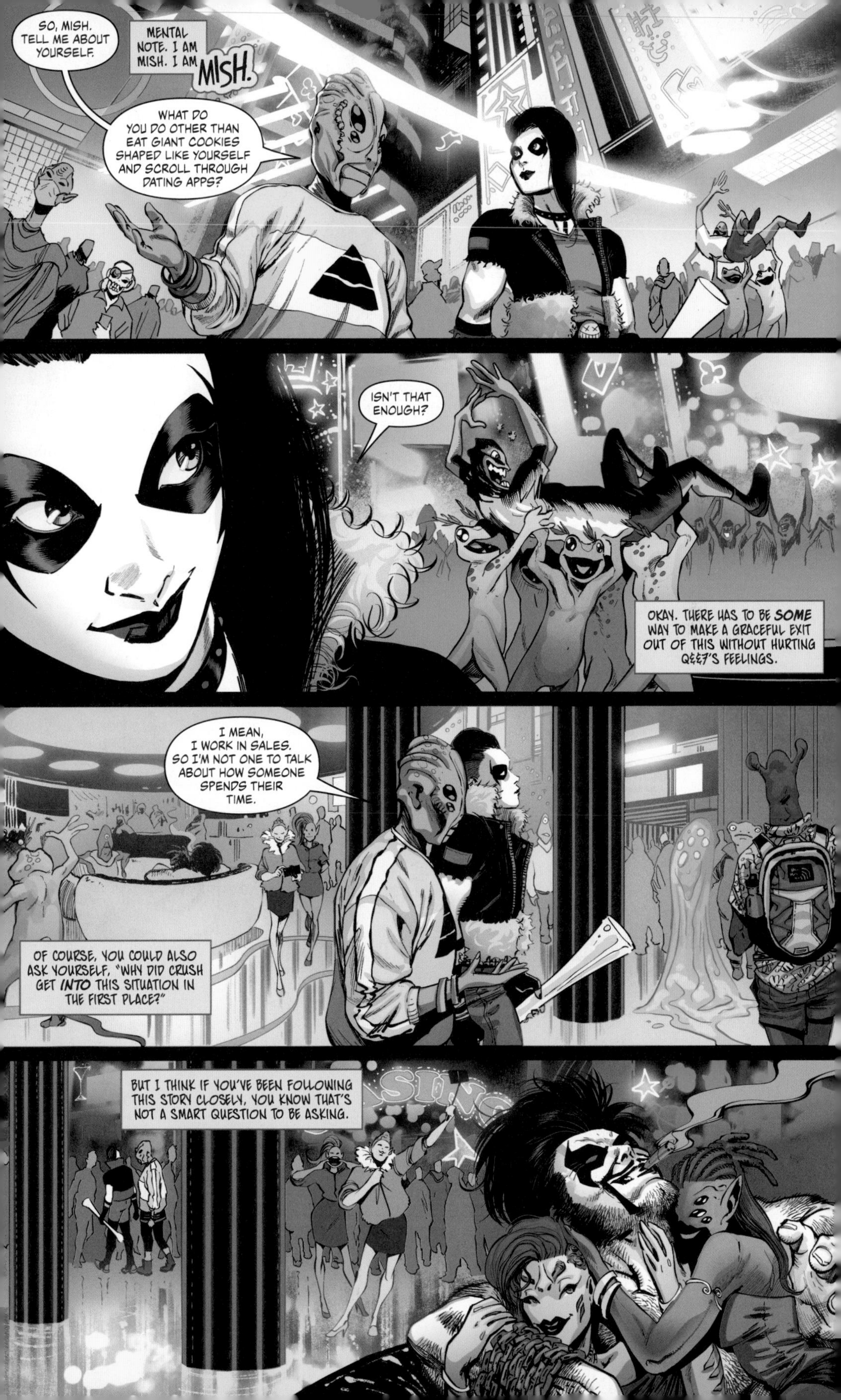
SO, MISH. TELL ME ABOUT YOURSELF.
MENTAL NOTE. I AM MISH. I AM MISH.
WHAT DO YOU DO OTHER THAN EAT GIANT COOKIES SHAPED LIKE YOURSELF AND SCROLL THROUGH DATING APPS?
ISN'T THAT ENOUGH?
OKAY. THERE HAS TO BE SOME WAY TO MAKE A GRACEFUL EXIT OUT OF THIS WITHOUT HURTING Q&&7'S FEELINGS.
I MEAN, I WORK IN SALES. SO I'M NOT ONE TO TALK ABOUT HOW SOMEONE SPENDS THEIR TIME.
OF COURSE, YOU COULD ALSO ASK YOURSELF, "WHY DID CRUSH GET INTO THIS SITUATION IN THE FIRST PLACE?"
BUT I THINK IF YOU'VE BEEN FOLLOWING THIS STORY CLOSELY, YOU KNOW THAT'S NOT A SMART QUESTION TO BE ASKING.

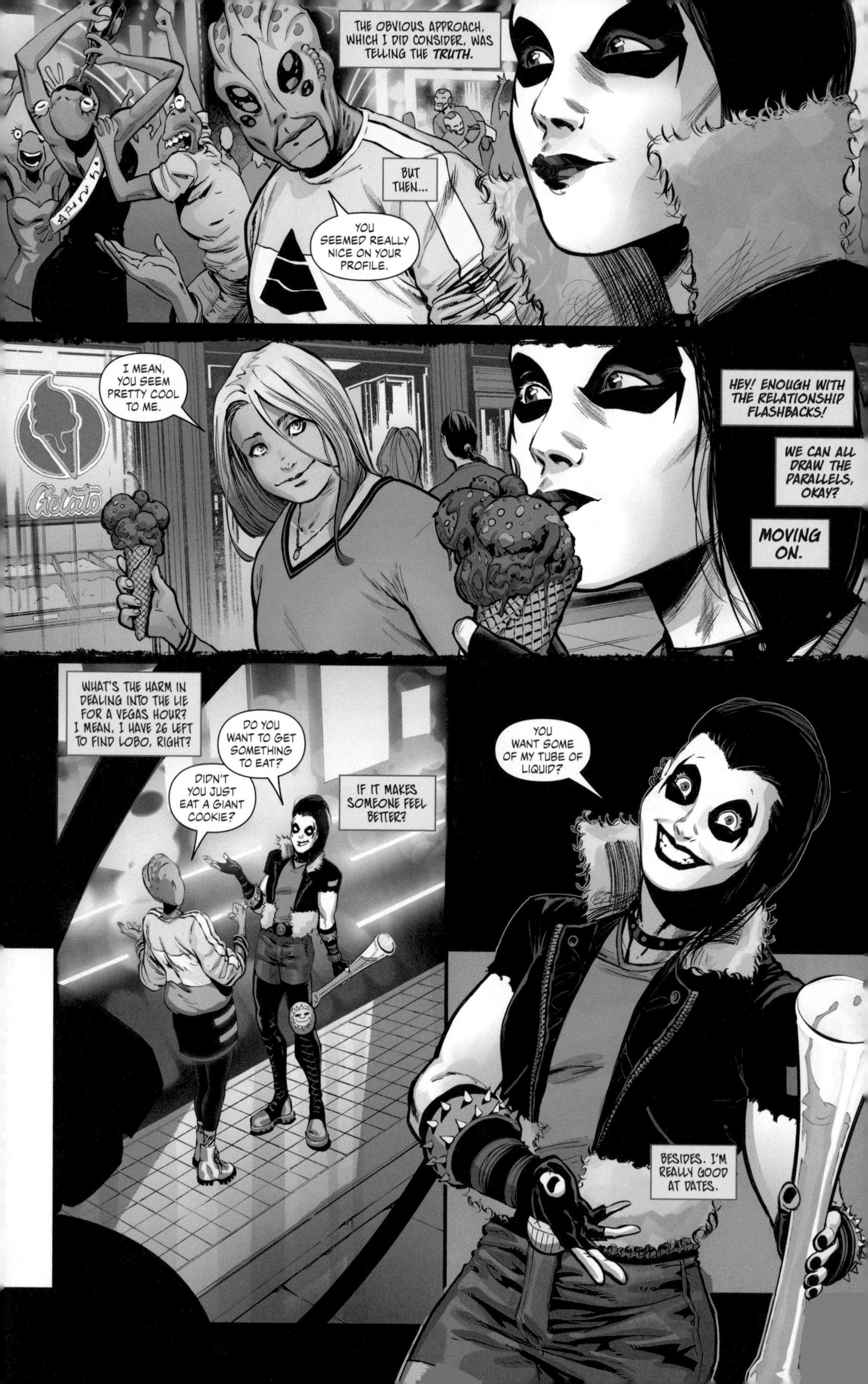
THE OBVIOUS APPROACH, WHICH I DID CONSIDER, WAS TELLING THE TRUTH.
BUT THEN...
YOU SEEMED REALLY NICE ON YOUR PROFILE.
I MEAN, YOU SEEM PRETTY COOL TO ME.
Gelato
HEY! ENOUGH WITH THE RELATIONSHIP FLASHBACKS!
WE CAN ALL DRAW THE PARALLELS, OKAY?
MOVING ON.
WHAT'S THE HARM IN DEALING INTO THE LIE FOR A VEGAS HOUR? I MEAN, I HAVE 26 LEFT TO FIND LOBO, RIGHT?
DO YOU WANT TO GET SOMETHING TO EAT?
DIDN'T YOU JUST EAT A GIANT COOKIE?
IF IT MAKES SOMEONE FEEL BETTER?
YOU WANT SOME OF MY TUBE OF LIQUID?
BESIDES. I'M REALLY GOOD AT DATES.

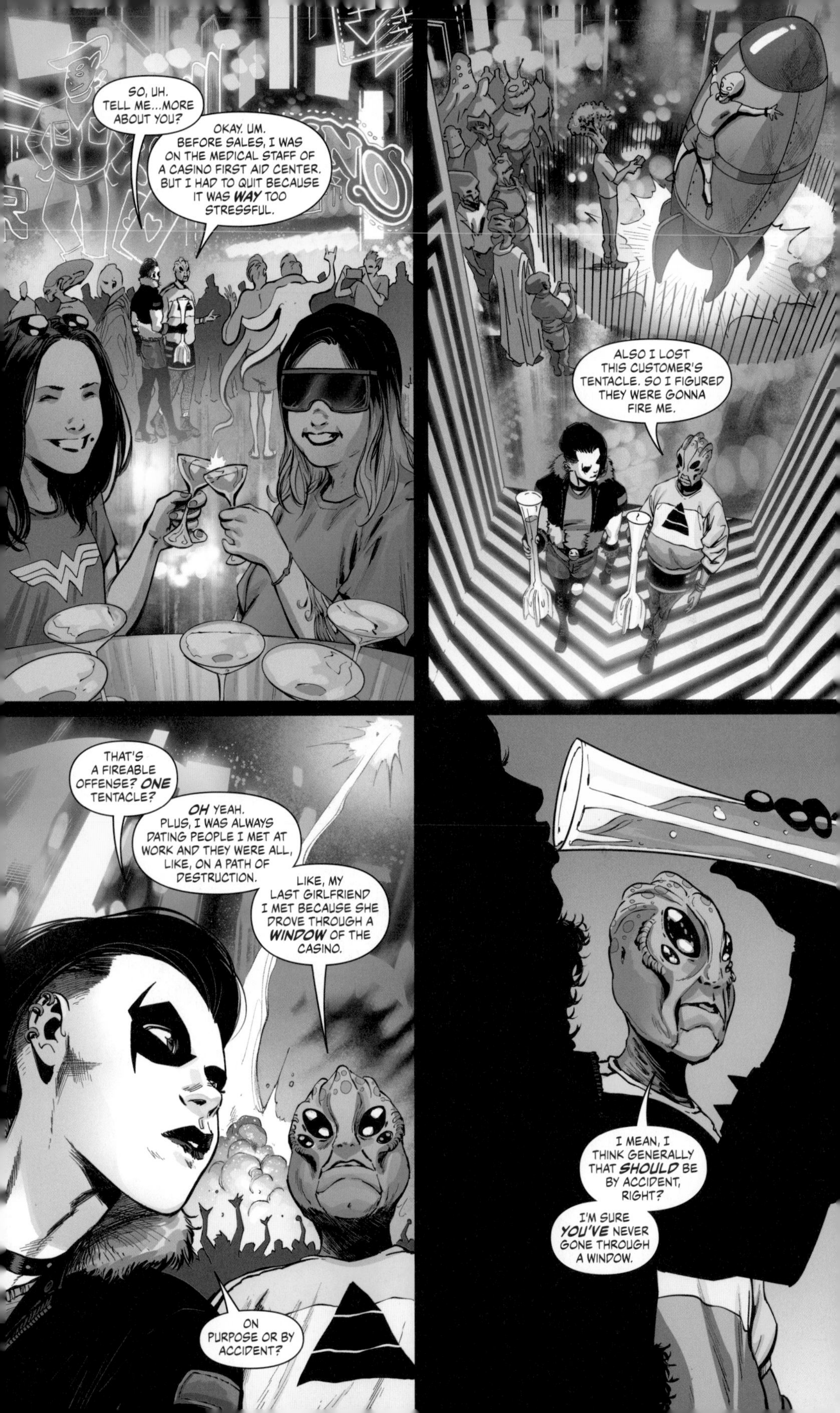

SO, UH. TELL ME...MORE ABOUT YOU?
OKAY. UM. BEFORE SALES, I WAS ON THE MEDICAL STAFF OF A CASINO FIRST AID CENTER. BUT I HAD TO QUIT BECAUSE IT WAS **WAY** TOO STRESSFUL.
ALSO I LOST THIS CUSTOMER'S TENTACLE. SO I FIGURED THEY WERE GONNA FIRE ME.
THAT'S A FIREABLE OFFENSE? **ONE** TENTACLE?
OH YEAH. PLUS, I WAS ALWAYS DATING PEOPLE I MET AT WORK AND THEY WERE ALL, LIKE, ON A PATH OF DESTRUCTION.
LIKE, MY LAST GIRLFRIEND I MET BECAUSE SHE DROVE THROUGH A **WINDOW** OF THE CASINO.
ON PURPOSE OR BY ACCIDENT?
I MEAN, I THINK GENERALLY THAT **SHOULD** BE BY ACCIDENT, RIGHT?
I'M SURE **YOU'VE** NEVER GONE THROUGH A WINDOW.

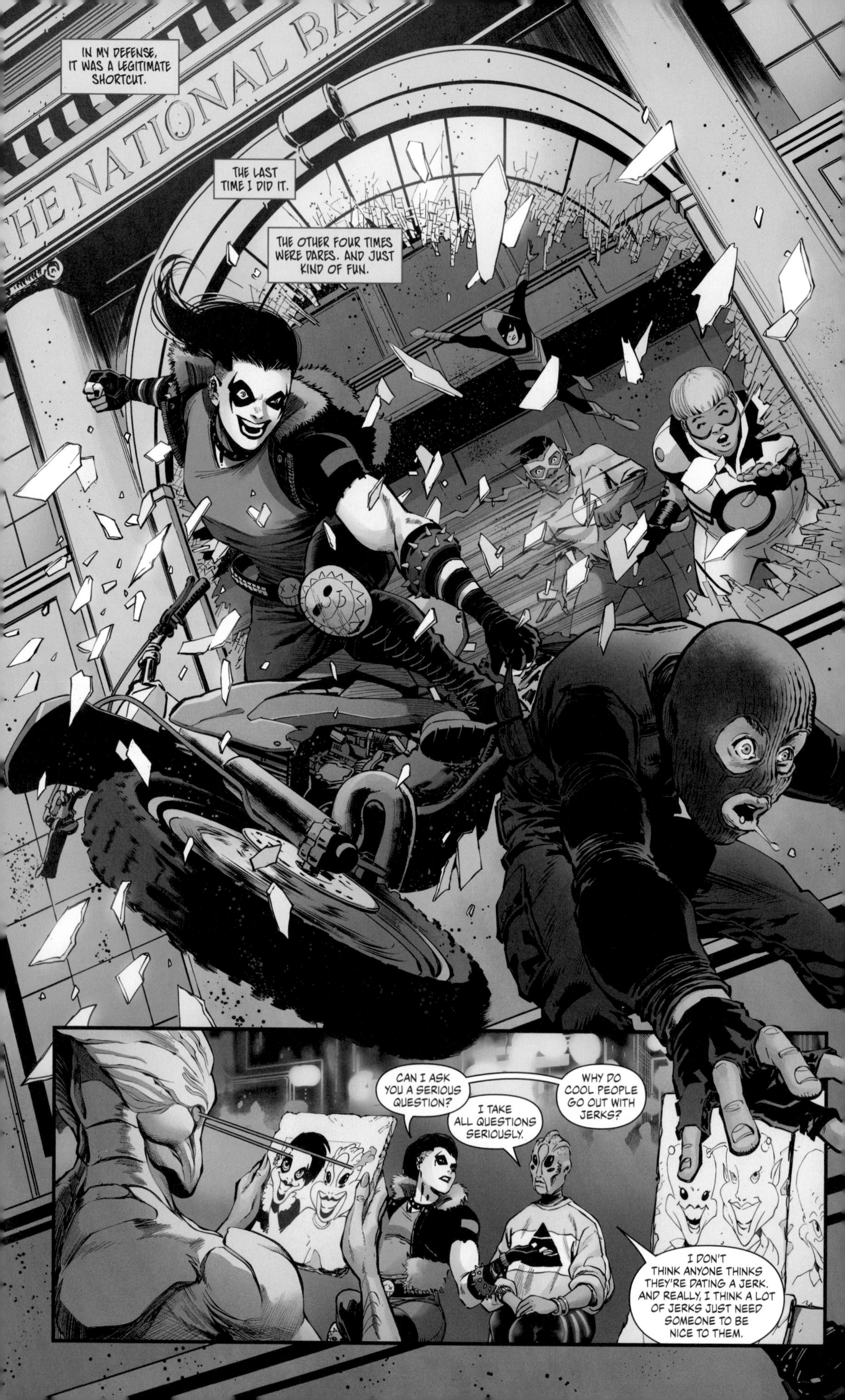
IN MY DEFENSE, IT WAS A LEGITIMATE SHORTCUT.
THE NATIONAL BA
THE LAST TIME I DID IT.
THE OTHER FOUR TIMES WERE DARES. AND JUST KIND OF FUN.
CAN I ASK YOU A SERIOUS QUESTION?
I TAKE ALL QUESTIONS SERIOUSLY.
WHY DO COOL PEOPLE GO OUT WITH JERKS?
I DON'T THINK ANYONE THINKS THEY'RE DATING A JERK. AND REALLY, I THINK A LOT OF JERKS JUST NEED SOMEONE TO BE NICE TO THEM.

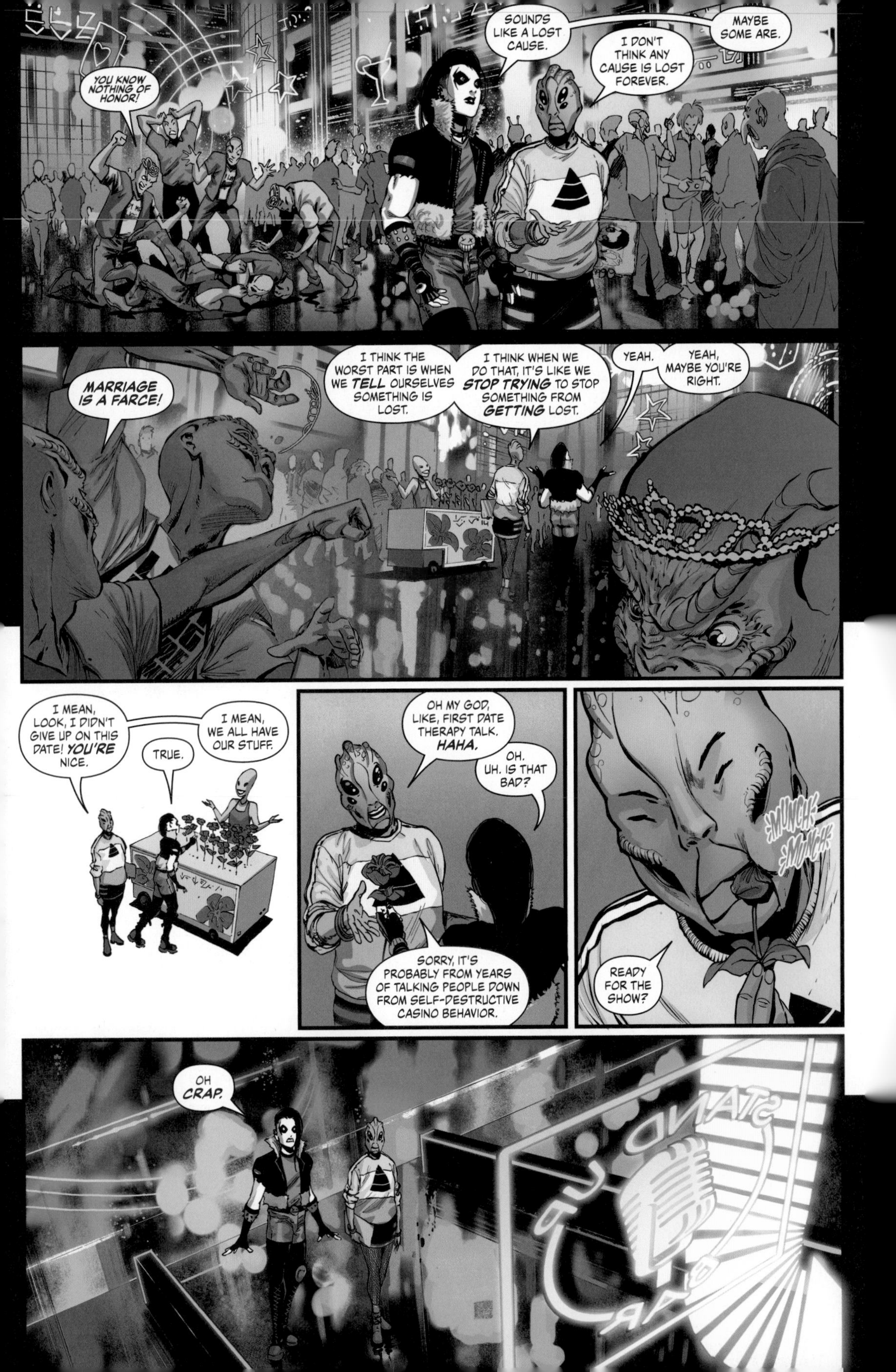
YOU KNOW NOTHING OF HONOR!
SOUNDS LIKE A LOST CAUSE.
MAYBE SOME ARE.
I DON'T THINK ANY CAUSE IS LOST FOREVER.
MARRIAGE IS A FARCE!
I THINK THE WORST PART IS WHEN WE TELL OURSELVES SOMETHING IS LOST.
I THINK WHEN WE DO THAT, IT'S LIKE WE STOP TRYING TO STOP SOMETHING FROM GETTING LOST.
YEAH.
YEAH, MAYBE YOU'RE RIGHT.
I MEAN, LOOK, I DIDN'T GIVE UP ON THIS DATE! YOU'RE NICE.
I MEAN, WE ALL HAVE OUR STUFF.
TRUE.
OH MY GOD, LIKE, FIRST DATE THERAPY TALK. HAHA.
OH. UH. IS THAT BAD?
SORRY, IT'S PROBABLY FROM YEARS OF TALKING PEOPLE DOWN FROM SELF-DESTRUCTIVE CASINO BEHAVIOR.
MUNCH
MUNCH
READY FOR THE SHOW?
OH CRAP.
STAND UP BAR

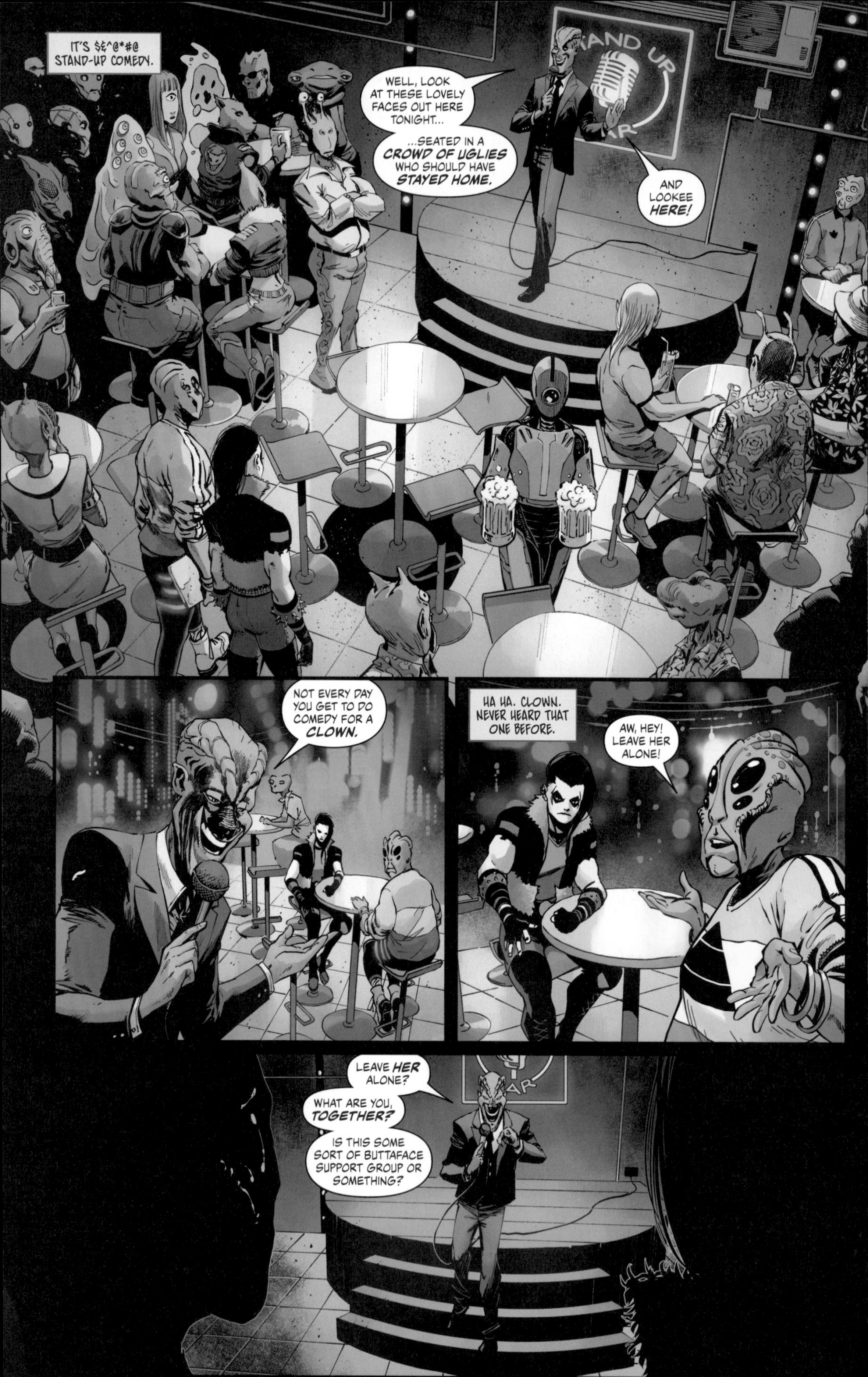
IT'S $£^@*#@ STAND-UP COMEDY.
STAND UP BAR
WELL, LOOK AT THESE LOVELY FACES OUT HERE TONIGHT...
...SEATED IN A CROWD OF UGLIES WHO SHOULD HAVE STAYED HOME.
AND LOOKEE HERE!
NOT EVERY DAY YOU GET TO DO COMEDY FOR A CLOWN.
HA HA. CLOWN. NEVER HEARD THAT ONE BEFORE.
AW, HEY! LEAVE HER ALONE!
LEAVE HER ALONE?
WHAT ARE YOU, TOGETHER?
IS THIS SOME SORT OF BUTTAFACE SUPPORT GROUP OR SOMETHING?

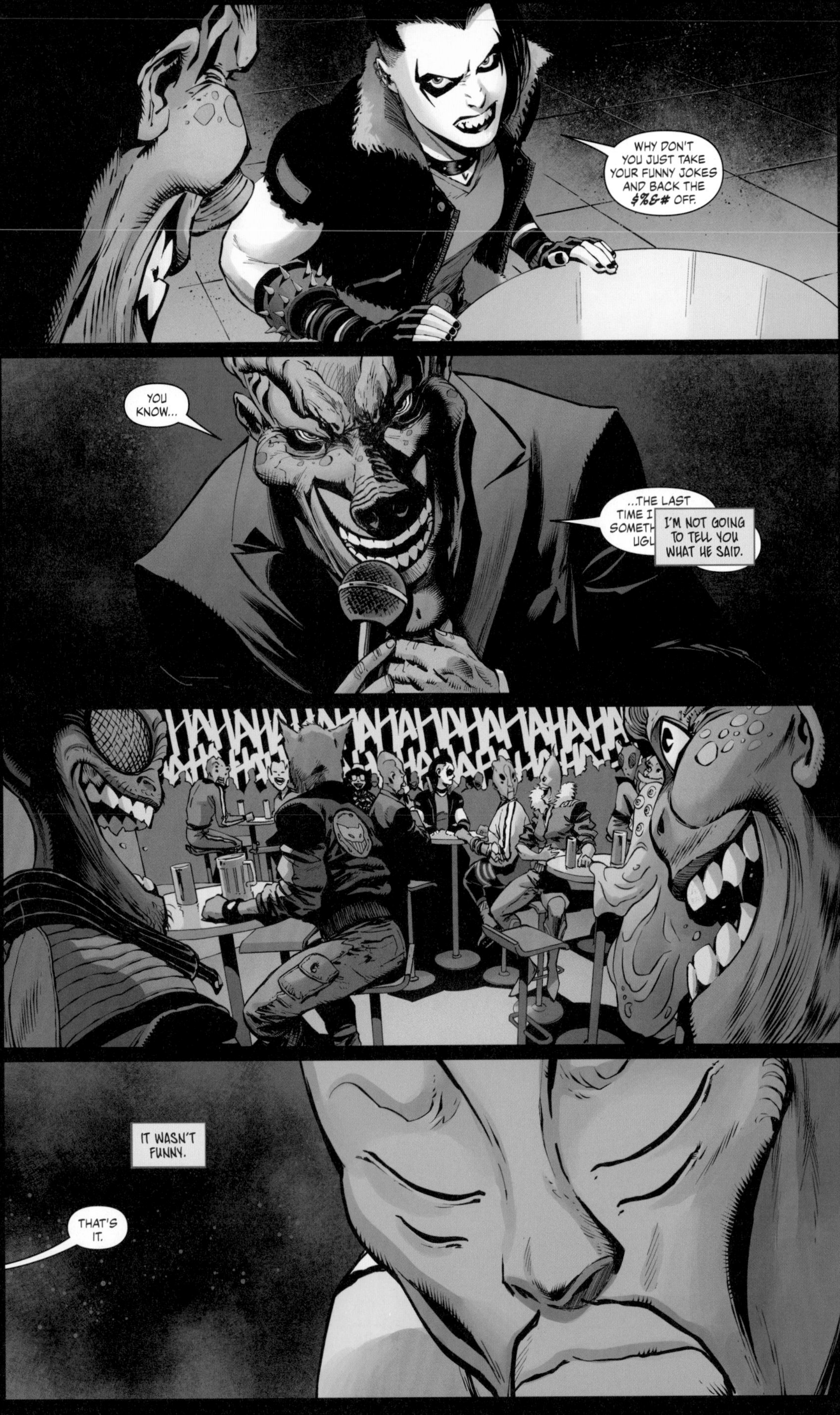
WHY DON'T YOU JUST TAKE YOUR FUNNY JOKES AND BACK THE $%&# OFF.
YOU KNOW...
...THE LAST TIME I SOMETH UGL
I'M NOT GOING TO TELL YOU WHAT HE SAID.
IT WASN'T FUNNY.
THAT'S IT.

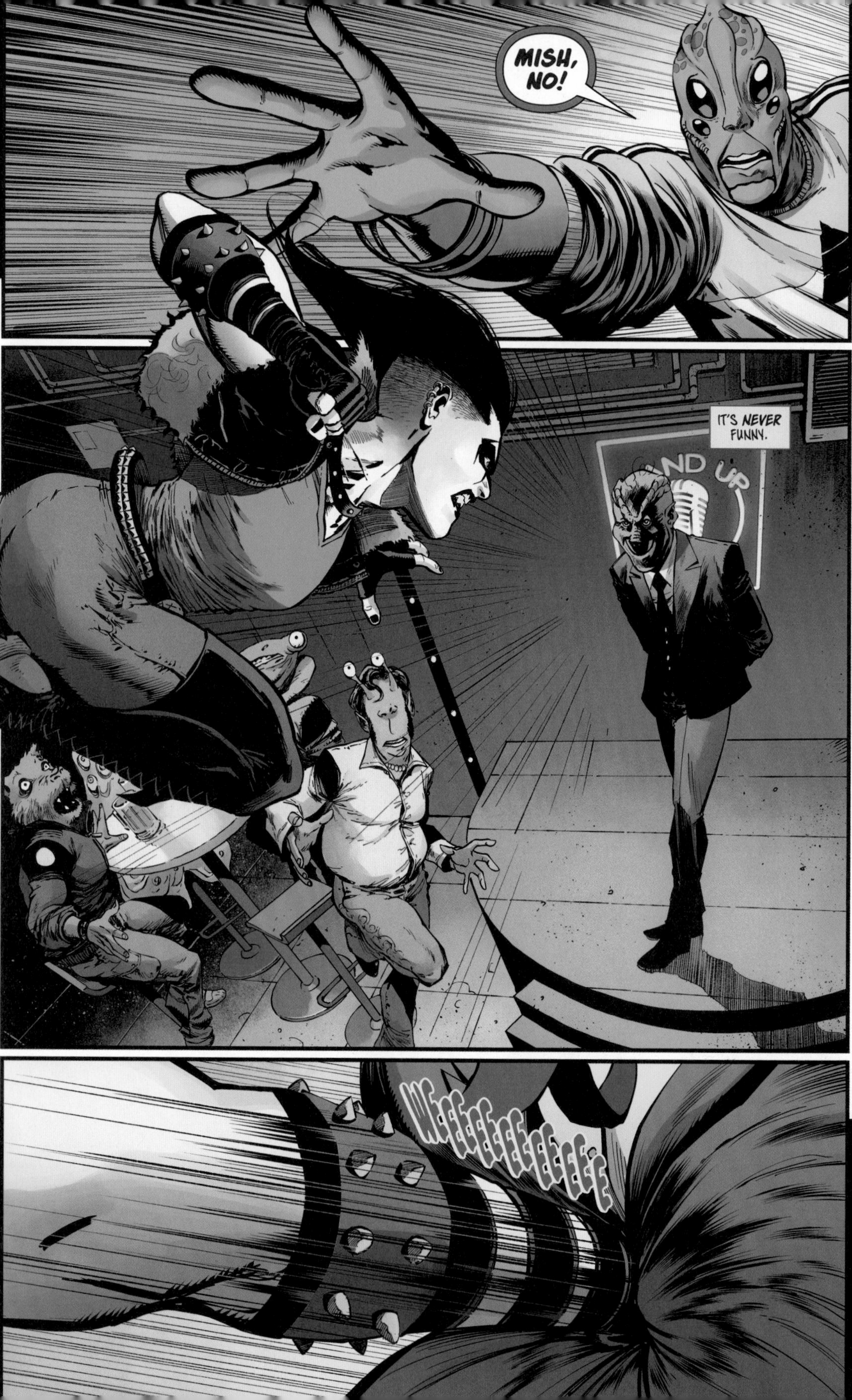
MISH, NO!
IT'S NEVER FUNNY.
WEEEEEEEEEEEEE

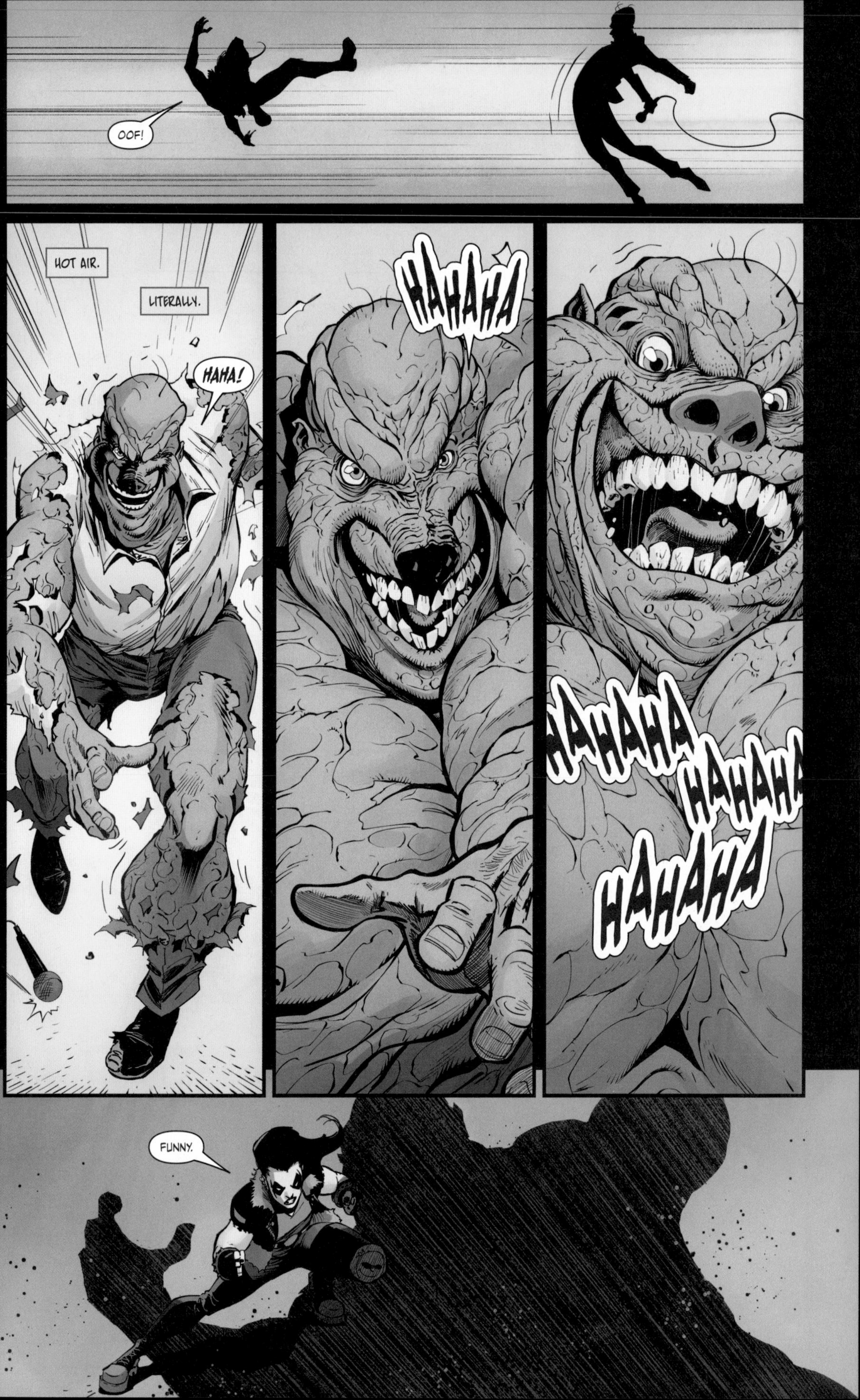
OOF!
HOT AIR.
LITERALLY.
HAHA!
HAHAHA
HAHAHA
HAHAHA
HAHAHA
FUNNY.

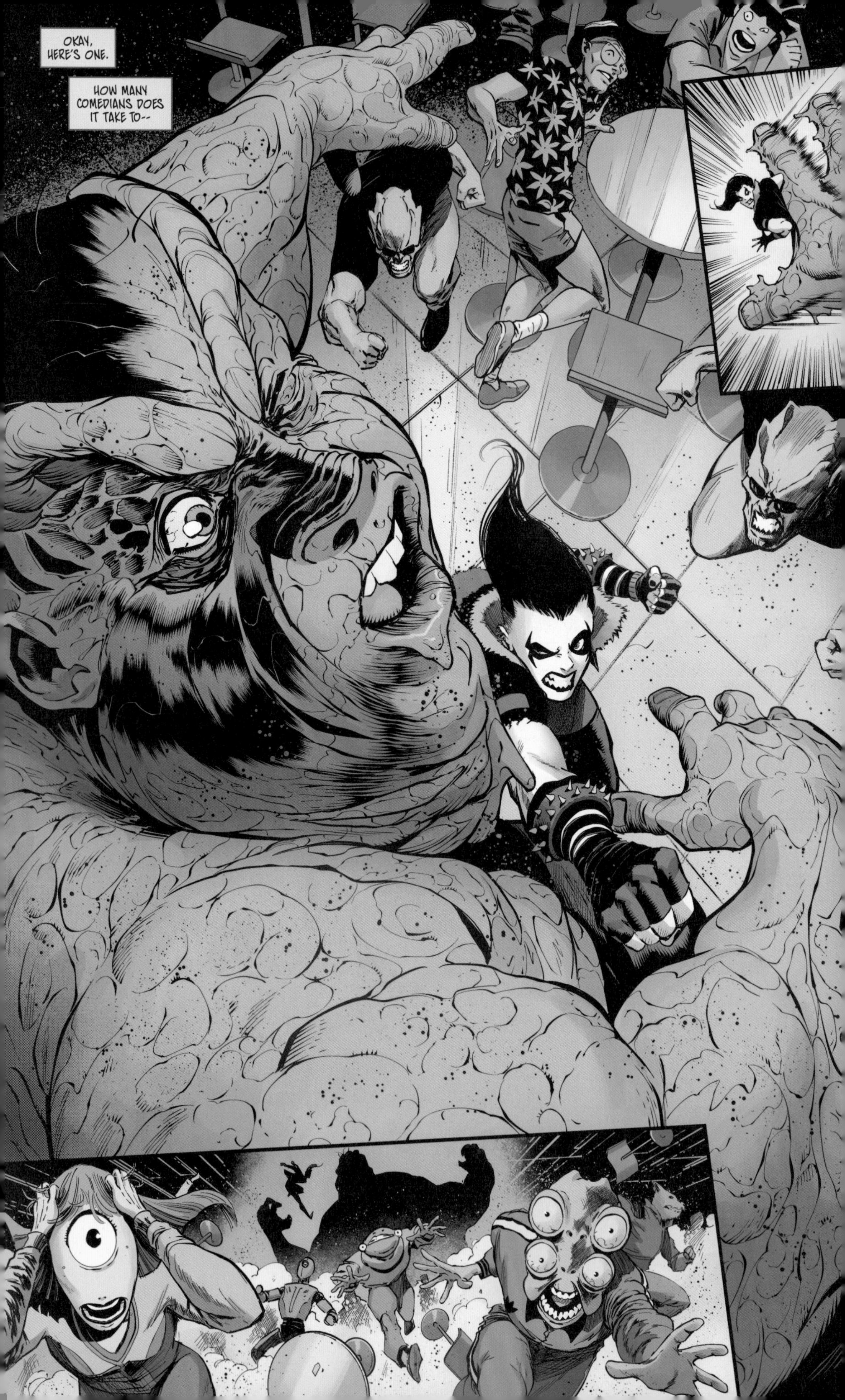
OKAY, HERE'S ONE.
HOW MANY COMEDIANS DOES IT TAKE TO--

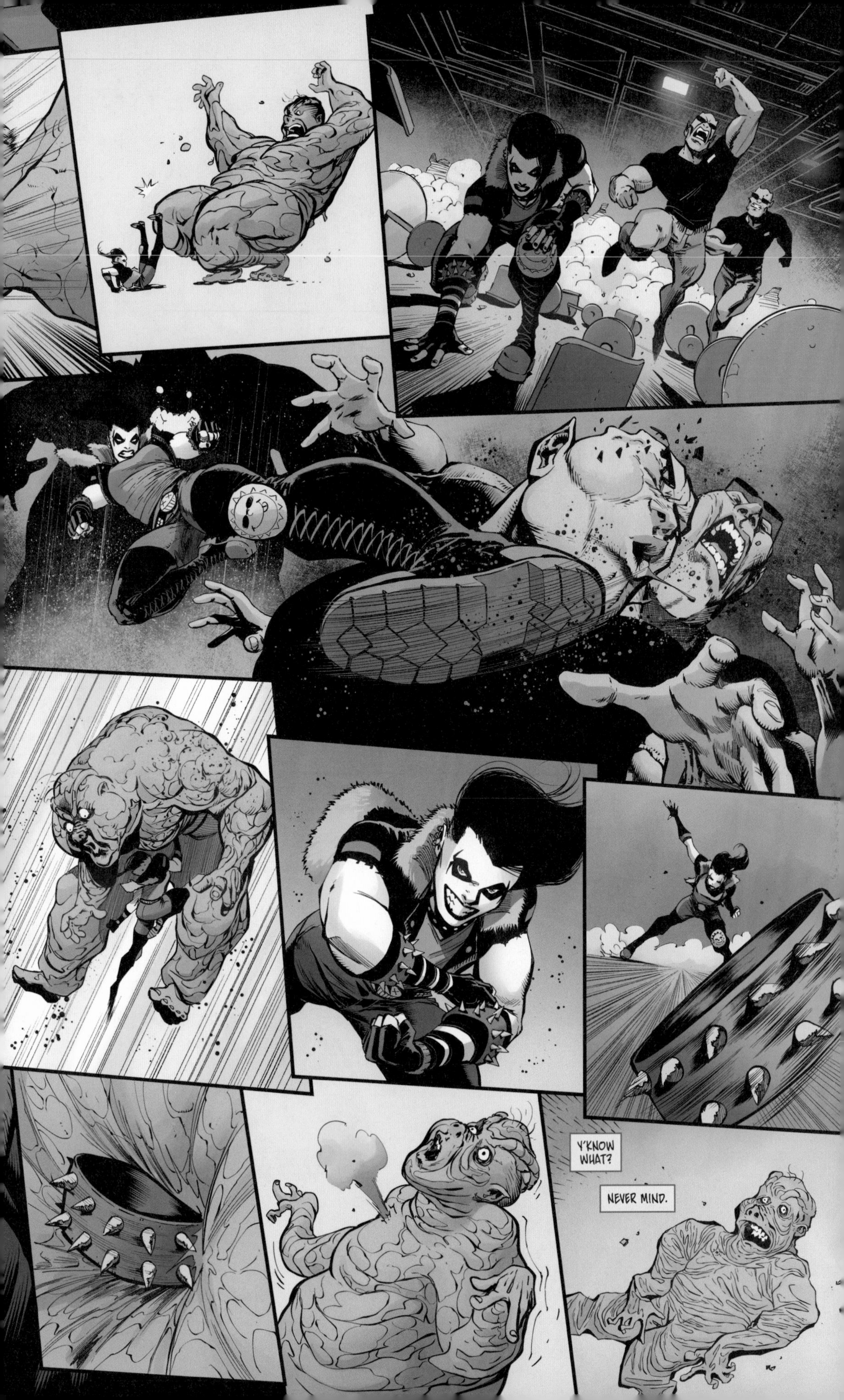
Y'KNOW WHAT?
NEVER MIND.

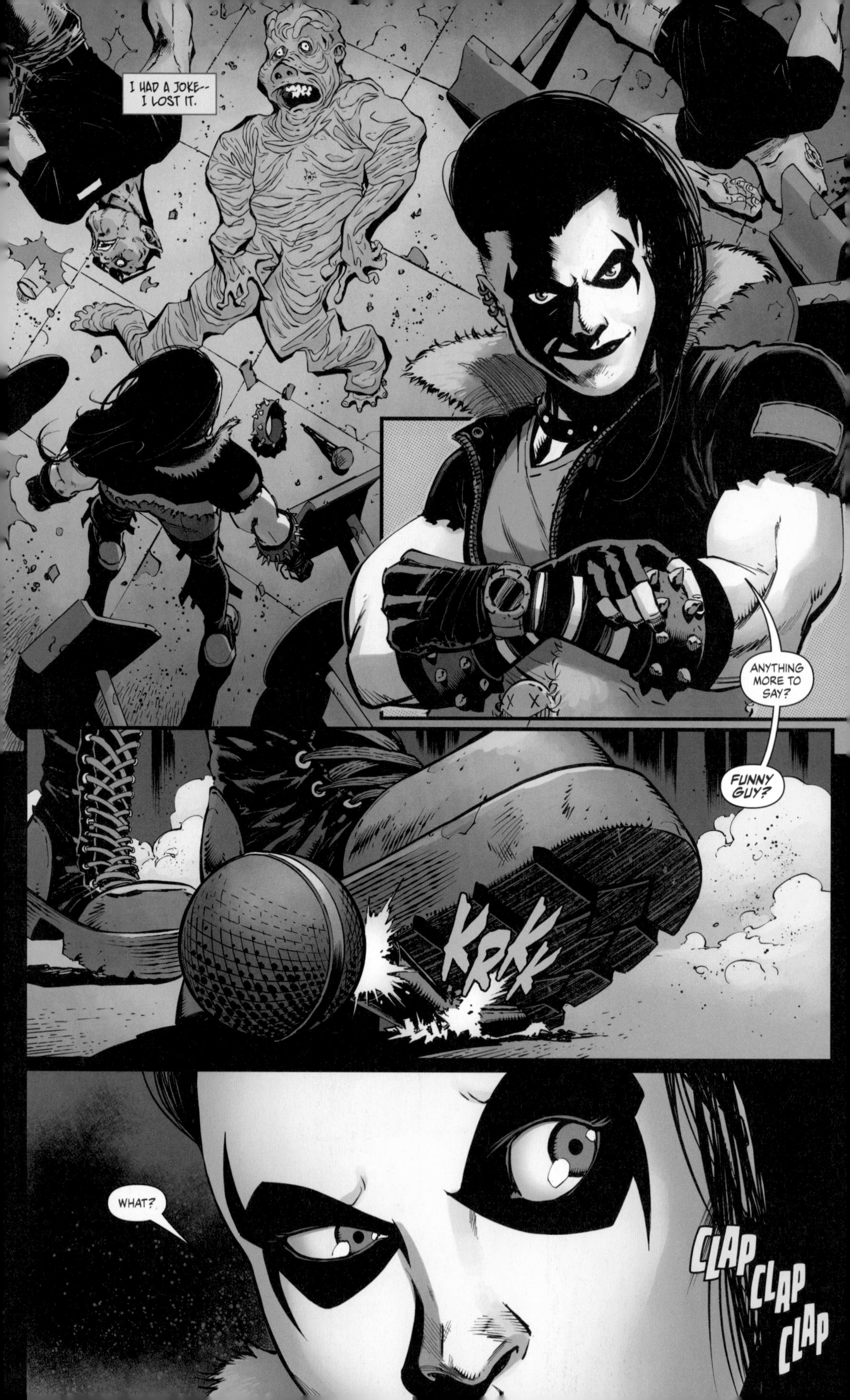
I HAD A JOKE--
I LOST IT.
ANYTHING MORE TO SAY?
FUNNY GUY?
KRKK
WHAT?
CLAP CLAP CLAP

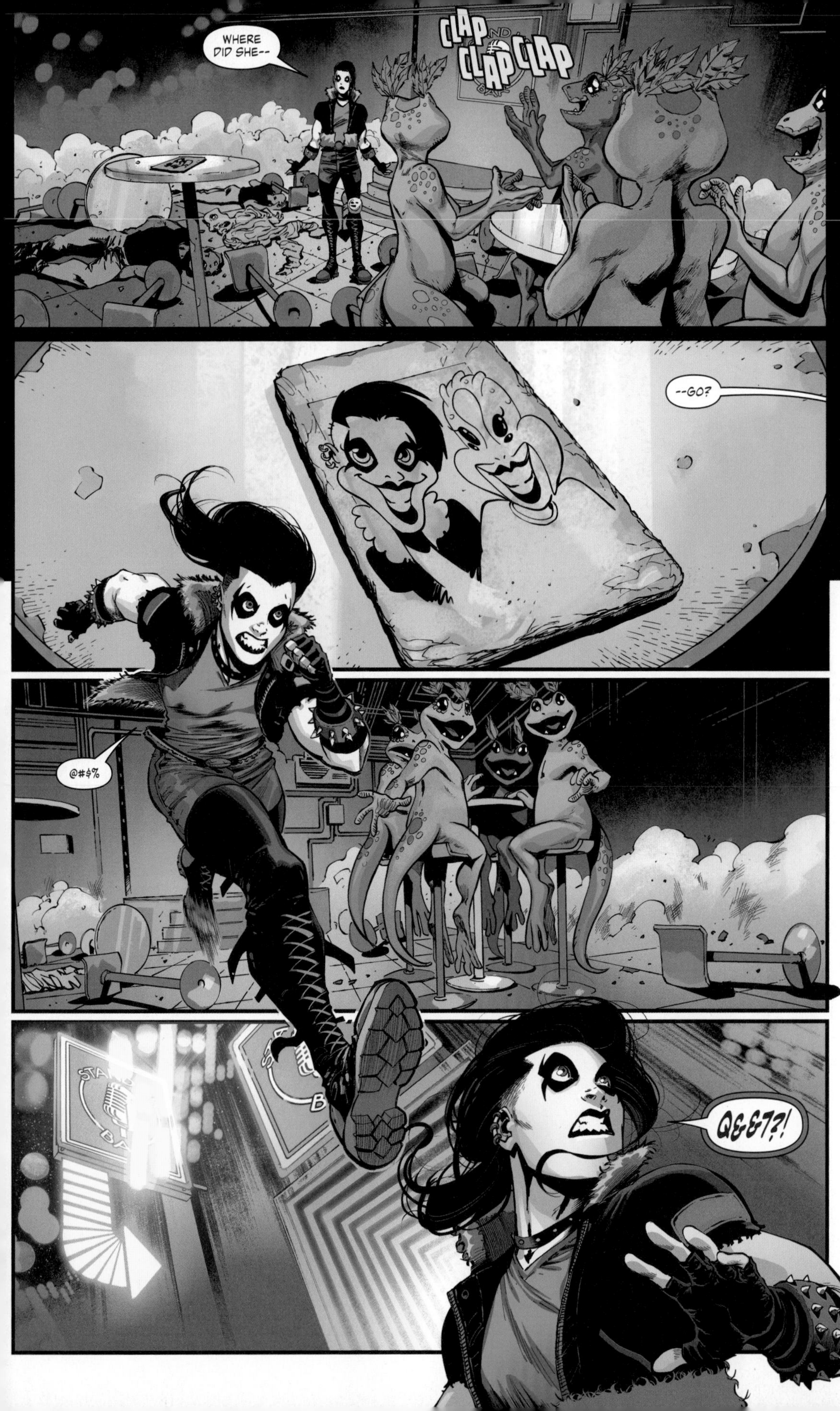
WHERE DID SHE--
CLAP CLAP CLAP
--GO?
@#$%
Q&&7?!

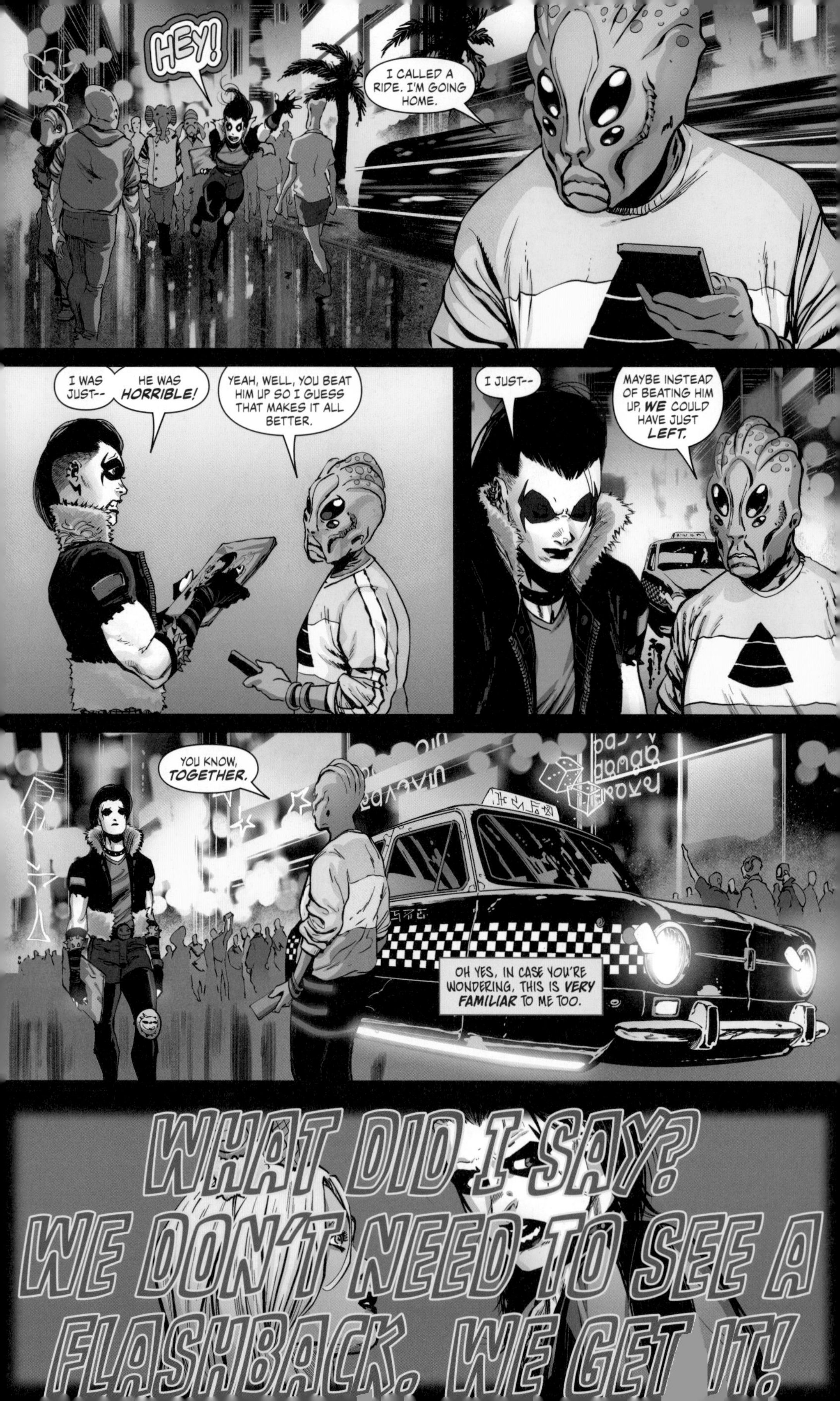
HEY!
I CALLED A RIDE. I'M GOING HOME.
I WAS JUST--
HE WAS *HORRIBLE!*
YEAH, WELL, YOU BEAT HIM UP SO I GUESS THAT MAKES IT ALL BETTER.
I JUST--
MAYBE INSTEAD OF BEATING HIM UP, *WE* COULD HAVE JUST *LEFT.*
YOU KNOW, *TOGETHER.*
OH YES, IN CASE YOU'RE WONDERING, THIS IS *VERY FAMILIAR* TO ME TOO.
WHAT DID I SAY? WE DON'T NEED TO SEE A FLASHBACK. WE GET IT!

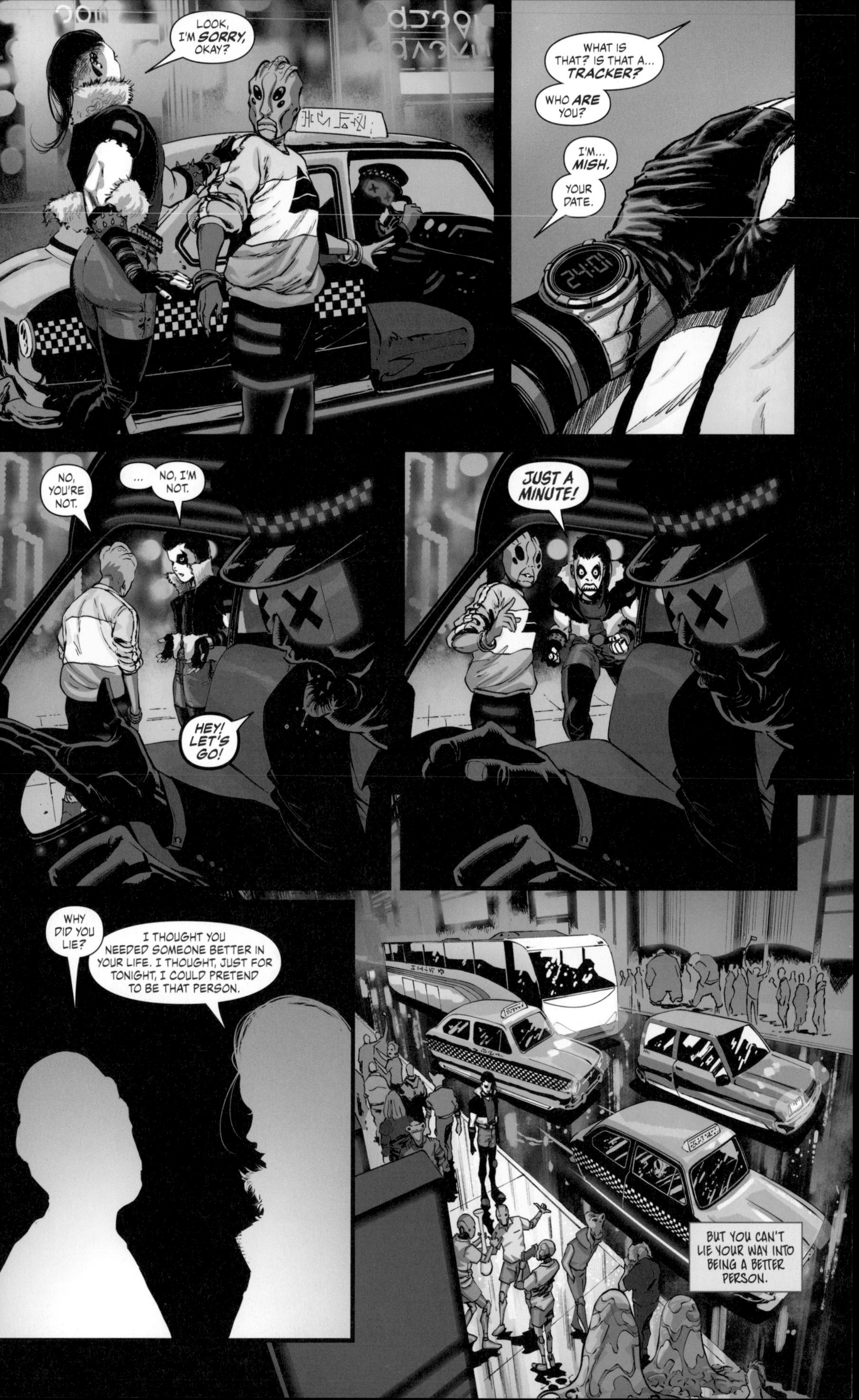
LOOK, I'M SORRY, OKAY?
WHAT IS THAT? IS THAT A... TRACKER?
WHO ARE YOU?
I'M... MISH.
YOUR DATE.
NO, YOU'RE NOT.
... NO, I'M NOT.
HEY! LET'S GO!
JUST A MINUTE!
WHY DID YOU LIE?
I THOUGHT YOU NEEDED SOMEONE BETTER IN YOUR LIFE. I THOUGHT, JUST FOR TONIGHT, I COULD PRETEND TO BE THAT PERSON.
BUT YOU CAN'T LIE YOUR WAY INTO BEING A BETTER PERSON.

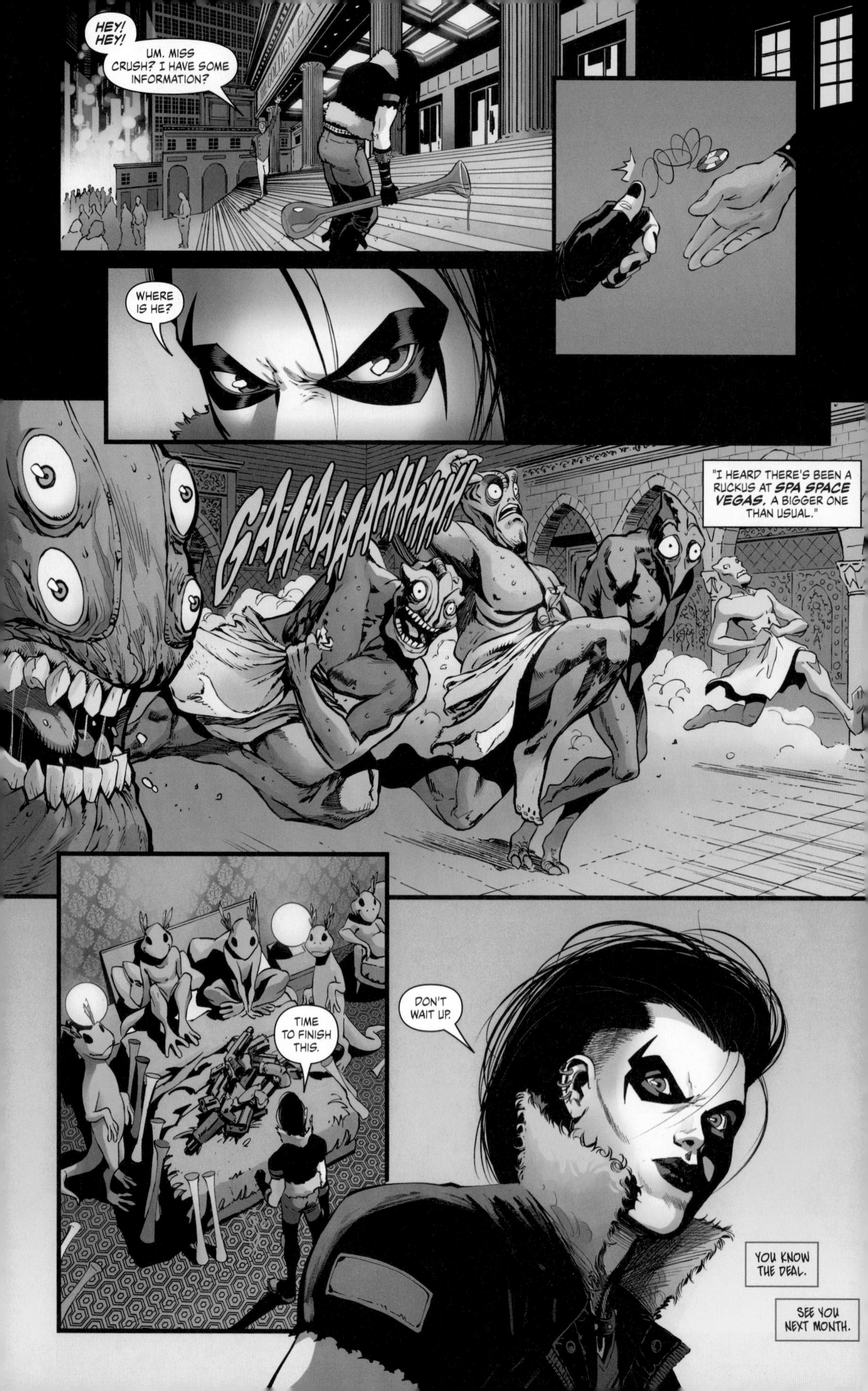
HEY! HEY!
UM. MISS CRUSH? I HAVE SOME INFORMATION?
WHERE IS HE?
"I HEARD THERE'S BEEN A RUCKUS AT SPA SPACE VEGAS. A BIGGER ONE THAN USUAL."
GAAAAAAHHHHH
TIME TO FINISH THIS.
DON'T WAIT UP.
YOU KNOW THE DEAL.
SEE YOU NEXT MONTH.

CRUSH & LOBO #7 COVER BY W. SCOTT FORBES

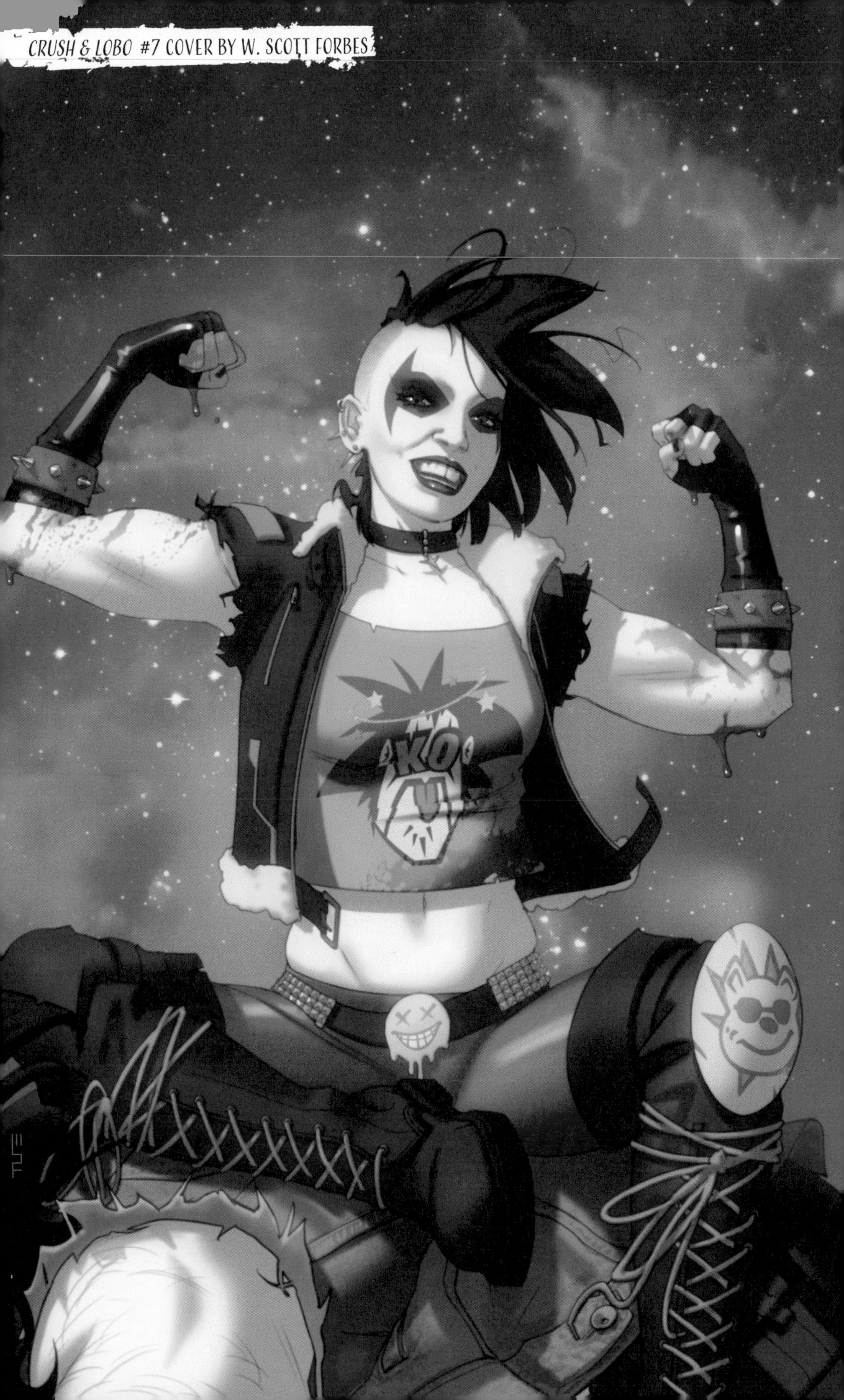
KO

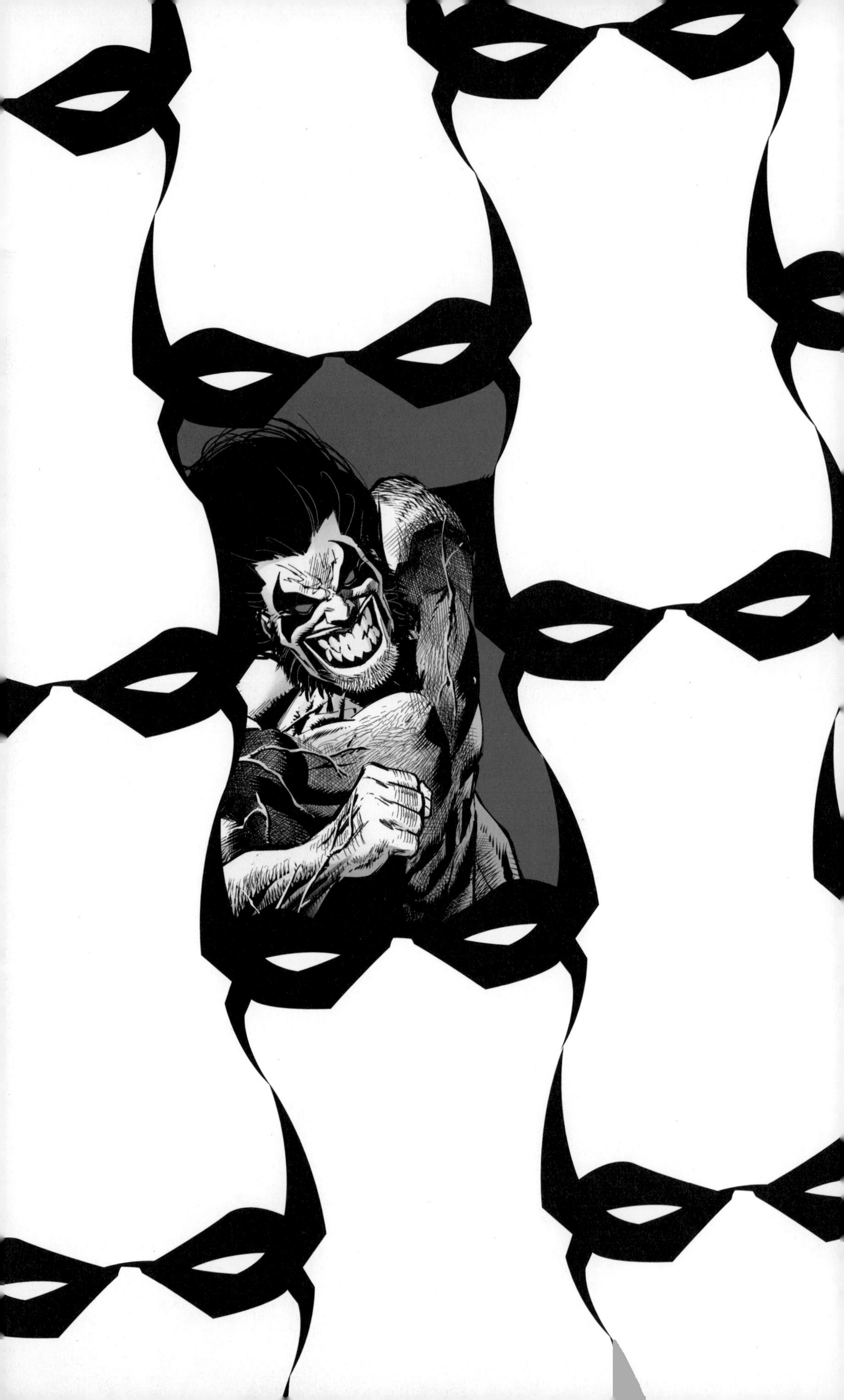

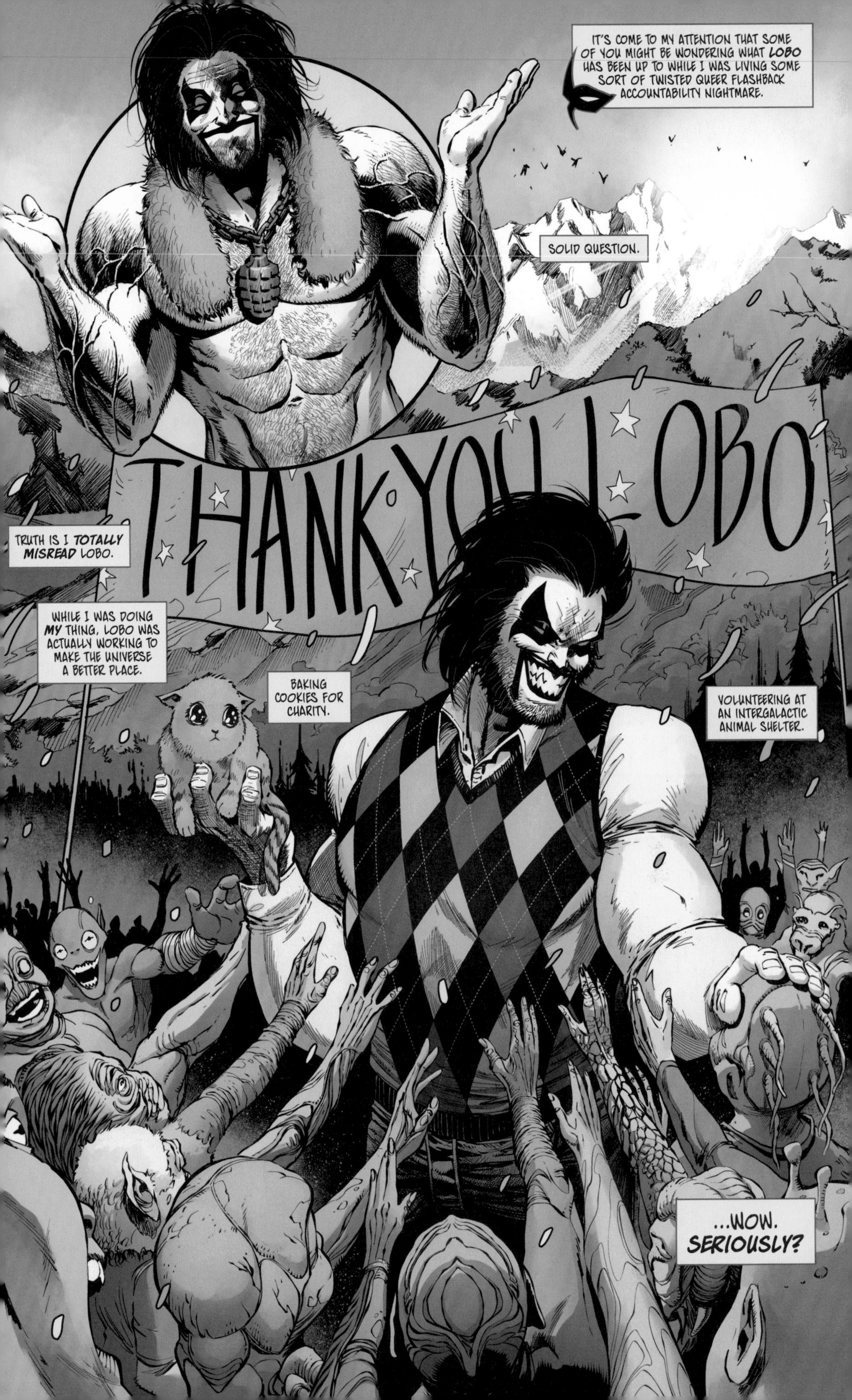
IT'S COME TO MY ATTENTION THAT SOME OF YOU MIGHT BE WONDERING WHAT LOBO HAS BEEN UP TO WHILE I WAS LIVING SOME SORT OF TWISTED QUEER FLASHBACK ACCOUNTABILITY NIGHTMARE.
SOLID QUESTION.
THANK YOU LOBO
TRUTH IS I TOTALLY MISREAD LOBO.
WHILE I WAS DOING MY THING, LOBO WAS ACTUALLY WORKING TO MAKE THE UNIVERSE A BETTER PLACE.
BAKING COOKIES FOR CHARITY.
VOLUNTEERING AT AN INTERGALACTIC ANIMAL SHELTER.
...WOW. SERIOUSLY?

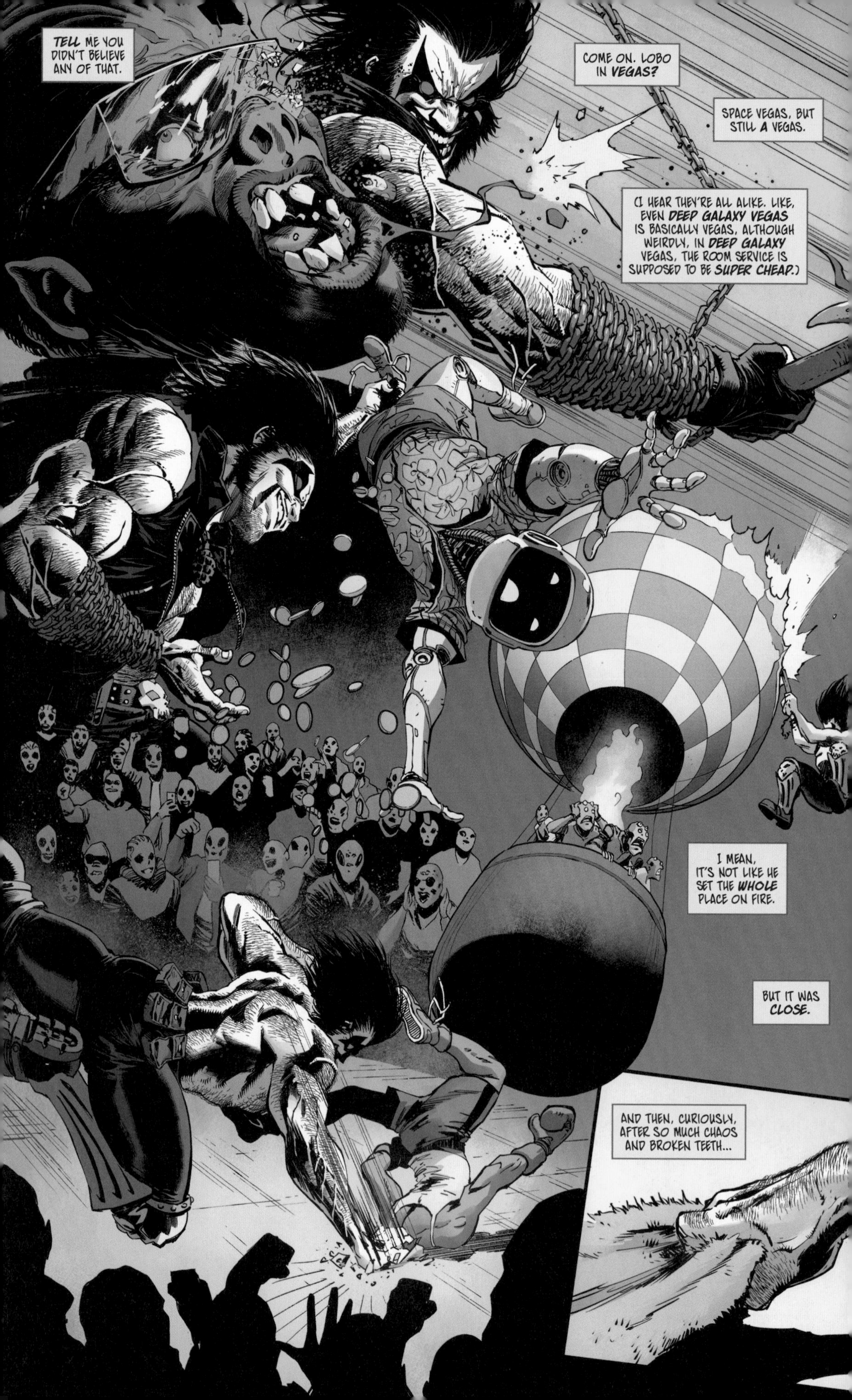

TELL ME YOU DIDN'T BELIEVE ANY OF THAT.
COME ON. LOBO IN VEGAS?
SPACE VEGAS, BUT STILL A VEGAS.
(I HEAR THEY'RE ALL ALIKE. LIKE, EVEN DEEP GALAXY VEGAS IS BASICALLY VEGAS, ALTHOUGH WEIRDLY, IN DEEP GALAXY VEGAS, THE ROOM SERVICE IS SUPPOSED TO BE SUPER CHEAP.)
I MEAN, IT'S NOT LIKE HE SET THE WHOLE PLACE ON FIRE.
BUT IT WAS CLOSE.
AND THEN, CURIOUSLY, AFTER SO MUCH CHAOS AND BROKEN TEETH...

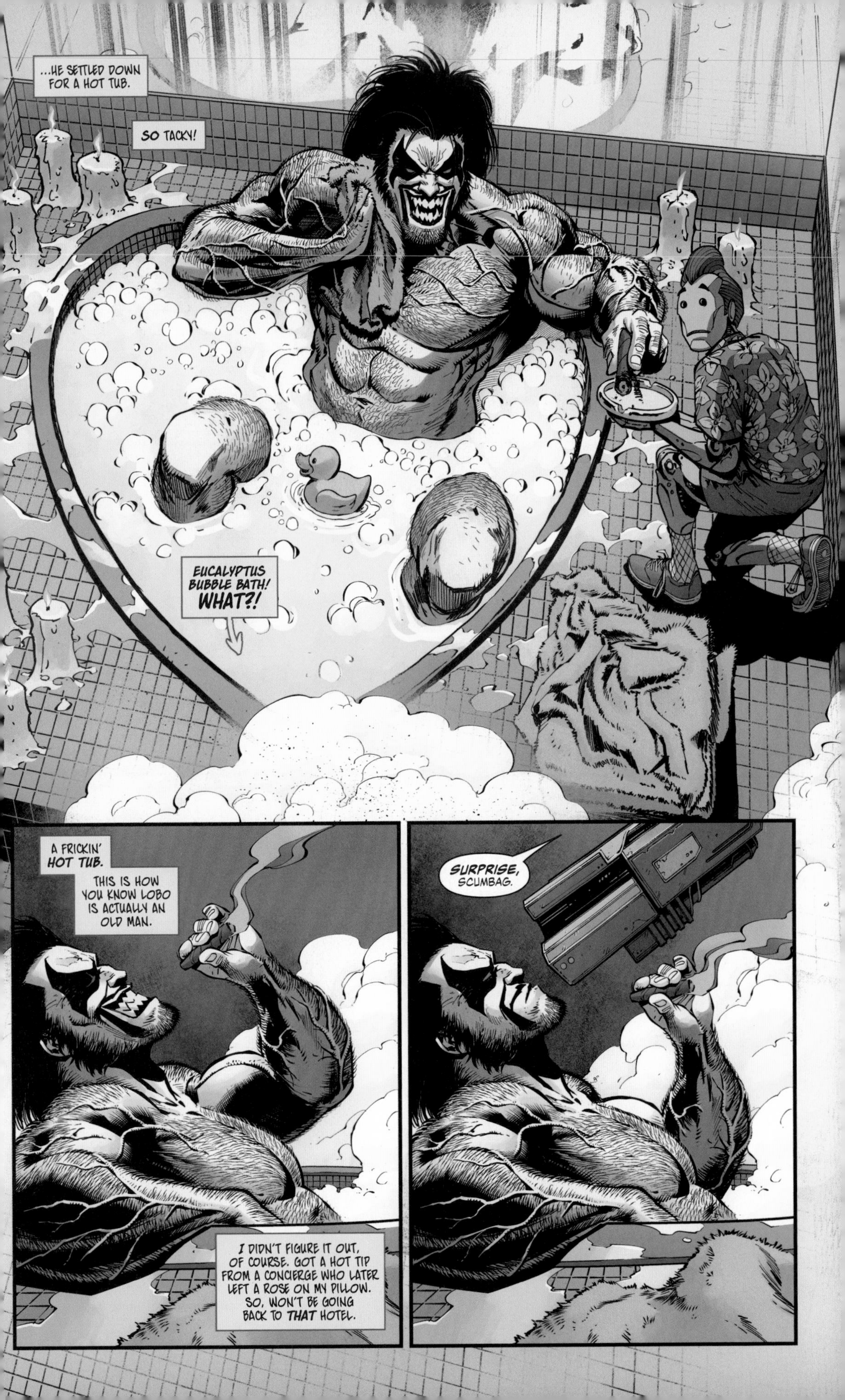
...HE SETTLED DOWN FOR A HOT TUB.
SO TACKY!
EUCALYPTUS BUBBLE BATH! WHAT?!
A FRICKIN' HOT TUB.
THIS IS HOW YOU KNOW LOBO IS ACTUALLY AN OLD MAN.
I DIDN'T FIGURE IT OUT, OF COURSE. GOT A HOT TIP FROM A CONCIERGE WHO LATER LEFT A ROSE ON MY PILLOW. SO, WON'T BE GOING BACK TO THAT HOTEL.
SURPRISE, SCUMBAG.

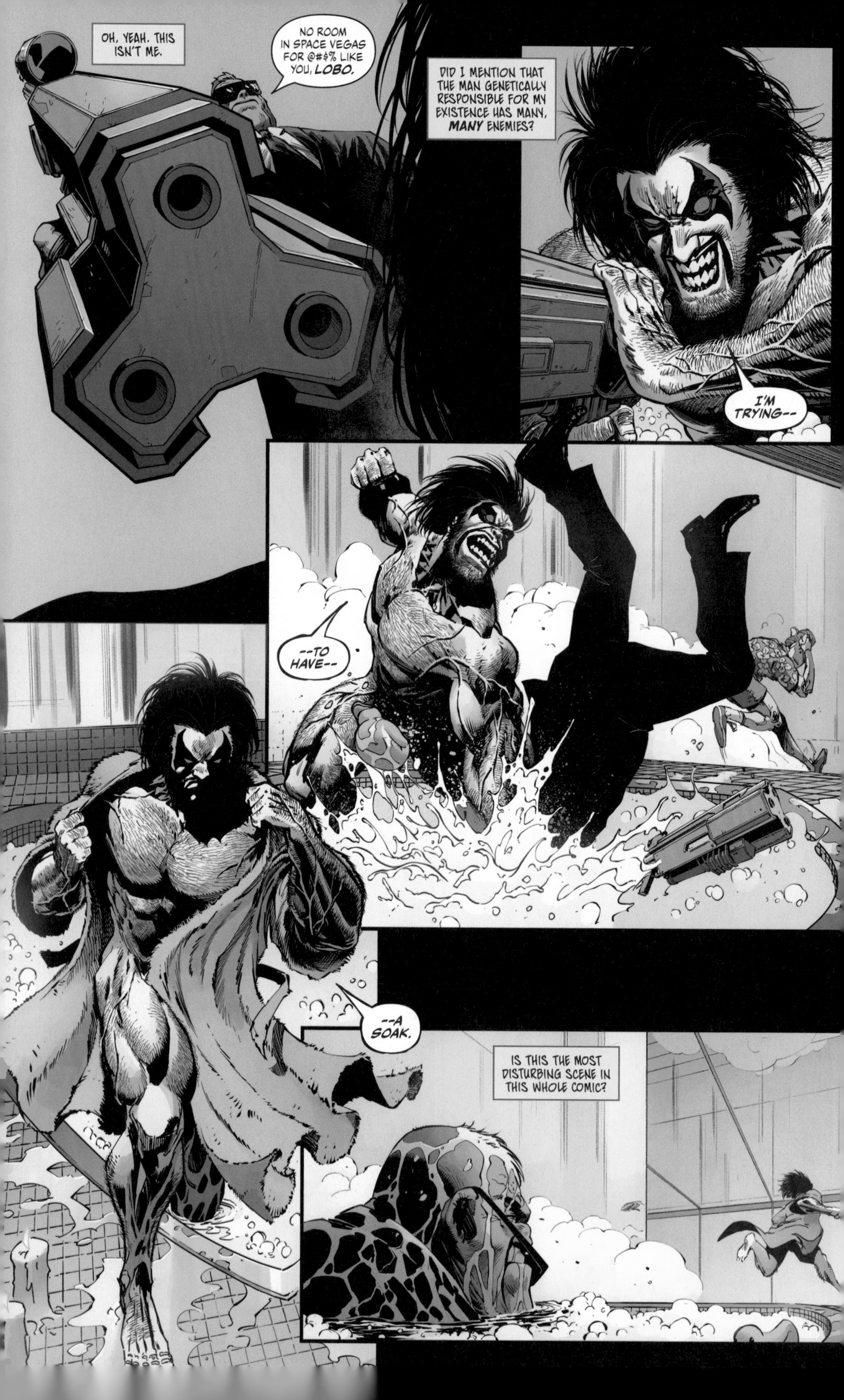
OH, YEAH. THIS ISN'T ME.
NO ROOM IN SPACE VEGAS FOR @#$% LIKE YOU, LOBO.
DID I MENTION THAT THE MAN GENETICALLY RESPONSIBLE FOR MY EXISTENCE HAS MANY, MANY ENEMIES?
I'M TRYING--
--TO HAVE--
--A SOAK.
IS THIS THE MOST DISTURBING SCENE IN THIS WHOLE COMIC?

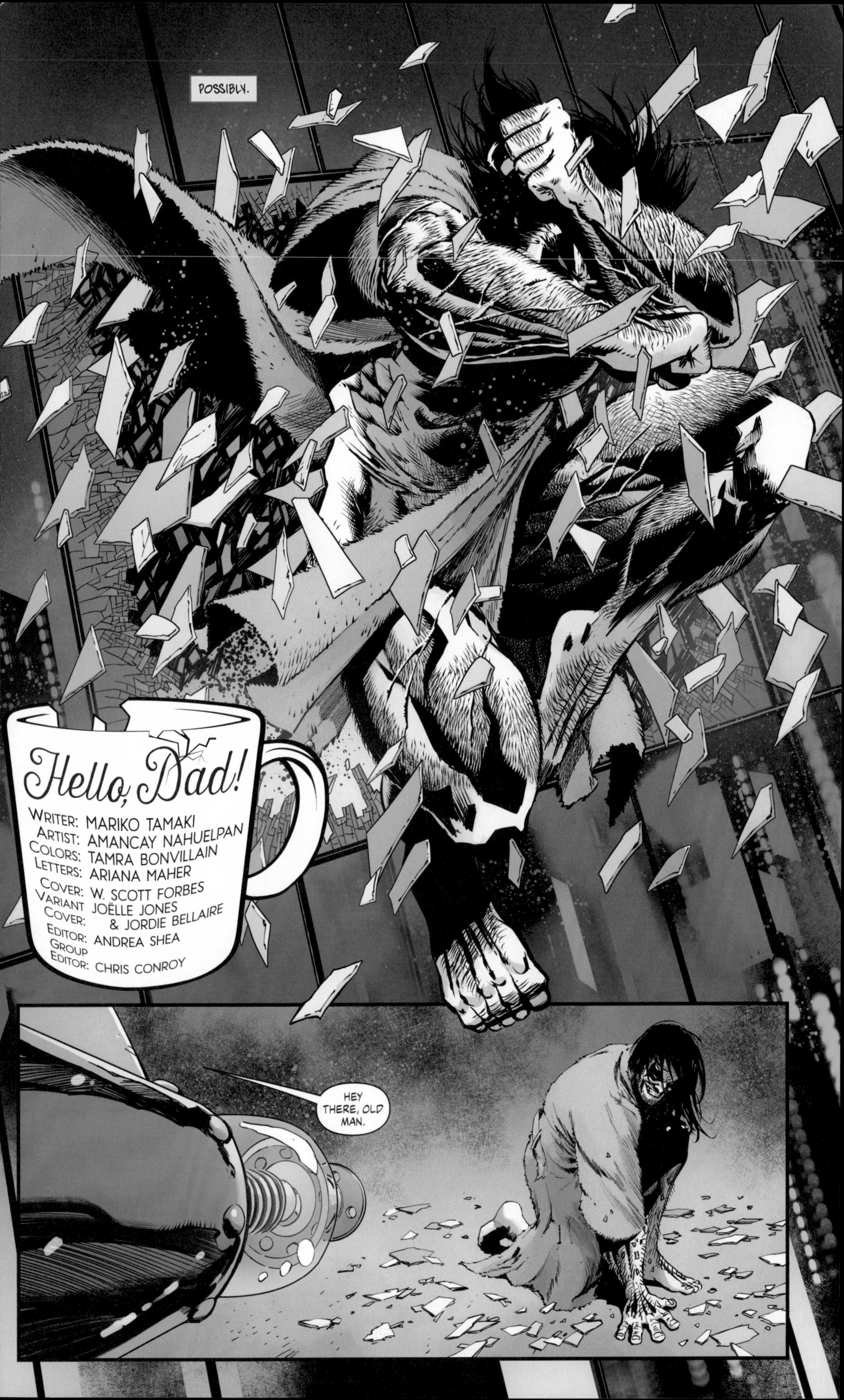
POSSIBLY.
Hello, Dad!
WRITER: MARIKO TAMAKI
ARTIST: AMANCAY NAHUELPAN
COLORS: TAMRA BONVILLAIN
LETTERS: ARIANA MAHER
COVER: W. SCOTT FORBES
VARIANT COVER: JOËLLE JONES & JORDIE BELLAIRE
EDITOR: ANDREA SHEA
GROUP EDITOR: CHRIS CONROY
HEY THERE, OLD MAN.

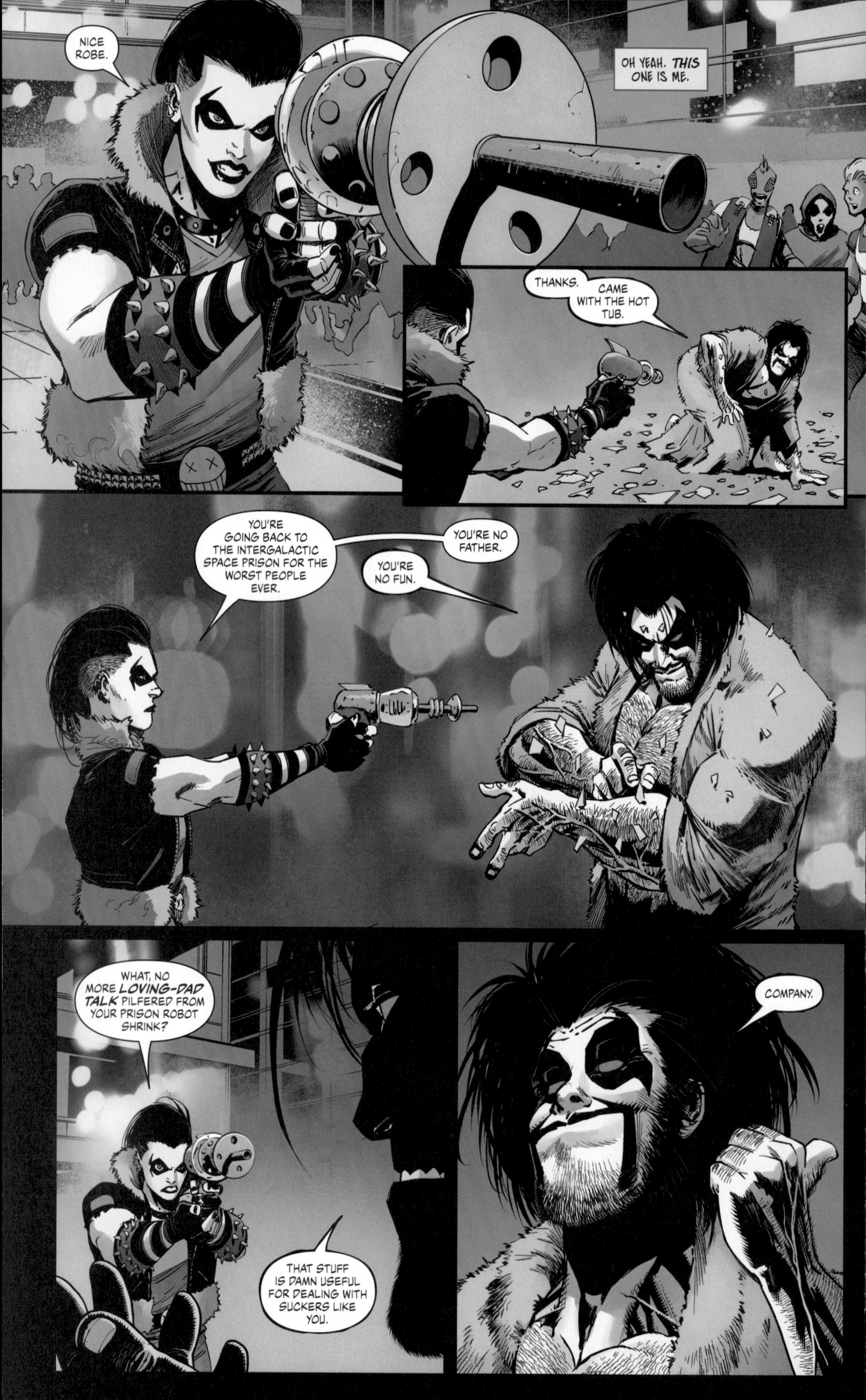
NICE ROBE.
OH YEAH. THIS ONE IS ME.
THANKS.
CAME WITH THE HOT TUB.
YOU'RE GOING BACK TO THE INTERGALACTIC SPACE PRISON FOR THE WORST PEOPLE EVER.
YOU'RE NO FATHER.
YOU'RE NO FUN.
WHAT, NO MORE LOVING-DAD TALK PILFERED FROM YOUR PRISON ROBOT SHRINK?
THAT STUFF IS DAMN USEFUL FOR DEALING WITH SUCKERS LIKE YOU.
COMPANY.

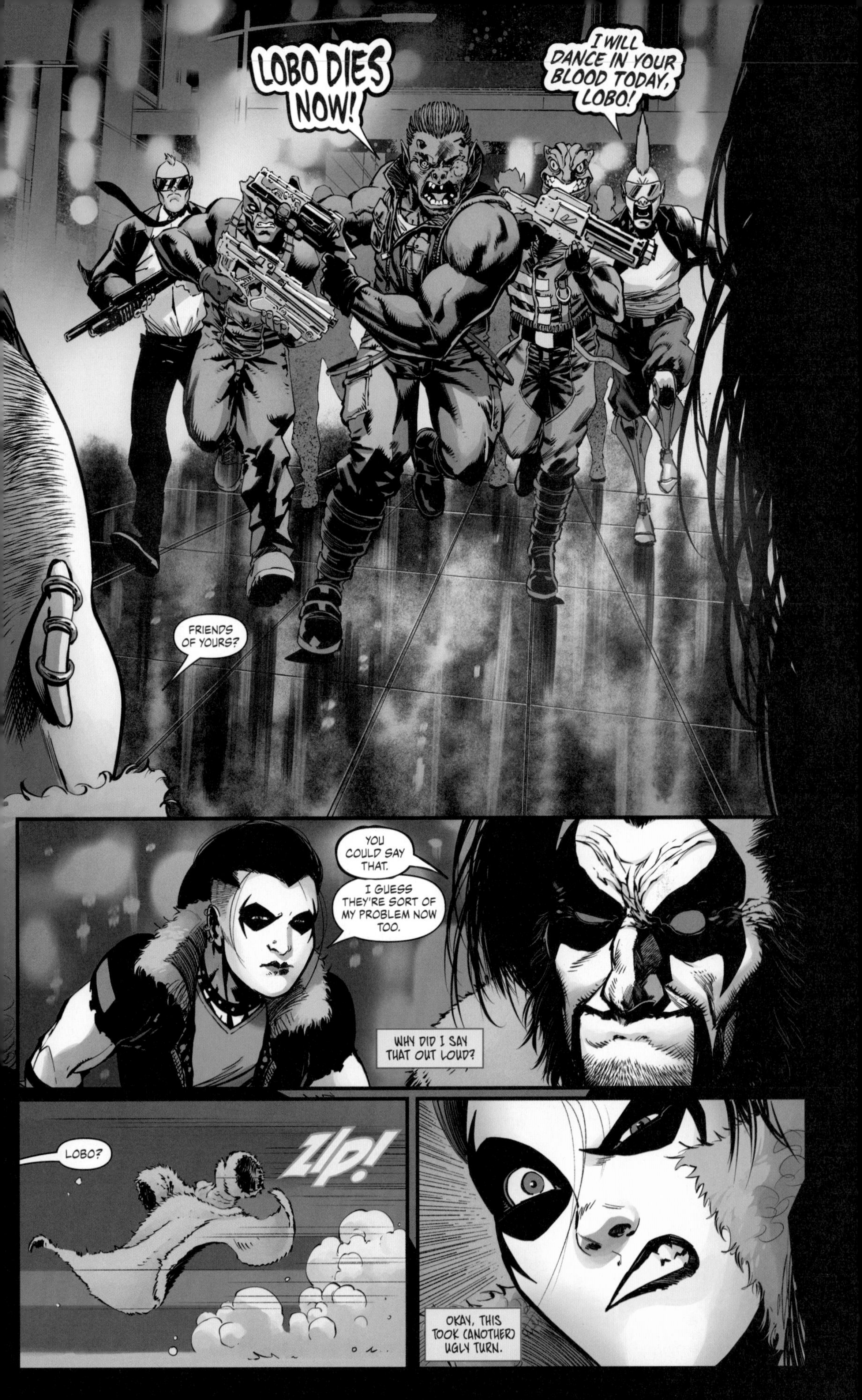
LOBO DIES NOW!
I WILL DANCE IN YOUR BLOOD TODAY, LOBO!
FRIENDS OF YOURS?
YOU COULD SAY THAT.
I GUESS THEY'RE SORT OF MY PROBLEM NOW TOO.
WHY DID I SAY THAT OUT LOUD?
LOBO?
ZIP!
OKAY, THIS TOOK (ANOTHER) UGLY TURN.

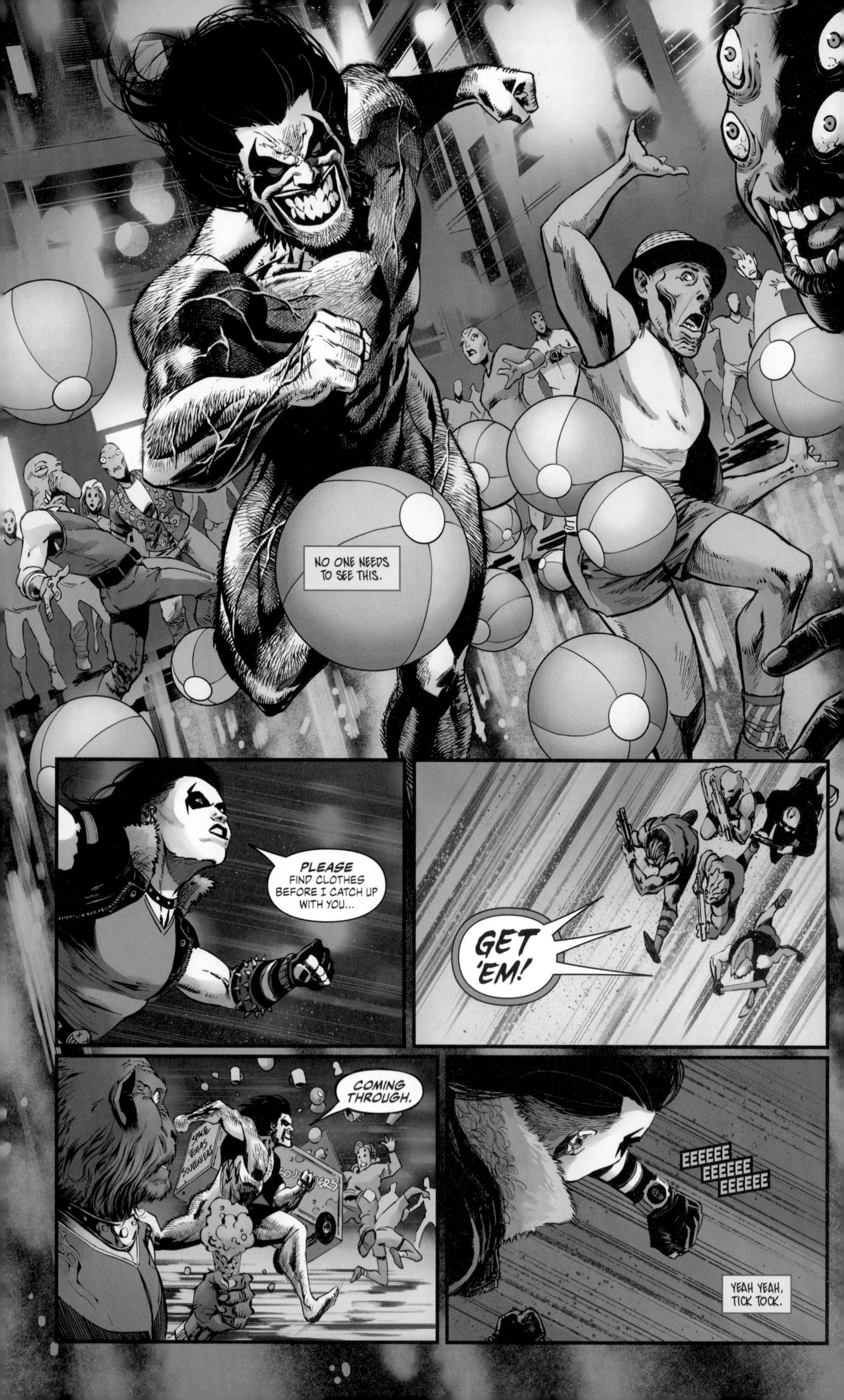

NO ONE NEEDS TO SEE THIS.
PLEASE FIND CLOTHES BEFORE I CATCH UP WITH YOU...
GET 'EM!
COMING THROUGH.
SPACE VEGAS SOUVENIRS
EEEEEE EEEEEE EEEEEE
YEAH YEAH, TICK TOCK.

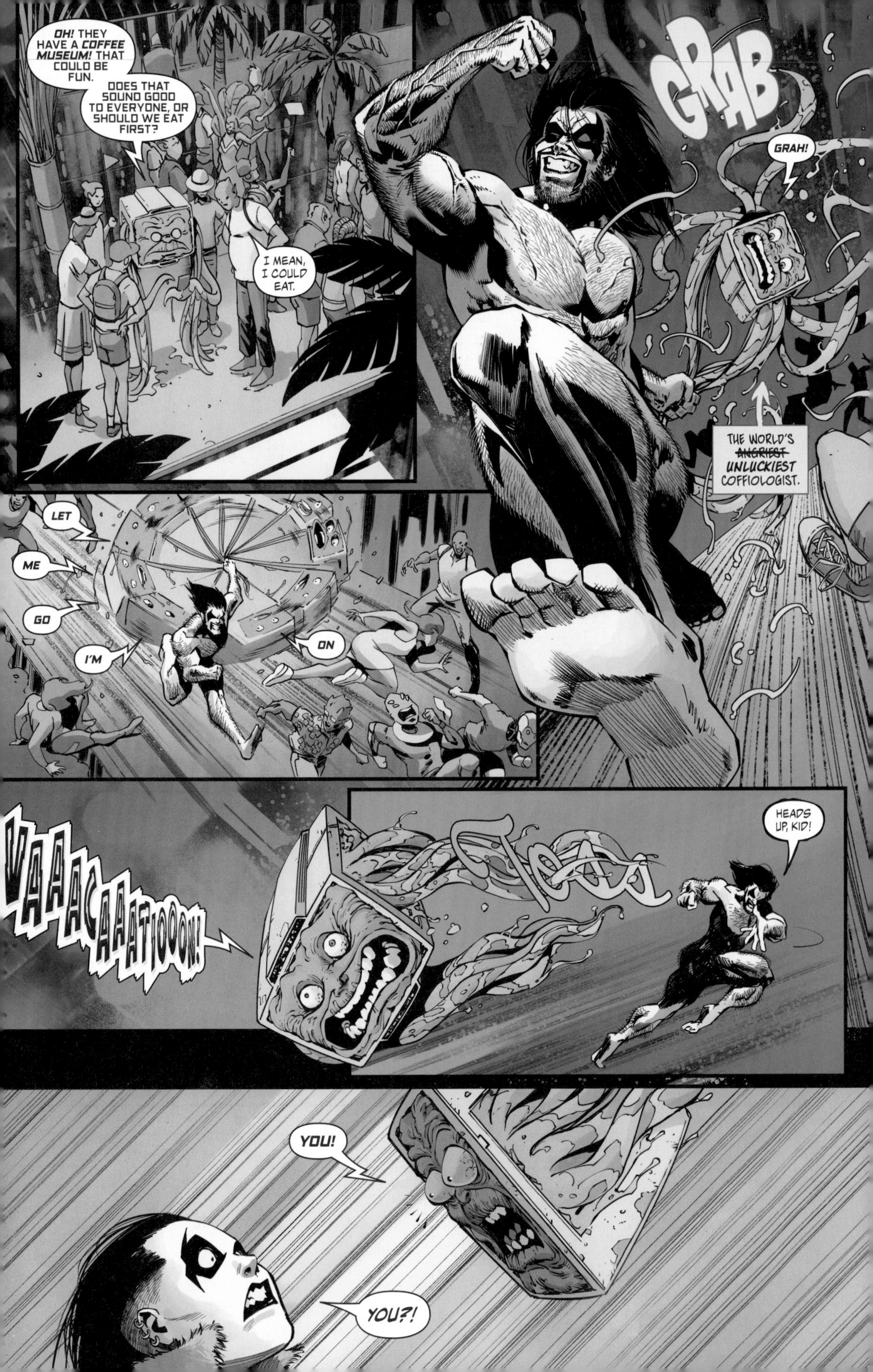
OH! THEY HAVE A COFFEE MUSEUM! THAT COULD BE FUN.
DOES THAT SOUND GOOD TO EVERYONE, OR SHOULD WE EAT FIRST?
I MEAN, I COULD EAT.
GRAB
GRAH!
THE WORLD'S ~~ANGRIEST~~ UNLUCKIEST COFFIOLOGIST.
LET
ME
GO
I'M
ON
VAAACAAATIOOON!
HEADS UP, KID!
YOU!
YOU?!

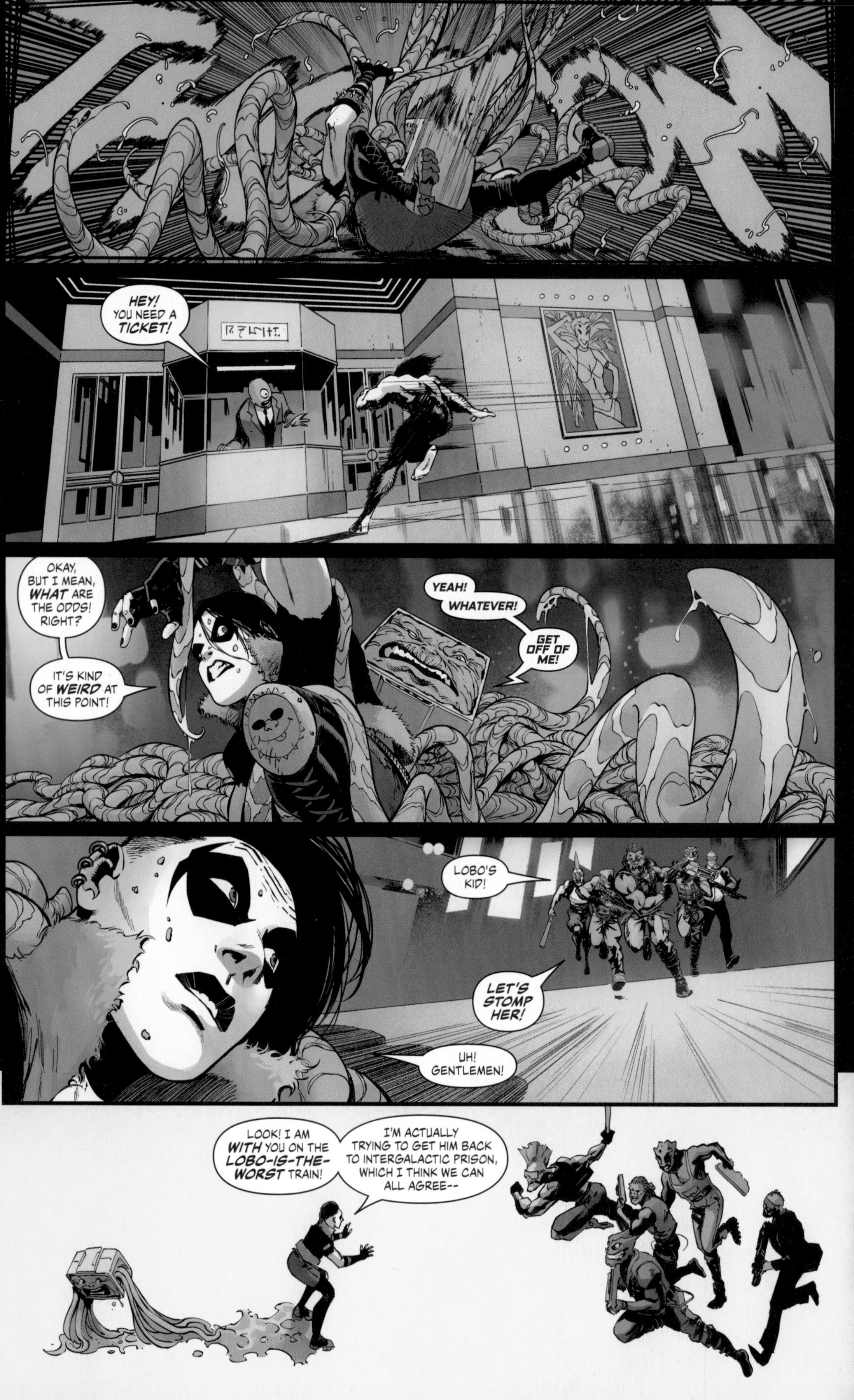

HEY! YOU NEED A TICKET!
OKAY, BUT I MEAN, WHAT ARE THE ODDS! RIGHT?
IT'S KIND OF WEIRD AT THIS POINT!
YEAH! WHATEVER!
GET OFF OF ME!
LOBO'S KID!
LET'S STOMP HER!
UH! GENTLEMEN!
LOOK! I AM WITH YOU ON THE LOBO-IS-THE-WORST TRAIN!
I'M ACTUALLY TRYING TO GET HIM BACK TO INTERGALACTIC PRISON, WHICH I THINK WE CAN ALL AGREE--

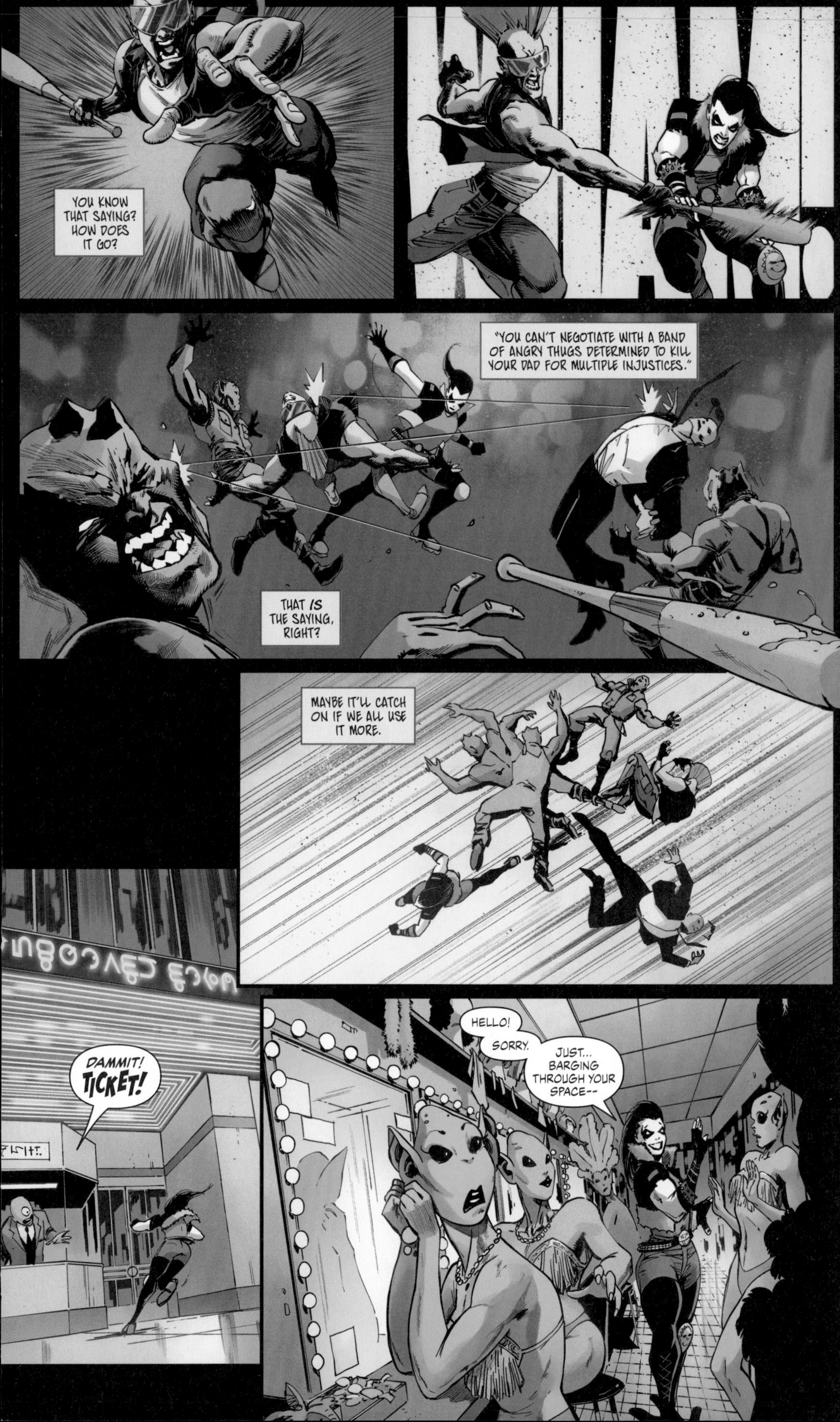
YOU KNOW THAT SAYING? HOW DOES IT GO?
"YOU CAN'T NEGOTIATE WITH A BAND OF ANGRY THUGS DETERMINED TO KILL YOUR DAD FOR MULTIPLE INJUSTICES."
THAT IS THE SAYING, RIGHT?
MAYBE IT'LL CATCH ON IF WE ALL USE IT MORE.
DAMMIT! TICKET!
HELLO!
SORRY.
JUST... BARGING THROUGH YOUR SPACE--

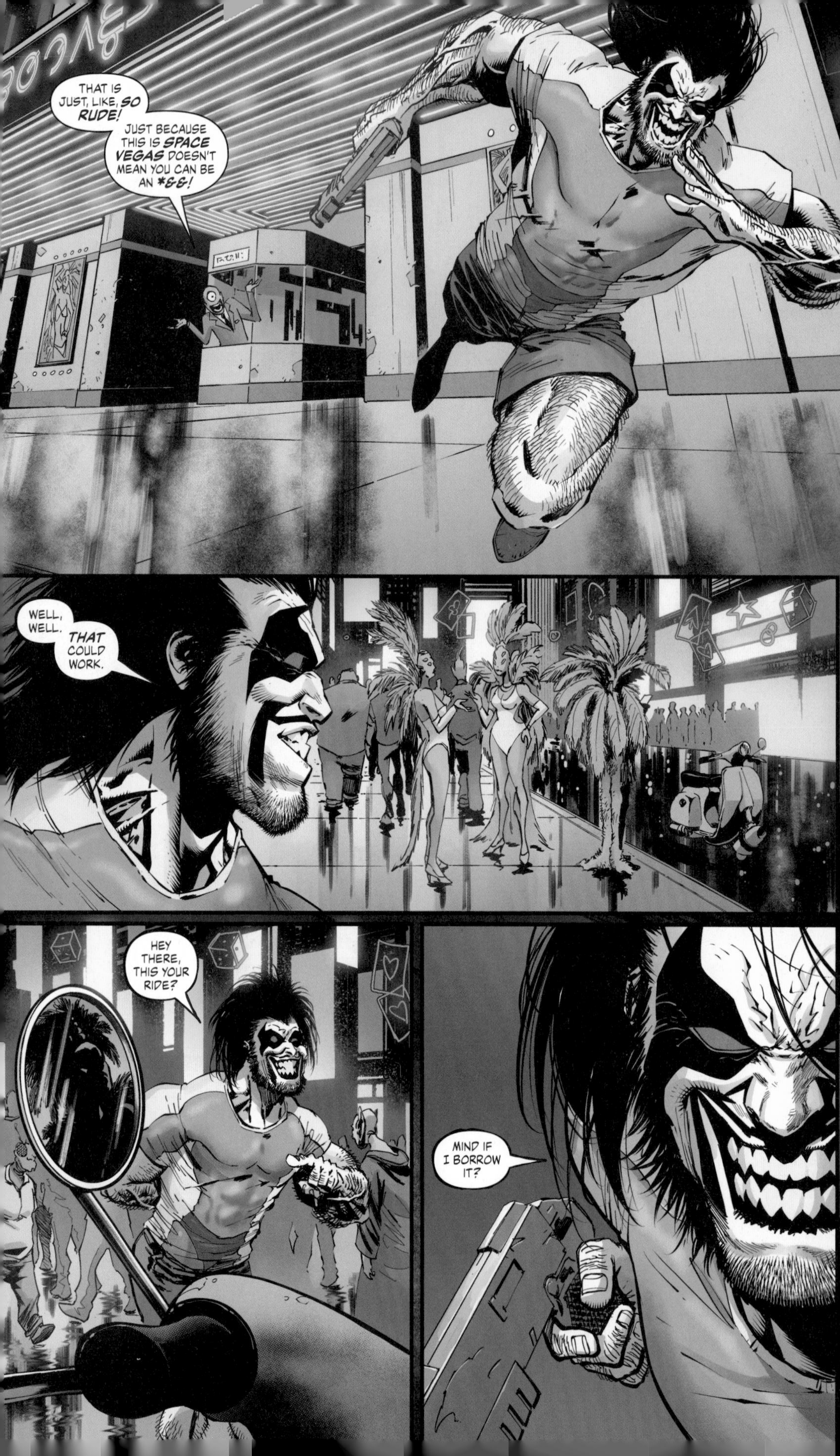
THAT IS JUST, LIKE, SO RUDE!
JUST BECAUSE THIS IS SPACE VEGAS DOESN'T MEAN YOU CAN BE AN *&&!
WELL, WELL. THAT COULD WORK.
HEY THERE, THIS YOUR RIDE?
MIND IF I BORROW IT?

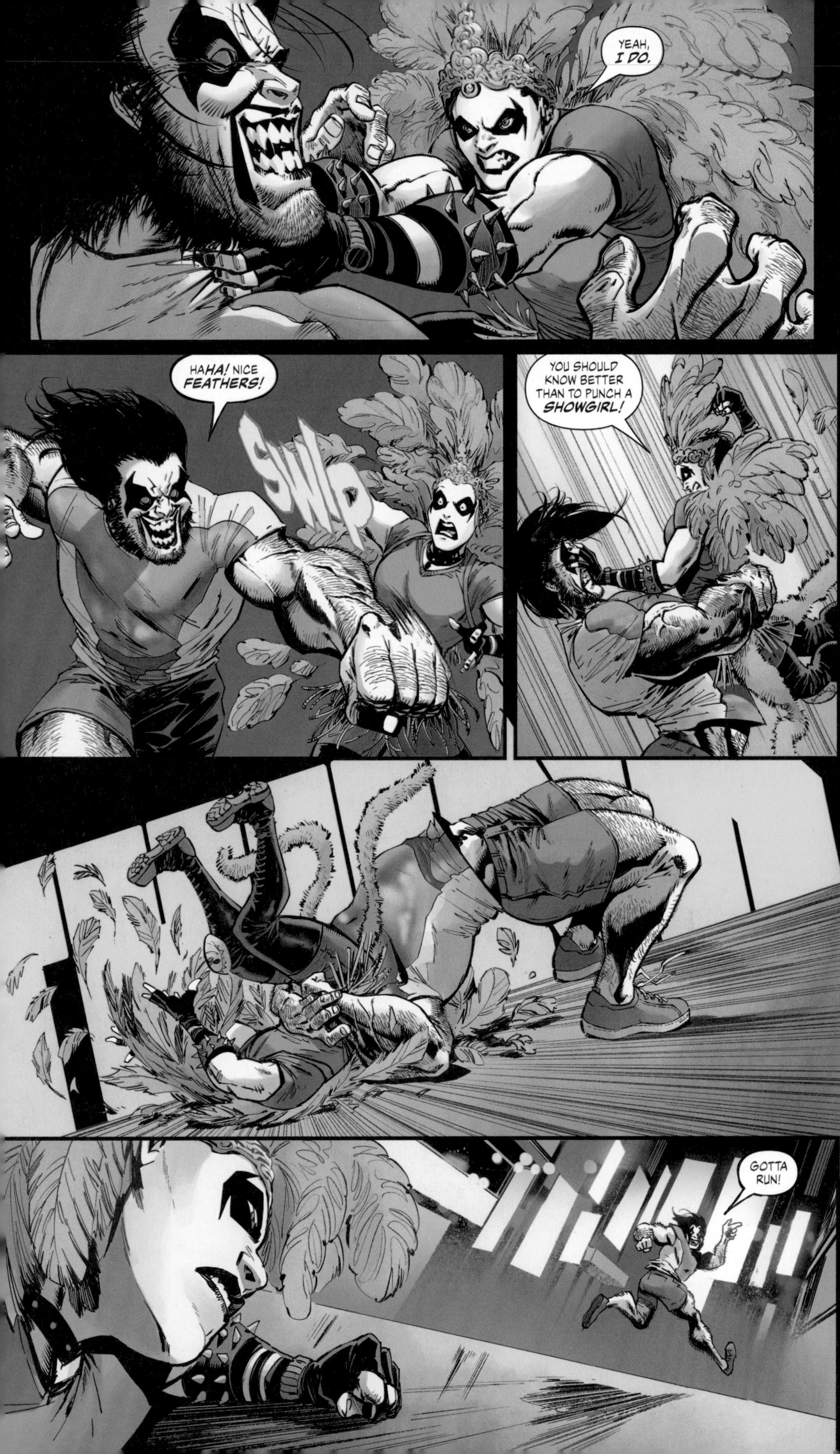

YEAH, I DO.
HAHA! NICE FEATHERS!
SWIP
YOU SHOULD KNOW BETTER THAN TO PUNCH A SHOWGIRL!
GOTTA RUN!

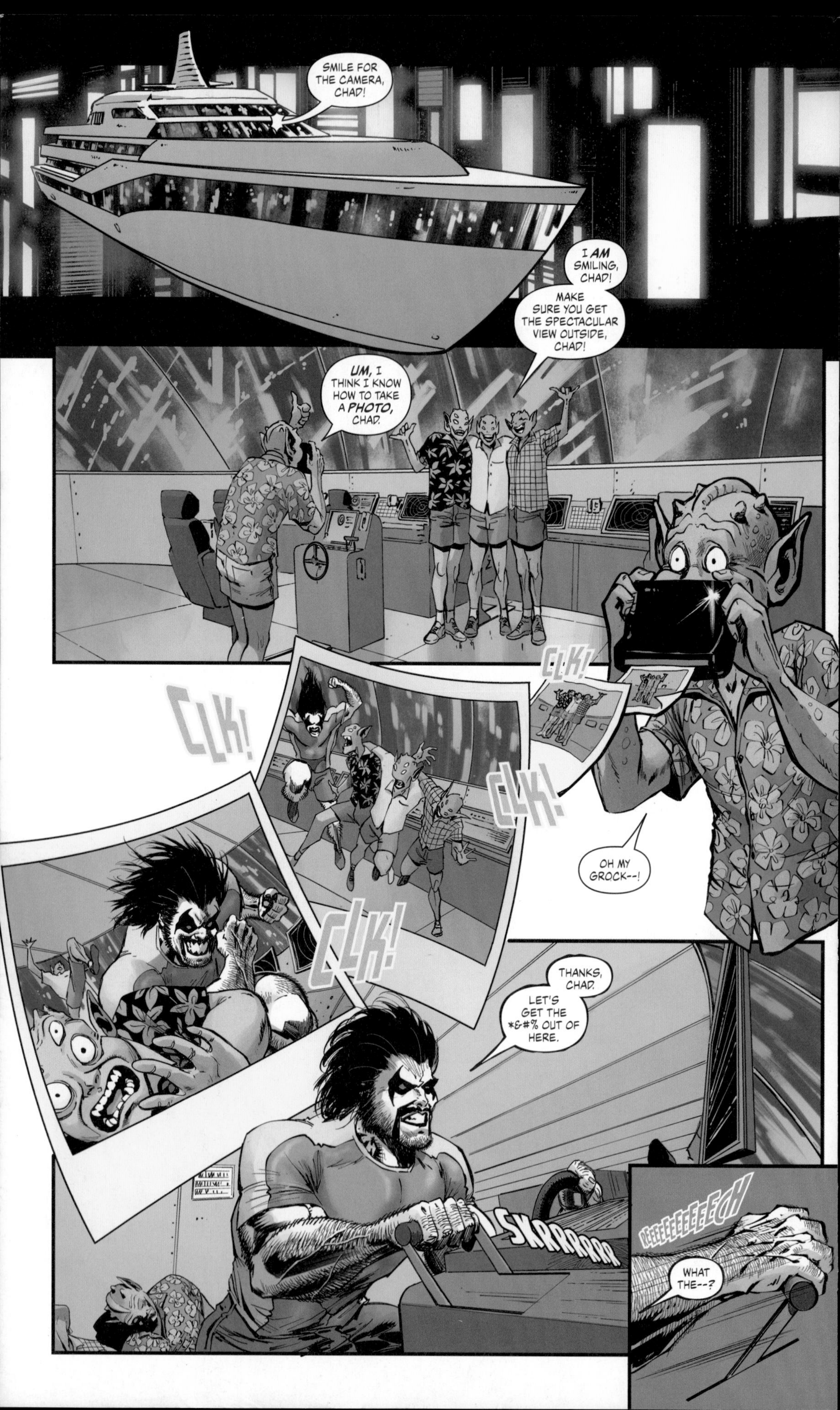

SMILE FOR THE CAMERA, CHAD!
I AM SMILING, CHAD!
MAKE SURE YOU GET THE SPECTACULAR VIEW OUTSIDE, CHAD!
UM, I THINK I KNOW HOW TO TAKE A PHOTO, CHAD.
CLK!
CLK!
CLK!
OH MY GROCK--!
CLK!
THANKS, CHAD.
LET'S GET THE *&#% OUT OF HERE.
SKRRRRRRR
REEEEEEEEEEEECH
WHAT THE--?

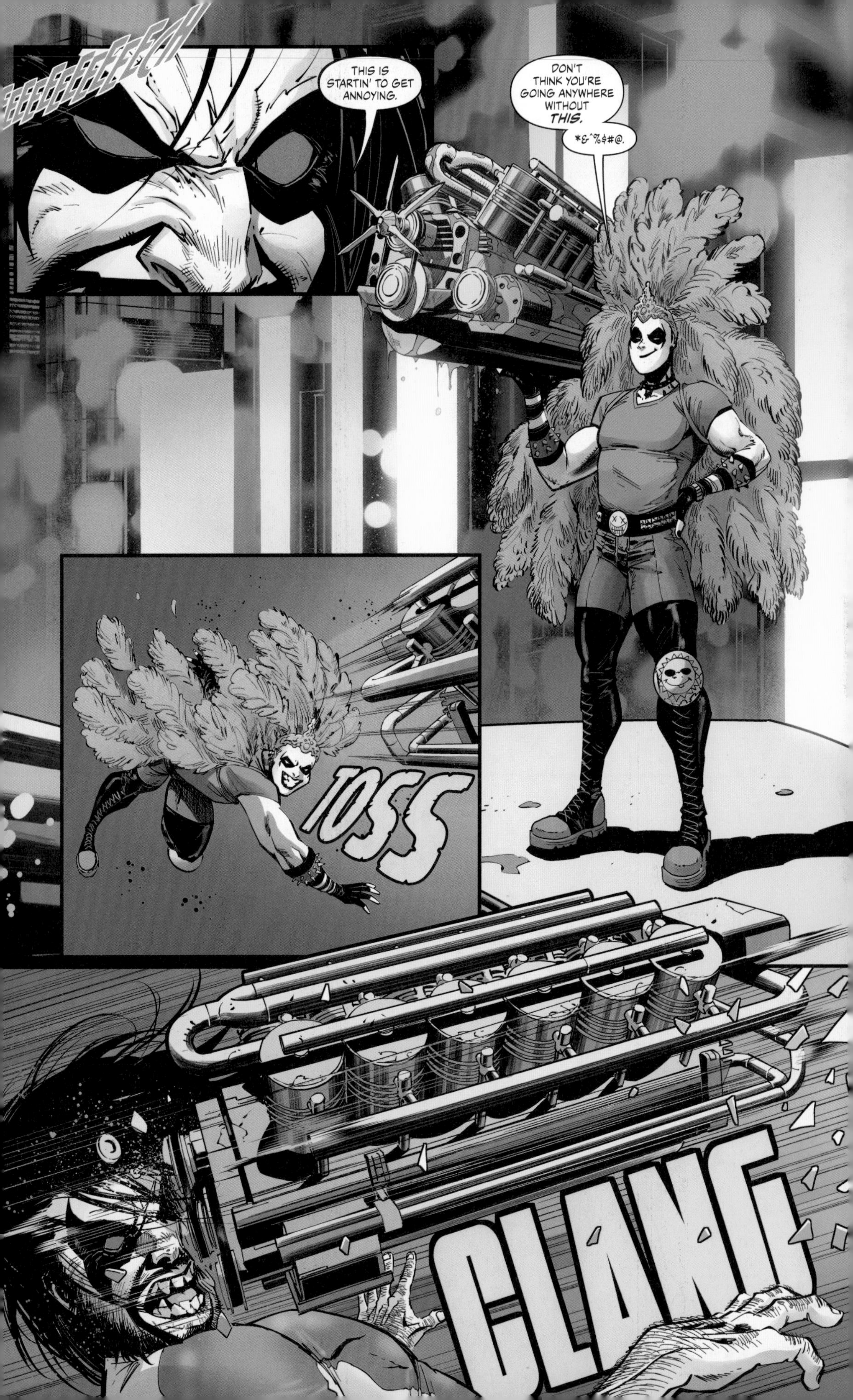
EEEEEEEEEEEEECH
THIS IS STARTIN' TO GET ANNOYING.
DON'T THINK YOU'RE GOING ANYWHERE WITHOUT *THIS.*
*&^%$#@.
TOSS
CLANG

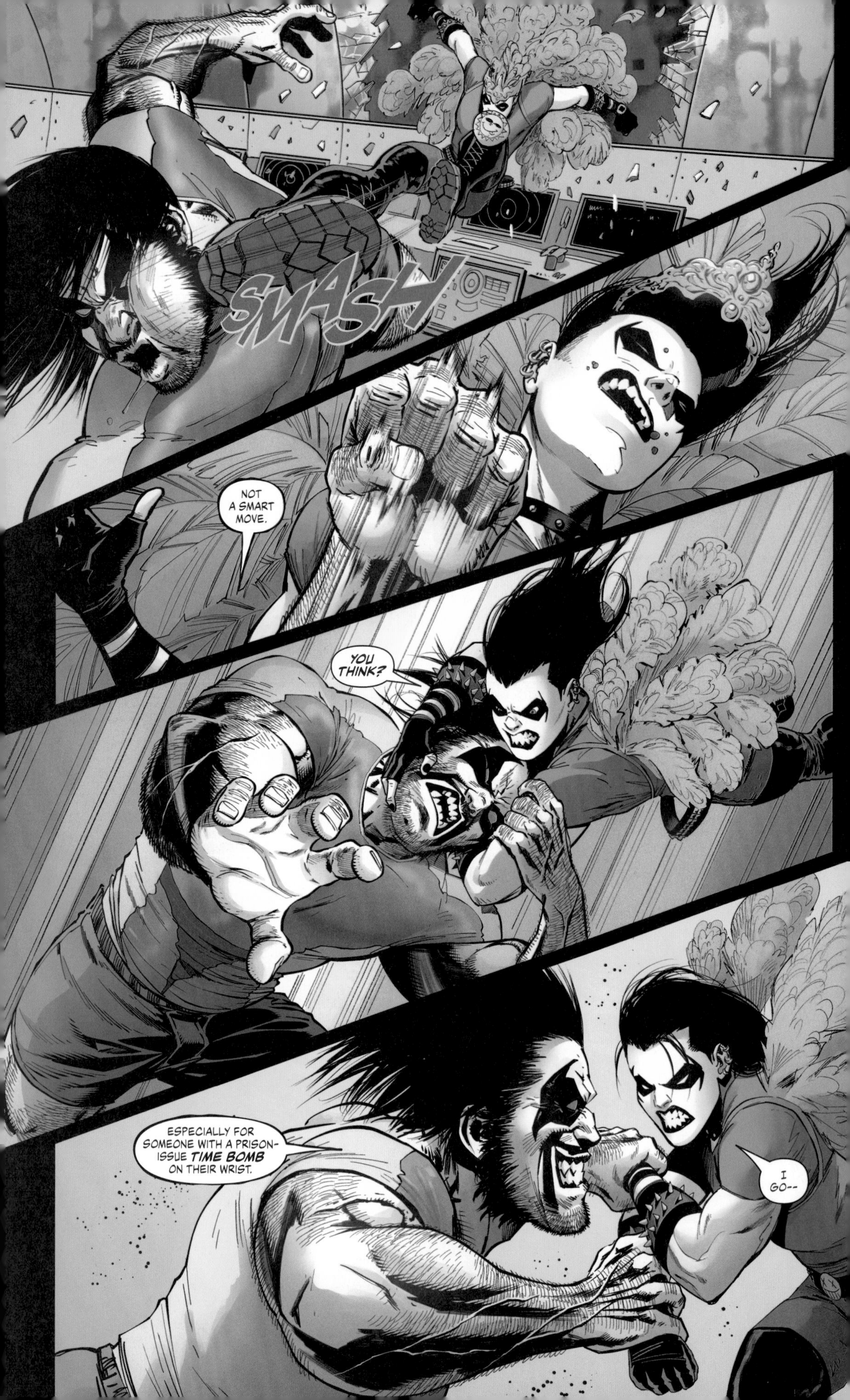
SMASH
NOT A SMART MOVE.
YOU THINK?
ESPECIALLY FOR SOMEONE WITH A PRISON-ISSUE TIME BOMB ON THEIR WRIST.
I GO--

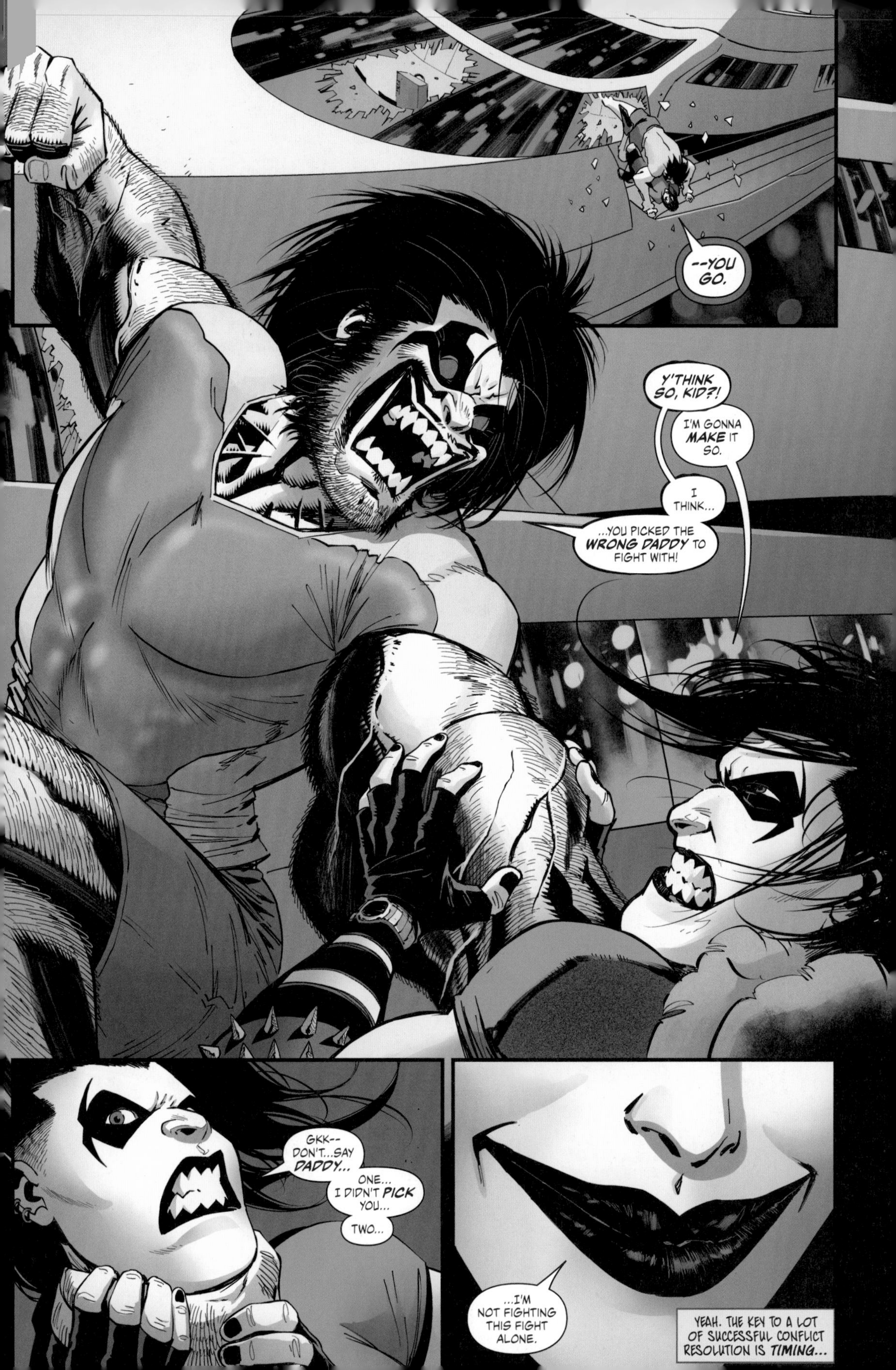

--YOU GO.
Y'THINK SO, KID?!
I'M GONNA MAKE IT SO.
I THINK...
...YOU PICKED THE WRONG DADDY TO FIGHT WITH!
GKK-- DON'T...SAY DADDY...
ONE... I DIDN'T PICK YOU...
TWO...
...I'M NOT FIGHTING THIS FIGHT ALONE.
YEAH. THE KEY TO A LOT OF SUCCESSFUL CONFLICT RESOLUTION IS TIMING...

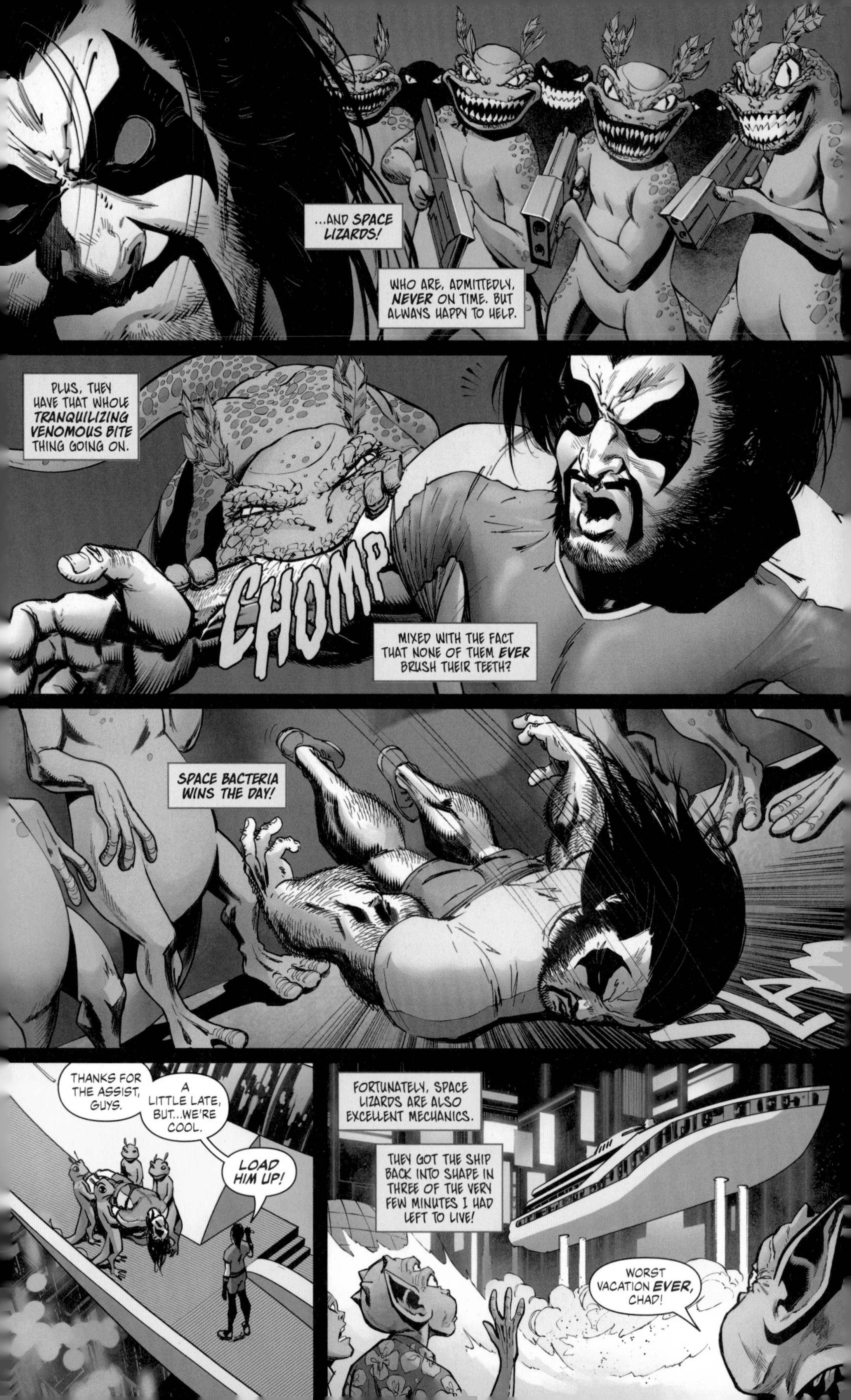
...AND SPACE LIZARDS!
WHO ARE, ADMITTEDLY, NEVER ON TIME. BUT ALWAYS HAPPY TO HELP.
PLUS, THEY HAVE THAT WHOLE TRANQUILIZING VENOMOUS BITE THING GOING ON.
CHOMP
MIXED WITH THE FACT THAT NONE OF THEM EVER BRUSH THEIR TEETH?
SPACE BACTERIA WINS THE DAY!
THANKS FOR THE ASSIST, GUYS.
A LITTLE LATE, BUT...WE'RE COOL.
LOAD HIM UP!
FORTUNATELY, SPACE LIZARDS ARE ALSO EXCELLENT MECHANICS.
THEY GOT THE SHIP BACK INTO SHAPE IN THREE OF THE VERY FEW MINUTES I HAD LEFT TO LIVE!
WORST VACATION EVER, CHAD!

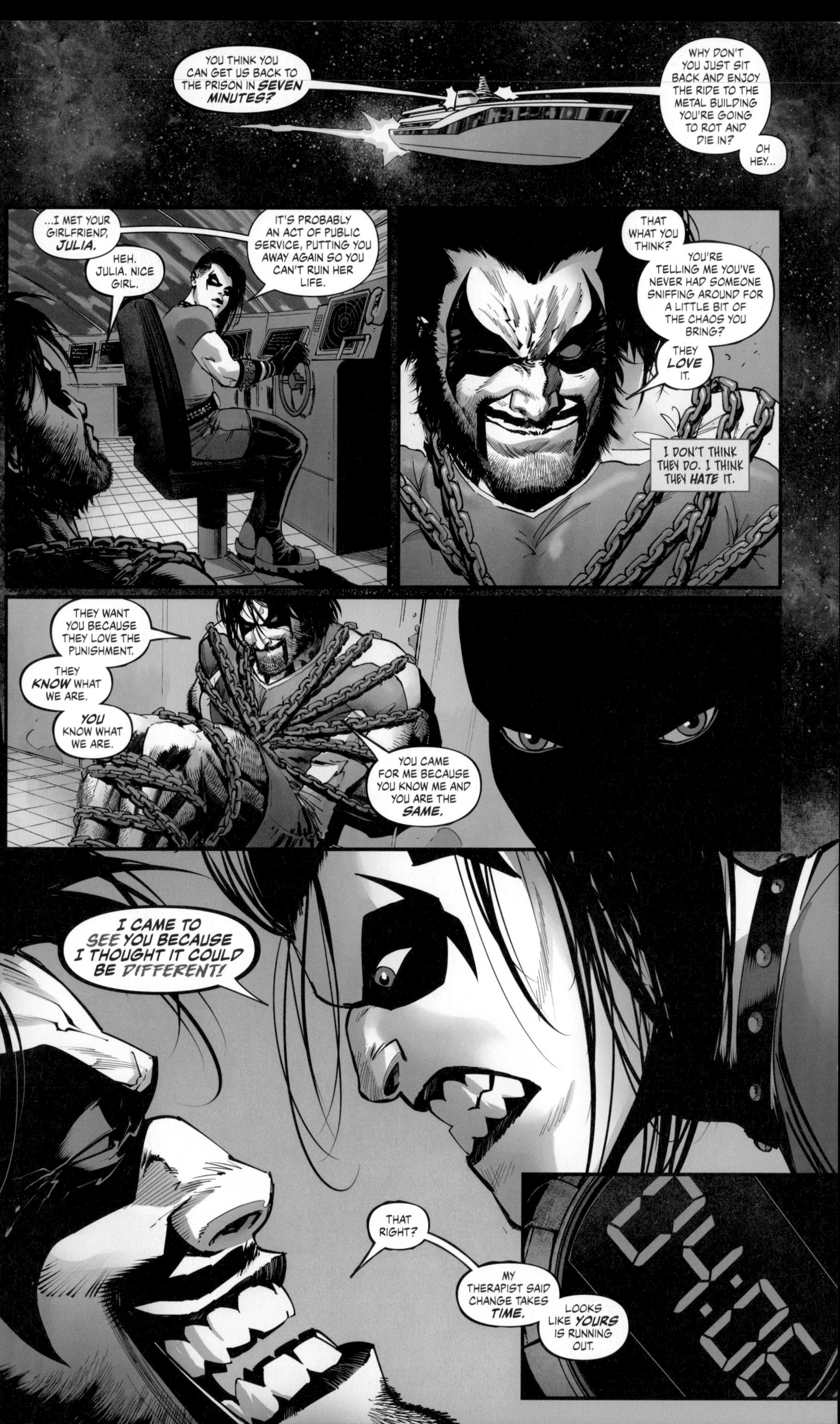
YOU THINK YOU CAN GET US BACK TO THE PRISON IN SEVEN MINUTES?
WHY DON'T YOU JUST SIT BACK AND ENJOY THE RIDE TO THE METAL BUILDING YOU'RE GOING TO ROT AND DIE IN?
OH HEY...
...I MET YOUR GIRLFRIEND, JULIA.
HEH. JULIA. NICE GIRL.
IT'S PROBABLY AN ACT OF PUBLIC SERVICE, PUTTING YOU AWAY AGAIN SO YOU CAN'T RUIN HER LIFE.
THAT WHAT YOU THINK?
YOU'RE TELLING ME YOU'VE NEVER HAD SOMEONE SNIFFING AROUND FOR A LITTLE BIT OF THE CHAOS YOU BRING?
THEY LOVE IT.
I DON'T THINK THEY DO. I THINK THEY HATE IT.
THEY WANT YOU BECAUSE THEY LOVE THE PUNISHMENT.
THEY KNOW WHAT WE ARE.
YOU KNOW WHAT WE ARE.
YOU CAME FOR ME BECAUSE YOU KNOW ME AND YOU ARE THE SAME.
I CAME TO SEE YOU BECAUSE I THOUGHT IT COULD BE DIFFERENT!
THAT RIGHT?
MY THERAPIST SAID CHANGE TAKES TIME.
LOOKS LIKE YOURS IS RUNNING OUT.

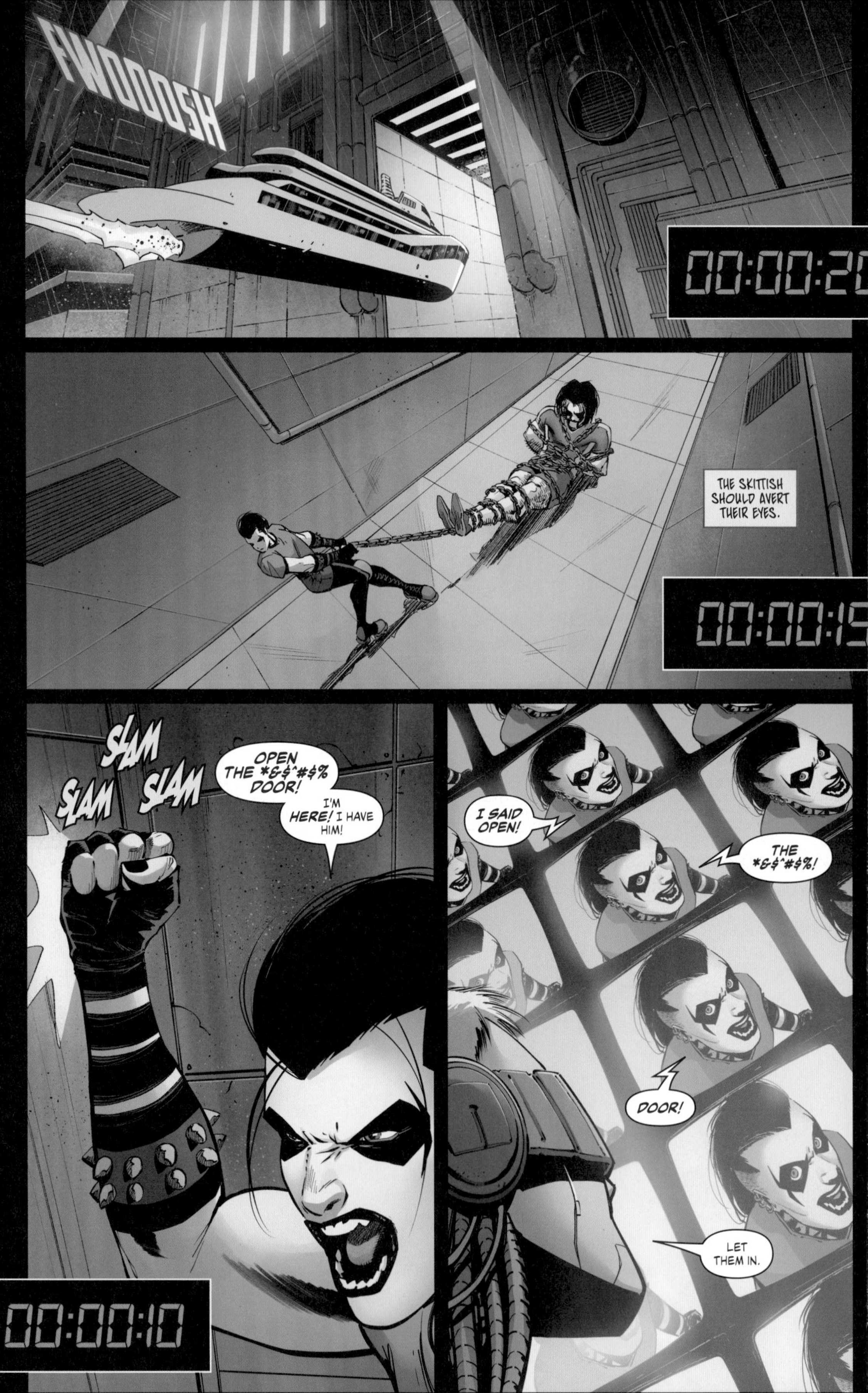
FWOOOSH
00:00:20
THE SKITTISH SHOULD AVERT THEIR EYES.
00:00:15
SLAM
SLAM
SLAM
OPEN THE *&$^#$% DOOR!
I'M HERE! I HAVE HIM!
00:00:10
I SAID OPEN!
THE *&$^#$%!
DOOR!
LET THEM IN.

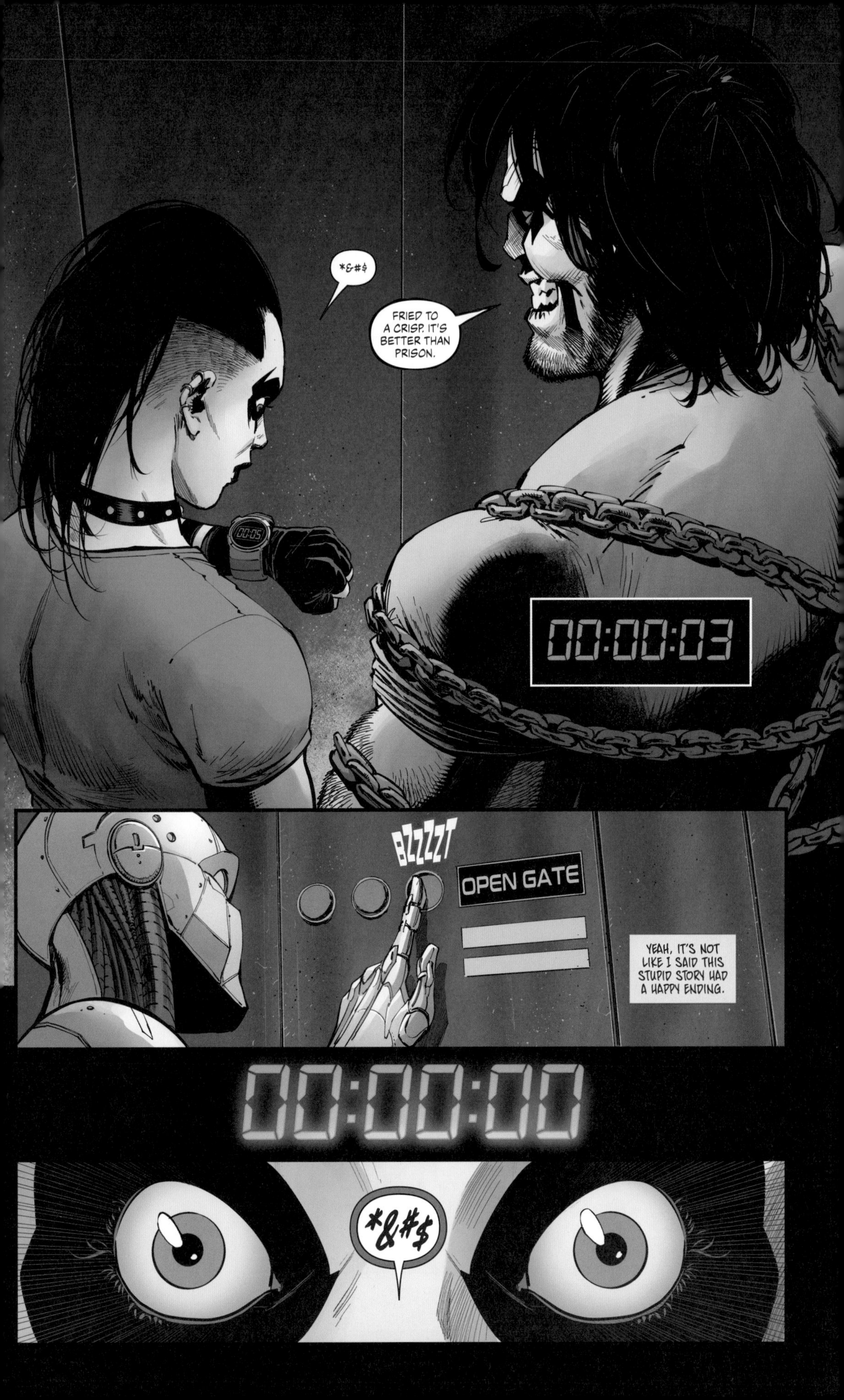
*&#$
FRIED TO A CRISP. IT'S BETTER THAN PRISON.
00:05
00:00:03
BZZZZT
OPEN GATE
YEAH, IT'S NOT LIKE I SAID THIS STUPID STORY HAD A HAPPY ENDING.
00:00:00
*&#$

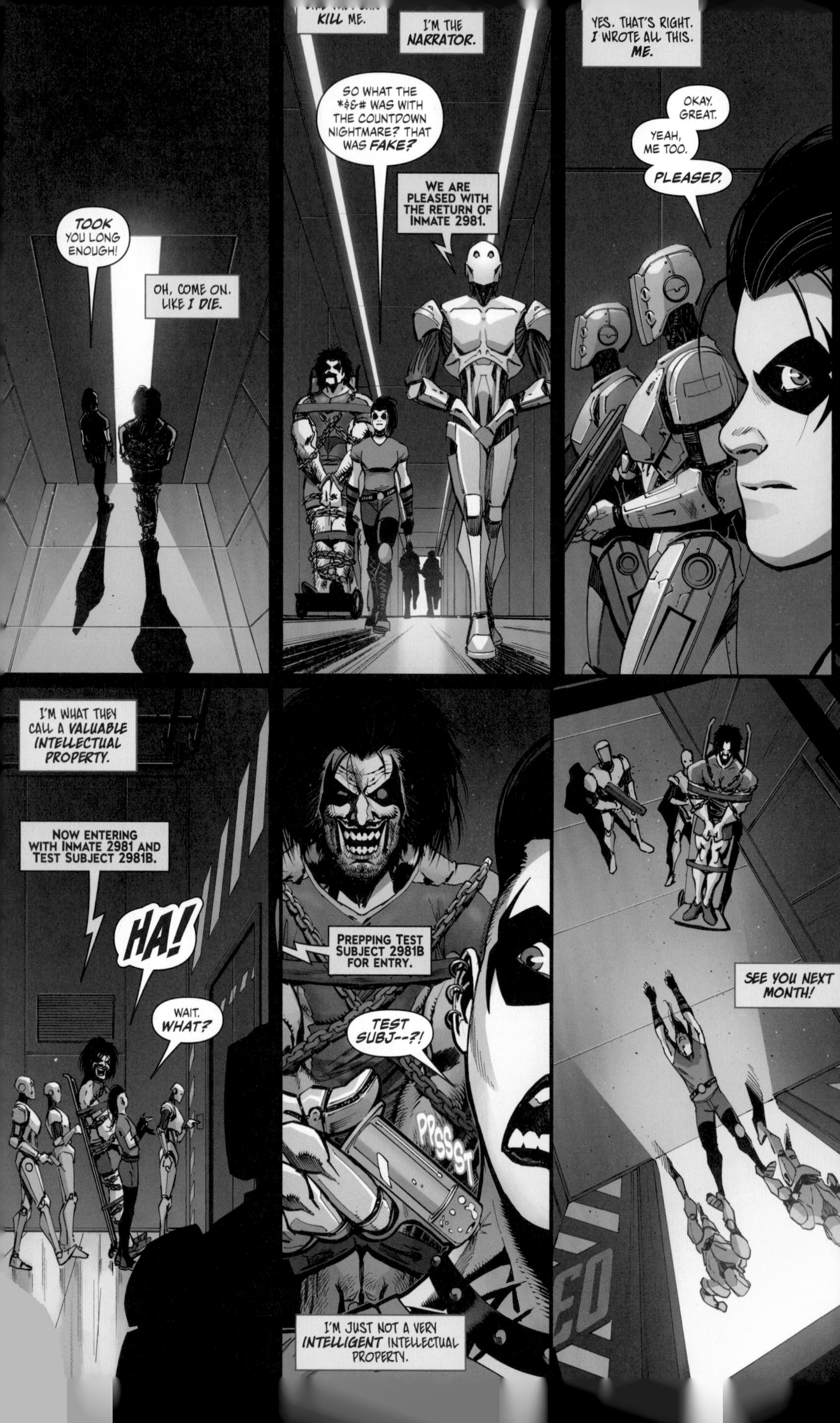
TOOK YOU LONG ENOUGH!
OH, COME ON. LIKE I DIE.
KILL ME.
I'M THE NARRATOR.
SO WHAT THE *$&# WAS WITH THE COUNTDOWN NIGHTMARE? THAT WAS FAKE?
WE ARE PLEASED WITH THE RETURN OF INMATE 2981.
YES. THAT'S RIGHT. I WROTE ALL THIS. ME.
OKAY. GREAT.
YEAH, ME TOO.
PLEASED.
I'M WHAT THEY CALL A VALUABLE INTELLECTUAL PROPERTY.
NOW ENTERING WITH INMATE 2981 AND TEST SUBJECT 2981B.
HA!
WAIT. WHAT?
PREPPING TEST SUBJECT 2981B FOR ENTRY.
TEST SUBJ--?!
PPSSST
I'M JUST NOT A VERY INTELLIGENT INTELLECTUAL PROPERTY.
SEE YOU NEXT MONTH!

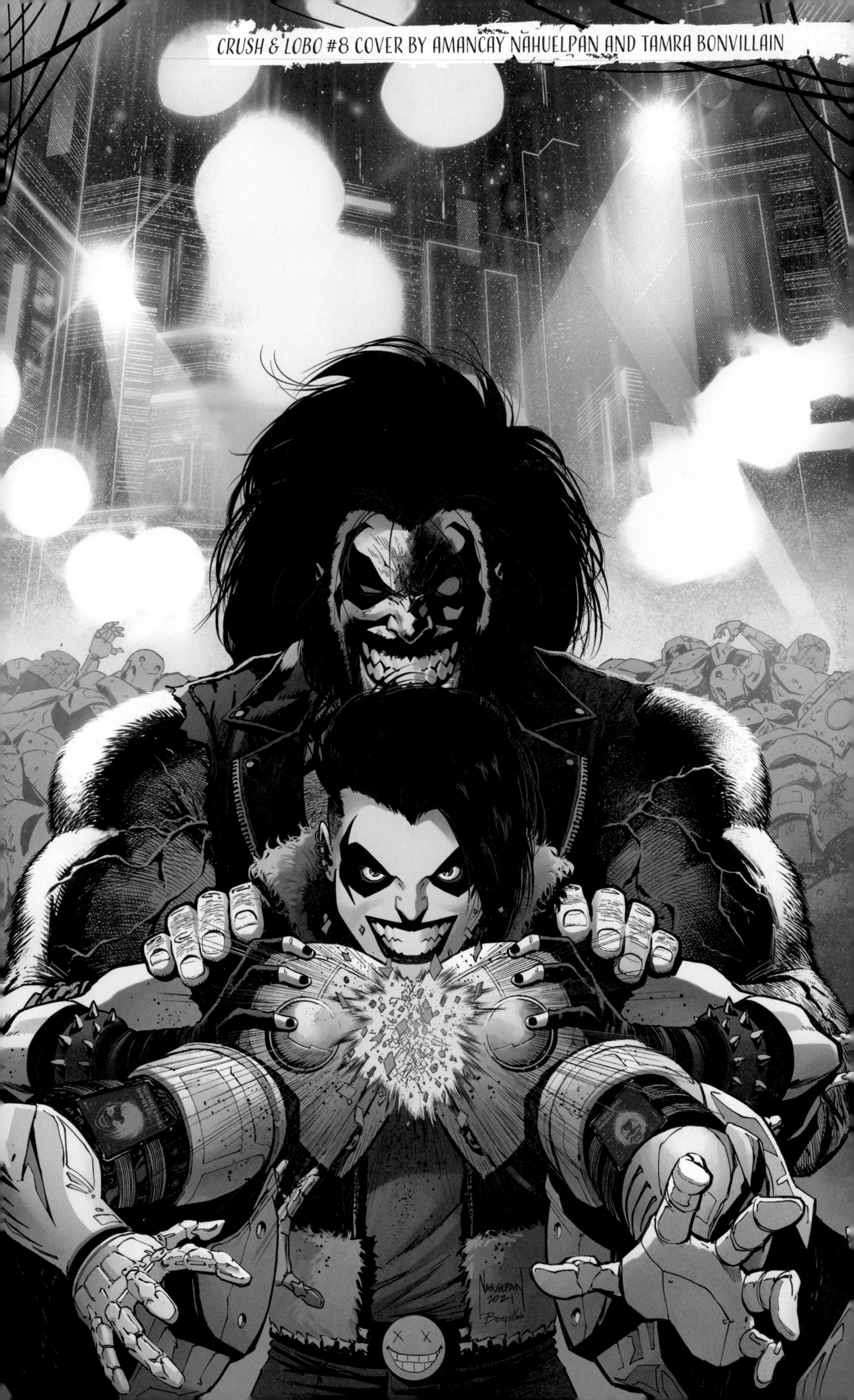
NAHUELPAN 2021
Bonvillain
CRUSH & LOBO #8 COVER BY AMANCAY NAHUELPAN AND TAMRA BONVILLAIN

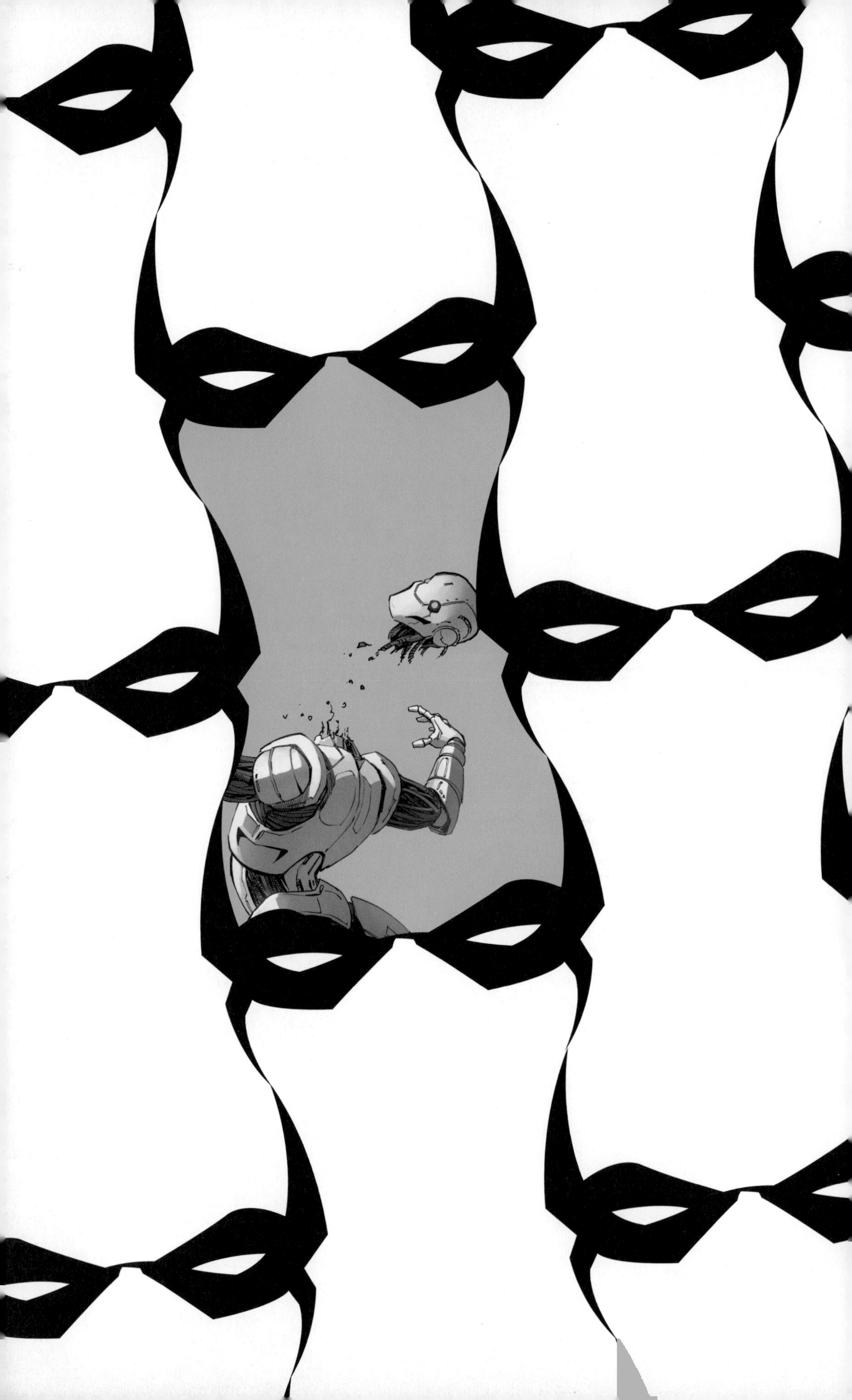

ROBOT THERAPISTS SUCK

Writer: Mariko Tamaki
Artist: Amancay Nahuelpan
Colors: Tamra Bonvillain
Letters: Ariana Maher
Cover: Amancay Nahuelpan & Tamra Bonvillain
Variant Cover: Jen Bartel
Editor: Andrea Shea
Group Editor: Chris Conroy

LOBO created by ROGER SLIFER and KEITH GIFFEN.

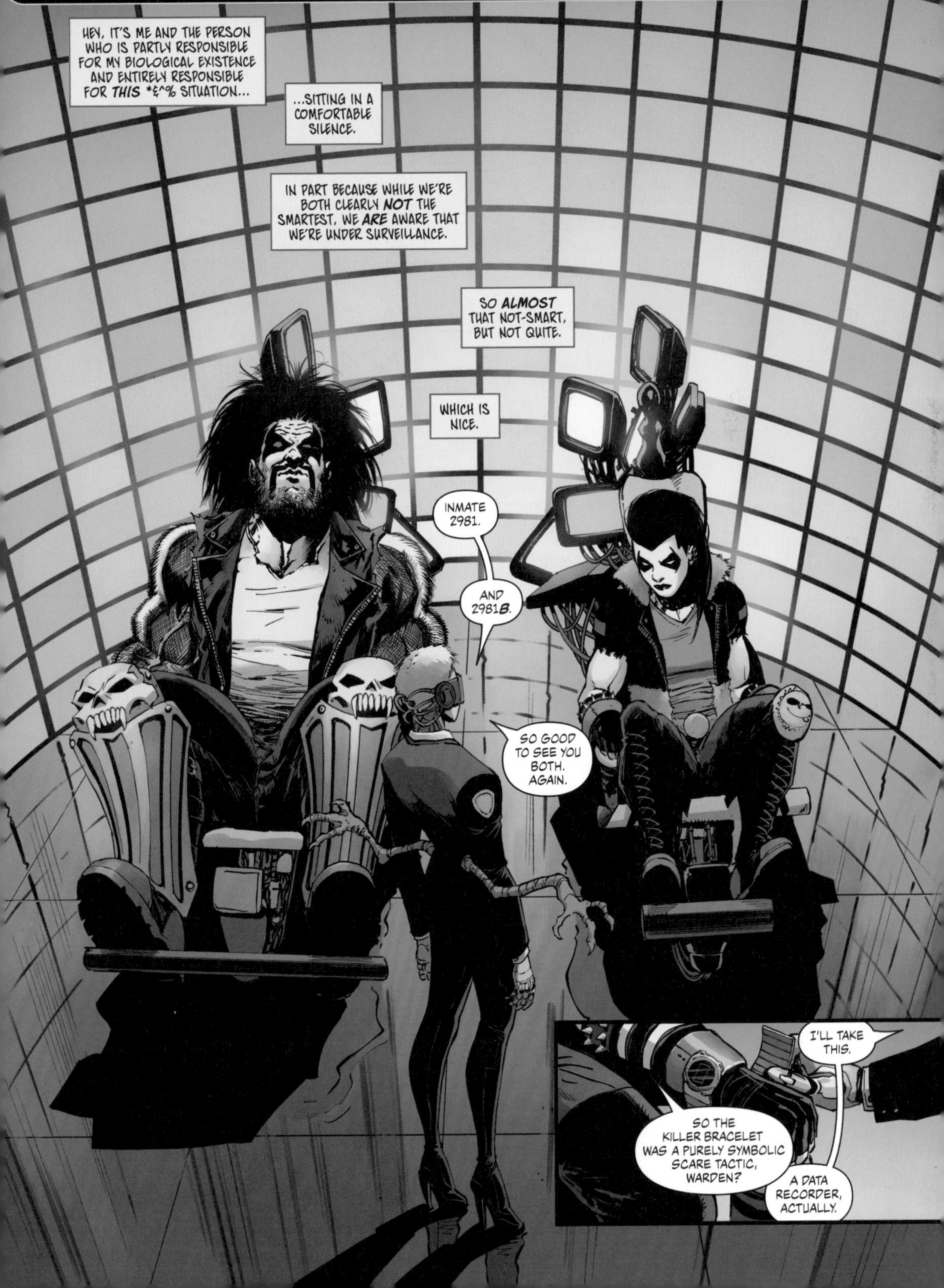

HEY, IT'S ME AND THE PERSON WHO IS PARTLY RESPONSIBLE FOR MY BIOLOGICAL EXISTENCE AND ENTIRELY RESPONSIBLE FOR *THIS* *&^% SITUATION...
...SITTING IN A COMFORTABLE SILENCE.
IN PART BECAUSE WHILE WE'RE BOTH CLEARLY **NOT** THE SMARTEST, WE **ARE** AWARE THAT WE'RE UNDER SURVEILLANCE.
SO **ALMOST** THAT NOT-SMART, BUT NOT QUITE.
WHICH IS NICE.
INMATE 2981.
AND 2981**B**.
SO GOOD TO SEE YOU BOTH. AGAIN.
I'LL TAKE THIS.
SO THE KILLER BRACELET WAS A PURELY SYMBOLIC SCARE TACTIC, WARDEN?
A DATA RECORDER, ACTUALLY.

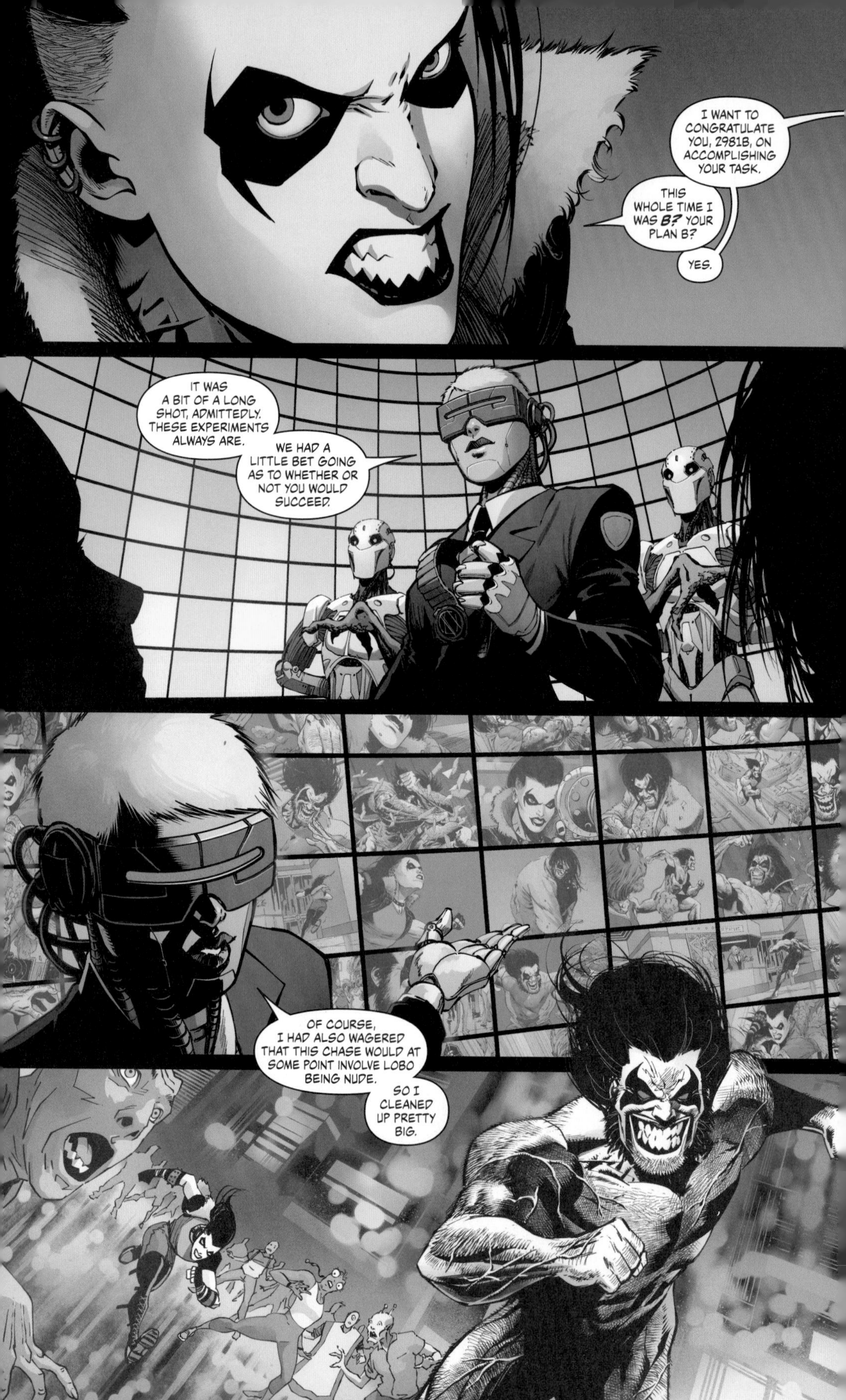
I WANT TO CONGRATULATE YOU, 2981B, ON ACCOMPLISHING YOUR TASK.
THIS WHOLE TIME I WAS B? YOUR PLAN B?
YES.
IT WAS A BIT OF A LONG SHOT, ADMITTEDLY. THESE EXPERIMENTS ALWAYS ARE.
WE HAD A LITTLE BET GOING AS TO WHETHER OR NOT YOU WOULD SUCCEED.
OF COURSE, I HAD ALSO WAGERED THAT THIS CHASE WOULD AT SOME POINT INVOLVE LOBO BEING NUDE.
SO I CLEANED UP PRETTY BIG.

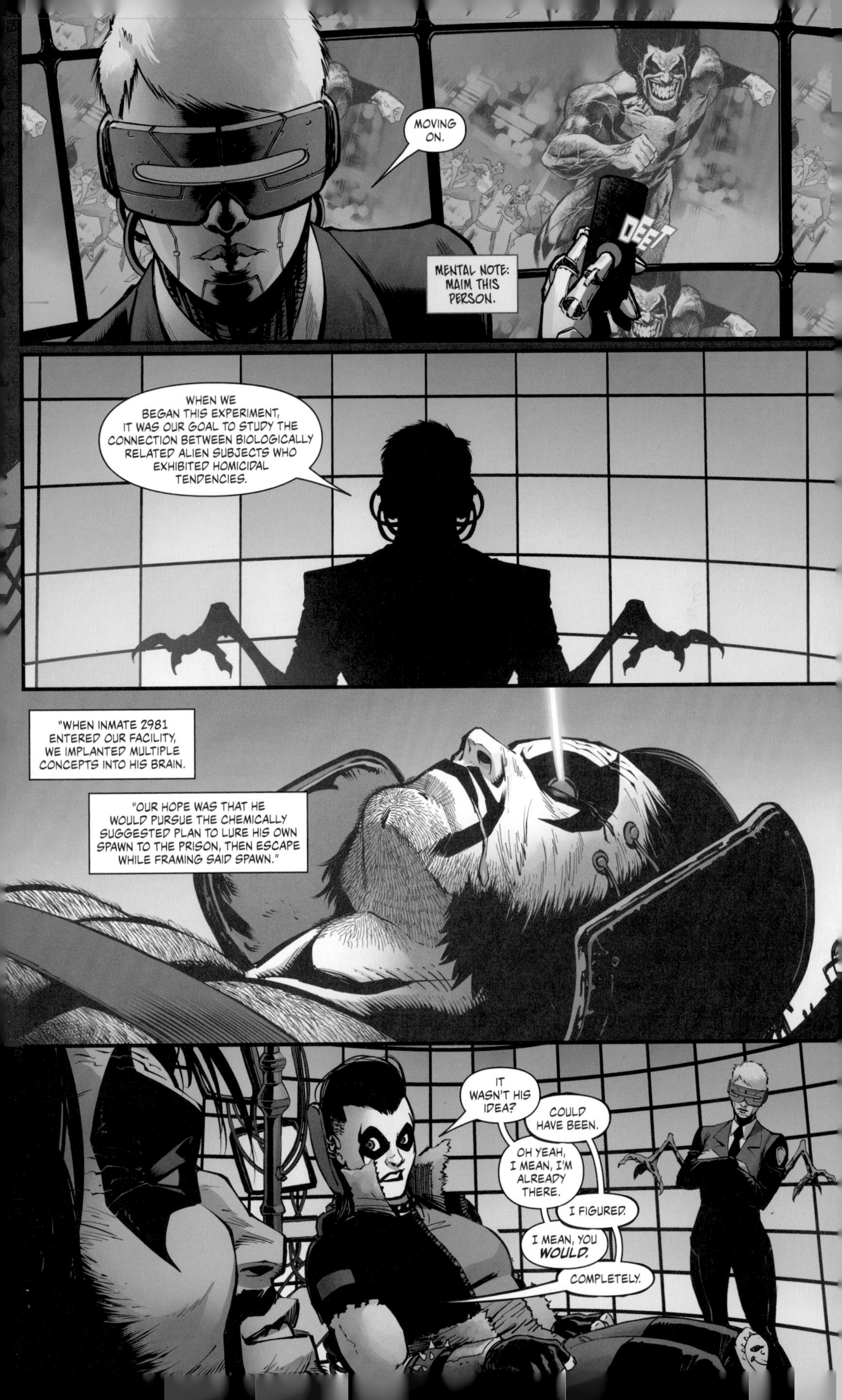
MOVING ON.
DEET
MENTAL NOTE: MAIM THIS PERSON.
WHEN WE BEGAN THIS EXPERIMENT, IT WAS OUR GOAL TO STUDY THE CONNECTION BETWEEN BIOLOGICALLY RELATED ALIEN SUBJECTS WHO EXHIBITED HOMICIDAL TENDENCIES.
"WHEN INMATE 2981 ENTERED OUR FACILITY, WE IMPLANTED MULTIPLE CONCEPTS INTO HIS BRAIN.
"OUR HOPE WAS THAT HE WOULD PURSUE THE CHEMICALLY SUGGESTED PLAN TO LURE HIS OWN SPAWN TO THE PRISON, THEN ESCAPE WHILE FRAMING SAID SPAWN."
IT WASN'T HIS IDEA?
COULD HAVE BEEN.
OH YEAH, I MEAN, I'M ALREADY THERE.
I FIGURED.
I MEAN, YOU *WOULD.*
COMPLETELY.

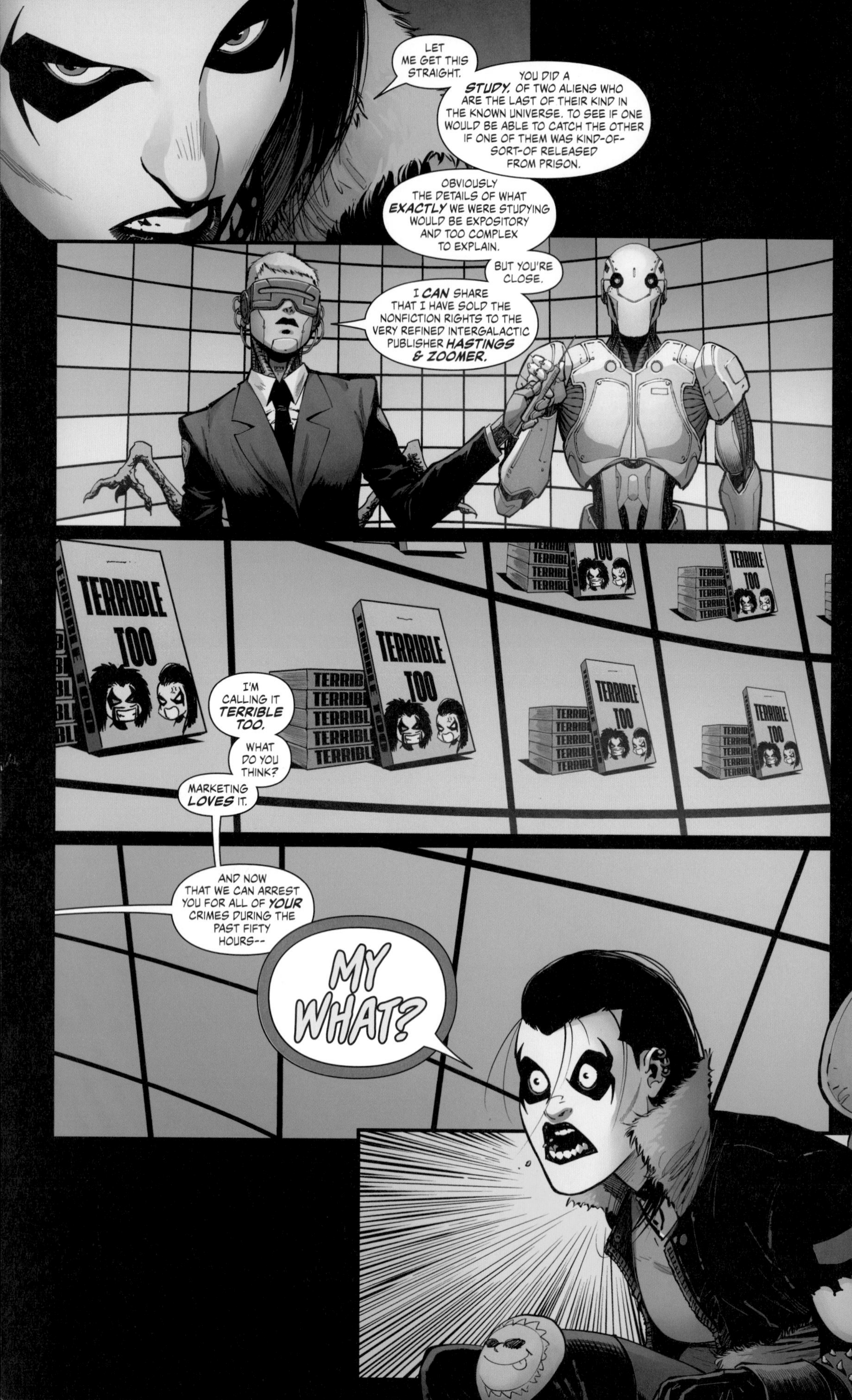
LET ME GET THIS STRAIGHT.
YOU DID A STUDY, OF TWO ALIENS WHO ARE THE LAST OF THEIR KIND IN THE KNOWN UNIVERSE. TO SEE IF ONE WOULD BE ABLE TO CATCH THE OTHER IF ONE OF THEM WAS KIND-OF-SORT-OF RELEASED FROM PRISON.
OBVIOUSLY THE DETAILS OF WHAT EXACTLY WE WERE STUDYING WOULD BE EXPOSITORY AND TOO COMPLEX TO EXPLAIN.
BUT YOU'RE CLOSE.
I CAN SHARE THAT I HAVE SOLD THE NONFICTION RIGHTS TO THE VERY REFINED INTERGALACTIC PUBLISHER HASTINGS & ZOOMER.
TERRIBLE TOO
I'M CALLING IT TERRIBLE TOO.
WHAT DO YOU THINK?
MARKETING LOVES IT.
AND NOW THAT WE CAN ARREST YOU FOR ALL OF YOUR CRIMES DURING THE PAST FIFTY HOURS--
MY WHAT?

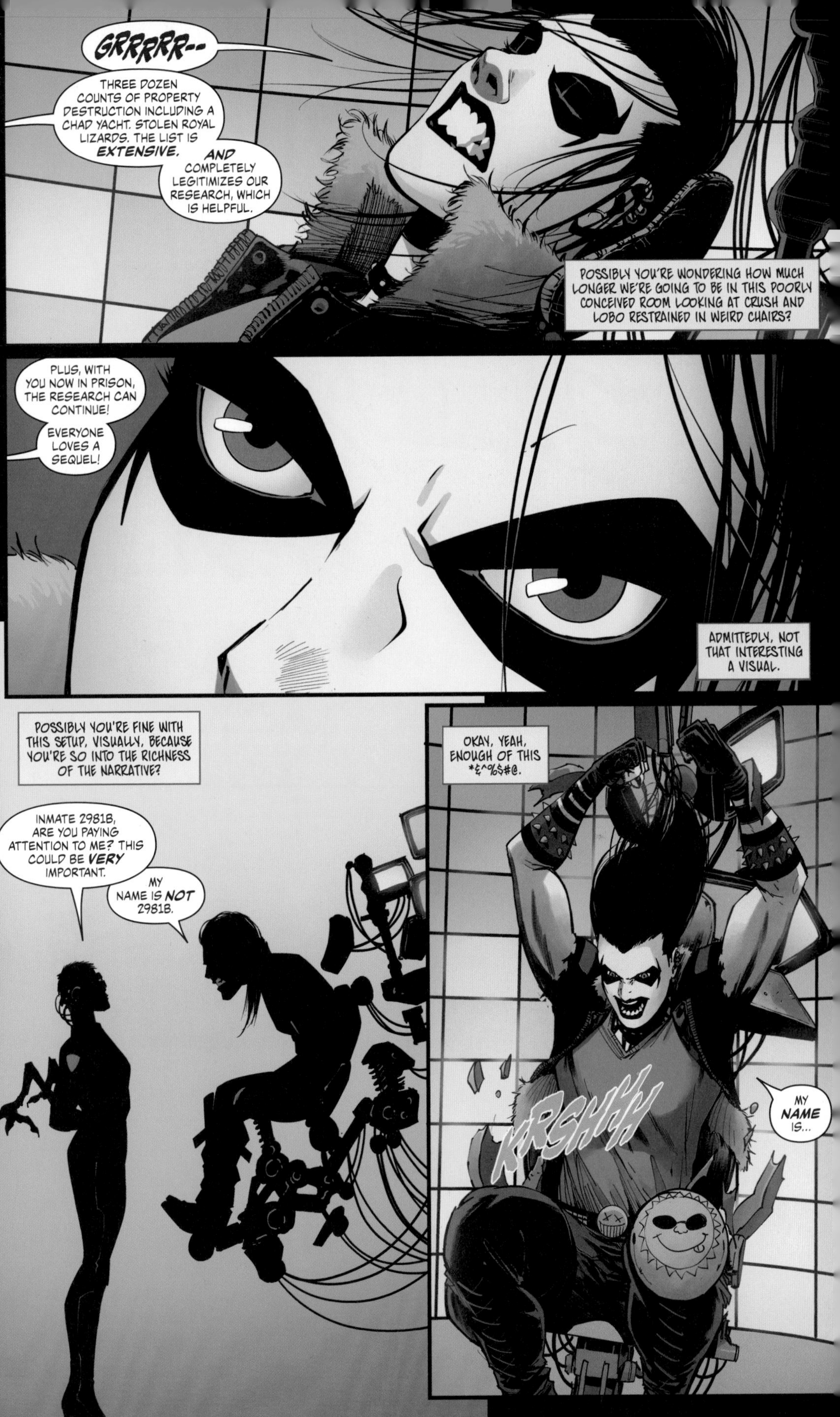
GRRRRR--
THREE DOZEN COUNTS OF PROPERTY DESTRUCTION INCLUDING A CHAD YACHT. STOLEN ROYAL LIZARDS. THE LIST IS EXTENSIVE.
AND COMPLETELY LEGITIMIZES OUR RESEARCH, WHICH IS HELPFUL.
POSSIBLY YOU'RE WONDERING HOW MUCH LONGER WE'RE GOING TO BE IN THIS POORLY CONCEIVED ROOM LOOKING AT CRUSH AND LOBO RESTRAINED IN WEIRD CHAIRS?
PLUS, WITH YOU NOW IN PRISON, THE RESEARCH CAN CONTINUE!
EVERYONE LOVES A SEQUEL!
ADMITTEDLY, NOT THAT INTERESTING A VISUAL.
POSSIBLY YOU'RE FINE WITH THIS SETUP, VISUALLY, BECAUSE YOU'RE SO INTO THE RICHNESS OF THE NARRATIVE?
INMATE 2981B, ARE YOU PAYING ATTENTION TO ME? THIS COULD BE VERY IMPORTANT.
MY NAME IS NOT 2981B.
OKAY, YEAH, ENOUGH OF THIS *&^%$#@.
KRSHHH
MY NAME IS...

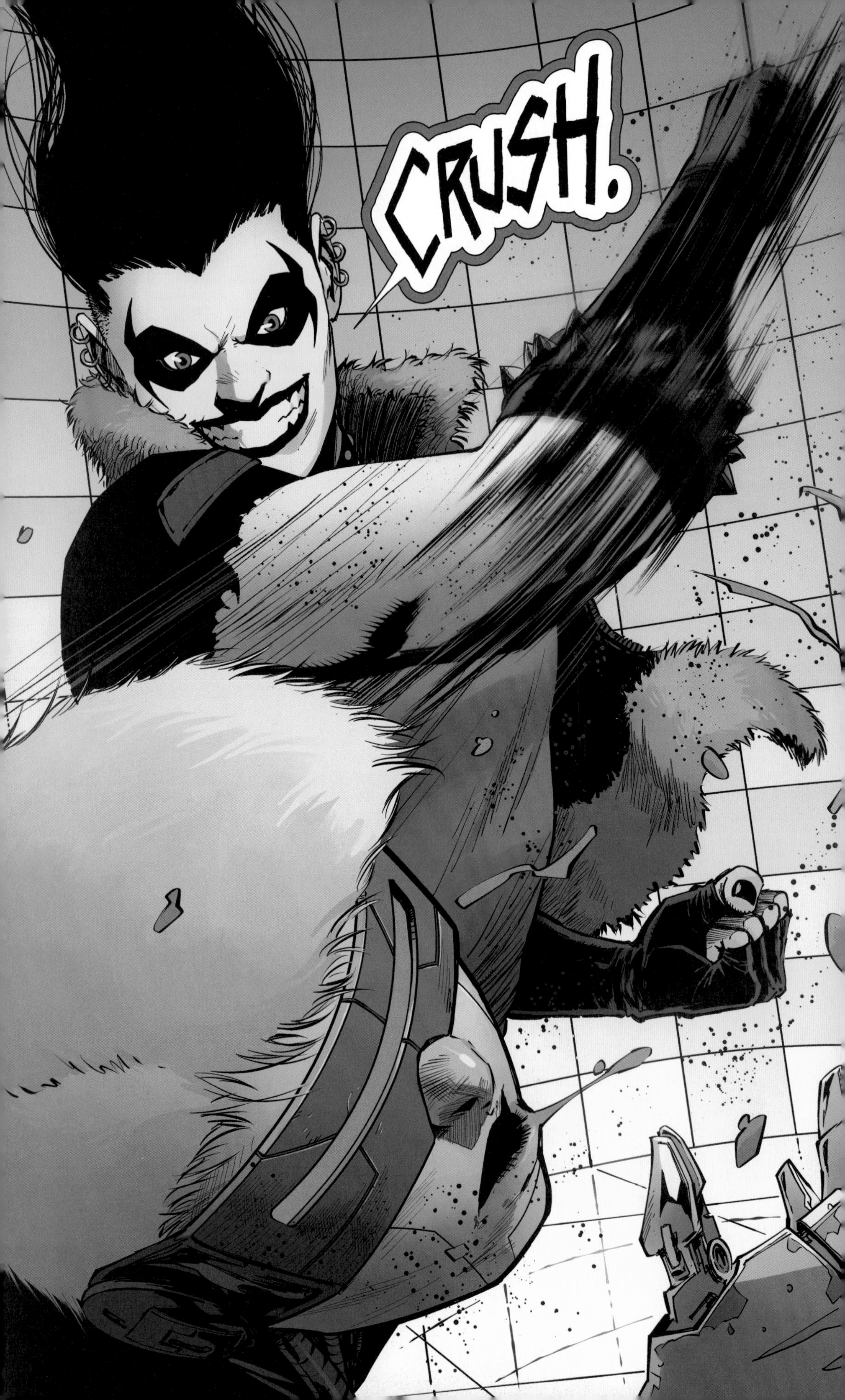
CRUSH.

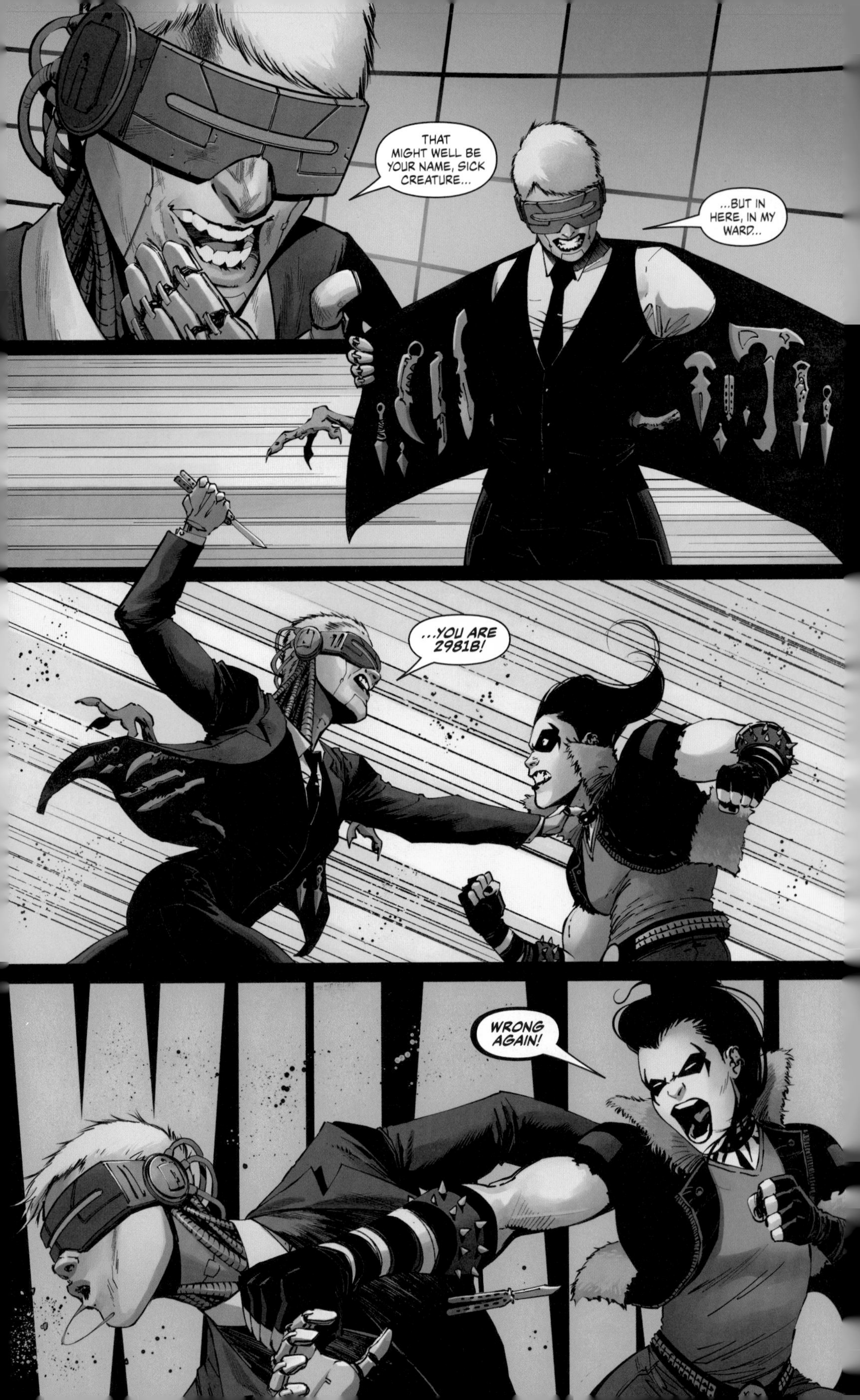
THAT MIGHT WELL BE YOUR NAME, SICK CREATURE...
...BUT IN HERE, IN MY WARD...
...YOU ARE 2981B!
WRONG AGAIN!

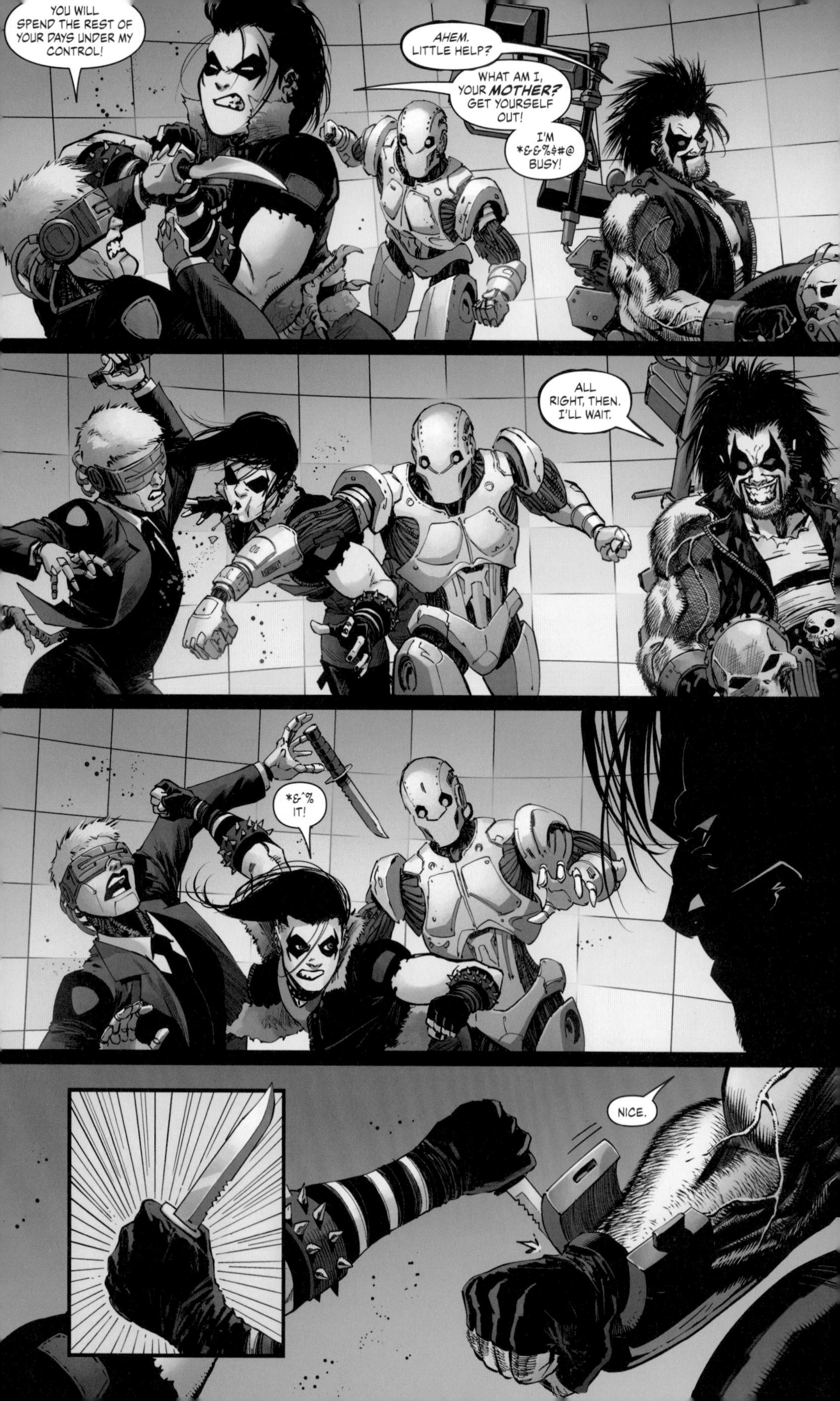
YOU WILL SPEND THE REST OF YOUR DAYS UNDER MY CONTROL!
AHEM. LITTLE HELP?
WHAT AM I, YOUR MOTHER? GET YOURSELF OUT!
I'M *&&%$#@ BUSY!
ALL RIGHT, THEN. I'LL WAIT.
*&^% IT!
NICE.

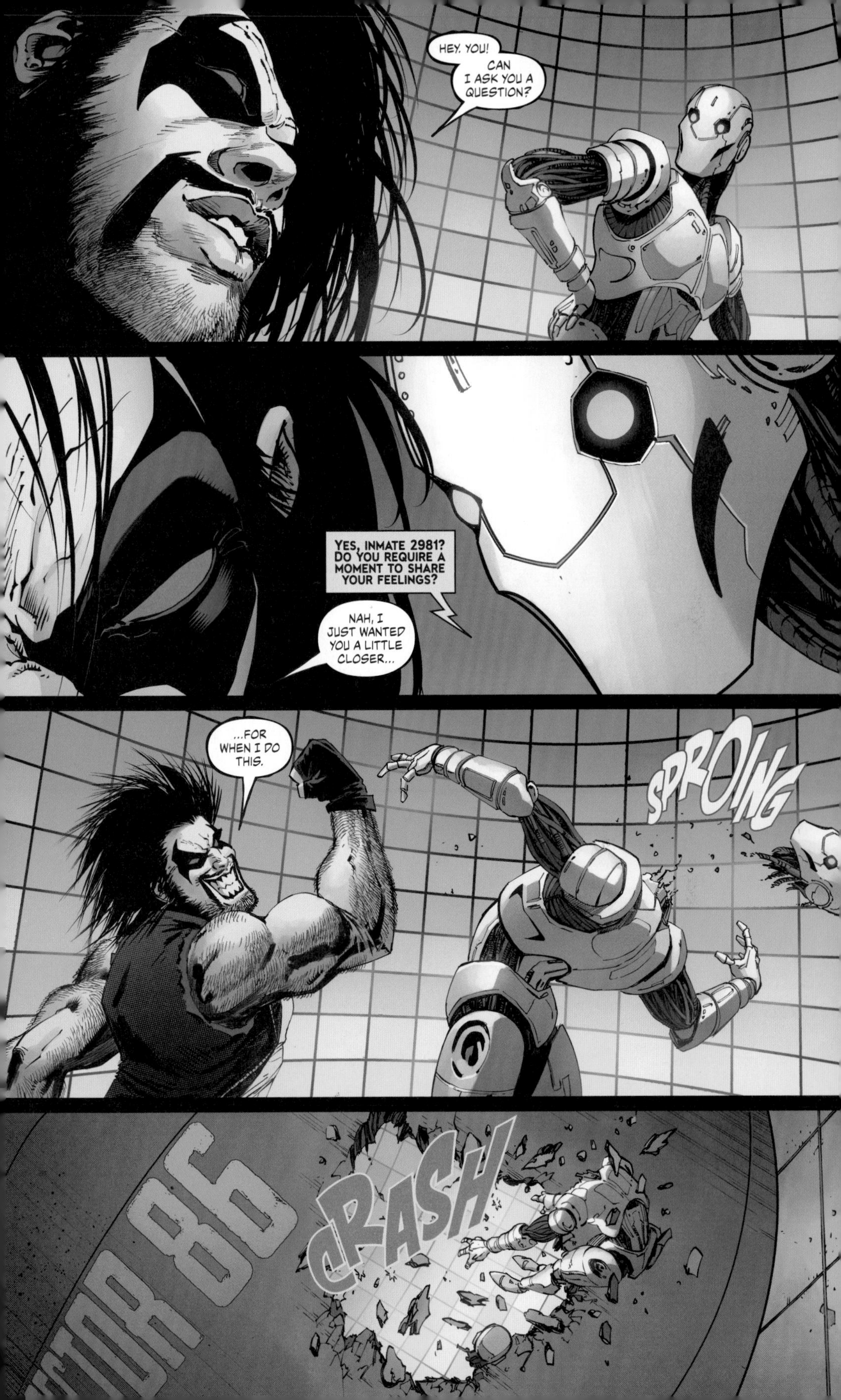
HEY. YOU!
CAN I ASK YOU A QUESTION?
YES, INMATE 2981? DO YOU REQUIRE A MOMENT TO SHARE YOUR FEELINGS?
NAH, I JUST WANTED YOU A LITTLE CLOSER...
...FOR WHEN I DO THIS.
SPROING
CRASH

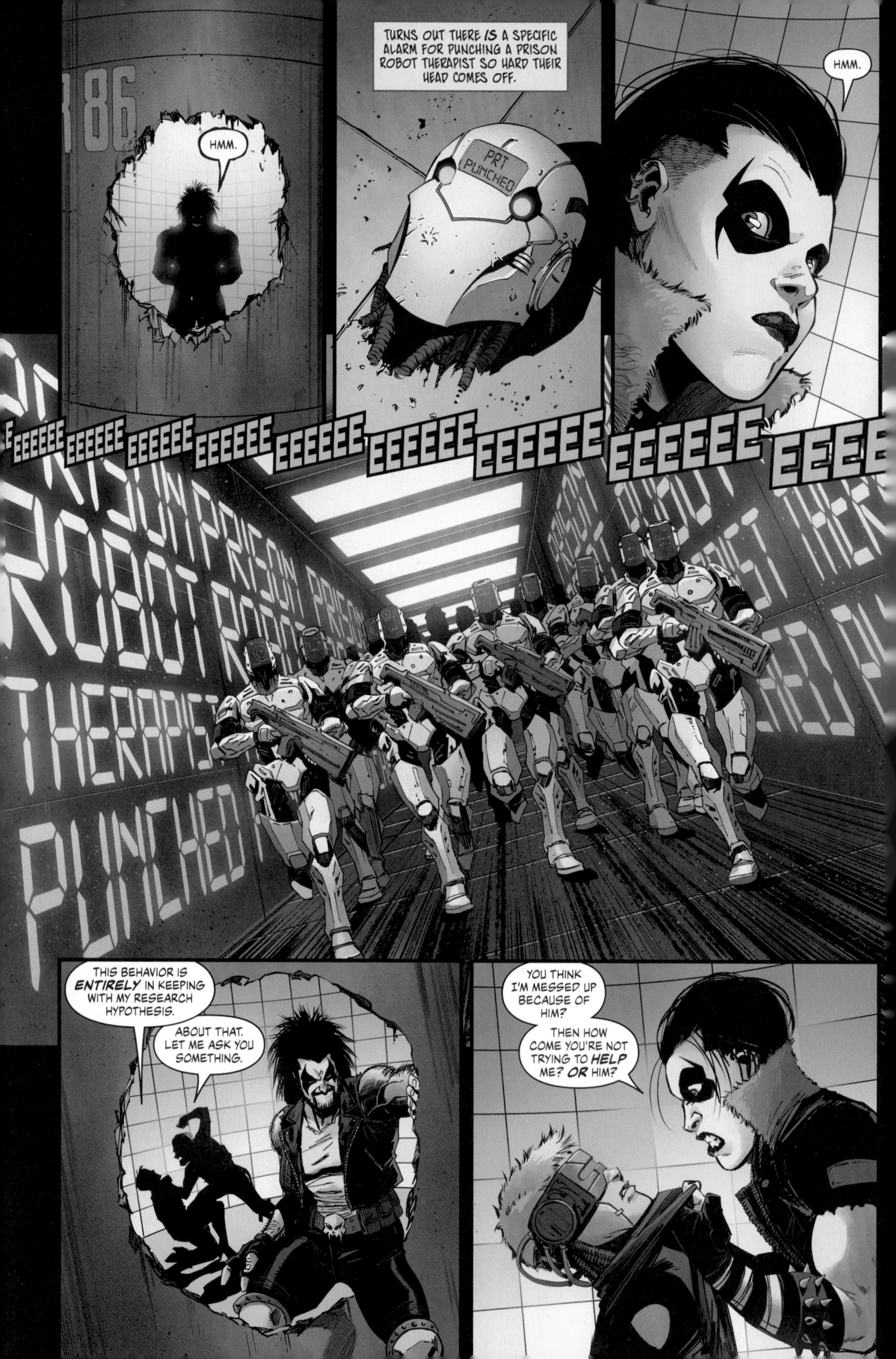

HMM.
TURNS OUT THERE *IS* A SPECIFIC ALARM FOR PUNCHING A PRISON ROBOT THERAPIST SO HARD THEIR HEAD COMES OFF.
PRT PUNCHED
HMM.
EEEEEE EEEEEE EEEEEE EEEEEE EEEEEE EEEEEE EEEEEE EEEEEE EEEE
PRISON
ROBOT
THERAPIST
PUNCHED
THIS BEHAVIOR IS ***ENTIRELY*** IN KEEPING WITH MY RESEARCH HYPOTHESIS.
ABOUT THAT. LET ME ASK YOU SOMETHING.
YOU THINK I'M MESSED UP BECAUSE OF HIM?
THEN HOW COME YOU'RE NOT TRYING TO ***HELP*** ME? ***OR*** HIM?

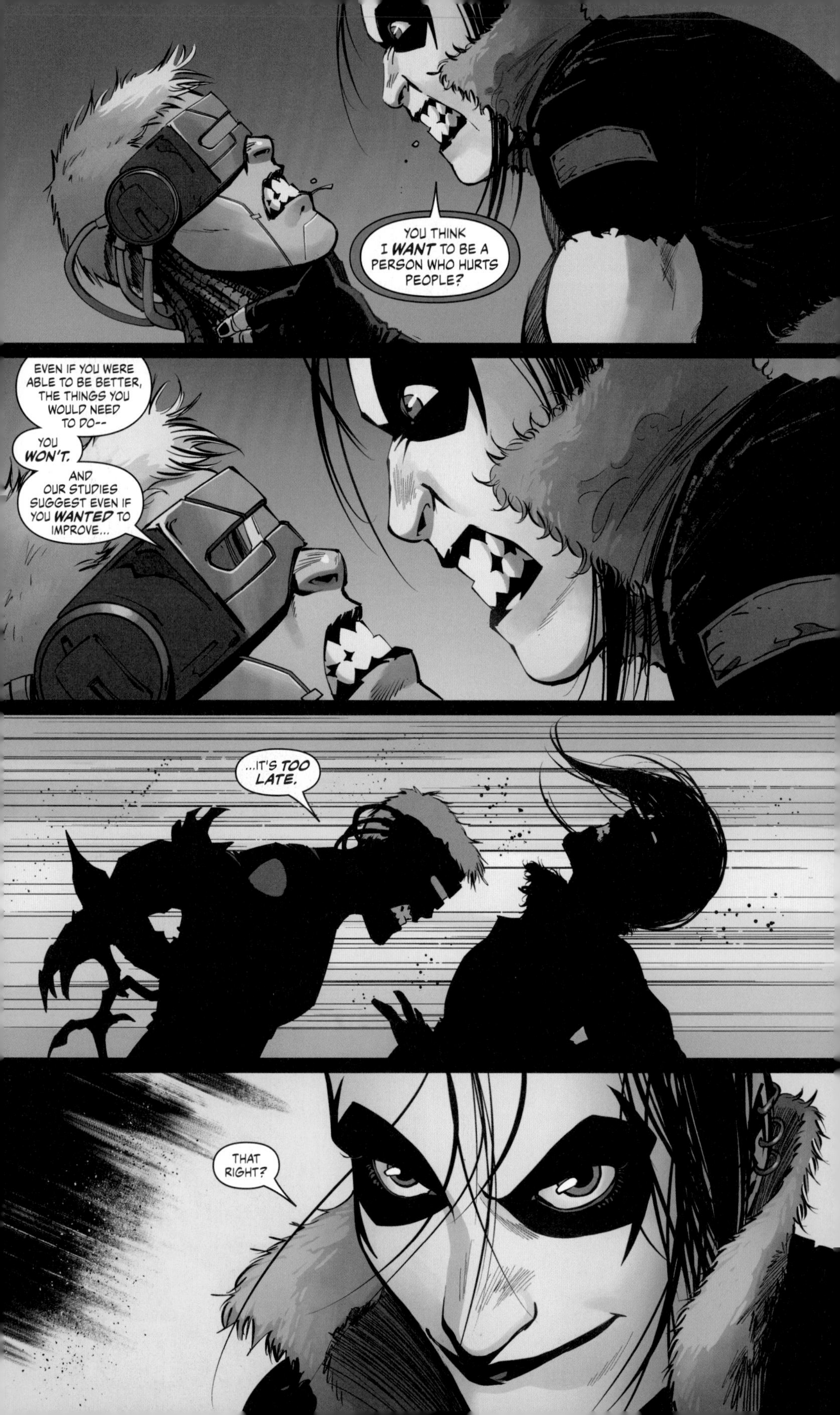
YOU THINK I WANT TO BE A PERSON WHO HURTS PEOPLE?
EVEN IF YOU WERE ABLE TO BE BETTER, THE THINGS YOU WOULD NEED TO DO--
YOU WON'T.
AND OUR STUDIES SUGGEST EVEN IF YOU WANTED TO IMPROVE...
...IT'S TOO LATE.
THAT RIGHT?

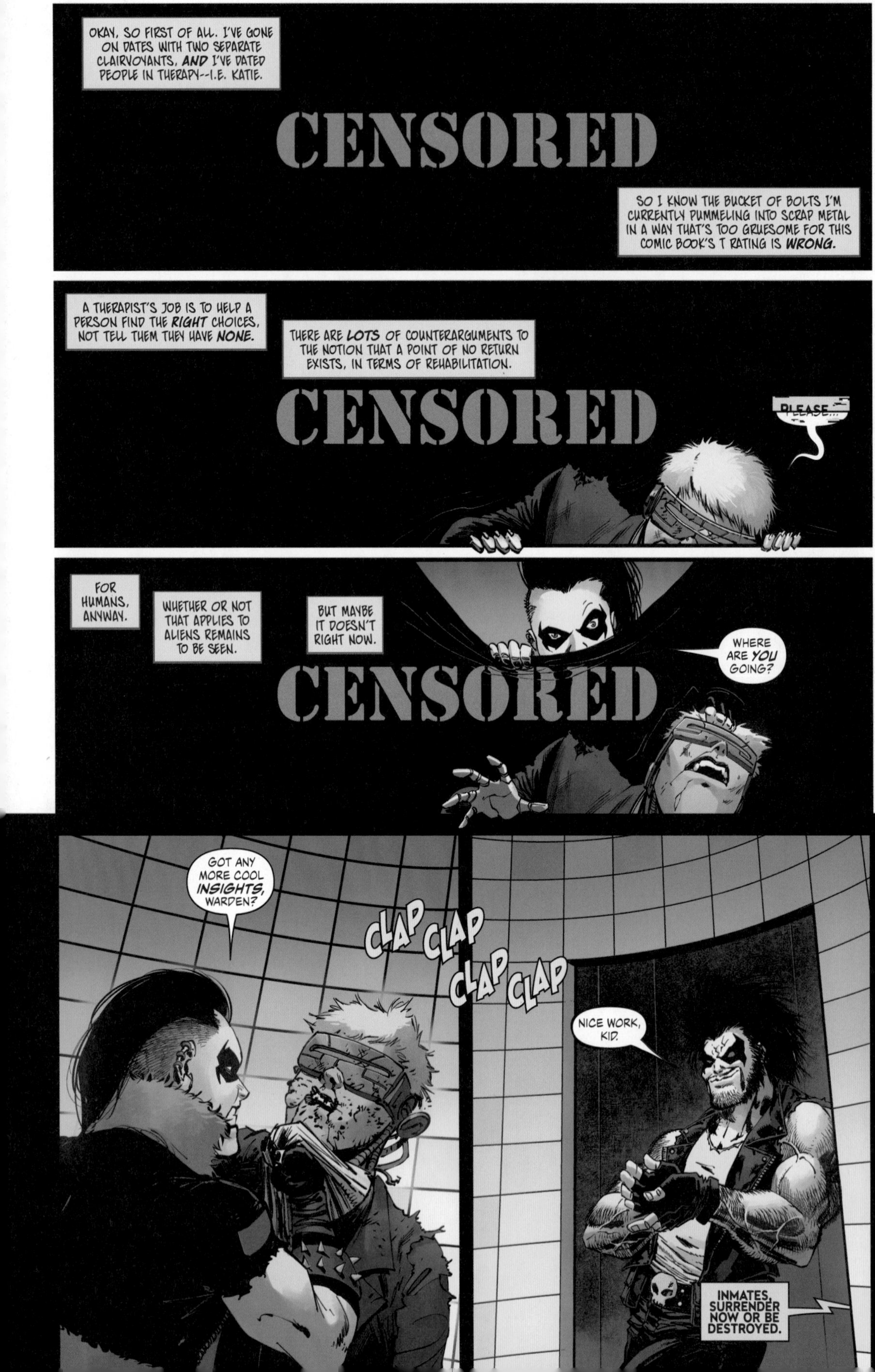

OKAY, SO FIRST OF ALL. I'VE GONE ON DATES WITH TWO SEPARATE CLAIRVOYANTS, AND I'VE DATED PEOPLE IN THERAPY--I.E. KATIE.
CENSORED
SO I KNOW THE BUCKET OF BOLTS I'M CURRENTLY PUMMELING INTO SCRAP METAL IN A WAY THAT'S TOO GRUESOME FOR THIS COMIC BOOK'S T RATING IS WRONG.
A THERAPIST'S JOB IS TO HELP A PERSON FIND THE RIGHT CHOICES, NOT TELL THEM THEY HAVE NONE.
THERE ARE LOTS OF COUNTERARGUMENTS TO THE NOTION THAT A POINT OF NO RETURN EXISTS, IN TERMS OF REHABILITATION.
CENSORED
PLEASE...
FOR HUMANS, ANYWAY.
WHETHER OR NOT THAT APPLIES TO ALIENS REMAINS TO BE SEEN.
BUT MAYBE IT DOESN'T RIGHT NOW.
WHERE ARE YOU GOING?
CENSORED
GOT ANY MORE COOL INSIGHTS, WARDEN?
CLAP CLAP CLAP CLAP
NICE WORK, KID.
INMATES, SURRENDER NOW OR BE DESTROYED.

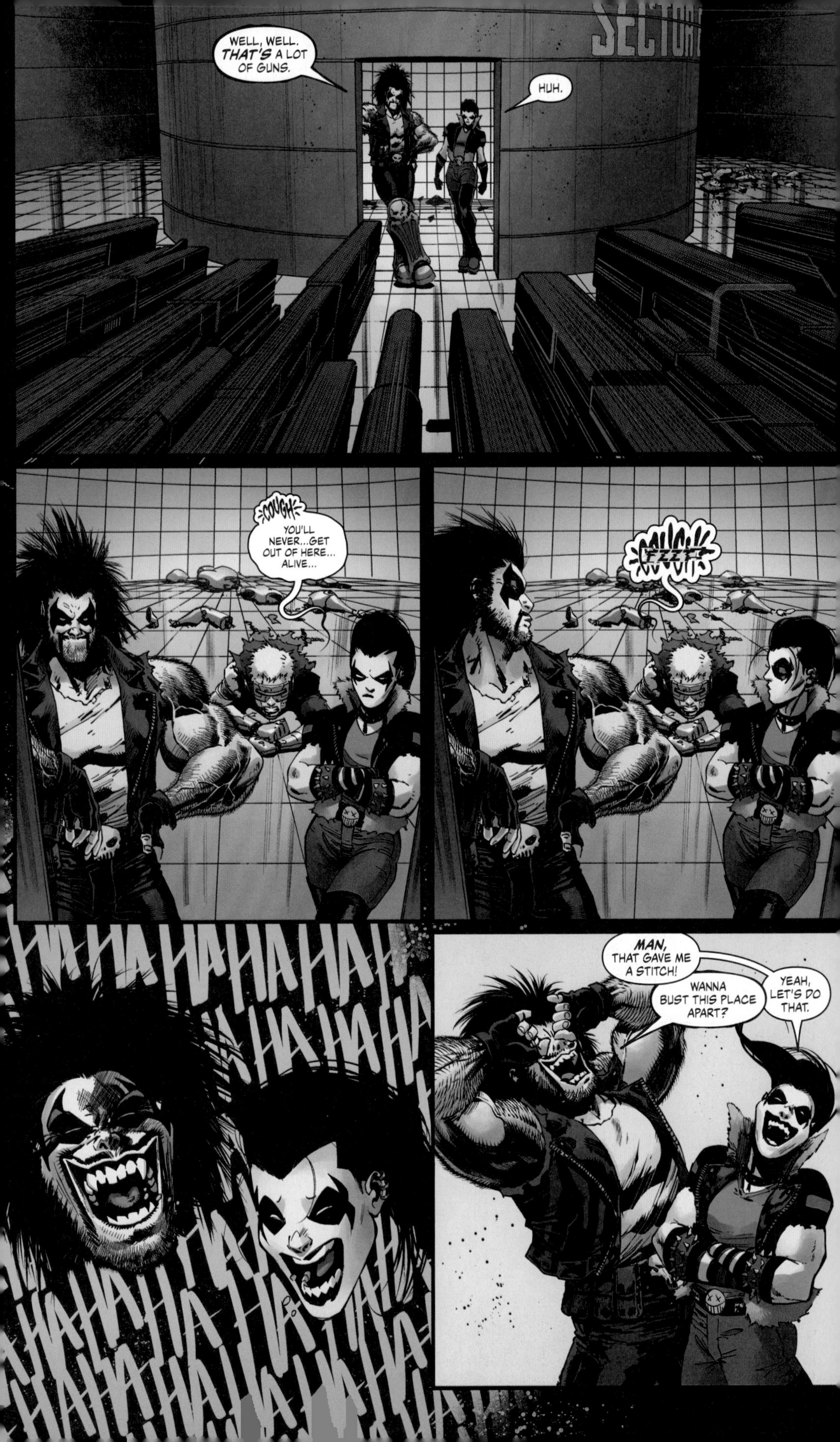
SECTOR
WELL, WELL. *THAT'S* A LOT OF GUNS.
HUH.
COUGH
YOU'LL NEVER...GET OUT OF HERE... ALIVE...
FZZT
HAHAHAHAHAHA
HAHAHAHAHA
HAHAHAHAHAHA
MAN, THAT GAVE ME A STITCH!
YEAH, LET'S DO THAT.
WANNA BUST THIS PLACE APART?

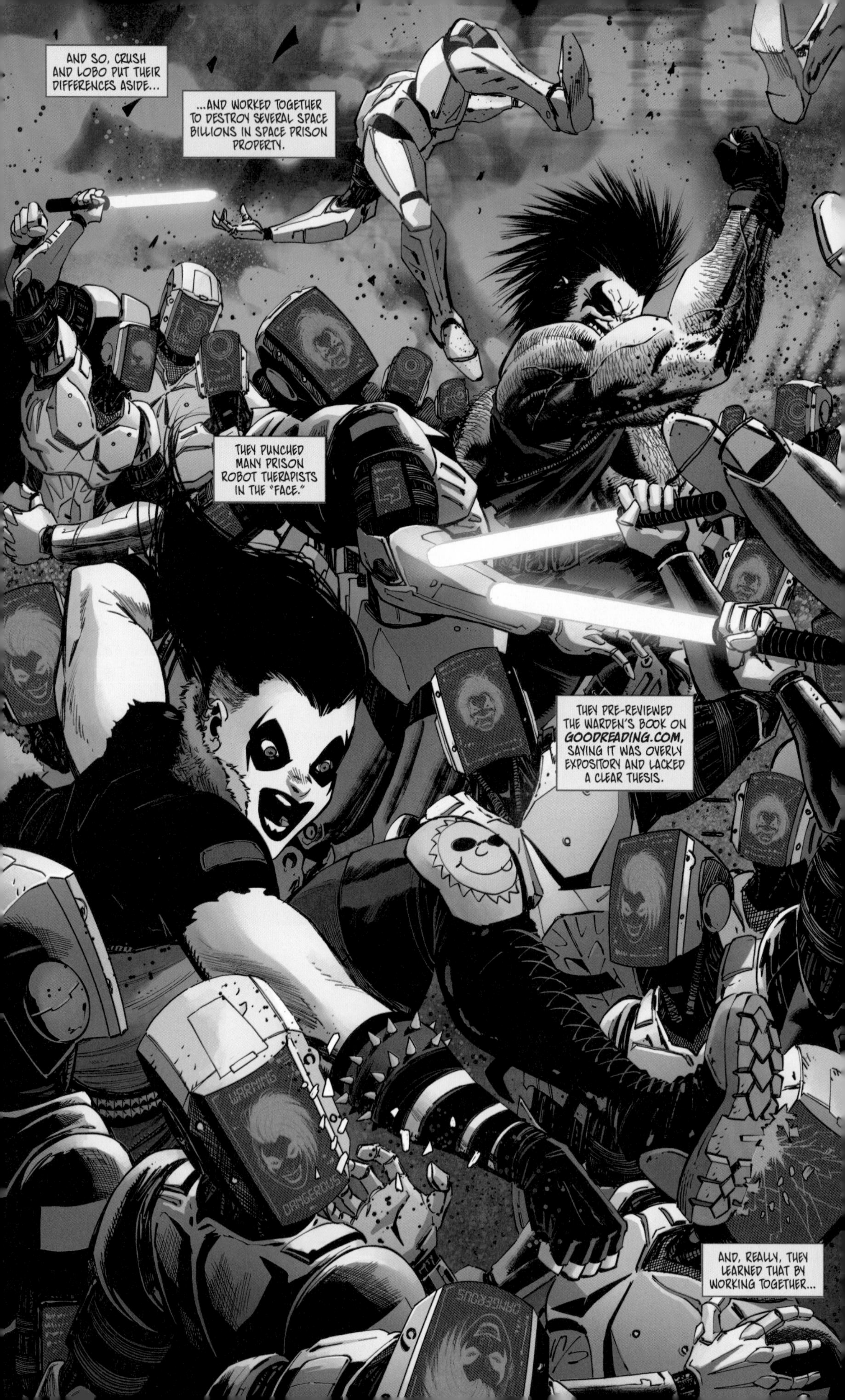
AND SO, CRUSH AND LOBO PUT THEIR DIFFERENCES ASIDE...
...AND WORKED TOGETHER TO DESTROY SEVERAL SPACE BILLIONS IN SPACE PRISON PROPERTY.
THEY PUNCHED MANY PRISON ROBOT THERAPISTS IN THE "FACE."
THEY PRE-REVIEWED THE WARDEN'S BOOK ON GOODREADING.COM, SAYING IT WAS OVERLY EXPOSITORY AND LACKED A CLEAR THESIS.
AND, REALLY, THEY LEARNED THAT BY WORKING TOGETHER...

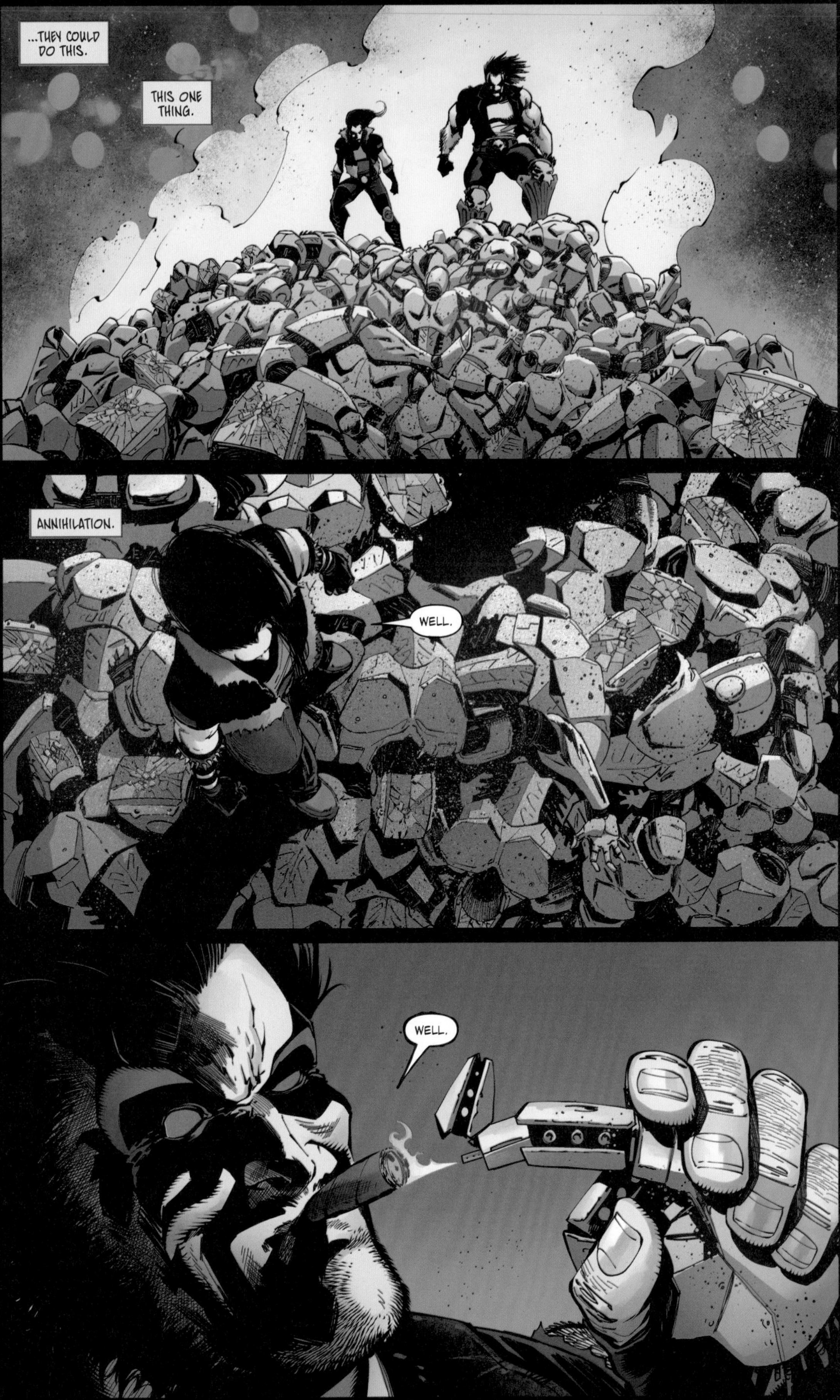
...THEY COULD DO THIS.
THIS ONE THING.
ANNIHILATION.
WELL.
WELL.

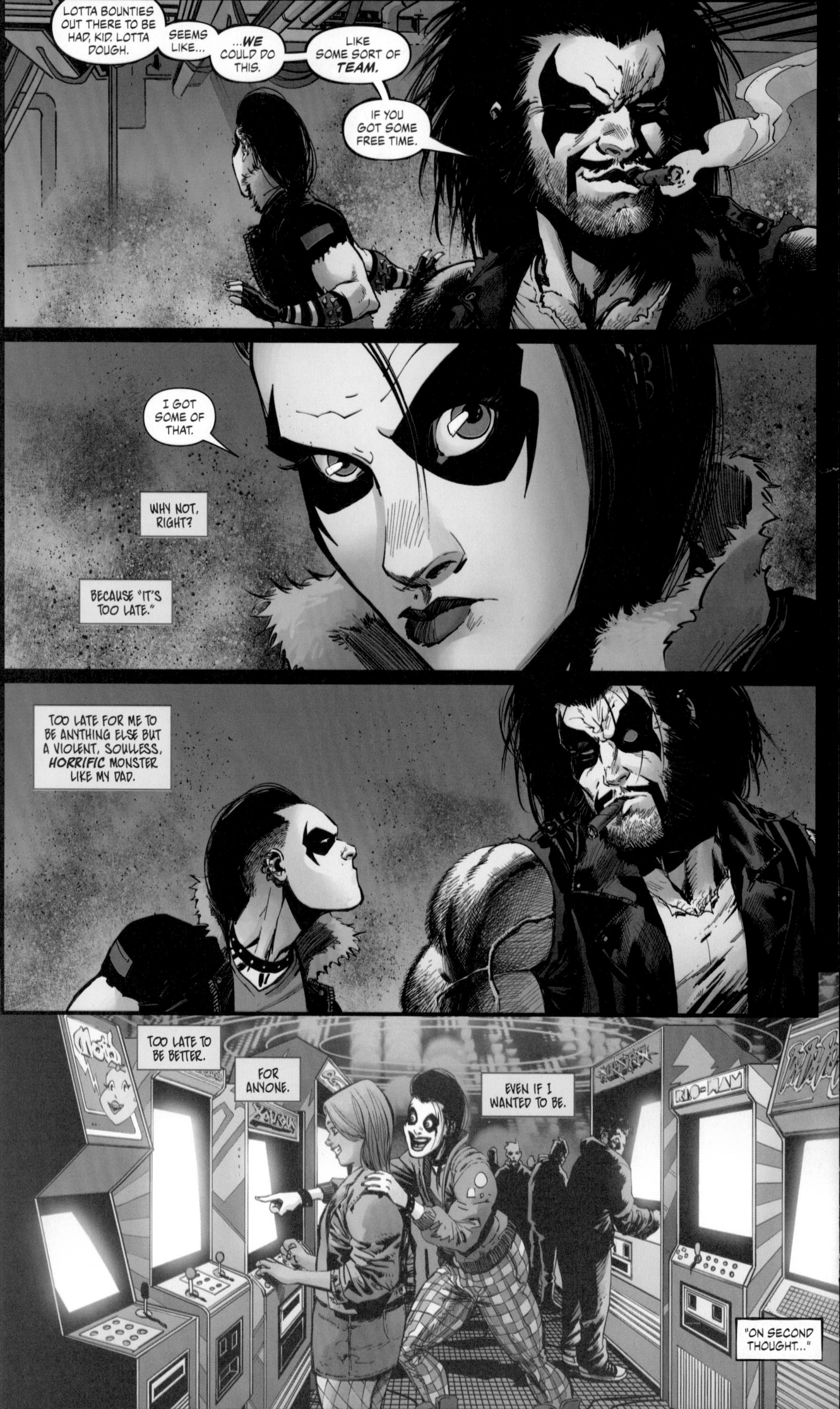
LOTTA BOUNTIES OUT THERE TO BE HAD, KID. LOTTA DOUGH.
SEEMS LIKE...
...WE COULD DO THIS.
LIKE SOME SORT OF TEAM.
IF YOU GOT SOME FREE TIME.
I GOT SOME OF THAT.
WHY NOT, RIGHT?
BECAUSE "IT'S TOO LATE."
TOO LATE FOR ME TO BE ANYTHING ELSE BUT A VIOLENT, SOULLESS, HORRIFIC MONSTER LIKE MY DAD.
TOO LATE TO BE BETTER.
FOR ANYONE.
EVEN IF I WANTED TO BE.
"ON SECOND THOUGHT..."

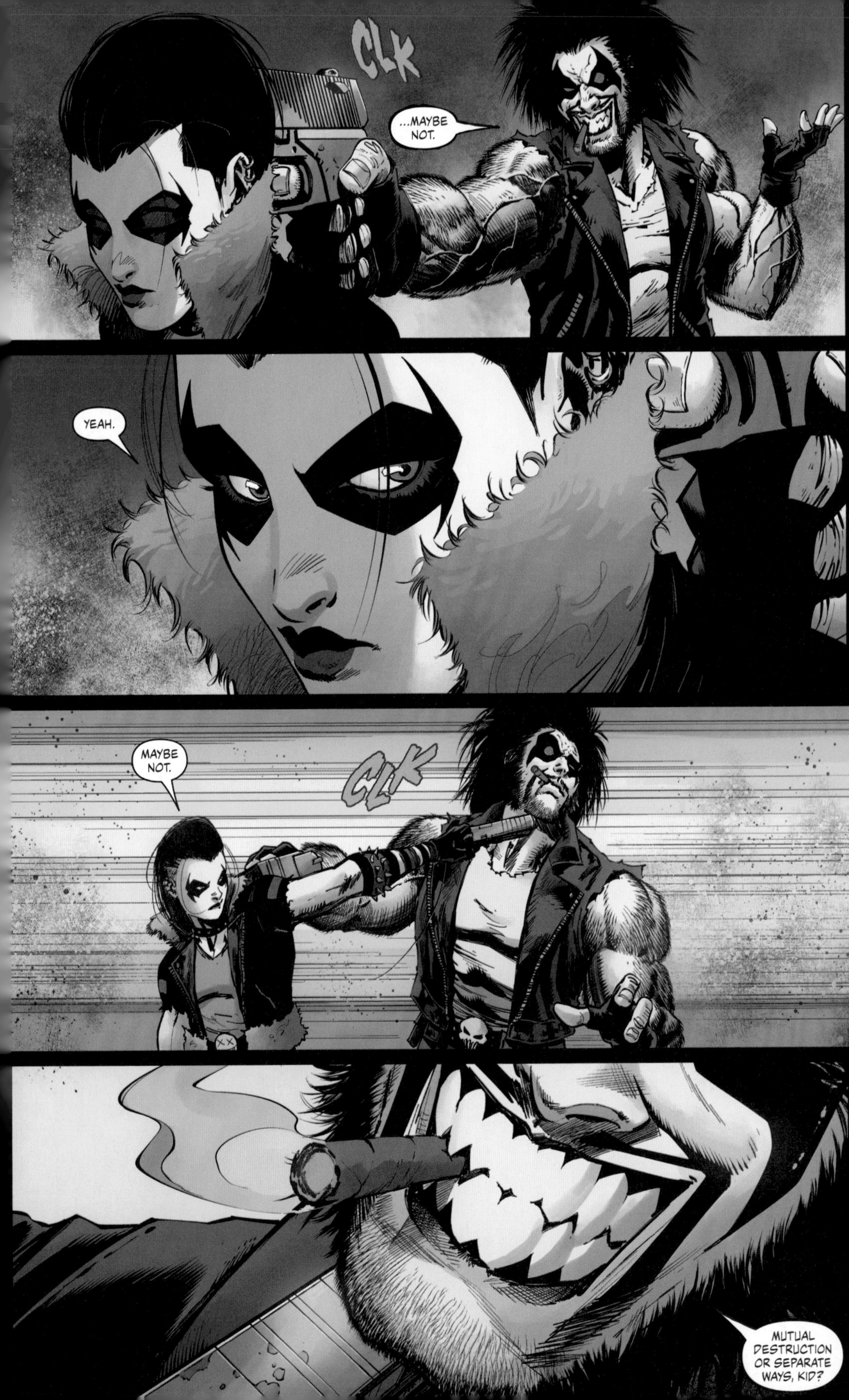
CLK
...MAYBE NOT.
YEAH.
MAYBE NOT.
CLK
MUTUAL DESTRUCTION OR SEPARATE WAYS, KID?

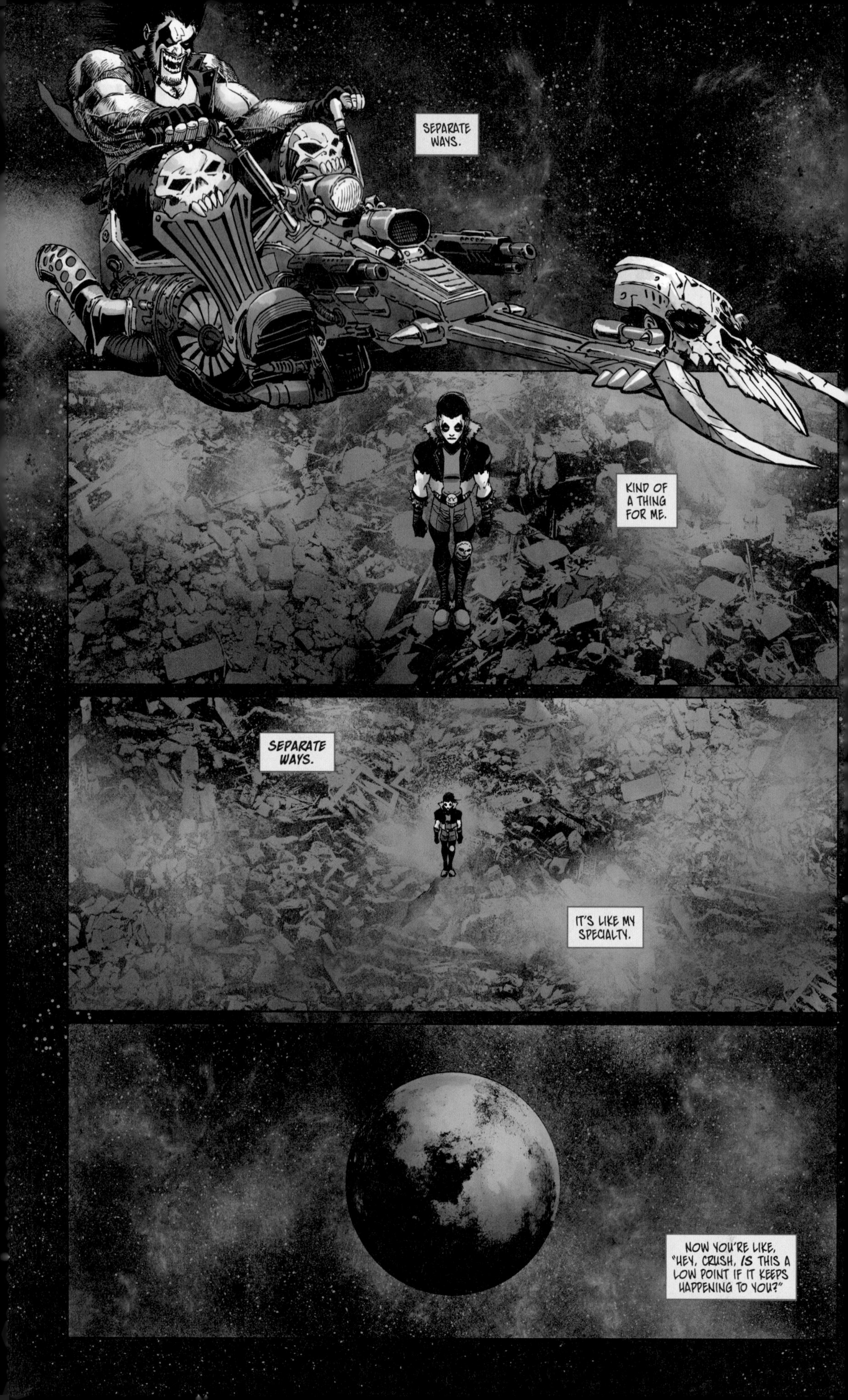
SEPARATE WAYS.
KIND OF A THING FOR ME.
SEPARATE WAYS.
IT'S LIKE MY SPECIALTY.
NOW YOU'RE LIKE, "HEY, CRUSH, IS THIS A LOW POINT IF IT KEEPS HAPPENING TO YOU?"

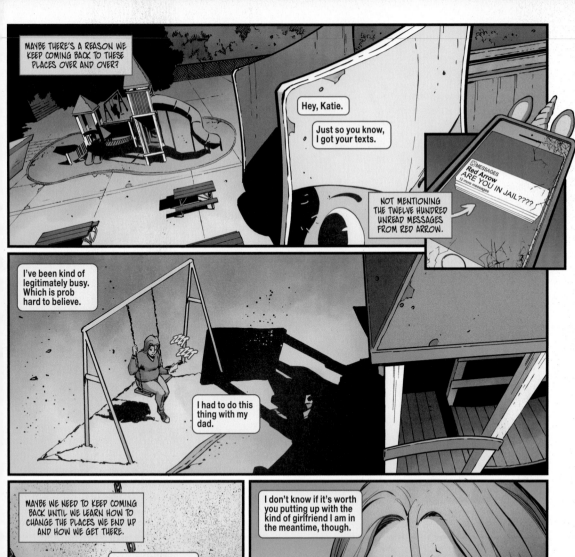

MAYBE THERE'S A REASON WE KEEP COMING BACK TO THESE PLACES OVER AND OVER?

Hey, Katie.

Just so you know, I got your texts.

NOT MENTIONING THE TWELVE HUNDRED UNREAD MESSAGES FROM RED ARROW.

MESSAGES
Red Arrow
ARE YOU IN JAIL????
12 more messages

I've been kind of legitimately busy. Which is prob hard to believe.

I had to do this thing with my dad.

MAYBE WE NEED TO KEEP COMING BACK UNTIL WE LEARN HOW TO CHANGE THE PLACES WE END UP AND HOW WE GET THERE.

I just wanted to say.

I want to be...not the worst girlfriend ever.

I don't know if it's worth you putting up with the kind of girlfriend I am in the meantime, though.

I hope you'll give me a chance to change.

I hope it's not too late.

...give me ...ance to change.

I hope it's not too late.

Let me think about it, OK?

<3

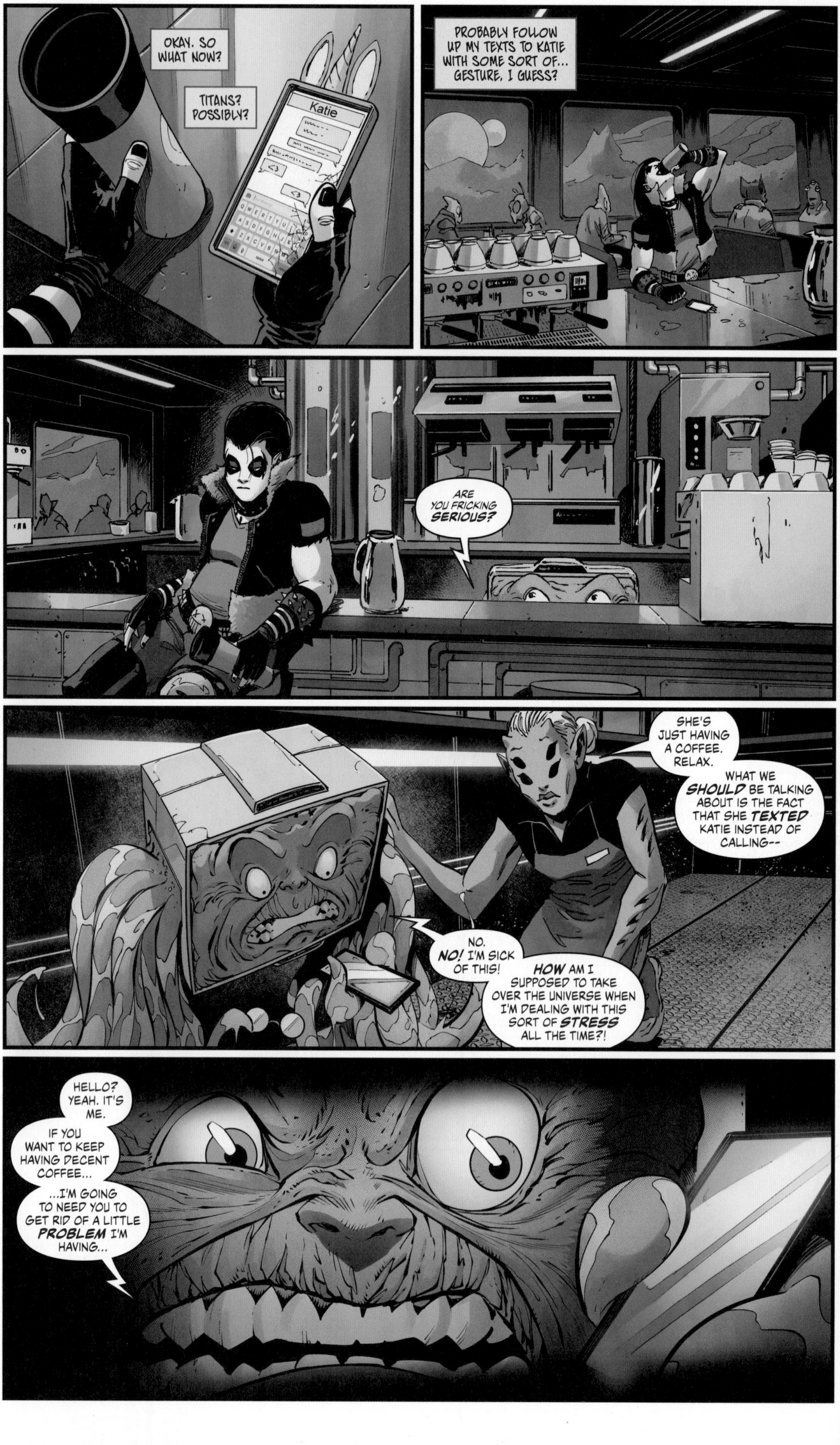
OKAY. SO WHAT NOW?
TITANS? POSSIBLY?
Katie
<3
<3
PROBABLY FOLLOW UP MY TEXTS TO KATIE WITH SOME SORT OF... GESTURE, I GUESS?
ARE YOU FRICKING SERIOUS?
SHE'S JUST HAVING A COFFEE. RELAX.
WHAT WE SHOULD BE TALKING ABOUT IS THE FACT THAT SHE TEXTED KATIE INSTEAD OF CALLING--
NO. NO! I'M SICK OF THIS!
HOW AM I SUPPOSED TO TAKE OVER THE UNIVERSE WHEN I'M DEALING WITH THIS SORT OF STRESS ALL THE TIME?!
HELLO? YEAH. IT'S ME.
IF YOU WANT TO KEEP HAVING DECENT COFFEE...
...I'M GOING TO NEED YOU TO GET RID OF A LITTLE PROBLEM I'M HAVING...

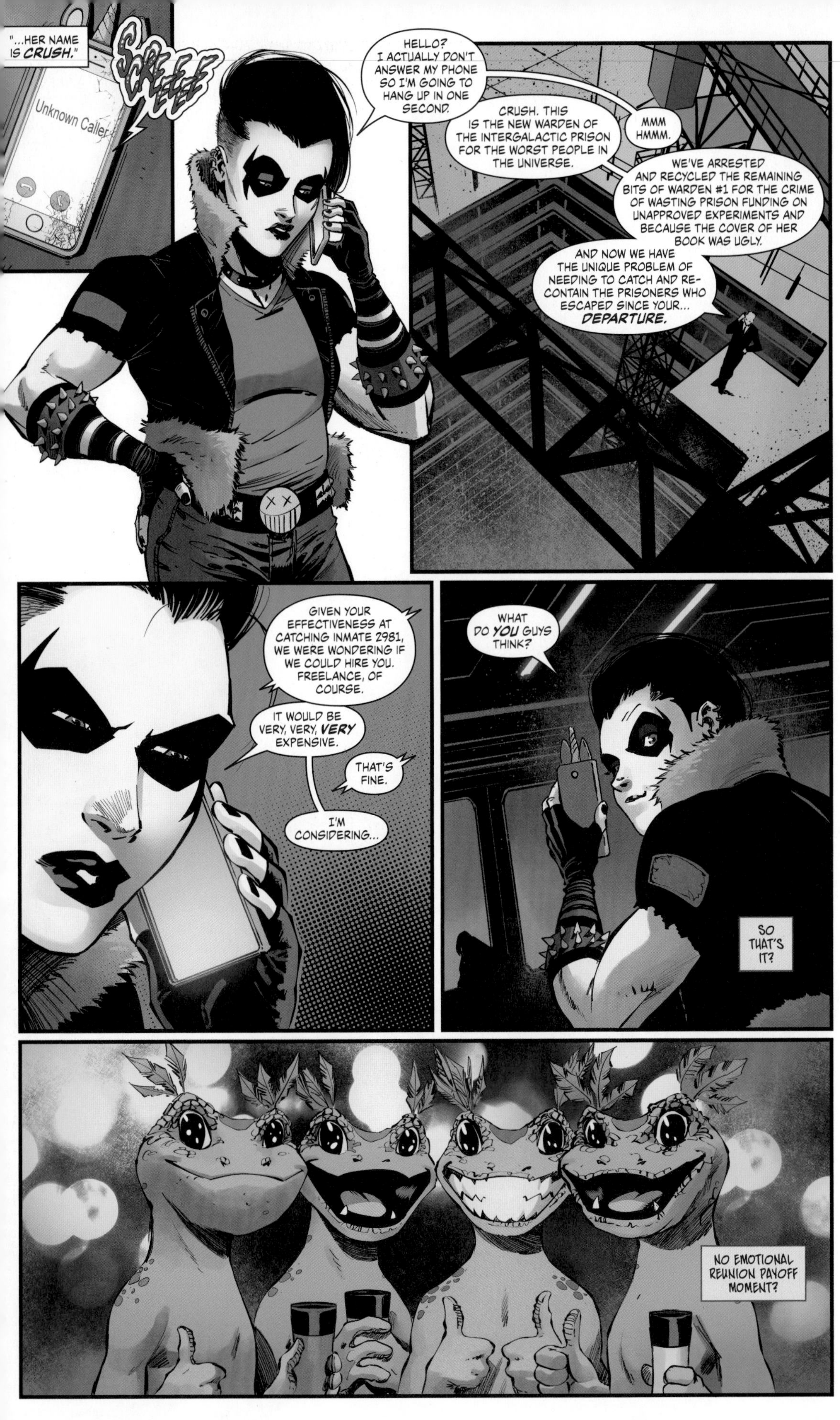

"...HER NAME IS CRUSH."
SCREEEEE
Unknown Caller
HELLO? I ACTUALLY DON'T ANSWER MY PHONE SO I'M GOING TO HANG UP IN ONE SECOND.
CRUSH. THIS IS THE NEW WARDEN OF THE INTERGALACTIC PRISON FOR THE WORST PEOPLE IN THE UNIVERSE.
MMM HMMM.
WE'VE ARRESTED AND RECYCLED THE REMAINING BITS OF WARDEN #1 FOR THE CRIME OF WASTING PRISON FUNDING ON UNAPPROVED EXPERIMENTS AND BECAUSE THE COVER OF HER BOOK WAS UGLY.
AND NOW WE HAVE THE UNIQUE PROBLEM OF NEEDING TO CATCH AND RE-CONTAIN THE PRISONERS WHO ESCAPED SINCE YOUR... DEPARTURE.
GIVEN YOUR EFFECTIVENESS AT CATCHING INMATE 2981, WE WERE WONDERING IF WE COULD HIRE YOU. FREELANCE, OF COURSE.
IT WOULD BE VERY, VERY, VERY EXPENSIVE.
THAT'S FINE.
I'M CONSIDERING...
WHAT DO YOU GUYS THINK?
SO THAT'S IT?
NO EMOTIONAL REUNION PAYOFF MOMENT?

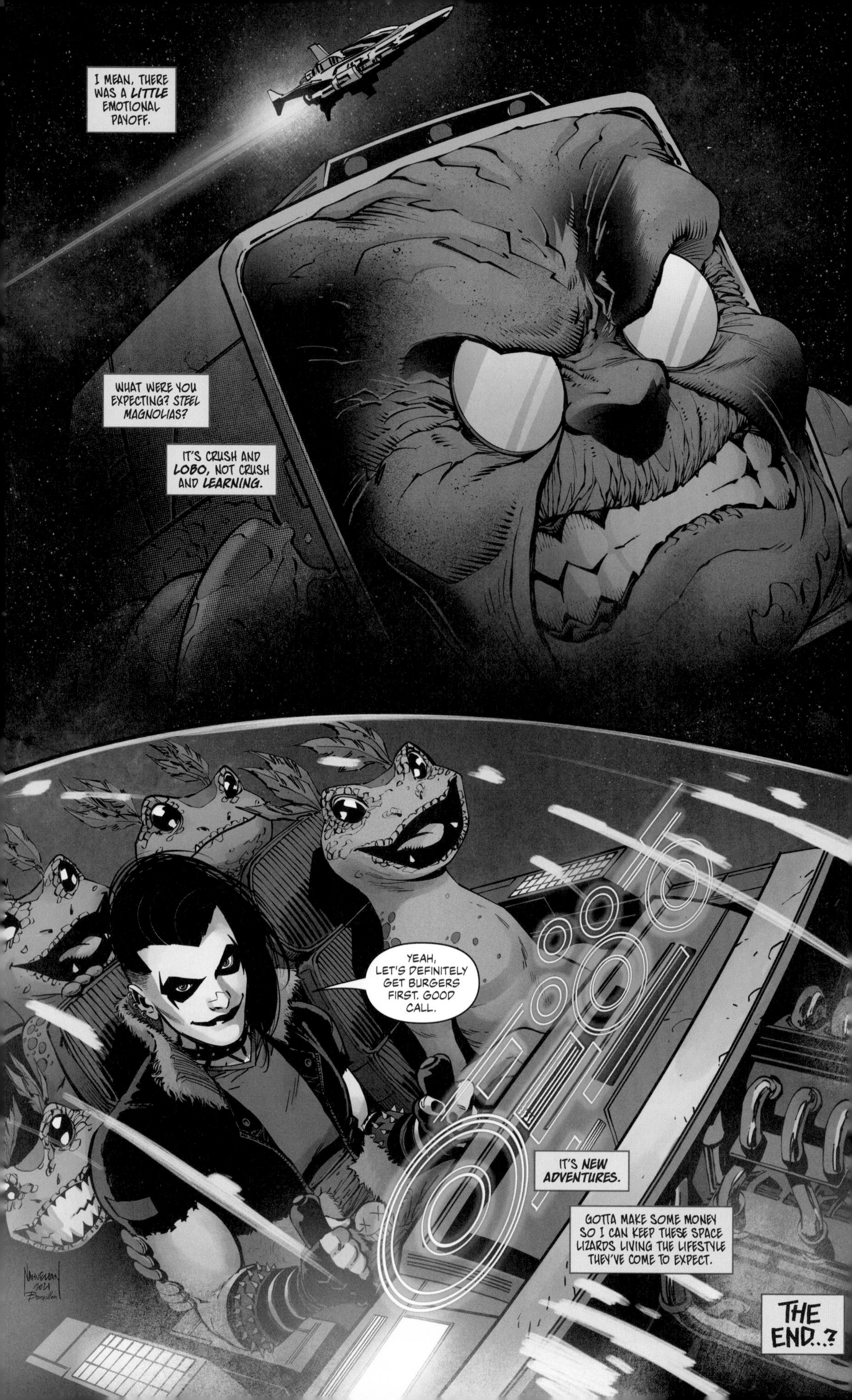
I MEAN, THERE WAS A LITTLE EMOTIONAL PAYOFF.
WHAT WERE YOU EXPECTING? STEEL MAGNOLIAS?
IT'S CRUSH AND LOBO, NOT CRUSH AND LEARNING.
YEAH, LET'S DEFINITELY GET BURGERS FIRST. GOOD CALL.
IT'S NEW ADVENTURES.
GOTTA MAKE SOME MONEY SO I CAN KEEP THESE SPACE LIZARDS LIVING THE LIFESTYLE THEY'VE COME TO EXPECT.
THE END..?

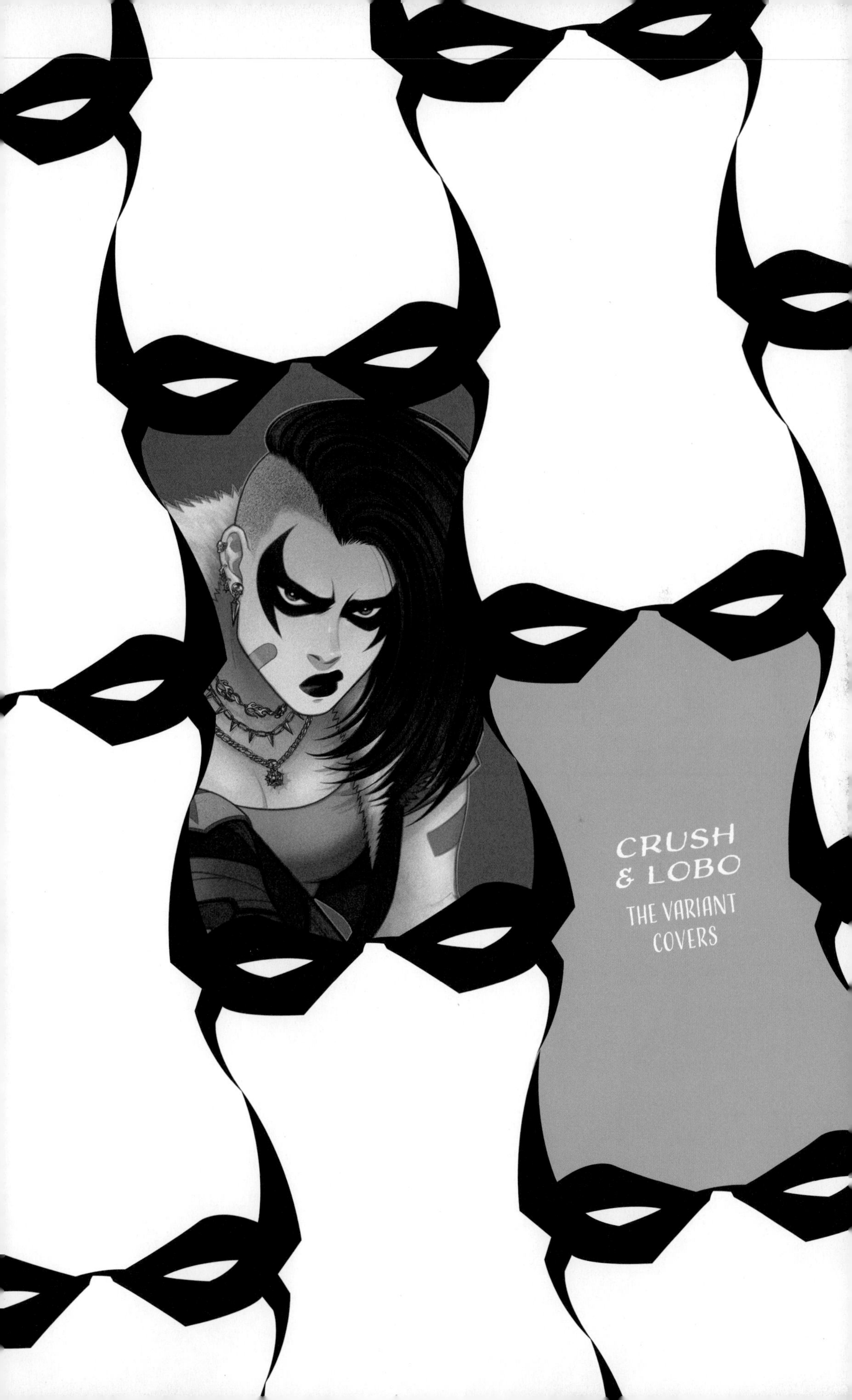
CRUSH
& LOBO
THE VARIANT
COVERS

CRUSH & LOBO #1 PRIDE VARIANT COVER BY YOSHI YOSHITANI

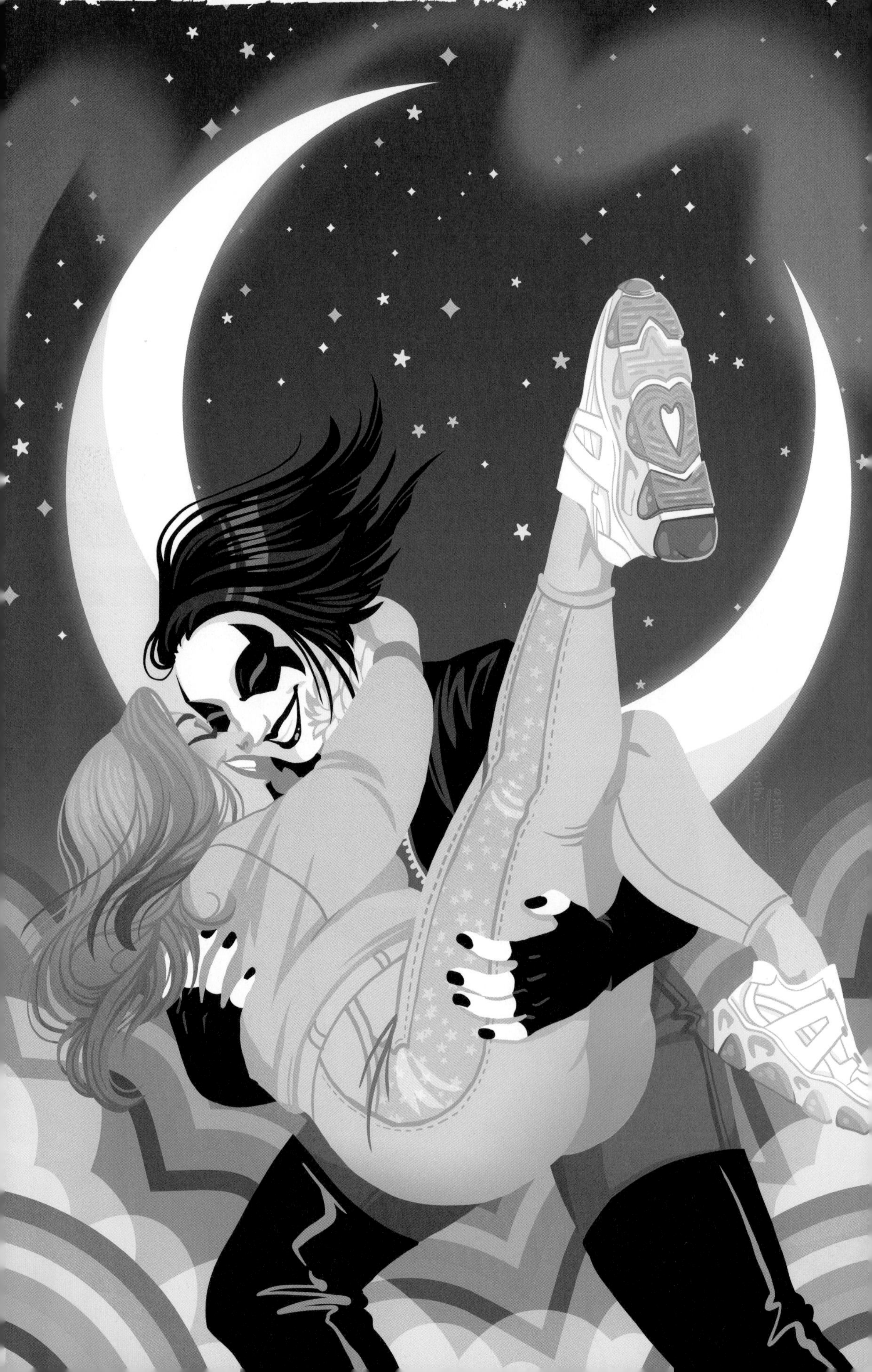

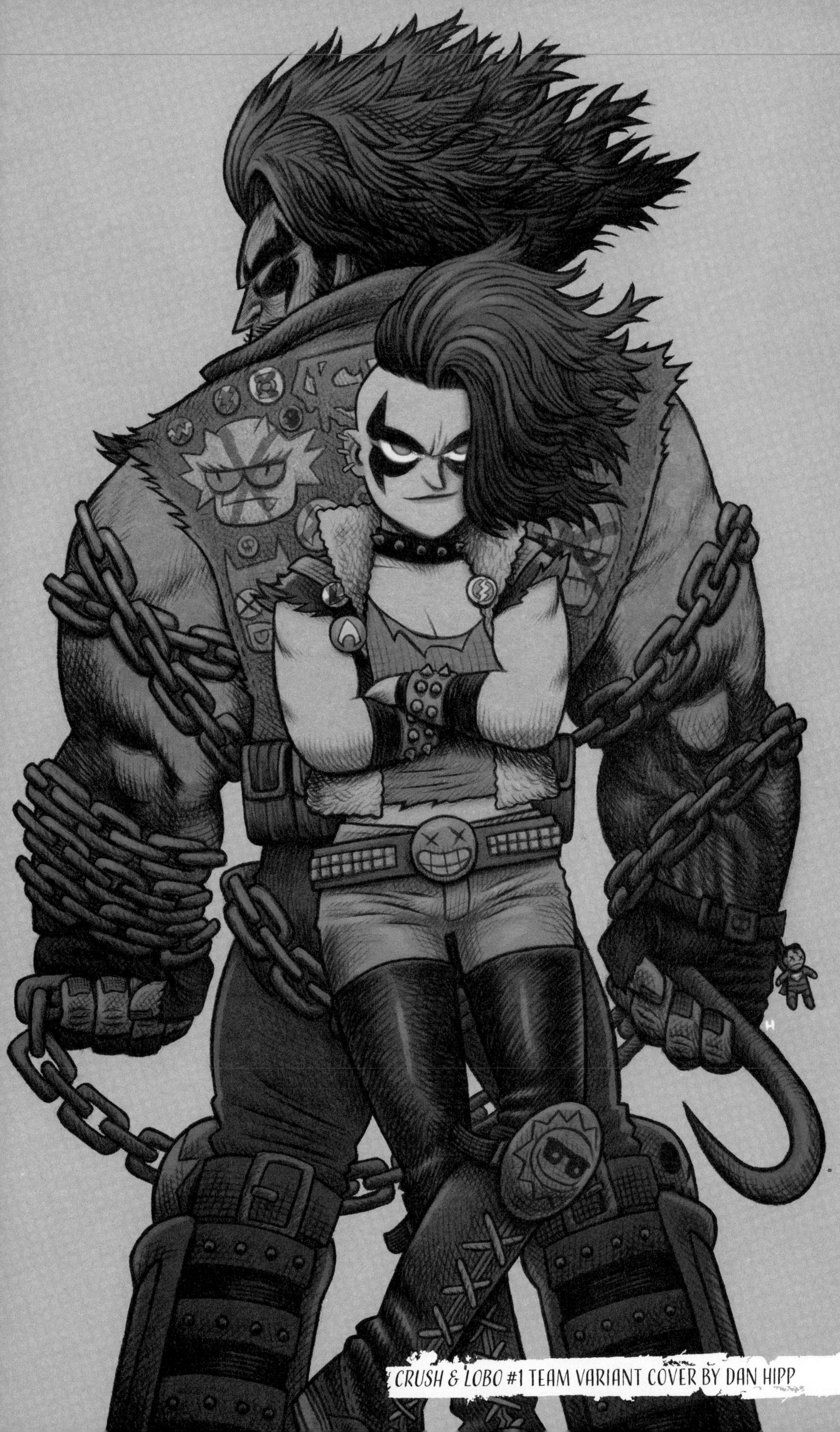

CRUSH & LOBO #1 TEAM VARIANT COVER BY DAN HIPP

CRUSH & LOBO #1 RATIO VARIANT COVER BY CHRISTIAN WARD

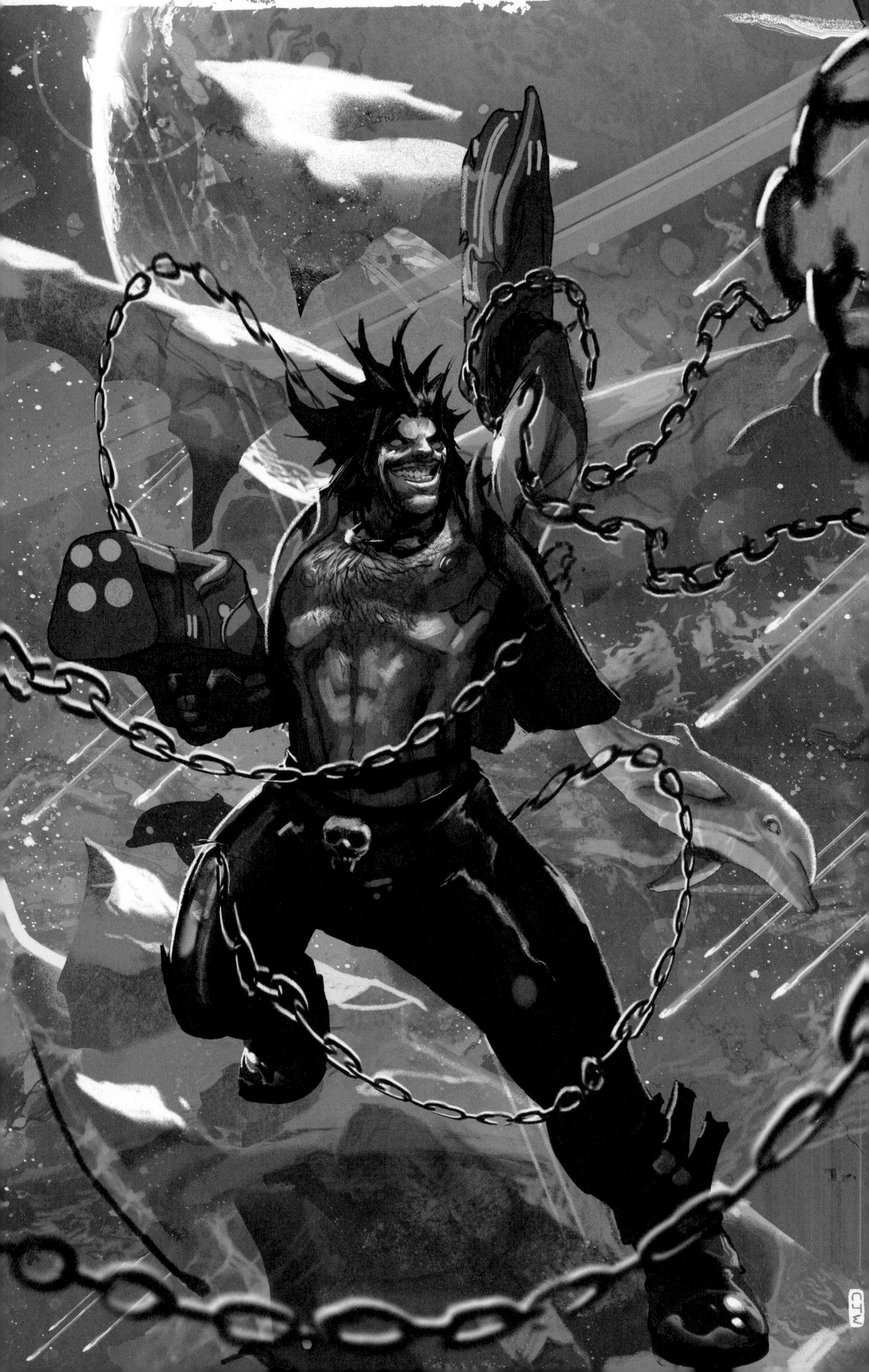

CRUSH & LOBO #2 VARIANT COVER BY DAN MORA

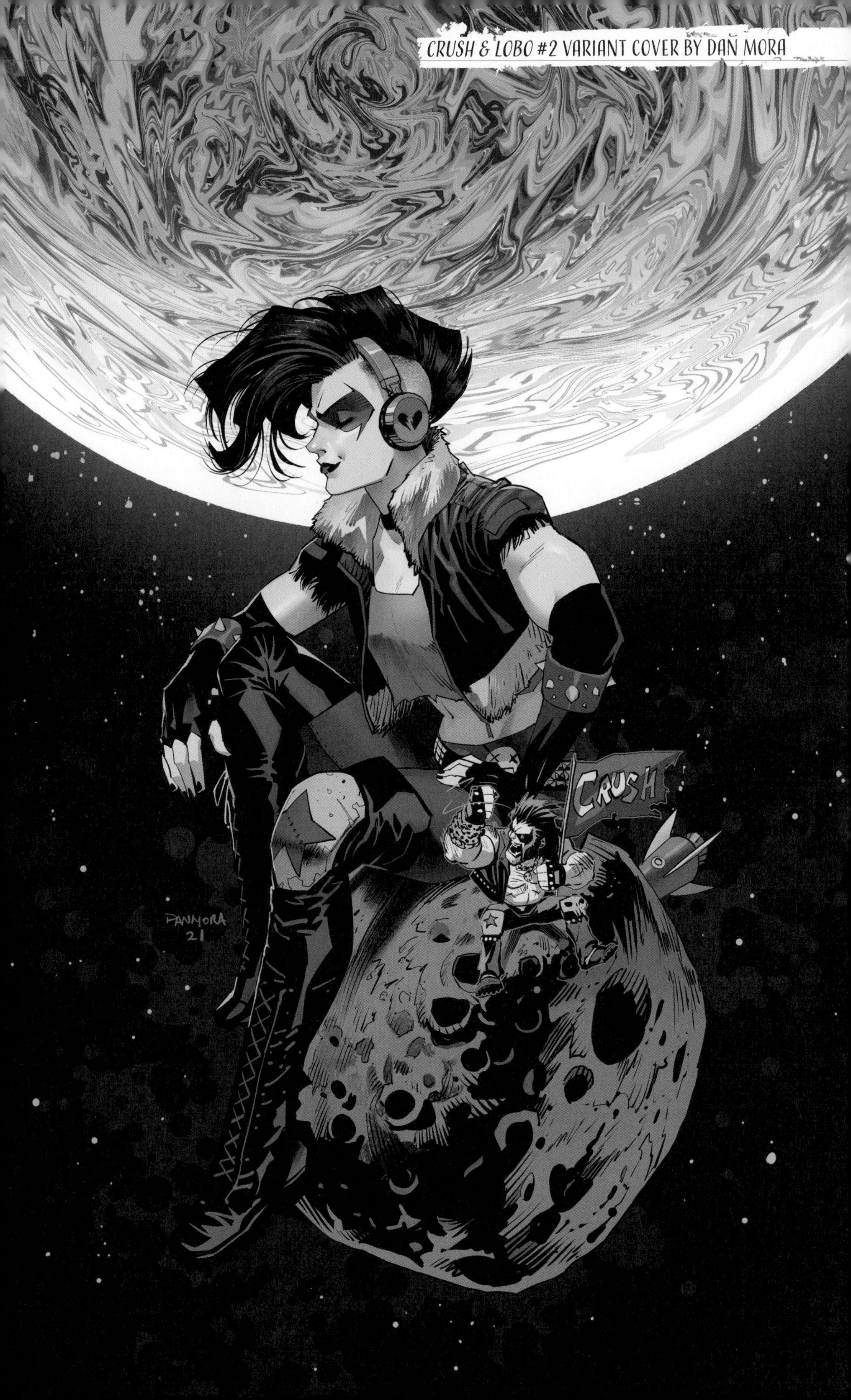
CRUSH
DANMORA
21

CRUSH & LOBO #3 VARIANT COVER BY KHARY RANDOLPH AND PETER STEIGERWALD

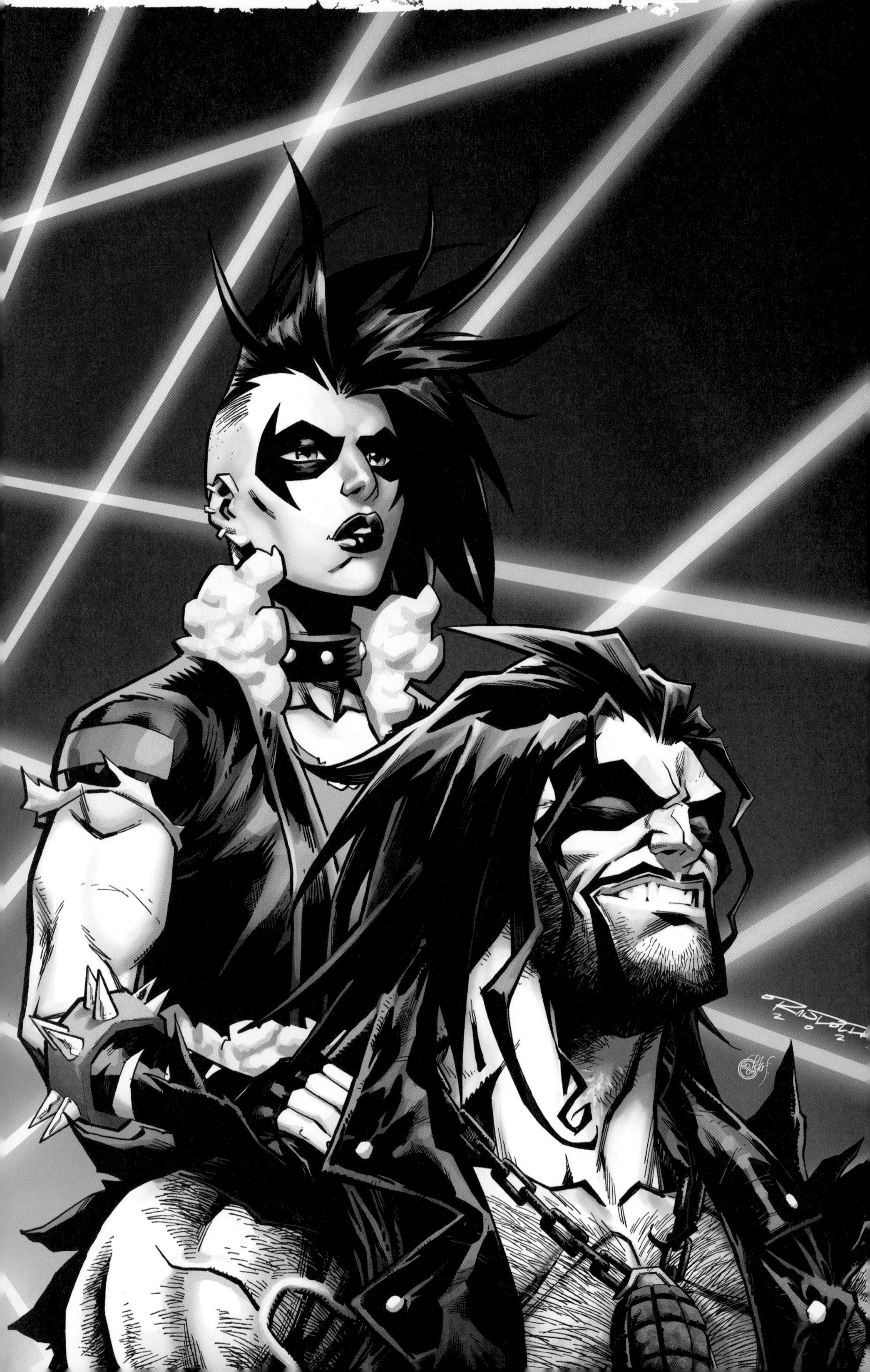

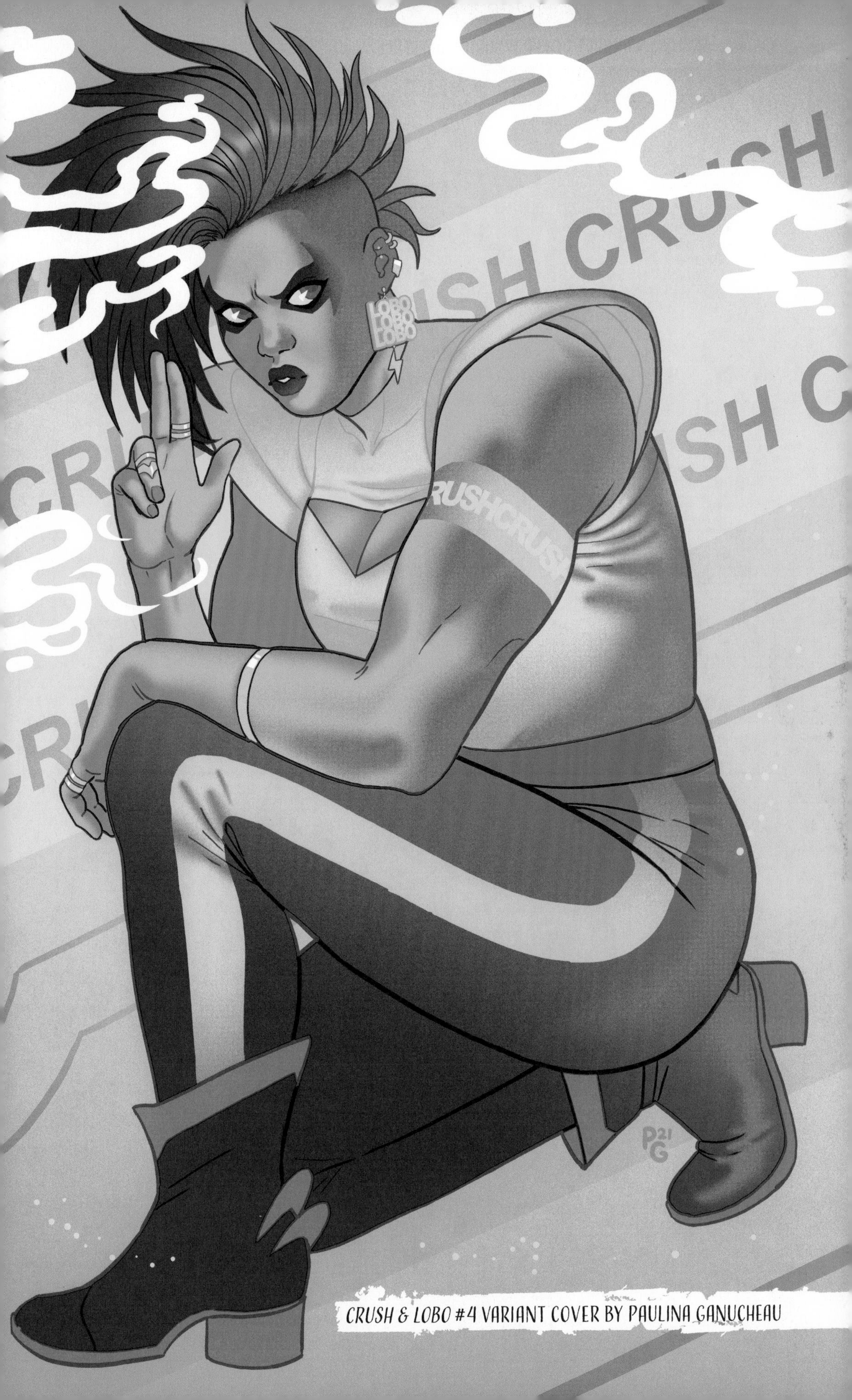
CRUSH
LOBO
LOBO
LOBO
RUSHCRUSH
CRUSH & LOBO #4 VARIANT COVER BY PAULINA GANUCHEAU

CRUSH & LOBO #5 VARIANT COVER BY BRIAN STELFREEZE

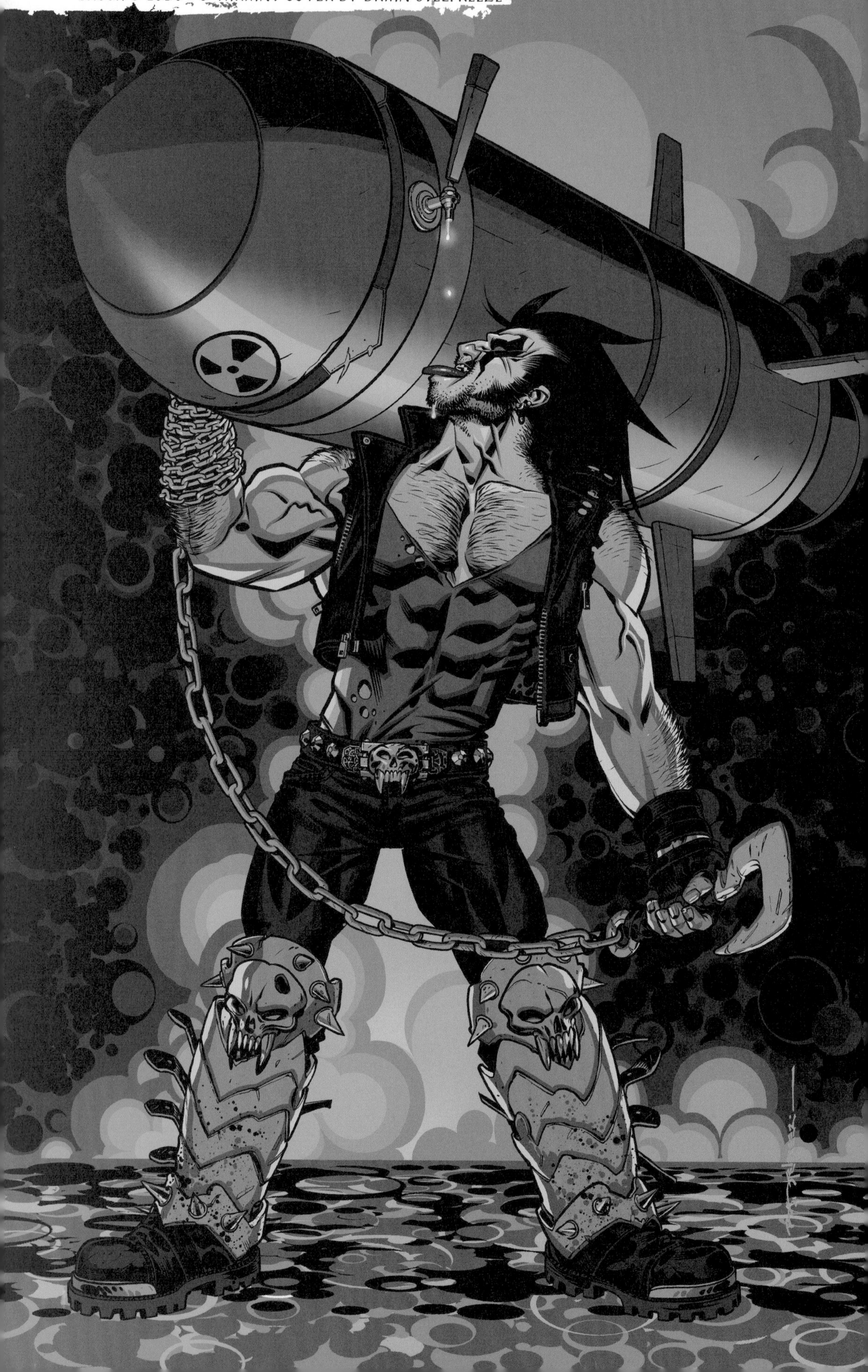

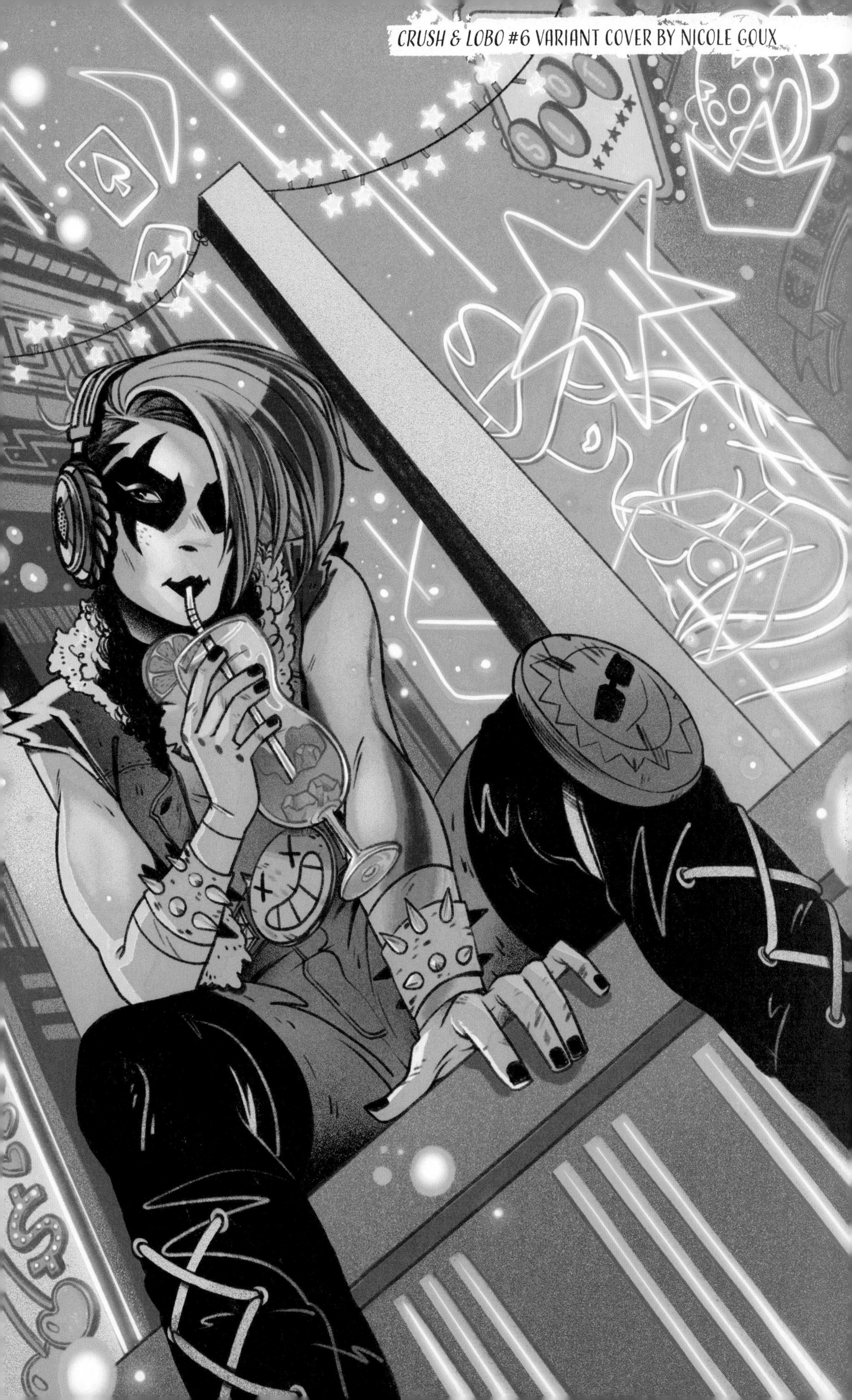

CRUSH & LOBO #6 VARIANT COVER BY NICOLE GOUX

CRUSH & LOBO #7 VARIANT COVER BY JOËLLE JONES AND JORDIE BELLAIRE

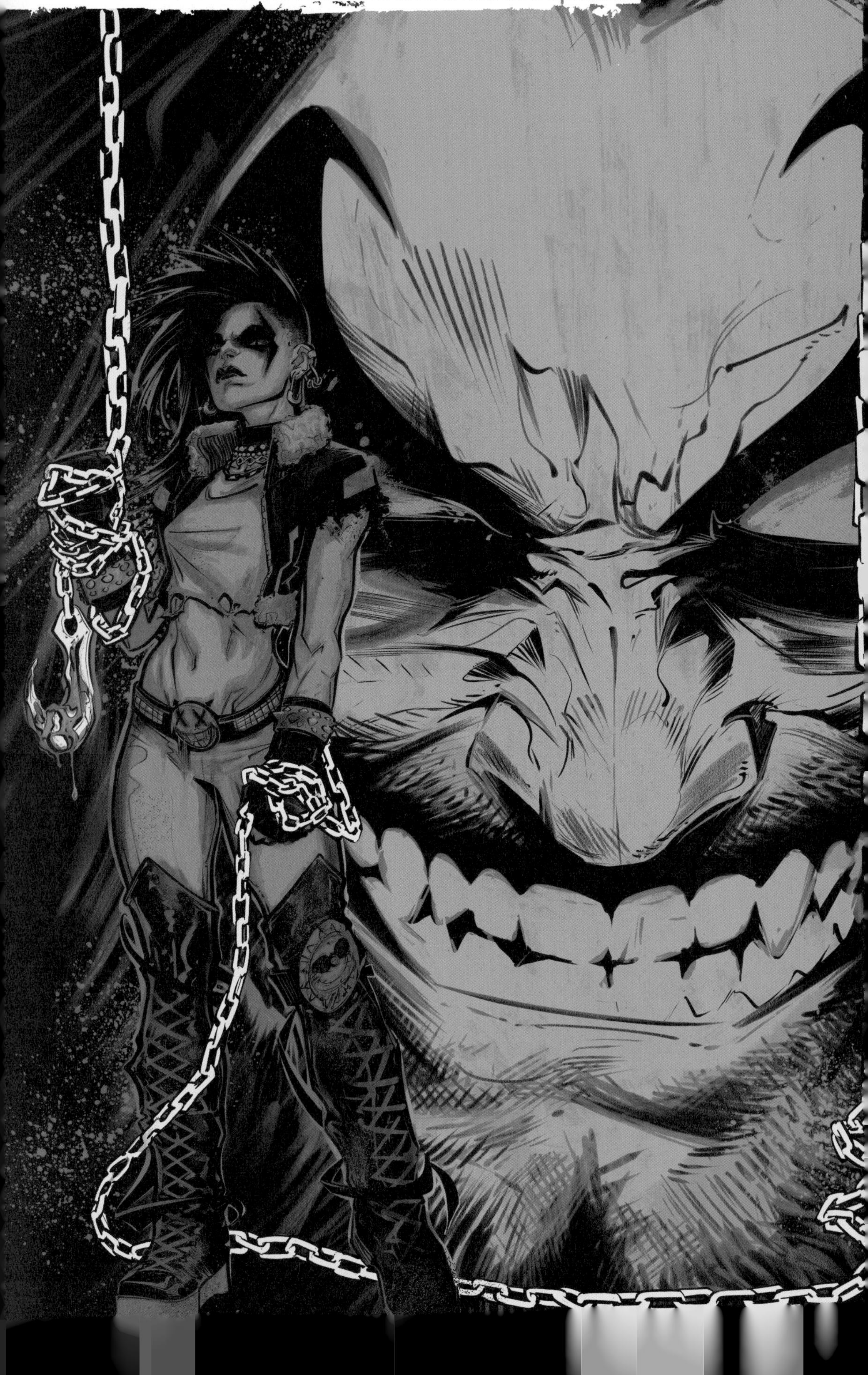

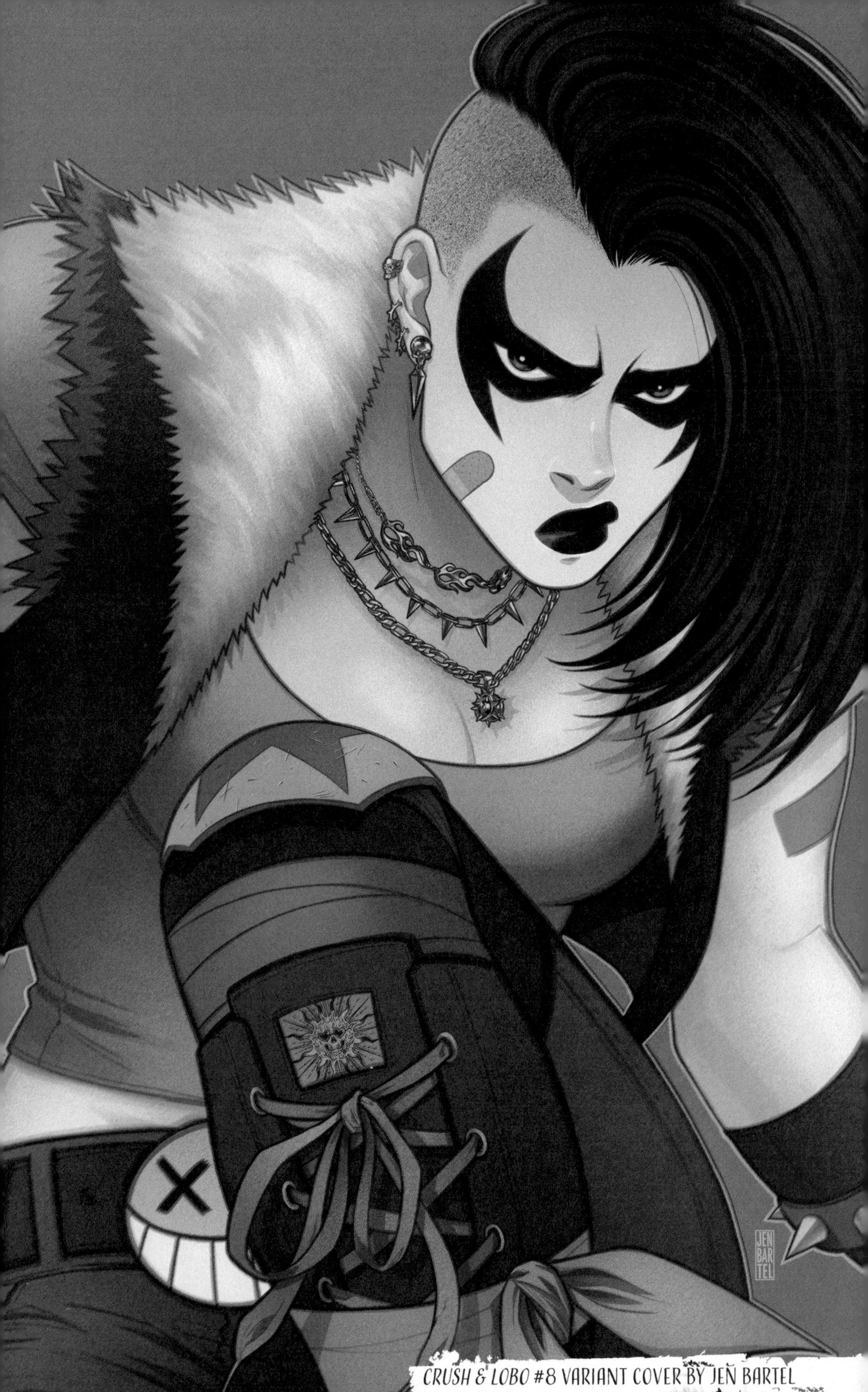
JEN BARTEL
CRUSH & LOBO #8 VARIANT COVER BY JEN BARTEL

DESIGNS BY AMANCAY NAHUELPAN

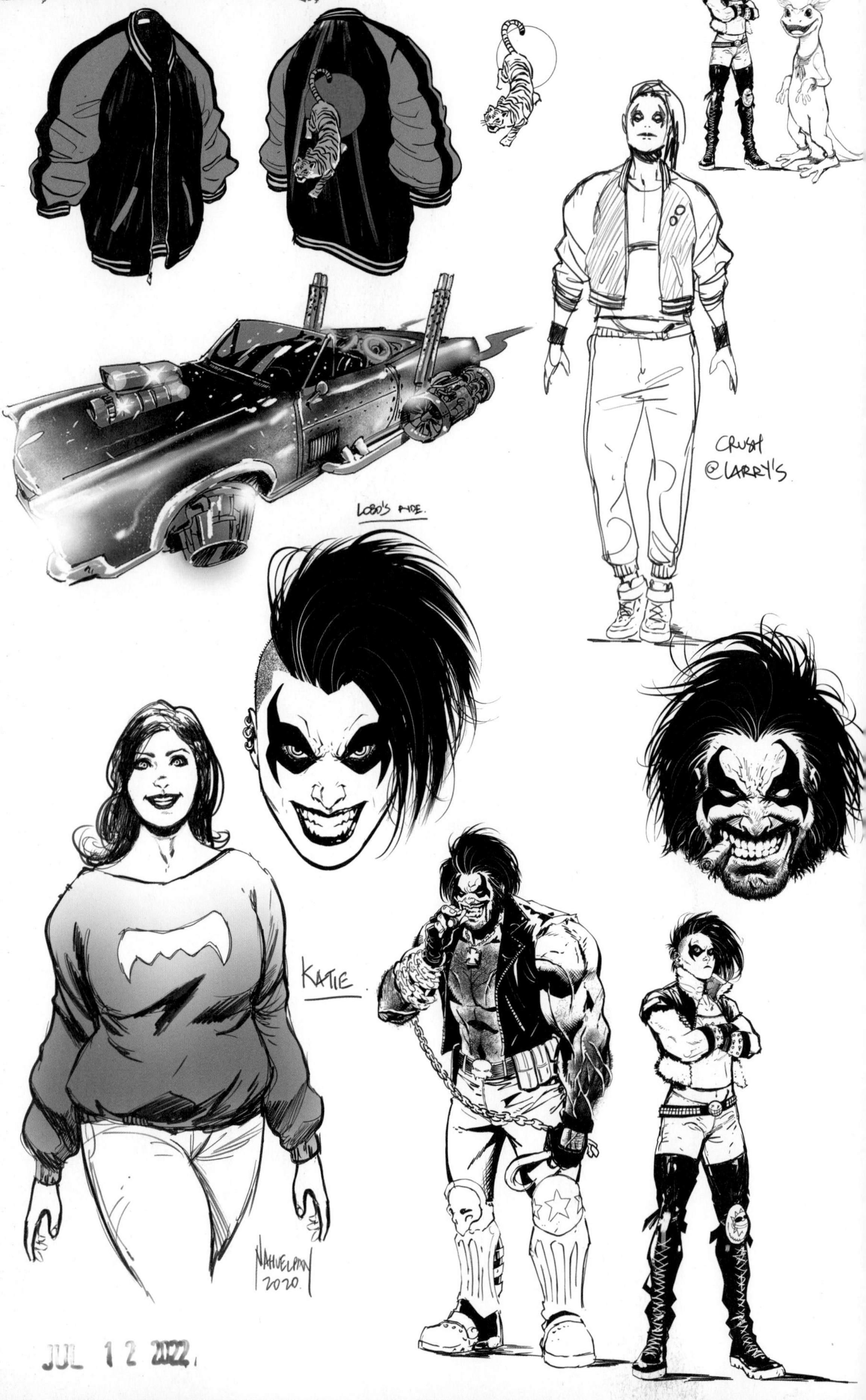
LOBO'S RIDE.
CRUSH
@LARRY'S
KATIE.
NAHUELPAN
2020.